THE LANGUAGE
OF THE
CIVIL WAR

THE LANGUAGE
OF THE
CIVIL WAR

John D. Wright

Oryx Press
Westport, Connecticut • London

The rare Arabian Oryx is believed to have inspired the myth of the unicorn. This desert antelope became virtually extinct in the early 1960s. At that time, several groups of international conservationists arranged to have nine animals sent to the Phoenix Zoo to be the nucleus of a captive breeding herd. Today, the Oryx population is over 1,000, and over 500 have been returned to the Middle East.

Library of Congress Cataloging-in-Publication Data

Wright, John D., 1938–
    The language of the Civil War / John D. Wright.
        p. cm.
    Includes bibliographical references and index.
    ISBN 1-57356-135-5 (alk. paper)
    1. United States—History—Civil War, 1861-1865—Language—Dictionaries. 2. United States—History—Civil War, 1861-1865—Social aspects—Dictionaries. 3. Soldiers—United States—Language—Dictionaries. 4. English language—United States—Usage—Dictionaries. 5. Americanisms—Dictionaries.   I. Title.

E468.9.W755 2001
973.7'1—dc21

                                                                                    2001034825

British Library Cataloguing in Publication Data is available.

Library of Congress Catalog Card Number: 2001034825
ISBN: 1-57356-135-5

First published in 2001

Oryx Press, 88 Post Road West, Westport, CT 06881
An imprint of Greenwood Publishing Group, Inc.
www.oryxpress.com

Printed in the United States of America

♾™

The paper used in this book complies with the Permanent Paper Standard issued by the National Information Standards Organization (Z39.48–1984).

10 9 8 7 6 5 4 3 2 1

For my wife
Inge
and children
Melissa and Kevin
who now know it takes longer to write about the Civil War than to fight it.

CONTENTS

PREFACE

THE AMERICAN SOLDIER has never been at a loss for words, and the intensity of the Civil War, our own tragic backyard battle, made those words march, charge, and explode. Generals became historians, gunners became humorists, and pickets became poets. The home front was also at work on the language, with ladies keeping diaries, journalists puffing up reports, and politicians, as always, spinning golden webs of words.

This book is an eclectic collection of the special language spoken by people who experienced the war. It is an attempt—the first, I believe—to draw together the words and phrases that soldiers used in camp, on the battlefield, and at home: their curses, insults, nicknames, and slang; their familiar terms for equipment, food, diseases, games, songs, and books; and their names for organizations, carriages, clothes, photographs, and other familiar subjects.

What, indeed, did it all sound like?

This volume will create a personal image of everyday life in those traumatic years from 1861 to 1865. I have sought to put together an engaging book for the casual reader, a reference work for students, a special dictionary for the libraries of Civil War buffs, and a source of historical information for writers of reference and fictional works.

The entries have been assembled from the massive array of books and writings about the war, material that seems to "grow like Topsy" on a daily basis. This material includes the excellent histories, dictionaries, and other volumes I have listed in the selected bibliography, as well as magazine and newspaper articles, and even the battlefield letters of my great-grandfather, Captain William C. Baskin, who fought the hopeless Confederate cause with his fellow Mississippians in Martin's Cavalry Division, the Army of East Tennessee. After the war, he was mayor of Tupelo, Mississippi (1888-98). I also retrieved terms from *A History of Mississippi* written by my grandmother's uncle, Confederate General Robert Lowry of Mississippi, who commanded the Rankin Grays and John Adams's brigade. Following the war, he was a commissioner who requested the release of President Jefferson Davis and then served as governor of Mississippi (1881-89).

William Cander Baskin (1839-98), the author's great-grandfather.

My desire to capture an atmosphere with words led to various reasons for including entries. The special military terms and slang are obviously the core. Some words familiar today are included to show that they were used back then, especially if we consider them modern ("washing machine," "snack," "look out for number one," "rub someone out"). Others were added because their meanings during the war were different than they are today ("G.I.," "body bag," "telephone," "moonshine," "flunk out," "goose-step," "native American"). Some appear because they were first used at that time ("passport," "photo," "nifty," "face the music"), and some were included to anchor a broader explanation ("plough" to comment on British spellings during the war).

Battles and units have not been singled out, but some actions and groups are covered for exceptional reasons, such as Pickett's Charge to point out this unfair name for an attack that was not ordered or led by Major General George E. Pickett. On occasion, I could not resist the poetic phrase ("clouds of mounted men"), but quotes were avoided unless certain ones were repeatedly used by well-known people. A few delightful expressions by the unfamous are included ("links of one sausage, made out of one dog"). Offensive ethnic words have been included ("nigger," "Uncle") because they were unfortunately part of the era, but perhaps the prejudice scale is somewhat balanced by the many insulting names for whites ("cracker," "poor white trash"). To achieve an overview of the Civil War vocabulary, I have also included some familiar things that soldiers would talk about. The exciting concept of "evolution," for instance, was only two years old when the conflict began. "Base ball" and, strangely enough, "hop scotch" were popular forms of recreation in camp. "Barnum's American Museum" was a famous stop for Union soldiers in New York.

I have, of course, made personal selections from this rich cornucopia of wartime life. Each army horse had a name, but only a few ridden by the famous are listed. Numerous military prisons and hospitals existed, but Andersonville and The Confederate Hospital were among the infamous examples most discussed during the war. The

Alabama and a few other ships were universally known on both sides, and the Sanitary Commission and American Bible Society were two organizations supporting soldiers that were constant topics at social events. This choice of prime examples continues through the other main categories, from military equipment, fortifications, and departments to mottos, camp songs, medical terms, and profanity.

Two methods were used to select and write entries: Terms were either mined from contemporary and historical accounts of the war or selected from dictionaries.

Most terms had to be drawn from accounts of the war. The selection process involved innumerable hours of trawling through detailed narrative volumes, such as *The Personal Memoirs of Ulysses S. Grant*; Shelby Foote's comprehensive trilogy, *The Civil War: A Narrative*; and J. Thomas Scharf's *History of the Confederate States Navy*. Soldiers' slang and military terms, such as names for camp equipment, are delightfully explained in personal accounts like *"Co. Aytch"* by Sam R. Watkins, a Tennessee private during the war, and in Bell Irvin Wiley's two scholarly mid-twentieth-century volumes, *The Life of Johnny Reb* and *The Life of Billy Yank*. Everyday terms used on the home front are readily available in such books as Margaret Leech's account of life in the U.S. capital, *Reveille in Washington*, and the carefully recorded diaries and letters of people like Mary Custis Lee and Mary Chestnut in the South and Jane C. Hoge and Dorothea Lynde Dix in the North. These accounts are valuable for having the words and expressions in context, and they often explain the meanings. After the entries were selected, I could then mark them in other sources to build up well-rounded definitions.

An easier selection was made from dictionaries. These include some published during the war, like John Russell Bartlett's *The Dictionary of Americanisms*, and excellent recent volumes, such as *The Civil War Dictionary* by Mark M. Boatner III, who emphasizes biographical entries, and Paul Dickson's *War Slang*, which is partly devoted to the Civil War. The selected entries were then searched for in other contexts.

Quotations added to illustrate correct usage are either real, in which case they are attributed, or they are imaginary ones created for conciseness and given as examples without attribution or couched in a form similar to "a soldier might say."

Decisions also had to be made on military ranks that constantly changed during the war. In a general statement about a soldier, such as his nickname, I used his highest rank. If an entry mentions him in a particular battle or event, his rank at that time is used; thus, Ulysses Grant is given his lower rank of brigadier general in the entry for "the pie order," which he issued in 1861.

The Civil War was so momentous, histories were being written as it happened. The authors of *Harper's Pictorial History of the Great*

Rebellion in the United States, who began writing in 1863, said, "We have a solemn duty to perform—we are this day making history. We are writing a book whose pages can never be erased—it is the destiny of our country and of mankind."

Neither should the vigorous language and the euphemistic words of those times be erased. Some of them have been carefully gathered together for this book, an effort that was more of a loving quest than a solemn duty.

ACKNOWLEDGMENTS

IN ADDITION TO my wife and children, four people in particular supported this book, making the long hours of writing seem less lonely. They are my brother, the Rev. William B. Wright, an Episcopalian minister and the "buffest" of Civil War buffs, who kindly sent his reference books; my agent Edward Knappman who, among his many wise suggestions, provided the book's title; and two of Oryx's editors, Henry Rasof, for his encouragement, patience and sound advice; and John Wagner, who fine-tuned the manuscript with amazing precision.

GUIDE TO RELATED TOPICS

Abbreviations
A.A.D.C.
A.A.G.
ab
AD
A.D.C.
A-1
A.P.
app.
A.V.C.
A.W.O.L.
batch
BC
biz
C
commish
comp
CS
CSA
D
D and D
D.B.
D.G.
D.H.
F.F.V.
F.M.C.
G.D.
Grant, U. H.
H
I.C.
I.F.W.
"Jeffn"
M.D.
m.d.
m.e.
medic
MVM
NHV
non-com
O.K.

O.P.
OVM
P.A.C.S.
P.D.
photo
Q.M.
RC
SNY
sub
T
T.E.
U.S.A. Hosp Dept
U.S.C.T.
U.S.M.A.
U.S.M.R.R.
vet
VMM
W

Battle and Fortification Terms
abatis
Alexandria Line
ambuscade
artillery of position
bag the enemy
barbette tier
battles
blockhouse
breach
breast-to-breast fighting
breastwork
brothers truce
bulge, the
cannonade
casemate
cheval-de-frise
Chinese game, the
color line
concentrated force

cornfield, the
council of war
counter-reconnaissance
coup de main
coup d'oeil
defeat in detail
demonstration
"deserter"
ditch
ditching
dog fall
driving in the pickets
echelon attack
effective range
embrasure
encounter battle
en barbette
en embrasure
en echelon
enfilade
epaulment
esplanade
fascine
feeler
fieldwork
file closer
fire-sheet lightning
fire-step
flank
flankers
fortified town
gabion
guidon
hasty entrenchment
head-log
hollow square
hornwork
hors de combat
Hotchkiss maps
infantry parapet

inside track, the
interior lines
in the air
left wheel
lunette
machicoulis gallery
meeting engagement
mud truce
organized battle
over
parapet
plunging fire
"Pull her off!"
punching
racking
rammer
rampart
Rebel yell
reconnaissance in force
redan
redoubt
refused
revetment
rifle pit
round
run out a gun
running a battery
run up a gun
salient
sand-bag battery
sap
sap and parallel
seat of war
sidling movement
skid
skirmish
supporting distance
Sunday battle
tactical articulation
talking torch
terre-plein
tete de pont
tight place
traverse
trou de loup
war-look
water battery
wild fire

Books and Poems
American Dictionary of the English Language, An
Army and Navy Pocket Dictionary, The

"Barbara Frietchie"
"Charge of the Mule Brigade"
Cupid's Own Library
Daniel XI
dime novel
"Drummer Boy of Marblehead, The"
"Gone to the War"
"Hirling and the Slave, The"
Home Comforts
Hospital Sketches
"Hymn of Freedom"
Impending Crisis, The
"In the Hospital"
"Johnny Reb's Epistle to the Ladies, The"
Les Miserables
Macaria, or Altars of Sacrifice
"March"
McGuffey's Electic Reader
New Gymnastics for Men, Women and Children, The
"Old Heart of Oak"
"Our Country's Call"
Rakish Rhymer, The
"Sambo's Right to Be Kilt"
"Shiloh"
Soldier's Hymn Book, The
"Stonewall Jackson's Way"
"Sweet Little Man, The"
Tale of Two Cities, A
"Tardy George"
"Thanksgiving Day"
Uncle Tom's Cabin
"We Are Coming, Father Abraham"
Woman in White, A

Buildings and Rooms
"Arlington House"
Astor House, the
Barnum's American Museum
Beauvoir
Bowman House, the
Briarfield
Brockenbrough house
buttery

dead house
dwelling-house
drawing room
garret
Harvey's Oyster Saloon
"Liberty Hall"
lodgment
"Mess, The"
parlor
piazza
St. Paul's Episcopal Church
shebang
sitting room
slip
Soldier's Home
veranda
"Yorkshire"

Civilian Personal Possessions
baa-lamb
baby-house
Balmoral
bandbox
bee-gum
bertha
bishop
blank book
bloomers
bustle
carpet-bag
collarette
comforter
crash
cross-grained
dickey
dip
dot
doings
falderal
fireball
fireboard
flounce
Franklin stove
gallowses
galoshes
garibaldi
gewgaw
Giant of Battles
goose
hoop skirt
jeans
kiss-me-quick
leghorn

looking-glass
Mouchoir
nosegay
Osnaburg
paling
palisade
pantalets
pantaloons
pap-cup
pelerine
piggin
pocket money
poke-bonnet
portmanteau
port-monnaie
puffing
ragbag
raglan
roundabout
ruche
Russian stove
sabots
sack coat
sacking
salamander stove
Saratoga trunk
Sleepy Hollow chair
smoothing iron
sperm candle
sun fuel
taper
tarletan
tick
tidy
toilette
truckle bed
tucking-comb
Union bonnet
Vandyke collar
washing-machine
wrapper
yard-paling

Culture and Entertainment

baton
Battle of Bull Run, The
cork opera
domestic sentimentalists
Essayons, the
"Libby Lyceum, the"
lyceum
Marble Heart, The
necromancer

Our American Cousin
Richmond Howitzers
Still Waters Run Deep
tableau vivant
"Victory, General Grant"
Virginia Cavalier, The

Departments and Offices

Adjutant General's
   Department
Aeronautic Department
Army Intelligence Office
Bureau of Military
   Justice
Inspector General's
   Deparment
Ordnance Department
Pay Department
Post Office Department
Provost Marshal Depart-
   ment
Quartermaster Depart-
   ment
Subsistence Department

Euphemisms

agricultural laborer
ambia
avoirdupois
boarding-house
business, the
cash in one's checks
casket
consolation
cornerstone, the
Cyprian
expectorate
fallen angel
fallen into his last sleep
fancy girl
fast house
field hand
French fever
French leave
gay young duck
going down the line
gone above
gone home
gone up
hail Columbia
hand in (one's) checks
hang up one's fiddle
horizonal refreshment
house servants

involuntary labor
liberate
muster out
"my people"
off the country
"Old Scratch"
on the turf
parlor house
pass over the river
peculiar institution
pushing up daisies
ranch
retrograde movement
servant
sinks, the
sportsman
take off
tumble bug
use up

Food, Drink, and Cooking

alcoholism
anise seed cordial
apple brandy
apple butter
apple pie
army bread
asses' milk
baker's cake
barley wine
bean hole
beefsteak
beef tea
bimbo punch
bolted
Borden's milk
bracer
brandy sour
bread sauce
broma
broom-corn
bruise
bully soup
burnt brandy and peach
burnt sugar coffee
calibogus
candy pull
cane seed coffee
catfish
Charlotte Russe
chicken water
chinquapin coffee
cider cart

clabber
cochineal
coffee boiler
collards
cook-house
"cook-up"
corpus cup
corn cake
corncob "soda"
corn dodger
corn fritter
corn pone
corn juice
corn, salt, and apples
creeper
cush
dainty
dandyfunk
Delmonico's
desiccated potatoes
dinner
duff
egg-nog
elder wine
essence of coffee
fixings
fix-up
fizz
general treat
gill
ginger beer
ginger cake
goober
gooseberry vinegar
graham bread
Graham system
grape coffee
grog ration
ground pea
hardtack
hasty pudding
hoe-cake
horehound candy
jerked beef
lager
light cornbread
lobscouse
locomotive
marooning
Martinez
mess
mess gear
mess kettle
metheglin
middling

milk punch
mint julep
Mississippi punch
navy bean
okra coffee
pea coffee
pepper treatment
pork and eggs
potato and persimmon
  coffee
potato chip
raspberry tea
rose hip sauce
rye coffee
sack posset
salad
saleratus
sassafras tea
sea pie
set-down
sheep's head soup
singling
skillygalee
slapjack
sleeper
slosh
slumgullion
snack
soda biscuit
sora
sorgum molasses
sour milk
still-house
stone fence
store-bought bread
sugar cracker
sutler's pie
sweet oil
switchel
syllabub
waiter
war coffee
watermelon sherbet
whiskey cobbler

Geographical Areas
American Union, the
Avenue, the
banquette
Big Ditch, the
Big Drink
Big Pond, the
black North
block
Burnt Country, the

Burnt District, the
Central Park, the
chopping
cotton-belt
Cotton States, the
cul-de-sac
Far South, the
further West, the
Gervais Street
Kanawha
Little Round Top
Long Bridge
Mason and Dixon's Line
Middle States, the
Negro Hill
Nickajack
quarter section
real South, the
run
shoot
slashes, the
Swampoodle
Sweet Water Branch
Trans-Mississippi
Washington City

Government and Politics
"An Act to Provide for the
  Public Defense"
Blue-Book
bread riot
Commander-in-Chief
common agency
commutation fee
Confiscation Acts
Confederate Oath
Conscription Act
consolidation
Crittenden-Hohnson
  Resolution
"Day of National Humili-
  ation, Fasting, and
  Prayer"
"death without benefit of
  the clergy"
declension
"Dedicatory Remarks"
delegate
Dix's American Flag
  Dispatch
diplomatist
draft riots
Emancipation Proclama-
  tion
Enrollment Act, the

Freedmen's Bureau
General Government, the
Great Seal of the Confederacy, the
"Hail to the Chief"
income tax
Ironclad Oath, the
Loyalty Oath
mileage
Military Bill, the
Montgomery Issue, the
National Union Party
National Volunteers
nullification
one-term principle
Ordinance of Secession
Peace Convention
Peace Democrats
Proclamation of Amnesty and Reconstruction
Radical Republicans
red tape
Roll of Honor
specie
states' rights
ten-forty bonds
Ten Percent Plan
Thanksgiving
"Thanks of Congress"
three-hundred-dollar clause
War Democrats
Wide Awakes
Your Excellency

Hardware and Weapons
Absterdam
Adams
ammunition train
apron
Arman
arme blanche
arsenal
artillery fuze
"Artisavis, or Bird of Art"
axle-tree
balk
ball
Beadslee telegraph
Bengal light
blunderbuss
bowie knife
breeching rope
browning
buck and ball

buoyant torpedo
caisson
calcium light
camel
canister shot
carcass
cartridge
cascabel
cathead
cavalry lance
chase
cheek
coal torpedo
Colt revolver
derringer
dirk
double shot
elevating screw
field-artillery
field-piece
fougasse
Gatling gun
grape shot
Greek fire
hand-grenade
handspike
hot shot
infernal machine
Joe Brown Pike
keg torpedo
Ketcham's grenade
lanyard
light ball
limber
limber chest
lunette
Marsilly carriage
Maynard Tape Priming
minié ball
Model 1840
Model 1860
moored torpedo
mortar
musketry
Napoleon
Parrott
Pattern 1853
petard
piece
pintle
prolonge
raft torpedo
ramrod
rifled gun

rocket-propelled submarine torpedo
sabot
sand shot
Sharps carbine
siege artillery
sling cart
smoke ball
smoothbore gun
solid shot
spar torpedo
Spencer carbine
spherical case shot
sponge
Springfield rifle
stake torpedo
stock tail
tampion
thumbstall
truck carriage
trunnion
Turtle torpedo
Winan steam gun
windage
wire entanglements
worm

Horses
Ajax
artillery horse
Billy
Brown-Roan
buggy-nag
Burns
Cincinnati
Daniel Webster
Fox
Highfly
Jack
Jefferson Davis
Kangaroo
Lookout
Lucy Long
Old Sorrel
Plug Ugly
Richmond
Rienzi
span
Traveller
Virginia
wheel pair
whicker

Jobs and Commerce
amanuensis
avails

bar-keep
baster
billy
bounty agent
carman
cheap john
company fund
debt of honor
domestics
hostler
limner
lunch room
lunch stand
metallic coffin
midwife
modiste
out-walker
pick
pimp
pinchback
postillion
Queen of the Valley
puddler
slush fund
"Soldier's Joy"
spiritualism
sutler
teamster
train-boy
twist
Union tie
waiter girl
yeoman farmer

Journalism

*Army and Navy Official
    Gazette*
Army Argus
Associated Press
Atlantic Monthly, The
Bohemian Brigade
Cairo war correspondent
"Confederate War
    Etchings"
Daily Rebel Banner
"Dirt Eating papers"
exchange
Extra Press Edition
Faber No. 2
"fighting editor"
"Foreign News"
"Gentleman's Agree-
    ment"
Gold Hoax
Harper's Weekly

Libby Chronicle, The
Liberator, The
"most largely circulated
    journal in the world,
    the"
"Movements of Mrs.
    Lincoln"
occasional
official intelligence
our own correspondent"
pen printing
pick-lock journalism
"Prayer of Twenty
    Millions"
Rapid Ann, The
Rowlands, John
"Situation, The"
Southern Bureau
*Southern Field and
    Fireside*
Southern Illustrated News
Southern Punch
telegraphic account
"Triple Sheets"
Vidette
war department
write someone down

Medical

aergrotant
affection of the mucous
    membranes
Agnew
ague
ailments of Venus
ambulance
ambulance corpsman
ambustion
anasarca
ankylosis
aphonia
apoplexy
apothecary
bad blood
bandage-roller
Banner hospital
bilious fever
black tongue
blood disease
bloody flux, the
blow-fly
blue mass
boneset
Bright's disease
bronze john

California Plan
calomel
camp fever
camp itch
cannon fever
cantharide
castor oil
cephalalgia
chincough
chloride of lime
chloroform
Chimborazo Hospital
clap
close-stool
colic
Company Q
Confederate disease
Confederate Hospital, the
consumption
continued fever
contract surgeon
convalescent camp
copaiva
costiveness
court plaster
crowd poisoning
debility, the
dementia
diarrhea-dysentery
diet kitchen
doctoress
Dover's powder
dresser
dressing station
dropsy
dyspepsia
dyspnea
embalming surgeon
emotional instability
erysipelas
ether
field hospital
fleam
flux
general hospital
glanders
graveyard coughing
green sickness
healing by first intention
hospital bummer
Hospital Directory
hospital steward
Hospital Transport
    System
Hospital visitor

house
Innominata
intermittant fever
ipecacuanha
Jackson Hospital
Jefferson Hospital
laudable pus
laudanum
lavender water
Letterman Ambulance
    Plan, the
low diet
lung fever
mania
manikin   •
*Manual of Military
    Surgery, A*
Medical Corps
miasma
*Military Medical and
    Surgical Essays*
minim
morphia
mortify
mustard plaster
night blindness
nostalgia
noxious effluvia
Mansion House Hospital
operator
opiumized
pennyroyal
physic
pavilion hospital
points and blunts
poisonous vapors
pox
quinine
puerperal fever
pus in the blood
putrid fever
salts
sand-itch
scorbutus
Seidlitz powder
shakes, the
smudge
snakeroot
special hospital
spotted fever
stone-bruise
surgeon
surgeon's call
surgical fever
swamp fever

tartar emetic
valerian
vapors, the
variola
vinum
vivandiere
ward-master
watermelon juice
whitlow
winter fever

Mottos, Slogans, Sayings and Exclamations

Aide-toi et Dieu t'aidera
"All played out!"
"All we ask is to be let
    alone."
armed neutrality
"Beauty and Booty"
"Black Flag"
"bowels yearning for
    battle"
"Buttermilk or cornfed?"
(one's) cake is all dough
call up mourners
cap the climax
"captured but not
    conquored"
"Capture or be cap-
    tured."
carry a horse to water
"Chances for Travel and
    Promotion"
come out at the little end
    of the horn
come up to chalk
coming man, the
conquer peace
crooked as a Virginia
    fence
dark as hell's cellar
dead cock in the pit
"Deo Vindice"
"The devil is loose, the
    devil is loose"
dig up the hatchet
don't care whether school
    keeps or not
"don't swap horses while
    crossing the river"
"Draw it easy!"
draw your furrow
    straighter
drunk as a fool
"Emancipation!"

everybody and his cousin
every mother's son
"Fed and Cornfed"
"Fight it out on this line"
fight like fun
"Fight man fashion"
"fire in the rear"
"First in Vicksburg"
food for powder
"Forty Acres and a mule"
from A to Izzard
get the wrong pig by the
    tail
getting the starch out of
    one's shirt
"Go boil your shirt!"
"Go west, young man, go
    west."
"grinding up the seed
    corn"
hail fellow well met
"Haines!"
happy as clams at high
    water
hard row to hoe
have a brick in one's hat
have (one's) return
    innings
have the staff in one's
    own hand
hearty as a buck
"Here's your mule!"
"Hope and hang on when
    you are wrecked."
"How!"
"How are you, Sanitary?"
"How does your
    corporosity
    sagaciate?"
hurry up the cakes
"Hold the fort."
"Hot work!"
I Dad!
"I fights mit Sigel"
"If you see a head, hit it."
"In Cod We Trust"
"invincible in peace and
    invisible in war"
"I swan"
"I take pen in hand"
"It is an order."
"It takes a man's weight
    in lead for every
    soldier killed in
    battle."

keep a stiff upper lip
knee-high to a splinter
knocked into a cocked hat
knock someone into the middle of next week
know B from a bull's foot
know on
"Landsakes!"
lay it on heavy over
Let her rip!
like a duck hit on the head
like a thousand of brick
like shoveling flies across a barnyard
links of one sausage, made out of the same dog
living within oneself
long summer day, a
looking out for number one
mad as a wet hen
"Mail Must Get Through, The"
"make a good ready"
make a spoon or spoil a horn
make one's toilet
make small potatoes of someone
make the fur fly
make your better acquaintance
manifest destiny
military murder
more than you can shake a stick at
mortally scared to death
"my friends"
"my little bird"
"my little family"
"My name is Haines."
"My pen is bad, my ink is pale; my love for you shall never fail."
"Never kill a cat."
"New Orleans, and home again by summer!"
"No Colored People Allowed On This Car"
not all the gold in California

not born in the woods to be scared by an owl
not by a jugfull
not care a sou
not worth a pinch of salt
nuts for us
not worth a continental cent
"Oh, Cow!"
"One Irishman and three yards of flannel make a Zouave"
on one's high horse
on one's own hook
"On to Richmond!"
"On to Washington!"
over head and ears
over the bay
owning a body
"Peace to his ashes."
"people's war, a"
poor as Job's turkey
"Pope's headquarters is where his hindquarters belong."
Pshaw!
put one to the blush
put on style
"Rally on the sutler!"
"rich man's war, poor man's fight"
robbing the cradle and the grave
"Root, hog, or die."
rowed up Salt river
savage as a meat axe
scarce as hen's teeth
scuppers running blood
see how the cat jumps
see the elephant
sending a boy to the mill
"sharp sabers and sharp spurs"
Sic semper tyrannis
"sixty days"
sling a nasty ankle
"Smash 'em up! Smash 'em up!"
snug as a bug in a rug
"so help me, Hannah!"
sound on the goose
stand in one's own light
stand the gaff
stiff upper lip
sure as a gun

"Swallowed a bass drum?"
Sykes' yellow dog
take the shortening out of a gingercake without breaking the crust
taking a twist at the tiger
"Tell that to the Marines"
tell tuther from which
"there's no ho in him"
thicker than fleas on a dog's back
throw down the gage
"Thunder!"
"till death or distance do us part"
toe the mark
"Too many pigs for the tits."
top rail number one
touching a tiger's cubs
true as the needle to the pole
true Yankee grit
trying to catch a seagull with a pinch of salt
"Tumble up!"
turkey on one's back
"two years and a but"
"Unconditional Loyalty"
very long grace for a thin plate of soup, a
"Victory or Damned Badly Wounded"
"War is hell."
"War is war"
watch and ward
"Whar's you? Whar's you?"
"Whoopee!"
"Who steals my purse steals trash."
Who wouldn't be a soldier?
work off a dead horse
worse for wear, the
You can't catch a weasel asleep.
"Zou! Zou! Zou!"

New Words, Expressions, and Things (introduced just before or during the war)
burgle

butt
by (the) grapevine telegraph
cab
caboose
canned food
chin whiskers
chip in
class
comeuppance
copper
devil-may-care
dick
drunk
evolution
face the music
grapevine
grubstake
homesteader
lickety-split
mutton-chop whiskers
nickel
nifty
passports
peach
photo
rub the wrong way
sheep-skin
squeal
stiff
whitewash
wild West
yellow

Nicknames
"Ace of Spaces"
Acorn Boys
"Aim Low"
"Allegheny"
alligator
America's Bloodiest Day
Andy
"Angel of the Battlefield"
"Angel of Cairo"
"Angel of Light"
"Angel of Marye's Heights"
"Apostle to the Blacks"
aristocratic nigger
Arkansas toothpick
"armed rabble, an"
Army of Observation
"Army of the Lord, the"
"artillery hell"
Aspinwall

"Atlanta Express, the"
"Attila of the west"
Aunty
avalanche
"Avengers of Fort Pillow"
bad nigger
bag of wind
"Bald Eagle"
bald-face
"Baldy"
baled hay
bandbox army
barefoot coffee
bark juice
barnyard preacher
barracks lawyer
"barralita"
"Battle Above the Clouds, The"
"Baylor's Babes"
bear
"Beast"
beat
beater
beau
"Beauty"
beef dried on the hoof
"Bethel Failure"
Betsy
Betty
Biddy
big house
"big Indian war"
Big Tent, the
"Bishop"
Bizarre
blackberry
"Black David"
"Black Horse Harry"
"Black Jack"
black law
black Republicans
blacksnake
Black Terror, the
Black Thursday
blacky
Blalock, Sam
blister
blockhead
"bloodiest day of the war"
"bloodiest region in America, the"
"Bloody Bill"
"Bloody Angle, The"

"Bloody Lane, The"
"Bloody Pond, The"
bluebacks
blue belly
bluebird
bluecoat
blue-eyed Child of Fortune
Blue Jug, the
blue light
"Blue Monday"
blue plum
blue-skin
"Bobby Lee"
body guard
Bonnie Blue Flag, the
boudoir cabinet
"Bowie Knife Boys"
"bowlegs"
boy
"Boy General, the"
bracer
"brain, heart and bowels of the rebellion"
"Brains of the Confederacy, the"
brass missionary
bread
bread bag
breadbasket
breadbasket of the Confederacy
brevet eagle
brevet horse
brick
"Brother Lincoln"
bubba
Buck
Buckland Races
"Bucktails, The"
bud
"Buffalo Bill"
bug
bugger
bug-house
bug juice
bugology
"Bull"
"Bull of the Woods"
bull-head
bullpen
bumblebee whiskey
bun
bunch-of-fives
Bureau of Exemptions

burnt skull
"Butcher"
Butterflies, the
Buttermilk Brigade
"buttermilk cavalry"
Butternut
buzzard-bait
cabbage-head
"Cabinet Car"
"Cad"
calico
California Bible
"California Joe"
camp followers
"Camp Misery"
cap
"Captain Roberts"
card
Carolina potato
Carolina racehorse
carrot-head
catamaran
cauliflower
chained lightning
charcoal nigger
cheesebox on a raft
chewer of the weed
chicken gizzard
chicken guts
Chicken Hominy
chief cook and bottle
     washer
Chimneyville
Chivs, the
chowderhead
Christian soldier
chum
civilian soldier
circle of fire
clawhammer coat
clay-eater
"clouds of mounted men"
coal-heaver
"coffee-grinder"
"Colonel, The"
"Commissary"
civilian soldier
Colt four-pounder
"Commissary"
"common niggers"
"Company"
comrade
Confed
"Confederate beef"
Confederate candle

"Confederate white
     elephant, the"
"Confederacy's best
     friend, the"
consecrated milk
"Constitution"
coon
coon jigger
coon lover
"Coonskin"
coot
Copperhead
corn-cracker
cornstalk militia
Corn Exchange Regiment
corpse-reviver
cotton-clad
cottoncracy
Cotton Stealing Associa-
     tion of the United
     States Navy
country hunk
"Country Sam"
counter-jumper
cow
cow juice
cowskin
crab-apple
Crabtown
cracker barrel confer-
     ence, the
cracker line
cradel of secession, the
"Crazy"
"Crazy Bet"
"Crazy Tom"
creature, the
Crescent City, the
critter companies
creevels, the
croaker
crawl
crooked stick
crossroads wiseacre
cuffie
"Cump"
cupboard
"Curly"
curlyhead
"Czar of Pennsylvania"
damned old goggle-eyed
     snapping turtle
darbies
darky

"Daughter of the Confed-
     eracy"
dead card
dead cart
"Deaf Burke"
"Defender of Vicksburg"
devil fish
"Devil's Den"
"Dictator, The"
dirt-digger
dirty niggers
doc
"Doc"
doctor
doctor woman
dodger
dodunk
dog collar
dog robber
dogs
dogs' bodies
dog tent
do-little
doll baby
Doodle
dough
doughboy
dough-face
down-easter
drab
"Dragon Dix"
"Dr. Bull Run Russell"
Dr. Green
"Drummer Boy of
     Chickamauga"
"Dry Land *Merrimac*"
dry-land sailor
dry nursery
dry seaman
"Dudy"
dunderhead
dundreary
dust
Dutchman
eagle
ebonic
Eddie
educated soldier
egg-sucker
"Elephant, The"
Ellsworth's Avengers
"Emancipator, the"
embalmed beef
Emerald Guards
"Eno's folly"

Ericsson's folly
essence pedler
Ethiopian
evil genius
exempt
"Extra Billy"
eye-opener
"eyes and ears of my
   army"
"eyes of the army"
"Eye, The"
Falls City
fanny
"Fanny"
farmer
fast trick
"Father Abraham"
"Father Neptune"
"Father of Annapolis"
"Father of Waters, the"
fifth wheel
"Fighting Joe"
"Fighting McCooks, the"
"Fighting Parson, the"
"Fighting Phil"
"fighting suit"
"Finest army on the
   planet"
finif
fire-eater
fire laddie
first luff
fish trap
Fitz
flatfoot
flicker
flimsy
flub dubs
fly-away
Flying Cloud
fly-up-the-creek
"Fool Tom Jackson"
"Fort Greenhow"
"Fort Hell"
Fort Pillow massacre
forty
forty dead men
"forty-rod"
"Forty Thieves, the"
four corners
"four-finger drinker"
"four old friends"
"Fox of Kinderhook, the"
"Fox of the White House,
   the"

fresh fish
frog
"fun, the"
Gallant Hood, the
Gallant Pelham, the
galoot
galvanized Yankee
gallinippers
"Gamecock of the South"
Gath
"Gay Cavalier"
gelt
"General Horace"
"General Starvation"
General Tom Thumb
"General Tubman"
gentleman of color
Garibaldi Guard
ghost
"Gibraltar of the West"
gin barrel
"ginned cotton"
goatee
gone goose
goner
goniff
goober grabber
good egg
good fellow
gopher hole
gov
government suit
grafter
"Granny Lee"
"Grant's Jew Order"
grass
graybacks
Graybeard Regiment, the
"Gray Ghost, the"
gray ghost
grease
greaser
"Great Bear of Wall
   Street, the"
"greatest crime of the
   ages"
"Great Hammerer, the"
Great Skedaddle, the
Greek
greenbacks
greenhorn
groggery
grouse
growler
grub scout

grub time
"Grumble"
gump
gunboats
gut-winder
hair of the dog
half-and-half
Hamite
Hancock the Superb
hanger-on
hard cash
hardhead
hard lot
hardscrabble
hardware
Harrison's Landing letter,
   the
Hart, Charlie
hash driver
hat on a shingle
headsplitter
heifer
"Hell-Cat, the"
"Hell Hole, the"
"Hellmira"
Hell's Half-Acre
hen-fruit
"hero of the Trent"
high tide of the Confed-
   eracy
hissing
hog path
holiday soldier
home-made Yankees
"Honest Abe"
"Honest George"
"Honeybun"
"Hooker's Division"
hoosier
hop
hornet
"Hornet's Nest, the"
horse collar
hoss
housewife
Hovey's Babies
howker
Hub, the
huckleberry
huguenot
humbug
hurra's nest
huzzaher
"hypo, the"
Ik. Marvel

"Immortal Regiment, The"
"Immortal Six Hundred, The"
incapable
insurrectionist
"Iowa Grey Hounds"
"Irish Bridget"
Irisher
Iron Brigade
iron coffin
iron column
iron devil
jack
Jack
Jackson's foot cavalry
jail fever
janizary
Jayhawker
"Jeb"
Jeff Davis muddlehead
Jersey lightning
jigger
jiggermaree
Jim Crow
jimhickey
jim-jams
Job's turkey
joe
Joe Brown's Pets
john
John Barleycorn
Johnny
"Jonah"
joy juice
junk
kelter
kid-glove boy
Kilkenny-cat affair
"Kill Cavalry"
Kingdom Come
Kirby Smith-dom
kissing cousin
"Kit"
Klapperschlangenflagge
"la belle Rebelle"
lamp-post
"Land of Legree and the Home of the Slave, the"
landsman
last ditch, the
lead pills
leatherhead

"left wing of Lee's army, the"
leg case
"Lee's Miserables"
"Level Eye"
lickspittal
lier-out
life everlasting
Light Division, The
lighthouse
Lightning Brigade
Lincoln boys
Lincoln pies
Lincoln's soldier
"Little Aleck"
"Little Billy"
"Little Creole, the"
"Little Mac"
"Little Magician, the"
"Little Napoleon"
"Little Phil"
"Little 'Un"
"Lo"
lobster back
Loco-foco
"Lone Star flag"
long sweetening
"Long Tom"
"Loose Bowels"
lost army, the
"Lost Order, the"
"Lost tribes of Israel, the"
lucifer
lunk-head
lush
lush Betty
Lyss
"Mac"
Mackrelville
mail carrier
Main Street
"man of Sumter, the"
manure spreaders
"Marble Man, the"
"Marse Robert"
"Maryland"
"Massa Jeff"
"Matthew," "Mark," "Luke" and "John"
maulie
"McClellan's bodyguard"
mean whiskey
meat bag
"Merrimac No. 2"

mess-mate
"Miasma"
"Michigan Annie"
middy
Milledgeville myth, the
Milroy's weary boys
"Minute Men"
Mississippi Rifle
"Miss Nancy"
Mister
Mr. Banks
mixologist
moke
Molly Cotton Tail
monitor fever
monkey jacket
monkeyshines
monogahela
moonshine
mort
Mosby's Confederacy
"Moses"
"most shot-at man in the war"
mother
"Mother"
"Mother Bickerdyke"
"Mother of Chickamauga, the"
"Mother of Presidents"
mountain dew
"mountain fox, the"
mouse
Mr. Lincoln's gun
Mr. Lincoln's war
mud head
mud hook
Mud Lane
"Mud March, the"
mudsill
"Mudwall"
muggins
mule
Mule Shoe, The
multiform
music
muss
muttonhead
"my bad old man"
"my old war horse"
"my organ"
"my whip-lash"
nag
"nailhead, the"
"Napoleon"

"Nassau bacon"
national game, the
"Neighbor"
newsie
newsmonger
news walker
nick
"nigger cars"
"Negro cloth"
"nigger-driver"
"niggerhead"
"nigger heaven"
"nigger war"
nigger-worshiper
night owl
night rig
nine-monthling
nokum stiff
non-conscript
nullifier
odd fish
oddments
office
"Oh, Be Joyful"
oil of gladness
"Old Abe"
"Old Allegheny"
"Old Baldy"
"Old Bed"
"Old Beeswax"
"Old Blizzards"
"Old Blue-Light"
"Old Bory"
"Old Buck"
old bull
"Old Club Foot"
"Old Figgers"
old flag, the
"Old Fuss and Feathers"
"Old Gentleman Tipsy"
Old Glory
"Old Graybacks"
old haymaker
"Old Hero of Gettysburg"
"Old Jack"
"Old Joe"
"Old Jube"
"Old Lemon-Squeezer"
Old Man, the
"old man"
Old North State
"Old Opium Pills"
"old peach"
"Old Pete"
"Old Pills"

old plug
"Old Probabilities"
"Old Puke"
"Old Quinine"
"Old Red Eye"
"Old Reliable"
"Old Rosey"
"Old Rye"
"Old Slow Trot"
old soldier
"Old Straight"
"Old Tom"
"Old Virginny"
"Old Wooden Head"
old woodpecker
Old Wristbreaker
"Ole Master"
"Ole Miss"
"One-eyed Jeff"
Optic, Oliver
"Ordinanz numero eins!"
"Original Gorilla, the"
"Orphan Brigade"
orphan flag
"our best recruiting
    sergeant"
"Our Bob"
"Our George"
"our soil"
Paddy
"Paddy"
pale-face
Palmetto boys
Palmetto flag
pan
paper-collar soldier
pard
parlor soldier
"Parson"
"Pathfinder of the Seas"
Paw-paw militia
"Peas on a Trencher"
peeler
Pelican Rifles
penny packet
Pen, the
Perry's Saints
persuader
Peter
Petersburg crater
"Pet Lambs"
pet name
pet regiment
Philadelphia Confederate
    note

"Philippi Races, the"
phiz
Pickett's Charge
pick-up
pie eater
"pie order, the"
Pigeon
pile
pins
piss-pot
play-out
plebe
plucking board
Plug
plug
"plug ugly"
"poet laureate of the
    South"
Point, the
polack
polar star
"Polecat"
political general
Poliute
Polly
poltrune
pony, the
poor white trash
"Pop"
"Popeye"
pop-skull
"Porte Crayon"
possum
potato grabbers
powder monkey
"Prairie Dog Village"
Presidential grub, the
"Prince John"
"prince of darkness"
"prince of humbugs"
"prince of rails"
Promises-to-Pay
pumpkin
pumpkin slinger
puny list
puppy love
Quaker gun
quartermaster hunter
"Queen of Sheba"
"Queen Varina"
quiet man, the
"Quinine"
"Quinine Brigade"
Raccoon Roughs
rackansacker

Tennessee quick step
Tennessee Tories
"terrible door of death,
    the"
"terrible men"
"terrible wound, a"
"this damned old house"
Thompson, Franklin
"those people"
thug
"Thunderer, The"
ticket, the
"Tige"
tiger den
"Tiger John"
"Tiger Rifles"
tile
tin
"tin can on a shingle"
titty
toad stabber
toot
Tory
tough nut
Truth, Sojourner
turkey bumps
turkey shoot
Twain, Mark
Twelve Apostles, the
"twenty-nigger law"
"tycoon, the"
Uncle Abe
Uncle Billy
Uncle Dick
Uncle George
Uncle Gideon
Uncle Joe
Uncle John
Uncle Robert
Uncle Sam
Uncle Sambo
"Unconditional Surren-
    der"
underpinnings
Union-saver
"United South"
unknown land, the
unmentionables
upper ten
"Useless"
Valiant Val
Vallandighammer
vandal chief, the
veal
"Virginia Cavalier, The"

"Virginia Creeper, the
Virginia weed
vomit
wag
wage slave
wagon dog
walking ticket
walk-over
"war dog"
"warrant officers'
    champagne"
wash kettle
wash-tub on a raft
"Waterspout Man, the"
weak sister
webfoot
weed
wench
whaler
"Whatisit, the"
Wheat's tigers
wheel
"Whistling Dick"
white nigger
white oak chip
whirl-a-gust
white black
white gold
White House, the
white trash
whorehouse pimp
whoreson
"Widow Blakely"
wigwam
"Wild Bill"
Wild Cat Stampede
Willie
"wily Dutchman, the"
Winnie
"Wizard of the Saddle,
    the"
"Wizard of the Valley,
    the"
wooden coat
Woodstock Races
Woolly Head
woolly head
worm castles
wrinkle
Yankee anniversary, the
"Yankee nurse, the"
"Yates' Hellions"
yawper
yearling
yellow boy

yellow dog
yellow hammers
yellow jack
"Young Bloods of the
    South"
"Young Napoleon"
Zu-Zu

Official Names, Titles, Orders, and Expressions

absent with authority
"All aboard!"
allotment
"All's well"
"All up!"
"Assembly"
"Assembly of Buglers"
"Attention"
at the conn
"Boots and Saddles"
brevet
cadence step
caracol
cartel
cashier
"Cease firing!"
"Charge bayonets."
close up
color
"Column forward!"
common time
countersign
court-martial
double time
dress the line
drum-head court-martial
"Extinguish lights."
fatigue duty
"Fire at will."
foraging
"Form square!"
Fort Sumter Medal
"For Your Eyes Only"
Fourth of July
free delivery
Fremont's proclamation
furlough
"General, The"
General Orders No. 11
General Orders No. 28
Gillmore Medal of Honor
guide right
guide center to the colors
Hood's Second Sortie

hundred-gun salute
goosestep
"In battery."
Kearny Cross
Kearny Medal
letters of marque
"Limber to the rear!"
long roll
Medal of Honor
military commission
military court
morning roll call
"No bottom."
noncombatant
Oath of Muster
parade rest
parole
picketed
put through
pledging ceremony
policing
"Rally"
rank
red-letter pass
"Retreat"
"Reveille"
roll-book
route step
setting pickets
ship over
sick-permit
"Spice the main brace."
spike the gun
standard
standard gray
"Taps"
"Tattoo"
"three days' cooked
    rations and 40 rounds"
"Up!"
wig-wag

Operations and Campaigns
Anaconda Plan
buffalo hunt
Butternut Guerrillas
California Column, the
Dahlgren papers
"General"
Hampton's Cattle Raid
raid around the army

Photography
ambrotype

carte de visite
daguerreotype
dark wagon
fancy
photo
photographist
spirit photograph
stereoscope
take an image
tintype

Prisons
Andersonville
brig
Libby Prison
Old Capitol Prison

Profanity and Its Euphemisms
all-fired
all shit and no sugar
army Latin
"Begad!"
"Be jiminey!"
blamed
blue-blasted
"By ginger!"
"By Jukes!"
"By lightning!"
"By the gods!"
"By the widow Perkins!"
"Damn your eyes!"
"Dang it to hell!"
"Dickens take it all!"
"Doggone it!"
drat
don't care a hang
"Faugh!"
"Fire and brimstone!"
"Gee rod!"
"Gee whillikins!"
"Gorry!"
"Gosh almighty!"
"Gosh darn!"
Great Jerusalem!
Great Scott!
"Great snakes!"
hot as the hinges of hell
Hurrah for hell!
Jupiter!
"Kiss my arse"
"Moses!"
Oh, Perdition!
sacredamn
Shove it up your ass!

Punishments
ball and chain
barrel shirt
Black List
buck and gag
C
Company Q
D
dead line
death post
drumming-out
guard-house
"hog-skin cravat"
knapsack drill
"Libeler of the Press"
mock funeral
"Morgan's Mule"
Rip-Raps, the
shower bath
straggler's camp
T
tying up
W

Recreation, Relaxation, and Games
ace
acey-deucey
air ball
Alabama Flat-rock, The
a larking
alley
anagram
Antony over
ball
bandy
base ball
bathing
battledore
bluff
bowling
bucking the tiger
"Checkered Game of
    Life, The"
checkers
chess
chuck-a-luck
cock fighting
craps
cribbage
cricket
criss-cross
deck
Derby, the
dipping snuff

draughts
"Devil's Half-Acre"
euchre
faro
fox and geese
gaff
gander-pulling
greased pig contest
Great Snowball Battle,
  the
gunning
hog race
home
hop scotch
Hot Cockles
hot jackets
illumination
Jack's Alive
jackstraws
keno
loo
louse fight
louse race
marbles
monte
muggins
Old Capitol
old sledge
penny ante
poker
quoits
raffling
ring tournament
seining
skittles
ten-pins
tombola
twenty-one
Twenty Questions
whist
whittling

Ships and Boats

Alabama
Albemarle
America
blockade runner
bomb-ketch
bungo
David
droger
fire raft
fire-room
fire ship
flat

ironclad
iron-clad steam-battery
Jacob's-ladder
Keokuk
killick
mortar boat
obstruction sweeper
orlop deck
"Pook Turtle"
port stopper
powder boat
quoin
scow
smoke box
stack
steam ironclad floating
  battery
tinclad
trumpet

Slang and Informal Terms

about played out
above one's bend
absquat
acknowledge the corn
acquire
adios
advanced female
after someone with a
  sharp stick
Albany beef
alchy
all in three years
all sorts of
ambition
among the missing
ant killer
any manner of means
applesauce
apple-shaker
Arab
argufy
artificial oyster
a-soldiering
back-out
back talk
bad
bad-box
bad egg
bail one's own boat
bait
baggage smasher
balmy
bamboozle

banger
bat
battling stick
bazoo
beak
bean
beanpole
beanpole and cornstalk
  bridge
beast
beat-up
beef up
beehive
beer-jerker
bend the elbow
benders
big bug
bit
bite dog, bite bear
blenker
blizzard
blow
blow down
blower
blow on someone
blow-up
blue devils
blue-eyed
blue ruin
bobbery
body bag
bogus
bomb-proof
bone
boodle
booking
bore a hole in
born tired
bosh
boss
bounce
brass
breather
breezing
breezy
bruised
buck
buffalo chips
buffalo gnat
bull
bully
bum
bump
bunk it
bunkum

"Burn my skin!"
burst a boiler
buss
busser
buster
Butlerize
by the ears
C
caboodle
calaboose
call someone's hand
canoodle
case
catarumpus
catawampus
chalkies
chawed up
checker, the
chicken feed
chicken pie
chigger
chinch
chin music
chisel
chiv
chow
chuck
clam
clean thing, the
clip
clipper
coffin
coffin-meat
cold-meat cart
collar
comedown
clear the coop
con
conflab
conniption
cool
conacetic
corned
cousin
cow tick
crawfish
crawl
crib
crick
croak
crooked shoes
crusher
cunning
cut and run

cut a wide swath
cut dirt
cutlery
cut stick
cut up extras
cut up jack
dab
damaged
dead-alive
decoction of stump water
deep game
desecrated vegetables
devil's dye
ding
dingbat
dig
diked out
din
dip
dog cheap
dog-hungry
dog leg
dog-poor
done brown
done for
done gone
done up
dornick
do the big job
double harness
double team
down to the ground
dragged out
drinky
drunky
dull music
dumpish
Dutch fit
elbow-crooking
everywheres
every which way
fagged out
falderal
feel streaked
fetch up
fiddle-de-dee!
fig
fillip
fire away
flam
flapdoodle
flummox
flunk out
fogeyism

fore-handed
fox
frazzled
frolic
fuddled
full chisel
full drive
full split
full swing
gal-boy
gallanting
gam
gambado
get a beat on
get it
get the mitten
get up and get
gig
gimp
give someone goss
gloze
go callyhooting
go it bald-headed
go it blind
go it strong
goober
goose egg
gorm
go sparking
go the whole figure
go the whole hog
grab a root
grapey
grit
guy
hack
hacked
half-shot
hammer and tongs
hard-baked
hard run
hawing and geeing
hedge
hellabaloo
highfalutin
high feather
high-toned
hoofing it
hop the twig
horse sense
hornswoggle
"Hot work!"
how-come-you-so
hunk

hunky-dory
improvement
in a box
in a freeze
indeedy
indigo mud
in full feather
jam-up
jim-jams
jollification
jug
jug-steamed
jump
keep company
keep tavern
kick
kick and cuff
kick the bucket
kick up a dust
kill
knock off
knock up
larrup
law
leastways
lick
lip
liquor up
loblolly
long chalk
looseness
lousy
lousy with
low-down
mellow
mizzle
mop and mow
mush
navigate
nobby
no great scratch
no odds
offish
O.K.
old
one-horse
on the fly
Paddy-like
peach
peanut
peeling
pike
pipe down
pipe-laying

plank down
plant
play old soldier
play off
play smash
plug a tooth
pokerish
polt
poppycock
posted
power, a
puff
pull foot
put the licks in
rail it
railroad time
raise blazes
rambunctious
reading linen
refractory
rock
rocking someone
rocky
rope in
rub out
run (one's) gait
running the guard
rush
rusticate
sack
sail in
sass
saucy
scout
scratch gravel
sell
set store by
shackly
sharp-set
shell out
shenanigan
shift
shilly shally
shine a frog
shoddy
shovel fleas
sight
skedaddle
skirmishing
skylarking
slangwhang
slat
slewed
slip up
slope

slows, the
smell powder
snap
snapped
snatch
snatch bald-headed
snub
sobby
spanking good
spark it
splendiferous
spoon-fashion
spot
spread down
squiffed
stomach-jumped
streaky
stump
tailor fashion
take a shine to
take the cake
take the shine off some-
    one
talk large
tall
the go
thin
thirsty
thundering
ton
trophy
tumbled over
Turk-fashion
unco
unman
up a tree
vamose
vaunt
vitiate
wallpapered
wash
whipped
wiggle-waggle
wilt someone
wipe out
wool
Yankeeized
yep

Slavery and Negroes
"Abolition!"
abolitionized
Abraham
African
amalgamate

American Antislavery
  Society
article
Aunt
buckra
colored folk
colorphobia
contraband
crier
dozens, the
driver
gang
Gullah
head driver
Mammy
marriage abroad
manumission
mulatto
nanna
Negress
nigger
overseer
pickaninny
planter
quadroon
sold South
speculator
stewart
swaga buckra
title
track-hound
trash gang
Uncle
Undergound Railroad
viginal crop
village
yellow

Social Events
apple-bee
at-home
barbecue
basket-meeting
blow-out
infare
levee
open house
social
starvation party
tea party

Soldiers and Sailors
abolition soldiers
artillery driver
artilleryman

automaton
Blue, the
blue-water sailor
book-soldier
Boys in Blue
Boys in Gray
bummer
bunk-mates
Bushwhacker
cannonier
chasseur
color guard
conscript
courier
dragoon
effective
ensign
Federalists
field officer
flag officer
General-in-Chief
general officer
Gray, the
grayback
guerrilla
guidon
heavy
horse sergeant
leadsman
picket
pontonier
sharpshooter
soldier of the Republic
straggler
subaltern
three-months man
topical engineer
trooper
vedette
veteran volunteer
volunteer veteran
wagoner
Zouave

Soldiers' Equipment and Uniforms
accouterments
armored vest
bedroll
blacking
brogs
cap box
cartridge-box
clawbar
corps badge

cottonade
Davis boot
ditty-bag
drilling
duck trousers
equipage
facing
forage cap
frock coat
frogging
glass
great-coat
gutta-percha
Hardee hat
hardtack box
havelock
haversack
helmet
hickory shirt
holystone
Kearny patch
kepi
kersey
knapsack
Mackinaw blanket
marquee
McClellan cap
merino shirt
nail keg
necessaries
oil-cloth
opera-glass
percussion cap
polka jacket
rowel
rubber
saddle-skirt
shako
shaving glass
shell jacket
Sibley tent
slouch hat
talma
traps
whipple hat

Soldiers' Personal Items
actress cards
belly band
Beecham's Pills
"biled" shirt
boiled shirt
cockade
comfort-bag
identifier

identity disc
patchwork
Sanitary shirt
slush lamp
strop
tobacco bag
wafer
water-filterer

Songs, Dances, and Music

"All Hail the Power of Jesus' Name"
"All Quiet Along the Potomac To-night"
"Amazing Grace"
"Annie of the Vale"
"Arkansas Traveler"
"Auld Lang Syne"
"Aura Lee"
banjo
"Battle-Cry of Freedom, The"
"Battle Hymn of the Republic, The"
"Blue Tail Fly"
"Bonnie Blue Flag, The"
"Brass-Mounted Army, The"
"Dixie"
"Drummer Boy of Shiloh, The"
fife
"Gal on a Log"
galop
German, the
"God Save the South"
hoe-down
"Homespun Dress, The"
"Home Sweet Home"
Hood's Minstrels
Hutchinson Family Singers
"John Brown's Body"
Juba
"Kingdom Coming"
Lancers, The
"Lorena"
"Marching Song of the First Arkansas"
"Marching Through Georgia"
"Mary Had a Little Lamb"
"Mocking Bird, The"

"My Maryland"
"Old Folks at Home"
patting
pianoforte
polka
quadrille
"Rising of the People"
"Rogue's March, The"
schottische
slave songs
"Somebody's Darling"
"Song for our Soldiers"
"Spanish Fandango, The"
stag dance
"Tenting on the Old Camp Ground"
"Tramp, Tramp, Tramp, the Boys Are Marching"
"We'll Hang Jeff Davis from a Sour Apple Tree"
"When Johnny Comes Marching Home"
"When This Cruel War Is Over"
"Yankee Doodle"
"Yellow Rose of Texas, The"

Training

Annapolis
Artillerist's Manual
Elements of Military Art and Science
first classman
goose squad
goosestep
Hardee's Tactics
hay foot, straw foot
Maxims of War
receiving ship
System of Infantry Tactics
Uniform and Dress
West Pointer

Transportation

Atlanta & West Point Railroad
barouche
Black Maria
boxcars
buggy
bull train

carriage-way
carryall
chair
chaise
chay
common road
corduroy road
coupe
deck
dickey
dog-cart
dray
flying telegraph train
gig
hack
hansom
mail train
off-wheel horse
omnibus
pilot-engine
"Pioneer, The"
plank road
rockaway
shafts
shell road
sprung wagon
street-car
sulky
traces
United States Military Railroads
way-bill

Units

advance guard
armorer's gang
army
Army of Virginia
artillery
Awkward Squad
battalion
battery
Berdan's sharpshooters
Black Horse Cavalry, the
boatswain's gang
Border Brigade
Bridge Guard
brigade
burying squad
captain-of-the-hole's gang
carpenter's gang
Cherokee Mounted Rifles
company
conscription squad

corps
Corps d'Afrique
counter-battery
department
division
flying artillery
Georgia State Line
grand division
gunner's gand
high-number regiment
home guard
Indiana Legion
Indian Home Guard
legion
litter corps
master-at-arm's gang
military division
militia
Nauvoo Legion Militia
operational organization
partisan rangers
Pioneer Corps
platoon
regiment
sailmaker's gang
Secret Service
section
small-arms men
squadron
State Rangers
territorial organization
Union Light Guard
United States Colored
    Troops
Veteran Reserve Corps
Virginia State Line
Wild's African Brigade
wing
wood bee

Unusual or Popular Words, Spellings, or Language Constructions

at
bashaw
bravely
brickley
by and again
cafeteria
caitiff
calumniated
capital
chafe
cicerone

clever
columbarium
controul
countrified
cracklings
crinoline accident
cumshaw
cyclopean
day-dawn
daubing the chinks
depredating
disremember
discombobulate
do don't
do execute on (or upon)
drive well
dry wash
dundrearies
energize
English, the
environ
eventuate
excurt
extacy
fixed fact
freshet
front-door yard
go by
gone with
graft
Hayti
help
hern
hisn
holydays
houseless
hurryment
illuminator
kindlers
know on
lief
logicize
lover
imperial
magnetic telegraph
malison
"marble"
mean
mile
Mr. Grant
Mrs. President
musicianer
natheless
native American
Nicholson pavement

nohow
Norther
no sabe
nothing to nobody
obliged
orison
ourn
pair of stairs
pavement
personate
phonography
plough
police descent
private-hand letter
ratherish
reconnoissance
Robert Lee
rod
sawyer
scour
signalize
singular
skrimmage
smite
smooch
snag
Southron
Stonewall
studying
stuffening
summerset
telegraphic message
telephone
theirn
tierce
to
trust bearer
"United States are...."
us-all
veteranize
vitiate
we-uns
wrathy
yourn
you-uns
you-all

War-related Organizations and Businesses
American Bible Society
Christian Association
Christian Commission
European Legion, the
Fenian Brotherhood
"Haystack, The"

Knights of the Golden
  Circle
Ladies Defense Associa-
  tion
Madam Russell's Bake
  Oven
Monroe Guard, the
Nashville Plow Works
Paff's Cave
Peace and Constitutional
  Society
rolling mill
powder manufactory
refreshment saloon
Sanitary Commission
Sanitary Fair
sewing society
Soldier's Aid Society
Soldier's Friend League
Sword Test, the
Sisters of Charity
Southern Mothers'
  Association

spinning bee
Spotswood Hotel
Tredegar Iron Works
Union Refreshment
  Saloon
Wayside Home
Willard's Hotel
Wolf's Den, The

War-related Terms

ante-bellum
Confederate War, the
crape
Disunionist
earlier Revolution, the
Federal principle
Gentlemen
Glorious Cause, the
National Army
Northman
Old Army, the
peace meeting
Pittsburg Landing

ransom
refugeeing
Revolution, the
Second War for Indepen-
  dence, The
Sharpsburg
Southern Confederacy
Southern Republic
Trent Affair
Union Meetings
Unpleasantness, the
War Against the States
War Between the States
War for (or of) Indepen-
  dence, the
War for Separation, the
War for Southern
  Nationality, the
War of 1861, the
War of Secession
War of the Rebellion
Yankee Invasion, the

A

A.A.D.C. (or Add. A.D.C.). Abbreviations for additional aide-de-camp. The number of aides de camp in the Union Army swelled after August 5, 1861, when Congress authorized an unlimited number of the additional aide positions. *See also* A.D.C.

A.A.G. Abbreviation for assistant adjutant general, the most respected and personal member of a general's staff. Besides issuing and explaining his superior's orders to subordinates, the A.A.G. also did many thankless tasks. Confederate Brigadier General "STONEWALL" Jackson sent his A.A.G., Captain Henry Kyd Douglas, to deliver a message to a detachment "on the other side of the Blue Ridge Mountains, somewhere near Culpepper." When Douglas returned, worn and weary after a four-day journey of more than 200 miles, Jackson gave him a nod and dismissal: "Very good. You did get there in time. Good night."

ab. An abbreviation of "abolitionist" used by southerners as a nickname for a Union soldier.

abatis A defensive barricade of large branches placed close together with the ends sharpened and facing toward the enemy. The bottom ends were anchored into the ground. An emergency abatis could be quickly constructed by locking together limbs and vines.

"Abolition!" The slogan used by slavery abolitionists. It had previously been a colonial slogan for demanding the repeal of the British Stamp Act in 1765.

abolitionized A word that began to be used in the North in 1863 to describe the Lincoln administration's increased emphasis on abolition, as demonstrated by the Emancipation Proclamation. Some northerners believed that loyalty to the Union and the war effort was now being equated with one's support of abolition.

abolition soldiers A southern name for Union troops.

about played out About ready to quit. A tired, demoralized soldier might describe himself as "about played out"; the phrase was also sometimes used for whole units. *See also* "All played out!"; play-out.

above one's bend A slang expression meaning "above one's reach" or "beyond one's abilities"; e.g., "I could try to describe Susan's beauty, but it is above my bend."

Abraham The name of a slave who, on June 25, 1863, suffered only superficial injuries when blasted off a Confederate hilltop position by a Union mine dug into the southern lines during the siege of Vicksburg. Abraham, a cook, was adopted by an Iowa unit, which sequestered him in a tent and charged fellow soldiers five cents to view the miraculous man. Asked how high he had flown, Abraham calculated "bout tree mile."

absent with authority The official military designation for soldiers who had permission to leave their units. Often, the majority of men absent with authority were ill or disabled. *See also* A.W.O.L.

absent without official leave *See* A.W.O.L.

absquat (or absquattle or absquatulate) A slang term meaning "to leave or run away"; e.g., "The Yankees absquatulated pretty good when we opened fire." The word, meaning the opposite of squatting, was supposedly coined in the early nineteenth century in Kentucky.

Absterdam A Union army field-artillery projectile that was three inches long and solid.

accouterments A soldier's equipment other than his uniforms and weapons. Common accouterments included the CARTRIDGE BOX, CAP BOX, KNAPSACK, HAVERSACK, RUBBER (blanket), and cooking utensils.

ace A term for a run scored in BASE BALL.

"Ace of Spades" An early nickname given to Robert E. Lee for his enthusiastic orders to dig fortifications. Some of the most extensive spading by Lee's troops was done around Richmond and Charleston. The nickname was sometimes altered to "King of Spades" and "Spades Lee."

acey-deucey A slight variation of backgammon that was a popular game in camp and on ship. It often led to gambling, which was against regulations.

acknowledge the corn (or confess the corn) To admit you have done something wrong. A soldier accused of anything from lying to stealing someone's tobacco, might confess as follows: "You've got me, friend. I'll acknowledge the corn." The expression supposedly came from the trial of a man accused of stealing horses and corn, who said, "I acknowledge the corn," but not the horses. He was reportedly hanged. A similar expression today is "cop a plea."

"Acorn Boys" Nickname that the members of the U.S. 14th Army Corps of the Army of the Potomac gave themselves. They had once run low on rations when surrounded by Confederates, probably General Braxton Bragg's troops at Chattanooga, Tennessee, and the men had to gather and roast acorns. They adapted the acorn as their badge in 1864 to be worn on the centers of their caps.

acquire A euphemism meaning "to steal" or "to forage." It was especially used by the troops of Union Major General W.T. Sherman on their 1864 march through Mississippi and Georgia when they "acquired" everything from corn to cattle from local residents. So effective were his troops at obtaining supplies, that Sherman wrote: "I don't believe I will draw anything for them but salt."

actress cards Naughty photographs popular in both Union and Confederate camps. These early pinups, consisting of paper prints of American and European "actresses" in scanty clothes, were nailed to camp huts, pinned to tent walls, and carried from one battle to the next in KNAPSACKS.

AD The abbreviation for the AERONAUTIC DEPARTMENT of the Union army. Although its members were civilians, some wore the letters in brass on their caps until laughs and jokes from soldiers forced their removal. *See also* BC.

Adams A revolver imported from London. It was a more exotic weapon, often engraved with fancy designs and was normally used by officers. The gun, which had been adopted by the British War Department, was manufactured by R. Adams.

A.D.C. The abbreviation for aide-de-camp. An aide was on the staff of a general, a chief of artillery, or another commanding officer and performed a variety of official and personal duties. The Union's Major General W.T. Sherman would sometimes lie on a settee and dictate a dispatch to an aide who sat by his side while balancing the writing paper on one knee. *See also* A.A.D.C.

Add. A.D.C. *See* A.A.D.C.

adios This Spanish word for "goodbye" was about 30 years old during the war and was especially used by soldiers from the Southwest. It literally means "to God" with the implied blessing of "I commend you to God."

Adjutant General's Department The U.S. department responsible for military orders and regulations, manuals, recruiting, personnel records, and activating and deactivating volunteer units. It was headed by the adjutant general, who was a brigadier general, and had assistant adjutant generals in the various army headquarters. *See also* A.A.G.

advance guard (or advanced guard) The first troops to push into an area that was often occupied by the enemy. An advanced guard sometimes comprised cavalry and artillery supported by infantry.

advance station *See* dressing station.

advanced female A woman seeking equality with men; e.g., "The surgeon complained that advanced females were taking control of the hospital wards."

aergrotant The medical term for an ill person. An illness was formally called an aegrotantem.

Aeronautic Department The Union army's unit in charge of observation balloons. Thaddeus Lowe, a civilian officially titled Chief of Aeronauts, Army of the Potomac, and given the honorary title of "Professor," organized the Balloon Corps in 1861 and headed it after it became operational in January 1862. His seven balloons were filled by portable horse-drawn hydrogen generators that used sulfuric acid and iron filings to generate the gas. An ascent required about 12 volunteers to let out the line that always restrained the balloon, and other lines tethered it against possible winds. Lowe reported observations from his high advantage point using a telegraph key in his basket. The first U.S. balloon on the battlefield, the *Intrepid*, was ordered on April 5, 1862, by General George McClellan at Yorktown, Virginia, to determine the size of Major General John Magruder's forces. Magruder, however, got word of the balloon and had his small force march in a circle that passed a forest clearing, giving the impression of new troops continuously advancing. When Professor Lowe reported this gigantic force, McClellan had his troops dig in for a long siege, allowing the Confederates to escape. One of the observers of Lowe's early experiments was Count Ferdinand von Zeppelin, a Prussian who served in the Union army and who later developed the dirigible. Balloons were also later used to direct cannon fire to their targets. About 3,000 flights were made for the Union. *See also* AD, "most shot-at man in the war, the"; Silk Dress Balloon.

Professor Thaddeus S. Lowe of the Union Aeronautic Department preparing to observe the battle of Fair Oaks, Virginia, on May 31, 1862. *Library of Congress, Prints & Photographs Division, LC-B8171-2348.*

affection of the mucous membranes A euphemism for a venereal disease.

African A name sometimes used for a Negro, especially in the North. In his official report on an action occurring during the Vicksburg campaign on June 7, 1863, Union General Ulysses S. Grant wrote: "In this battle most of the troops engaged were Africans, who had little experience in the use of firearms. Their conduct is said, however, to have been most gallant, and I doubt not but with good officers they will make good troops."

after someone with a sharp stick An expression meaning "to seek revenge on," or "get satisfaction from," someone; e.g., "After Forrest's raids, we knew Sherman would be after him with a sharp stick."

Agnew A loose-fitting shirt worn by Union nurses. It became an unofficial uniform after 1862 when a nurse in the Peninsula campaign borrowed a shirt from Dr. Agnew. It was usually worn with an open collar, sleeves rolled up, and the tails untucked.

agricultural laborer A formal euphemism for a slave. Addressing the Confederate Congress on April 29, 1861, President Jefferson Davis reviewed the history of slaves in the South: "In a moral and social condition they had been elevated from brutal savages into docile, intelligent, and civilized agricultural laborers, and supplied not only with bodily comforts, but with careful religious instruction, under the supervision of a superior race."

ague A common name for malaria. One Illinois soldier wrote his family, "We are more afraid of the ague here than the enemy." The name was also generally used for fevers with intermittent chills.

aide-de-camp *See* A.D.C.

Aide-toi et Dieu t'aidera The motto of the Confederate commerce raider ALABAMA. The French words, meaning "Help yourself and God will help you," were inlaid in gilt on the ship's wheel. *See also* blockade runner.

aid station *See* dressing station (or advance station).

ailments of Venus The common name on both sides for venereal disease. More than 180,000 cases were reported in the Union army, which camped near cities more often than did the Confederate army.

"Aim Low" Nickname earned by Colonel Granville Moody of the 12th Ohio Regiment before the battle of Murfreesboro, or Stones River, in Tennessee on December 31, 1862. Moody was leading his troops in prayer. As he said, "Now, boys,

fight for your country and your God, and . . . ," a loud Confederate volley whizzed over them. Moody glanced up and quickly concluded with, ". . . and aim low!"

air ball A pop fly in a BASE BALL game.

Ajax One of the horses of Confederate General Robert E. Lee. It was a sorrel (light reddish brown) steed given to him in 1862 after the second battle of Bull Run. Lee stopped riding him because he said Ajax had "failed." See also Brown-Roan; Lucy Long; Richmond; Traveller.

Alabama The most famous Confederate raider, a 220-foot cruiser that captured 65 Union merchant ships around the world and virtually drove U.S. commerce from the high seas. Built in 1862 simply as the "290" by the Laird Company of Liverpool, England, it "sat upon the water with the lightness and grace of a swan," according to its commander, Rear Admiral Ralphael Semmes. It had three masts, steam power, eight guns, and 144 men and officers whom Semmes called "a precious set of rascals." The *Alabama* was sunk June 19, 1864, in the English Channel off Cherbourg, France, by the *Kearsarge*, a Union IRONCLAD disguised with wood. In the crowd viewing the battle on the French shore was a young painter, Edouard Manet. Semmes and 54 men escaped after being rescued by English and French boats, 70 of the crew became prisoners on the *Kearsarge*, and 21 died. The Alabama Claims in 1872 resulted in Great Britain paying $15.5 million to the U.S. for damages caused by the *Alabama* and two other ships built in England, the *Florida* and the *Shenandoah*.

The Alabama Flat-rock A lively country dance popular in the rural South. Union troops wintering in the Appalachians of Tennessee in 1863 made friends with the locals and "danced 'The Alabama Flat-rock' with mountain women."

a larking A joke played on new or naive soldiers by old hands. The victim was invited to "go a larking" in the woods, preferably on a frosty or rainy night, to hunt for nonexistent larks. He would be given an empty meal bag and shown how to crouch down (in a cramped position) and remain motionless and quiet while his camp-mates drove larks into the bag. The pranksters would then run off to their beds in camp, leaving the helper "holding the bag," often all night.

Albany beef A nickname for the sturgeon, which originated in New York State where the fish was plentiful in the Hudson River.

Albemarle A Confederate IRONCLAD ram that secured the vital Roanoke River down to Albemarle Sound on the North Carolina coast. It was 150 feet long and had two 6.4-inch Brooke rifles. Commissioned on April 17, 1864, and captained by Commander James W. Cooke, it soon damaged seven Union gunboats, without being hurt itself, in a three-hour battle in the Albemarle Sound. It was sunk October 26, 1864, by a small launch commanded by Lieutenant William B. Cushing with a crew of 14. They rammed a log wall protecting the *Albemarle*'s river berth, and Cushing used three lines tied to his wrists to swing a long pole over the enemy ship and activate a torpedo on the end of the pole. The launch was also swamped but Cushing survived.

alchy A slang name for alcohol.

alcoholism The word was first heard a year before the war began and became a common term during the conflict, which produced numerous alcoholics within the military forces. Union General Ulysses Grant was a heavy drinker who was often accused of alcoholism by his southern enemies and northern rivals.

Alexandria Line The area occupied by the Confederate forces before the first battle of Bull Run. Their headquarters were on the high plateau of Manassas Junction, which was about 30 miles east of Alexandria, Virginia.

"All aboard!" The warning call for passengers to come aboard a river boat about to sail. The term was later picked up by train conductors.

"Allegheny" The nickname for Confederate Major-General Edward Johnson, because in 1862 he commanded the Army of the Allegheny in Virginia's northern Shenandoah Valley. His troops then became part of General Lee's Army of Northern Virginia. Johnson and his Third Division saw action at many major battles, including Gettysburg. He was captured at the battle of Spotsylvania, and sent with 50 other prisoners to Morris Island near Charleston to be put in the line of Confederate fire. This plan was never carried out, and the 50 men were exchanged for 50 Yankee prisoners in Charleston.

alley A white marble used in the game of MARBLES.

all-fired A euphemism for "hell-fired." It often replaced "damn" although more innocent minds used it to mean "very," "extreme," or "extremely." A soldier might talk about an "all-fired retreat."

"All Hail the Power of Jesus' Name" A popular and stirring hymn on both sides. Chaplains often led the troops in singing its chorus to boost morale.

alligator The slang name for a tough boatman who lived in the swampy area of the lower Mississippi River. They used their local knowledge and fighting ability to harrass Union troops who occupied New Orleans after April 25, 1862.

Alligator See David.

all in three years An expression meaning "a problem will be solved eventually"; e.g., "When will McClellan go on the attack?" one of his privates asked. "All in three years," replied his messmate. The term was derived from the normal enlistment period of a Union volunteer soldier who was expected to get the job done "all in three years." *See also* "two years and a but."

allotment A payment plan that allowed Union soldiers to send part or all of their money to their wives, families, or friends. When the paymaster visited camp, they could sign a roll naming the amount and the person to receive it. The paymaster paid a soldier his requested portion and the remainder went by check to his chosen recipient.

"All played out!" The motto adopted in 1862 by soldiers in the Union Army of the Potomac, expressing their weariness of a war that their generals were badly managing. A popular song among the troops went: "Abram Lincoln, what yer 'bout?/ Hurrah! Hurrah!/ Stop this war. It's all played out./ Hurrah! Hurrah!" *See also* about played out; play-out.

"All Quiet Along the Potomac To-night" A sad, melancholy song sung by lonely soldiers in both armies. It was originally a poem written by the poet Ethelind Beers in 1861 at her home in Goshen, New York. It was based on a telegram dispatch from Major General George B. McClellan to the Secretary of War that declared "all is quiet tonight." Her poem was first published on November 30, 1861, in *HARPER'S WEEKLY*, then became a poem and song in the South after a copy was supposedly discovered on the body of a dead Union soldier. The last four lines are:

All quiet along the Potomac to-night,
No sound save the rush of the river;
While soft falls the dew on the face of the dead,
The picket's off duty forever.

The phrase was eventually used to mock McClellan, who developed the reputation for avoiding action. *See also* the slows.

all shit and no sugar A humorous variation on "all work and no play."

all sorts of A southern expression meaning excellent, expert, smart, etc. If you called an officer "all sorts of a leader" you meant he was a great leader. Soldiers also spoke of "all sorts of a horse."

"All's well" The hourly call of guards at night at many military prisons. The procedure was used primarily to inform their officers that they were awake at their posts. In the Confederacy's Pemberton Prison in Richmond, sentries called the hours by their post number, such as "Post Number 1. Two o'clock. All's well."

"All up!" A traditional morning camp call, especially in the Union Army, for soldiers to turn out of bed for assembly and roll call.

"All we ask is to be let alone." A Confederate slogan first proclaimed by President Jefferson Davis in his message to the Confederate Congress on April 29, 1861, about two weeks after the bombardment of Fort Sumter had begun the conflict.

amalgamate To mix the white and black races. The word and its nouns, "amalgamation" and "amalgamationist," were precursors of "integrate," "integration" and "integrationist." The term came from the process of amalgamating metals and was first used years before the war.

amanuensis A secretary or person who copies documents. After she had given birth, Cassie Smith wrote on October 10, 1862, to her husband, Confederate Lieutenant General Edmund Kirby Smith, to say the following: "As I am unable to give an account of myself, I have employed Nina to be my amanuensis."

"Amazing Grace" This famous hymn was a special favorite with Union and Confederate troops. It was written by John Newton, an English slave trader, after he accepted Christ and left his slave ship to become a minister.

ambia A southern euphemism for tobacco juice spittal; e.g., "Mrs. Lowry complained about the ambia on the sidewalk in front of his store."

ambition A southern term meaning "grudge." A soldier might have "an ambition against that damn captain."

ambrotype A early type of photograph that replaced the more expensive DAGUERREOTYPE in the mid-1850s. It was a glass negative with a background of black paper, paint, or velvet to make it seem a positive print. Practitioners of the art were called ambrotypists. E.M. Sammis, who had a studio in Olympia, Washington, advertised: "Secure the substance ere the shadow fades, Let Nature copy that which Nature made." Soldiers often carried a small case containing an ambrotype picture of their wives, sweethearts, or families. Because its image detail and tones were inferior to the daguerreotype, the ambrotype began to be replaced by the TINTYPE during the war.

ambulance The vehicle used on the battlefield was normally a two- or four-wheeled wagon drawn by two horses. It was often an open flatbed for quick retrieval of the wounded (who often shared it with dead officers), but sometimes had a canvas top and side sheets that could be rolled up.

ambulance corpsman A member of the ambulance corps that rescued soldiers on the battlefield and rushed them to surgeons behind the ranks. Anyone who was physically disqualified from fighting, including short men, could apply to become a corpsman.

ambuscade The more formal, though often preferred form, of "ambush."

ambustion The medical term for a burn or scald.

Ambulance wagons and drivers near Washington's Harewood Hospital in July 1863. *Library of Congress, Prints & Photographs Division, LC-B8171-2585.*

America The yacht that won the first America's Cup competition (then called the Queens' Cup) in 1851 in England. The Confederacy purchased it at the beginning of the war with the idea of converting it into a cruiser. However, when the Union blockade bottled up the yacht in the St. John's River in South Carolina, the Confederates sank it. It was raised by the U.S. Navy and used for the remainder of the war as a training yacht at the U.S. Naval Academy.

American Antislavery Society The abolitionist organization founded by William Lloyd Garrison and others in 1833. Garrison burned the U.S. Constitution because he said it supported slavery and in 1841 called on the North to secede. The activities of the Society were so controversial, a mob once dragged Garrison through Boston streets until he was rescued and put in jail for his protection. He first favored disunion, using the motto "No union with slaveholders," but then supported the war. He happily disbanded the Society the same year the South was defeated. *See also The Liberator.*

American Bible Society The organization that provided hundreds of thousands of Bibles, Testaments, and copies of the Lord's Prayer to Union soldiers. It even supplied Bibles to southern organizations servicing Rebel soldiers, including the Confederate Bible Society, which had split from it. In the first 18 months of the war, the American Bible Society distributed 490,000 Bibles and Testaments. These were distributed to Union troops by the CHRISTIAN COMMISSION. The materials were often found on the bodies of those killed in battle.

An American Dictionary of the English Language This popular dictionary with Civil War soldiers was first published by Noah Webster in 1828, revised in 1841 when Webster was 83, and then revised again during the war in 1864 in Springfield, Massachusetts, by G. and C. Merriam and their staff.

American Union A name sometimes used for the Union or the United States. In writing of the death of Confederate Lieutenant General "STONEWALL" Jackson, Union Major General Oliver O. Howard said: "Even his enemies praise him; but, providentially for us, it was the last battle which he waged against the American Union."

"America's bloodiest day" A name given to the battle of Antietam, which was fought along Antietam Creek in western Maryland on September 17, 1862. Some 13,700 Confederate and 12,350 Union casualties occurred there in about 12 hours of fighting. Confederate General Robert E. Lee's forces, making their first push into the North, were driven back by General George McClellan's Army of the Potomac.

ammunition chest *See* limber chest.

ammunition train A row of wagons carrying ammunition. The dilemma during a battle was to place the crucial train in easy reach of the artillerymen but out of direct enemy fire.

among the missing Absent, often with the idea of leaving or disappearing. If a soldier saw his sergeant coming and said he was "going to be among the missing," it meant he was about to run off.

Anaconda Plan The U.S. navy's operation to blockade Confederate ports, named for the snake that wraps itself around its prey and crushes it to death. Although half the southern blockade runners always made it through, the larger, slower trading ships could not. This eliminated the South's vital export of cotton and its import of war materials. Devised by General Winfield Scott, the Anaconda Plan was also known as "Scott's (Great) Snake" and "Scott's Anaconda."

"An Act to Provide for the Public Defense" The Confederacy's first conscription law, passed a year after the war began. It gave President Jefferson Davis control of all men over the age of 18 and under 35. Southern critics pointed out that the act violated the idea of states' rights that had created the Confederate States.

anagram The transposing of letters of words to create new words, a popular game during the war years (as now). "Flit on, cheering angel" is an anagram of the name of Florence Nightingale(1820-1910), the British nurse whose sanitary reforms were practiced by Union and Confederate nurses.

anasarca The medical term for a pronounced puffiness of the flesh, a generalized type of DROPSY or EDEMA.

anchylosis *See* ankylosis.

Andersonville The popular name of Camp Sumter, the South's most infamous military prison at Anderson Station near Andersonville, Georgia. The 20-foot fence was made of upright tree trunks. More than 33,000 men were crammed into 26 acres in the open, giving each inmate only 25 square feet. The inmates lacked adequate food, water, and medical care. More than 12,000 prisoners died, and Andersonville's Swiss-born commander, Major Henry Wirz, was the only Confederate executed after the war. *See also* dead line; Main Street; rolla pot; Sweet Water Branch.

Andy The nickname for Andrew Johnson, President Abraham Lincoln's vice president from Tennessee. Hearing criticism of Johnson for drinking on his inauguration day, Lincoln noted: "Andy ain't a drunkard." Johnson became president after Lincoln's assassination and was subjected to intense pressure from the RADICAL REPUBLICANS, who rode roughshod over his moderate Recon-

struction plans and failed to impeach him by one vote. "Andy is as hard as a knot and you can't kill him," assured one Tennesseean.

"Angel of Cairo" The nickname given by soldiers to Mary J. Safford, a young Union nurse who began caring for wounded soldiers in Cairo, Illinois. Her popularity was increased by her prettiness. She served with the SANITARY COMMISSION until she injured her spine after the battle of Shiloh.

"Angel of Light" A nickname given to abolitionist John Brown by writer and philosopher Henry David Thoreau.

"Angel of Marye's Heights" The nickname given by both sides to Sergeant Richard R. Kirkland of the 2nd South Carolina Volunteers at the battle of Fredericksburg. Kirkland put his life in jeopardy during the conflict when he brought water to Rebels and Yankees wounded on the battlefield.

"Angel of the Battlefield" The nickname for the Union's volunteer nurse Clara Barton. During the battle of Antietam, Barton had to replace a surgeon killed while he was drinking from a cup she had given him. In 1862, Union surgeon James L. Dunn wrote: "In my feeble estimation, General McClellan, with all his laurels, sinks into insignificance beside the true heroine of the age—the angel of the battle-field." After the war, Barton visited Andersonville prison to help identify and bury the dead. In 1881, she founded the American Red Cross.

anise seed cordial An alcoholic drink made of white brandy, aromatic anise seeds, sugar, water, and powdered COCHINEAL (for a red color).

ankylosis (or anchylosis) The medical term for a stiff joint, often caused by an injury, medical operation, or by a disease that caused bones to join.

Annapolis The Maryland home of the U.S. Naval Academy, established there in 1845. During 1861, when the state brimmed with southern sympathizers, the Academy left Annapolis for Fort Adams near Newport, Rhode Island, and then for a Newport hotel, the Atlantic House, until war's end. During this period, the Annapolis facilities were occupied by the U.S. army, including General Ambrose Burnside's troops.

"Annie of the Vale" A sentimental ballad that was popular during the war. Mrs. George Bailey entertained troops in Confederate camps with her well-known rendition.

ante-bellum Although now usually associated with southern plantation homes, the term was quickly applied during the war to anything that existed before the conflict. Confederate Private Sam R. Watkins even wrote about "ante-bellum friends." The term is also now used by historians to refer to the period immediately preceding the war.

antimacassar *See* tidy.

ant killer A humorous nickname for the foot, especially a large one.

Antony over A boy's popular ballgame. Two groups stand on either side of a house, or their school-house, and throw a ball back and forth over the roof.

any manner of means A glorious way of saying "any means." This usage would produce statements like "I'm getting a furlough by any manner of means possible."

A-1 Best or first class, in reference to things or people. Soldiers spoke of an "A-1 regiment" as well as an "A-1 captain." The phrase was sometimes altered to "A-number-1." The designation came from Lloyd's of London, the famous insurance company, which used this classification for ships in the best condition.

A.P. An abbreviation for the Union Army of the Potomac. After watching Major General W.T. Sherman's army pass by at the end of the war, Eliza Howland, a SANITARY COMMISSION volunteer, wrote: "They beat the A.P. all to pieces in their marching. . . ."

aphonia The medical term for loss of voice, either by a physical or psychological cause.

apoplexy The medical term for a stroke or cerebral accident, leading to loss of sensation or motion. The word is still used to describe the condition of any area of the body badly affected by a hemorrhage or restricted blood flow.

"Apostle to the Blacks" Nickname of Charles Colcock Jones, a Georgia planter and missionary who became an evangelist to slaves. Even northerners knew of the Apostle to the Blacks, and slaves who had received his Christian ministry gathered in sorrow at his graveside when he died in 1863. Jones's son, Charles, Jr., a Harvard-educated lawyer, became a Confederate artillery colonel, and his brother Joseph, a University of Pennsylvania medical graduate, was a CSA major who did research in Andersonville Prison on diseases of "those infamous Yankees."

apothecary The common name for a pharmacist during the war. A notice of the HOSPITAL TRANSPORT SERVICE of the Union's SANITARY COMMISSION stated: "A dispensary will be established on each vessel, and one or more apothecaries will be placed in charge of it."

app. Abbreviation for "approved." It often appeared on camp papers, such as furloughs.

apple-bee A fall community gathering and party for all ages to peel apples, usually in the kitchen of a farmhouse. Folklore said if a girl threw an apple peel over her shoulder it would fall and form the initials of the man she would wed.

apple brandy A brandy distilled from fermented cider, a special and rare camp treat. It was also called cider brandy and apple jack. Seven days before their Appomatox surrender, 500 ragged and barefooted troops of the Army of Northern Virginia received rations of apple brandy to wash down their meal of rancid pork and worm-riddled peas.

apple butter A thick smooth spread or sauce made of apples stewed down in cider with spices and sweetened. Camp cooks often produced the paste using apples gathered by soldiers during FORAGING expeditions.

apple jack *See* apple brandy.

apple pie A common, if unreliable, dessert that could fill up a hungry soldier. Local vendors would travel to camps with various concoctions that often lacked the vital ingredient of sugar. One soldier described the taste as being "a combination of rancid lard and crab apples."

applesauce A slang word for ridiculous or pretentious talk or nonsense; e.g., "I asked him direct questions and all he gave me was applesauce."

apple-shaker An insulting slang name for a uneducated rural person, e.g., "How can you teach military discipline to a bunch of apple-shakers?"

apron A small piece of leather that covered the vent on a cannon's breech. Gunner Number 3 held it in place until a cartridge was inserted in the gun, then lifted it to run a wire down the vent and pierce the powder bag of the cartridge. If the gun was hot and the vent not covered, oxygen could prematurely explode the powder. A very hot gun could be fired by the artilleryman simply removing his thumb from the vent.

Arab A slang name for an excitable person or one who behaved wildly. Each division had their Arabs whose intensity under battle conditions could produce either heroes or emotional wrecks.

argufy A contorted word for "argue," used by slaves and the most poorly educated in the population. It came from the GULLAH dialect of blacks on the coastal areas of Georgia and South Carolina.

aristocratic nigger A southern term for a black person who had an elegant bearing and manners, although the name was also sometimes used humorously for blacks "with pretensions."

Arkansas toothpick (or California toothpick) A humorous slang name for a large knife used in fighting, such as the BOWIE KNIFE. A popular version could be folded up into its handle. The Fire Zouaves (11th Regiment) of New York City used the name for their 16-inch knives. Bayonets were also called this.

"Arkansas Traveler" This spirited, jaunty song, especially popular in southern camps, was often played on a fiddle or Jew's harp.

"Arlington House" The home of Confederate General Robert

A large side knife such as might be called an Arkansas toothpick. *Copyright Inge Wright 1999.*

E. Lee, located across the Potomac River from Washington, D.C. From the heights of the property, one could see the U.S. Capitol. The 1,000-acre plantation estate was actually owned by Lee's wife, Mary Custis; they were married in the house and their children born there. Lee left Arlington House on April 22, 1861, and never saw it again. The estate was seized by the U.S. when the war began. The first Union dead were buried in a corner of it in 1864, and this developed into Arlington National Cemetery. The house is now managed by the National Park Service as a memorial to Lee. *See also* The Mess.

Arman A shipbuilding company in Bordeaux, France, that secretly build ironclads for the Confederacy. The warships were officially listed as being sold to Italy.

arme blanche The romantic French name ("white arm") sometimes used during the war for a sword, saber, bayonet, or other edged weapon. The name had also historically been applied to a cavalry.

armed neutrality The goal expressed early in the war by many people in Kentucky and Missouri. They wished to stay out of the conflict but retain defensive forces to protect their state from both sides. President Abraham Lincoln, in his message to Congress on July 5, 1861, addressed the question of "those who favor a policy which they call 'armed neutrality'—that is arming of those states to prevent the Union forces passing one way, or the Disunion the other, over their soil." Lincoln concluded that "under the guise of neutrality, it would tie the hands of Union men, and freely pass supplies from among them to the insurrectionists, which it could not do as an open enemy."

"an armed rabble" The description of the Union's western troops by Union Major General George Meade of the eastern Army of the Potomac.

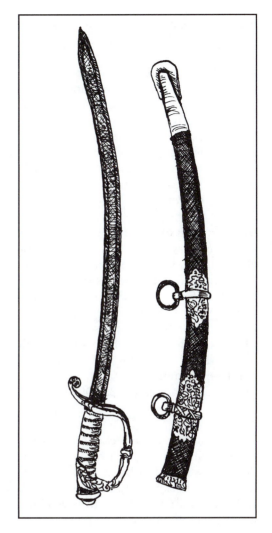

Swords, sabers, and similar weapons (depicted here is the sword and scabbard carried by the author's great-grandfather) were sometimes given the French name of *arme blanche. Copyright Inge Wright 1999.*

armored vest A defensive item bought by some soldiers early in the war, especially in the North. The vests were soon discarded because the steel armor and camp ridicule were equally heavy, with the latter including some unwanted reminders that the vest should cover the owner's behind during a battle.

armorer's gang On a navy ship, a company of men responsible for inspecting the ship's small arms, such as rifles, revolvers, swords, and cutlasses.

army The largest field command on both sides, consisting of one or more CORPS. The Union eventually had 16 armies, each commanded by a major general, and the Confederacy had 23, each led by a general. Armies were named for their DEPARTMENTS, such as the Union's Army of the Potomac which operated in the Department of the Potomac.

Army and Navy Official Gazette A Union military publication that often included Official Bulletins released by the War Department. One issue included Major General W.T. Sherman's 1864 Christmas message to President Abraham Lincoln: "I beg to present you, as a Christmas gift, the city of Savannah, with one hundred and fifty heavy guns and plenty of ammunition; and also about twenty-five thousand (25,000) bales of cotton."

The Army and Navy Pocket Dictionary A small dictionary used by Union soldiers. It was a thin book whose pages were not much larger than a playing card. A drawing of the Stars and Stripes proudly dominated the title page.

Army Argus A newspaper for Confederate soldiers published in Corinth, Mississippi. As well as news, it contained humor and satires about camp life.

army bread The more refined name for HARDTACK.

Army Intelligence Office The Confederate office that maintained lists of ill and wounded soldiers and kept their families informed of their conditions. Established in 1862, its "intelligence" was only of this nature and was not concerned with spying or confidential information.

army Latin A slang name for profanity; e.g., "Brewster missed morning roll call and got a earful of army Latin from the orderly sergeant."

Army of Observation The nickname for Union Major General W.T. Sherman's army during its siege of Vicksburg, Mississippi, in June 1863.

"The Army of the Lord" The name for a procession with music that traveled around the North with a 20-pound sack of flour that was auctioned many times in each town to raise money for the SANITARY COMMISSION. Each buyer immediately returned it to be reauctioned to the next person. The sack's journey began in Nevada where a Mr. Gridley began the first auction that raised $4,000 and several acres of land. (He got the idea after losing a local election bet and having to carry the sack on his back through his town.) The Army of the Lord raised $63,000 on the Pacific Coast alone.

Army of Virginia The short-lived Union army commanded by Major General John Pope. Its divisions were already famous for losing a series of battles under other commanders. Pope was called east in 1862 to "infuse a little western energy" into the ranks. He chastised the troops for their constant talk of "lines of retreat." In the army's first major action under Pope, it lost the second battle of Bull Run, quickly forming lines of retreat into Washington. Pope was relieved of his post, and later blamed the troops because they fought badly. The Army of Virginia immediately disappeared, its units incorporated into the Army of the Potomac.

arsenal A warehouse or other building in which arms and ammunition were kept under guard. In the later stages of the war, rapidly retreating Confederate troops often blew up their arsenal to keep the supplies from falling into Yankee hands. When Corinth, Mississippi, was evacuated and the arsenal set alight, one Confederate reported that it "was roaring and popping and bellowing like pandemonium turned loose."

article A term for a slave because slaves were considered to be "articles of merchandise." The term usually was preceded by a descriptive adjective, such as a "smart article" or a "strong article."

artificial oyster A southern substitution for an oyster during wartime restrictions. The creation was composed of green corn that was grated and mixed with butter and eggs before being rolled in batter and fried.

Artillerist's Manual A manual written in 1863 by John Gibbon for the Union army. It described the organization of batteries, the procedures of manning guns, the duties and personal attributes of artillerymen, and even the character traits required of artillery horses.

artillery The military branch concerned with large guns. It was divided into heavy (or seige) artillery and light (or field) artillery. Confederate artillery fired the first and last shots of the war at Fort Sumter and Appomattox, respectively.

artillery driver An artilleryman in charge of horses that pulled the cannon and attached LIMBER. Six horses and three drivers were normally used, with a driver for each pair of horses, called the lead, swing, and wheel teams. They were also called battery drivers in reference to their units.

artillery fuze A small fuse (the "z" spelling was then preferred) used with cannons. Fuses were usually carried by a gunner in a fuse box attached to his belt. Time fuses were used to explode shell and case shot at or near the target. Some were kept in smaller boxes labeled by time,

Union Eureka artillery shell. *Copyright Inge Wright 1999.*

such as "20 Second Fuzes," or Gunners 6 and 7 would cut the fuses to different lengths according to the estimated target distance. Percussion fuses used a spring or similar device to explode on impact.

"artillery hell" A nickname given to the battle of Antietam by Confederate Colonel Stephen D. Lee, who commanded artillery there.

artillery horse A horse used to pull heavy guns. They were also called battery horses. A BATTERY of six light guns needed about 110 horses, and the ideal animal was considered to be from 5 to 7 years old (preferable 7) and from 15 to 16 hands high. They were especially well treated, as seen in General Robert E. Lee's 1862 order saying anyone guilty of neglect of a battery horse would be punished. Artillery horses were also the frequent targets of the enemy to disable cannons. During the Battle of Gettysburg, the Union had 881 horses killed.

artilleryman (or artillerist) A soldier who operated a large gun BATTERY, either as a gunner or driver. Only about 6 percent of the war's soldiers were artillerymen. A full battery of 155 men would have 70 gunners and 52 drivers. The job was considered inferior to the dashing cavalryman and even the brave infantryman with his trusty rifle and shining bayonet. Cannons were loud, heavy, and dirty, requiring daily maintenance by artillerymen.

artillery of position The term used for artillery pieces that remained in one place, such as guns installed in forts for coastal defense.

"Artisavis or Bird of Art" The name given by R.O. Davidson, a clerk in the Confederate Quartermaster-General's Office, for a flying machine he had invented that would drop explosives on the enemy. He claimed that 1,000 of these devices would destroy an entire army within 12 hours and thus eventually eliminate all Union armies on southern soil and all Union fleets blockading ports. The Confederate War Department ignored Davidson's "aerial locomotion by man," even after he appealed for support in the Richmond *Whig*, which headed the story "Wonderful Bird of War."

a-soldiering The act or state of being a soldier. The term was often used during the war without the flippant connotation it would carry today. "I think every man who comes a-soldiering is a fool!" wrote a Union nurse, Mary Phinney von Olnhausen, on December 15, 1862, after attending to casualties from the battle of Fredericksburg.

Aspinwall The nickname for a loose worsted soldier's jacket that was donated to the 7th New York Regiment at the beginning of the war by wealthy William Aspinwall of New York City.

"Assembly" The name of a bugle call in camp that told soldiers to assemble. In the Union Army, it came in the mornings at

5:15 a.m., which was 15 minutes after the "ASSEMBLY OF BUGLERS" call, and in the evenings at about 6 p.m.

"Assembly of Buglers" The dreaded bugle call to rouse soldiers for the MORNING ROLL call. It was generally sounded at 5 a.m. during the summer and at 6 a.m. in the winter. The men would desperately strive to look presentable or get to the toilet in the 15 minutes left before the "Assembly" call. Almost everyone slept in his uniform, so the option always existed to take 15 more minutes of rest.

asses' milk An alcoholic drink made of rum and "aerated" lemonade and poured over crushed ice.

assistant adjutant general *See* A.A.G.

Associated Press This news service began in 1848 in New York and became important during the war when its general agent in Washington, D.C., was approved at the end of 1861 to receive and distribute all information released by government departments. Before this, some newspapers were given exclusive releases. The special access of the New York *Tribune* to the War Department finally aroused their competitors to demand the new system.

Astor House New York's most famous hotel, known for its political meetings and much favored by the Republicans. Occupying a full block on Broadway between Vesey and Barclay streets, it was built in 1831 by John Jacob Astor.

at The normal preposition used (instead of "in") to name a region of the country where something exists; e.g., "There have been riots at the North." "Our powers at the South have been impotent." "They live at the West."

at-home A social event when a lady would announce a day she would be at home for any friends who wished to visit. Tuesday was the general day for "at-homes" in Richmond, Virginia.

"The Atlanta Express" Nickname given by Union General W.T. Sherman's troops for any big shell used in their August 1864 bombardment of besieged Atlanta. Soldiers often yelled "There goes the Atlanta Express!" as the shells blasted off in 15-minute intervals.

The Atlantic Monthly The leading literary magazine in the North. It paid Julia Ward Howe $5 for writing the poem that became "The Battle Hymn of the Republic" and published it in February 1862. When Confederate President Jefferson Davis turned down peace without independence in 1864 and the Union negotiator wanted to publish Davis's uncompromising words in the *New York Tribune*, Lincoln advised him, "Can't you get it into *The Atlantic Monthly*? It would have less of a partisan look there." The magazine let Lincoln edit the text before publishing it.

"Attention" A bugle call to prepare soldiers for a more important one quickly following. In the Union Army, "Attention" was blown about 5:45 in the evening to prepare troops for the "Assembly" call preceding roll call.

at the conn On a warship, the position of a person who stands at the compass to see that the correct course is steered.

"Attila of the west" The nickname given to Union General W.T. Sherman by the *Macon Telegraph* in Georgia during Sherman's march through that state in 1864.

"Auld Lang Syne" The popular Scottish song was a favorite of Yanks and Rebs. It was played by several regimental bands in camps around Appomattox Court House during the three days from General Lee's defeat to the formal surrender ceremonies there.

Aunt A female slave, usually elderly, and often one who took care of white children. It was used with her first name, such as Aunt Sally.

Aunty Nickname given by Union soldiers to the army in its role as a supplier of everyday incidentals, which had to be paid for. They would pay Aunty to wash their clothes and provide everything from special pies to newspapers and tobacco.

"Aura Lee" A sentimental love song enjoyed by soldiers on both sides. It was composed by George R. Poulton with lyrics by W.W. Fosdick. The melody was later used for the Elvis Presley hit, *Love Me Tender*.

automaton A soldier who acted in a mechanical way (like a robot), obeying orders but often not knowing what the overall plan was. The name still applies to people who do things automatically.

avails Profits or proceeds, as from goods sold or rents; e.g., "There was nearly a riot in camp when someone calculated the sutler's large avails."

avalanche A playful corruption of "ambulance" that became the nickname for a small two-wheeled ambulance used in the Union army. It proved virtually useless because it tended to wobble and tip over, sliding its patients onto the ground.

A.V.C. (or AVC) The initials of the Alabama Volunteer Corps. In the various uniform changes through the war, the "A.V.C." was worn on buttons and the oval metal plates on belts. The early SHAKO HAT was decorated with a badge of an eagle under "AVC" in brass letters.

"Avengers of Fort Pillow" The name supposedly taken by some 1,200 black Union soldiers marching with General Samuel Sturgis in the summer of 1864. The *Atlanta Appeal* reported this and charged the soldiers with outrages on southern women. The FORT PILLOW MASSACRE of black soldiers by Confederate troops under Lieutenant General Nathan Bedford Forrest had taken place on April 12, 1864, in Tennessee.

The Avenue 1. A popular short name for Pennsylvania Avenue in Washington, D.C. 2. The popular name for Fifth Avenue in New York.

avoirdupois A euphemism for a person's heaviness or fatness. A soldier might be teased about his lady friend's "fine avoirdupois." The term is sometimes still heard and comes from the British and U.S. avoirdupois weight system in which a pound equals 16 ounces.

Awkward Squad The Union name for a special drilling squad to train uncoordi-nated soldiers. Their crimes included marching out of step, holding their guns incorrectly, stepping on those in front by violating the 13 inches space required, and failing to halt on command. If an Awkward Squad soldier showed no improvement, he was often subjected to the knapsack drill or other camp punishments.

A.W.O.L. Absent without official leave. This well-known military designation was used by the U.S. army before the war and by both sides during it. By 1865, more than 420,000 Union and Confederate soldiers were listed as A.W.O.L. Those caught on the Rebel side were forced to carry the initials on a sign around camp and suffer the taunts of their fellow soldiers. A.W.O.L. is now translated more briefly as Absent Without Leave. *See also* absent with authority.

axle-tree (or axle) The rod on which a wheel turned on a wagon or carriage.

B

baa-lamb A child's pet name for a lamb.

baby-house A common name for a dollhouse, since dolls were often called babies. At the Manhattan Fair of the SANITARY COMMISSION in New York on April 14, 1864, a Mrs. Chauncey sold her "baby-house" for $500.

back-out A slang word for cowardice or a lack of courage; e.g., "The sergeant has a severe case of back-out."

back talk The common term for replying to a superior officer in an insolent way.

bad A slang word meaning the opposite, good. Incorrectly considered to be a modern usage, it was part of a slave's GULLAH vocabulary, expressing approval of another slave who had done something bad in their master's opinion. It was pronounced long—"baaaad."

bad blood A common euphemism for syphilis.

bad-box A person was in a bad predicament when he was "in a bad-box." A soldier caught asleep on picket duty might tell his fellows he was now in a bad-box.

bad egg A dishonest, good-for-nothing, or evil person, e.g., "They shot Yates for desertion, but he wasn't such a bad egg."

bad nigger A complimentary term originally used by southern slaves and northern blacks for a black person, usually a man, who resisted white oppression. This was a hopeless and dangerous gesture on plantations but won the special admiration of the slave community.

baggage smasher A humorous slang name for a rough and careless type of person.

bag of wind A derogatory nickname for loud or pompous talkers. It was secretly given to Union Major General John Pope by his fellow officers.

bag the enemy To capture the enemy. The expression was often applied to a surprise flanking movement and march into the rear of the enemy, whose cannons are pointing away from the attack. The theory was good, but the "bagging procedure" seldom worked if the enemy had a larger force. Trains and military equipment could also be "bagged."

bail one's own boat To take care of one's own fate or business without waiting for assistance; e.g., "The reserve troops were late, so we had to bail our own boat."

bait A slang word for someone who was an intended victim, especially a person who was easy to swindle; e.g., "The new private was just the bait we needed for a fast poker game."

baker's cake A type of sponge cake laced with ammonia to make it light. It was covered with sweet colored icing.

bakery bread *See* store-bought bread.

"Bald Eagle" The nickname given by his men to Confederate Brigadier General Martin W. Gary, who was bald. He fought at many major battles, including both Bull Run encounters, Antietam, Fredericksburg, and Chickamauga. During the war, his infantry regiment was given horses to convert it to a cavalry. Gary was the last GENERAL OFFICER to pull out of Richmond when the Confederate capital fell, and he escorted the fleeing President Jefferson Davis and his cabinet from Greensboro, North Carolina, to the home of Gary's mother in Cokesbury, South Carolina, where they stayed on May 1, 1865.

bald-face A slang name for bad whiskey.

bald-faced shirt *See* boiled shirt.

"Baldy" 1. Nickname for the Union's Major General William F. Smith. His hair began to recede at the age of 18, and the name was stuck on him as a cadet at West Point. During the war, Smith became a favorite of Ulysses Grant, who had been two years ahead of him at the academy. Grant, however, relieved him of his command on July 19, 1864, partly because he failed to carry out orders properly. 2. The name of Union General George Meade's bay horse that had a white face and feet. Meade bought the horse after it was seriously wounded at the first battle of Bull Run. Baldy was known for its strange gait that was not quite a trot. The horse was wounded in the neck during the battle of Antietam (left for dead on the battlefield but found the next day contently grazing there) and shot between the ribs at Gettysburg. It survived Meade, being led behind his funeral procession seven years after the war's end.

baled hay A Union nickname for the commissary's dissicated (dehydrated) vegetables because of a suspicion that straw and grass were ground and added to them. They were also maligned as "desecrated vegetables."

balk A timber used on pontoon bridges supported by boats. A "balk party" laid five continous lines of balks parallel to one another over the boats from one bank to the other. Planks were then placed sideways on the balks to form the bridge's floor. One balk was 25 1/2 feet long. The Union army had bridges of this type over the James, Chickahominy, and Appomattox rivers.

ball 1. The soldier's usual word for a cannon ball or MINIÉ BALL. One picket recalled after the war that "Balls were passing over our heads, both coming and going." 2. A basic type of football played in camps on both sides. 3. A slang name for a battle. *See also* open the ball.

ball and chain A form of military punishment for moderately serious offenses, such as insubordination. A cannon ball, normally 30 pounds, was chained to the soldier's leg for several hours. His only options were to drag or carry the burden about camp, and this soon exhausted even the strongest of men.

Balloon Corps *See* Aeronautic Department.

Balmoral A woolen petticoat looped up in front and usually printed with figures.

It was named for Queen Victoria's Scottish castle. The Confederate spy Belle Edmondson, living in occupied Memphis, once smuggled out gray cloth for soldiers' uniforms by forming it into a Balmoral.

balmy A delightfully misleading slang word for being intoxicated or drunk. See DRUNK for numerous other terms referring to intoxication.

bamboozled A slang term describing someone who was intoxicated or drunk. See DRUNK for numerous other terms referring to intoxication.

bandage-roller A device found in many homes that allowed women to roll bandages for soldiers, an active pursuit during the war. A bandage-roller was often attached to a table and several women or family members would gather to roll and package the vital items. Abby Woolsey of New York noted that "for months bandage-rolling was the family fancywork, and other festivities really ceased."

bandbox A light, round box used to keep and carry hats, caps, shirt collars, and other items. The name came from its original purpose of holding collars, then called bands or neck-bands.

bandbox army Term used by western U.S. troops for their more regulated eastern compatriots who often drilled with a regimental band. The scornful reference was frequently applied to "the bandbox Army of the Potomac." The joke derived from a BANDBOX used to carry fine hats.

bandy An early form of tennis played by Union and Confederate soldiers in most camps.

banger A slang name for a club, sturdy stick, or cane.

banjo A popular musical instrument in camps, especially southern ones. Confederate Major General Jeb Stuart played it, had his own banjo-player follow him, and often went into battles humming a tune.

Banner hospital One of the modern hospitals built in and around Washington, D.C., about half-way through the war. They were among the first to include special diet meals.

banquette A sidewalk. The French name was used in some southern towns and cities.

"Barbara Frietchie" John Greenleaf Whittier's well-known poem was inspired by the Confederate occupation of Frederick, Maryland, in September 1862. It embellished an event when a 90-year-old woman hung the U.S. flag from her window. In Whittier's version, she was fired on, bullets cut the flag free, and Frietchie leaned out dangerously to catch it. The poem said Brigadier General "STONEWALL" Jackson, leading his troops on the street below, ordered:

> "Who touches a hair of yon gray head,
> Dies like a dog! March on!" he said.

"Barbara Frietchie" was published in Whittier's collection *In War Time* (1864). The *Richmond Examiner* bemoaned the power of the Yankee verse "to play such havoc with Southern histories of the war."

barbecue A barbecue in the South was the roasting of a whole animal, usually a hog, on a gridiron over a charcoal fire. Before wartime restrictions, this was a big social event with other foods included. The barbecue was originally the name of the iron framework that supported the meat over the fire, and this usage was recorded in the first half of the eighteenth century. The name evolved from the Haitian language where it meant a framework of sticks on posts.

barbette tier (or barbette) In a fort, a high platform that supports cannons (called "barbette guns") pointed and firing over the wall instead of through EM-BRASURES (openings). Such guns are said to be "in barbette." Almost all of Fort Sumter's barbette tier and its guns faced the sea to defend the U.S. against foreign ships. This contributed to its poor defense when Confederates attacked from the Charleston side.

barefoot coffee (or barefooted coffee) A slang name for black coffee. And "barefoot liquor" was drunk straight.

bark juice An amusing name for liquor.

bar-keep A common but informal name for a barkeeper or bartender.

barley wine An drink composed of white wine, barley water, barley, sugar, lemons, rosewater, water, and the herbs clary (of the mint family) and borage.

Barnum's American Museum The New York museum of collected oddities owned by P.T. Barnum. It remained popular during the war, featuring the midget GENERAL TOM THUMB, a live hippopotamus, two white whales, a (fake) mermaid, and other curiosities. On November 25, 1864, when eight Confederate agents from Canada set 19 fires in New York City within an hour, Barnum's was the only building seriously injured, with the bales of hay for animals burning quickly. Only one of the arsonists was captured, in Michigan, and later executed. *See also* "Prince of Humbugs."

barnyard preacher A nickname for an amateur or part-time preacher.

barouche A four-wheeled carriage with double seats for two couples to sit facing each other. The driver sat in a box seat in front, and the carriage's half top could be folded down. For his first inauguration in 1861, Abraham Lincoln traveled with outgoing President James Buchanan in an open barouche to the Capitol building.

barracks lawyer A soldier who knew army regulations so well he could use them against officers. A Confederate lieutenant cursed a troublemaker in his Virginia company, but had to immediately apologize after the man threatened to report him for violating a regulation forbidding cursing. Some officers could outwit barracks lawyers. When one Confederate private, drunk in a bar, refused to continue a march to Virginia because his company had not been officially mustered into service, he changed his mind when the captain informed him that his uniform would be stripped from him on the street to go to Virginia because it belonged to the state of Alabama.

"barrelita" Confederate Brigadier General Nathan G. Evans's pet name for a small barrel of whiskey that accompanied him throughout the war. It was carried and protected by a special orderly.

barrel shirt A humiliating punishment for minor military infractions. The offender was forced to march around camp wearing a flour barrel with the bottom knocked out and holes for his head and arms. He was often marched at the point of a bayonet. If the punishment was during a dress parade, the regimental band might strike up "The ROGUE'S MARCH." Often placards were hung from offenders' necks to describe their crimes, such as "thief," "robbing a comrade," "absent without leave," or "drunk." Confederate General Joseph E. Johnston even had barrel-shirt brigades that were forced to march on drill and parade. "Come out of that barrel," campmates would taunt, "I can see your head and feet sticking out."

base ball (Usually spelled as two words during the war.) The most popular sport in camp on both sides. The pitching was underhanded, and there was no regulation ball—a soft ball was used for what was called "Boston base ball" and a hard ball and more modern rules for "New

York base ball." Another version of the game was "town ball" with two bases. Some balls in camp were made of walnuts covered with yarn. In one game version, a base runner was also out if someone hit him with the ball, so minor injuries occurred. Organized teams from Union regiments played against one another. Camp games produced amazing scores, such as the 62 to 20 drubbing the 13th Massachusetts once gave the 104th New York. The usual winner, however, was the team that first scored 21 points. Rebels also loved the game; members of the 24th Alabama Regiment played it in Georgia as they awaited the advance by Major General W.T. Sherman's troops.

bashaw A proud, tyrannical man. As civilians in Columbia, South Carolina, fretted over Major General W.T. Sherman's approach, Malvina Gist wrote in her diary: "You would think Sherman was a three-tailed bashaw, to hear some of them talk." The name was another spelling of "pasha," a Turkish viceroy.

basket-meeting A picnic to which each person or couple brought their food and other provisions in a basket.

baster A woman who sewed clothes loosely together before the articles were carefully sewn. During the war, a baster of cavalry pantaloons in New York was paid about 32 cents for a 12-hour workday.

bat A slang term for an orgy of drinking or for a spree, binge, etc. Soldiers looked forward to visiting a town to "go on a bat."

batch (or bach) A popular shortened name for "bachelor."

bathing The early name for swimming, still used in Great Britain. "Sea bathing" during the war usually consisted of sitting in the shallow water in a costume that only revealed the feet. Feminine heads were often protected by wide-brim hats or parasols.

baton The long wooden stick used by military bandleaders. It usually had a metal knob for the hand and a metal tip at the other end.

battalion A military unit in the REGULAR ARMY on both sides that was left over from the OLD ARMY. One battalion often made up a COMPANY and two or more comprised a REGIMENT. In the cavalry, a battalion was composed of two squadrons, while three battalions made up a regiment.

battering gun *See* siege artillery.

battery A basic unit of artillery and artillerymen, corresponding to an infantry company. From 8 to 12 batteries made up an artillery REGIMENT. Union batteries normally had six cannons and Confederate ones usually had four. They had such names as the Third Company of Howitzers. By the end of the war, the Union had 432 batteries, about 12 percent of its total units, and the Confederary had 268 artillery groups divided into batteries, battalions, and regiments, nearly 18 percent of its units. *See also* counter-battery; water battery.

battery driver *See* artillery driver.

battery horse *See* artillery horse.

"Battle Above the Clouds" Nickname for the battle of Lookout Mountain at Chattanooga, Tennessee, a Union victory won by General Ulysses S. Grant's troops over General Braxton Bragg's on November 24, 1863. The imposing 400-foot mountainside of Missionary Ridge was stormed by the troops of Major General Philip Sheridan who had only been instructed to take the first rifle pits. Sheridan sent a request below to take the ridge and, receiving no reply, took a drink of whiskey and stormed up the mountain with his men. The amazing advance of blue uniforms resulted in 6,700 Confederates killed, wounded, or captured. Sheridan's soldiers were the only ones who forgot their exhaustion long enough to pursue the retreating Rebels. *See also* "How!"

"The Battle-Cry of Freedom" A patriotic Union war song written by George F. Root, a native of Massachusetts, and sung by the troops and throughout the North, often by school children. During a vicious battle at the Wilderness on May 6, 1864, members of the 45th Pennsylvania began to sing the song, and it was picked up by other regiments and rose over the battlefield. The song began:

> Yes, we'll rally round the flag, boys, we'll rally once again,
> Shouting the battle-cry of Freedom;
> We will rally from the hill-side, we'll gather from the plain,
> Shouting the battle-cry of Freedom.

And the chorus:

> The Union forever, hurrah! boys, hurrah!
> Down with the traitor, up with the star;
> While we rally round the flag, boys, rally once again,
> Shouting the battle-cry of Freedom.

"Rally round the flag, boys!" was supposedly first said by Andrew Jackson at the battle of New Orleans in 1815. Root also penned "TRAMP, TRAMP, TRAMP, THE BOYS ARE MARCHING" and "Just Before the Battle, Mother."

battledore The name of both a game and the paddle used in it to strike a ball or shuttlecock. The game, also called "battledore and shuttlecock," was a forerunner of badminton. Battledore paddles were popular gift items during the war.

"The Battle Hymn of the Republic" The stirring and most popular U.S. battle hymn. Julia Ward Howe, a well-known author, wrote the new lyrics to the tune of the pre-war song, "JOHN BROWN'S BODY"

after she visited Washington, D.C. Her "Battle Hymn" was first published in February 1862 in the *ATLANTIC MONTHLY*, which bought it for $5.

The Battle of Bull Run A play presented at the Broadway Music Hall in New York in 1861 shortly after the real battle took place. Called a "drama of intense interest," the subject of the northern defeat was still a strange choice. A few months later, John Wilkes Booth performed as Richard III at the theatre, then renamed Mary Provost's Theater.

battles The plural form was sometimes used for one battle, to indicate several different confrontations had occurred, often over several days. In his two-hour address at the dedication of the Gettysburg cemetery before President Abraham Lincoln spoke, Edward Everett referred to "the Battles of Gettysburg."

battling stick A slave's name for a sturdy stick. It was normally the one used to stir clothes being cleaned in a boiling pot or one used by the plantation owner or overseer to beat the slaves.

"Baylor's Babes" The nickname for the young Texas soldiers commanded by Lieutenant Colonel John R. Baylor. They joined his "BUFFALO HUNT" in December 1860 and captured Fort Fillmore in the Arizona Territory on July 27, 1861.

bazoo A slang name for the mouth; e.g., "Just once I'd like to tell the sergeant to shut his big bazoo."

BC The abbreviation for the Balloon Corps of the Union army. Its members wore the letters in brass on their civilian caps until this produced wry comments from soldiers. *See also* AD; Aeronautical Department.

Beardslee telegraph A portable Union telegraph system used in the field. It had an alphabet dial instead of a key and was powered by hand-turned magnetos. George W. Beardslee developed the system, and Colonel Albert J. Myer, the Union's first signal officer, adapted it for military use. Some 70 instruments were in use and followed the troops in FLYING TELEGRAPH trains. The system was first employed on May 24, 1862, in the Peninsula Campaign. The Beardslee had a limited range of only 10 miles and suffered from a slow transmission, so by the end of 1863 it had been replaced.

beak A slang name for a judge or magistrate. The word is still used in Great Britain for a magistrate.

bean A slang term for a $5 U.S. gold coin. Early in the nineteenth century, the name had been used for any coin.

bean hole A hole in the ground in Union camps, especially those with soldiers from lumbering regions, in which a covered iron pot with beans, often pork and beans, was covered with hot embers. This method of cooking lasted all night.

beanpole This familiar nickname for a tall, thin person was commonly used among soldiers during the war.

beanpole and cornstalk bridge The nickname given by President Abraham Lincoln to a railroad bridge constructed over the Potomac Creek because its thin trestle-work reminded him of those country items. He marveled that "there is nothing in it but beanpoles and cornstalks." Completed on May 13, 1862, the bridge was 400 feet long and 80 feet high. Amazingly, the bridge had been put together in two weeks by relatively untrained workers with a shortage of tools. It survived until destroyed by the Union forces as Major General Ambrose Burnside retreated after the defeat at Fredericksburg, Virginia, on December 13, 1862.

bear (or wild or slow bear) A hog. The bogus name was especially used by Confederate soldiers on the march who had been ordered not to steal hogs from farmers. After enjoying a special pork dinner, they would openly brag about the wild bear they had shot and eaten.

beast A common, but not insulting, name for a horse, especially in the South.

"Beast" The nickname for Union Major General Benjamin F. Butler. The name resulted from Butler's repressive and insulting actions as the commander of troops occupying New Orleans, especially his GENERAL ORDERS NO. 28 of May 15, 1862, which compared disrespectful women of that city with prostitutes. He

For ordering his men to treat the Confederate ladies of New Orleans as prostitutes, Union Major General Benjamin F. Butler was known throughout the South as "Beast" Butler. *Library of Congress, Prints & Photographs Division, LC-B8172-1406.*

later claimed he had copied it from a book of London Statutes, changing "London" to "New Orleans." He said the London newspapers were unaware of this "and called me 'Beast Butler' for adopting one of their own laws." His first Proclamation of May 1 had listed many punishments, including the burning of any house or building in which a Union soldier was killed, even if the owner was not involved in the murder. Other examples abounded, including his hanging of a citizen for wearing part of a torn U.S. flag. He also had a woman arrested who crossed the street to avoid walking under the U.S. flag (while he was under it smoking a cigar). Butler had a guard walk her back and forth under the flag for 30 minutes. The nickname followed him the remainder of his life. Even when he addressed a crowd in front of New York's City Hall to support Horace Greeley's election to Congress, hecklers yelled "Down with the Beast!" *See also* Butlerize; spoons.

beat 1. A nickname for a soldier who was lazy or lacked self-discipline. Beats were known for avoiding duties, and they often lost their own camp items and had to borrow from others. 2. A journalist's story that is printed before his competitor's; e.g., "The New York *Herald* had the beat on the battle of Shiloh." The current term is "scoop."

beater A nickname for a person who surpasses or defeats others; e.g., "He's taken more than his share of criticism, but Old Abe is a beater."

beat-up A slang term for being worn out and exhausted; e.g., "We marched all day and were beat-up before we reached the seat of war."

beau A common name for the sweetheart of a woman or girl. The term continued in popular use into the 1930s.

"Beauty" The derisive nickname given by classmates to the unhandsome, chinless "JEB" Stuart while he attended WEST POINT. Later, as a Confederate major general, he was known for his charm and beautiful, self-designed uniforms. *See also* "eyes of the army"; "Gay Cavalier"; raid around the army.

"Beauty and Booty" (or "Booty and Beauty") The two prizes that Yankee invaders were after, according to Confederate General P.G.T. Beauregard. In his proclamation issued in Virginia on June 1, 1861, he warned that

> A reckless and unprincipled tyrant has invaded your soil. Abraham Lincoln, regardless of all moral, legal, and constitutional restraints, has thrown his Abolitionist hosts among you, who are murdering and imprisoning your citizens, confiscating and destroying your property, and committing other acts of violence and outrage, too shocking and revolting to humanity to be enumerated. All rules of civilized warfare are abandoned, and they proclaim by their acts, if not on their banners, that their warcry is "BEAUTY AND BOOTY." All that is dear to man—your honor and that of your wives and daughters—your fortunes and your lives, are involved in this momentous contest.

Beauvoir The home of Jefferson Davis during the last 12 years of his life. It is at Biloxi, Mississippi, overlooking the Gulf of Mexico. In 1877, when Davis was financially ruined, his old friend and the owner of Beauvoir, Mrs. Sarah Dorsey, gave him a cottage on the property to write his history of the war. When she died of cancer in 1879, she left the property to him. Beauvoir is now a museum. *See also* Briarfield.

bedroll Blankets rolled with personal items and carried by soldiers on the march. One version was called a HORSE COLLAR.

Beecham's Pills A medicine used mainly for headaches and stomach problems, although the company advertised it as a cure for "Bilious and Nervous Disorders, such as Wind and Pain in the Stomach, Sick Headache, Giddiness, Fulness, and Swelling after Meals, Dizziness and Drowsiness, Cold Chills, Fushings of Heat, Loss of Appetite, Shortness of Breath, COSTIVENESS, Scurvy, Blotches on the Skin, Disturbed Sleep, Frightful Dreams, and all Nervous and Trembling Sensations, &c." Originally British, Beecham's Pills were sold in the U.S. for 25 cents, with the slogan "Worth a Guinea a Box."

beef dried on the hoof A nickname for bad beef among the troops of Union General Ulysses Grant.

beefsteak The normal name for a steak when the war began, but the shorter form evolved before it ended. It was served commercially in a beefsteak house. A well-known variety was the porterhouse beefsteak.

beef tea A soupy drink made by simmering chopped beef in water and draining off the juice. It was served in military hospitals as an easily digested stimulant and to provide quick nourishment, although one Confederate nurse wrote that her patients refused to drink it "in common with all soldiers and I believe men."

beef up A slang term, still used, for adding strength or vigor to something. Civil War soldiers might talk about the need to beef up morale or troop numbers.

bee-gum A southern nickname for a high-crowned hat or a woman's hairstyle in which her hair is piled high on top of her head. "Bee gum" is a southern name for a hollow gum tree that often contains a beehive.

beehive A slang term for a KNAPSACK.

beer-jerker A slang name for a person who drew beer from a keg into glasses, usually in a drinking establishment.

"Begad!" A euphemism for "By God!" but considered too profane for polite society during the war.

"Be jiminey!" A mild exclamation of surprise or emotion, being a form of the later "by jiminy." It is a seventeenth-century oath that supposedly came from either *"Jesu domine"* or "by Gemini," referring to Castor and Pollux, the sons of Zeus.

belly band A wide bandage made of flannel that some soldiers wrapped around their stomachs because an old wives' tale said it cured dysentery.

benders A slang word for a person's legs.

bend the elbow (or crook the elbow) A slang expression meaning to drink alcohol or have a drink.

Bengal light A bright blue steady signal light, used at sea and to illuminate a land area. It was usually composed of sulfur, niter, and the black sulfide of antimony. Bengal lights were also used during festive events. Eleanor Jackson, a resident of Montgomery, Alabama, recalled the inauguration of Confederate President Jefferson Davis, followed by evening celebrations when "Rocketts and bengal lights were thrown from the opposite sides of the street constantly."

Berdan's sharpshooters The common name for the famous 1st and 2nd Regiments of U.S. Sharpshooters. They were named for Colonel Hiram Berdan of the 1st Regiment. Every man selected for the units had to come within five inches of the bullseye with 10 shots at a range of 200 yards. The most famous member was "CALIFORNIA JOE." The sharpshooters, used as snipers and skirmishers, were given the best available rifles, .52 caliber

Sharps with telescopic sights. They dressed in dark green, for camouflage and probably to emulate the rifle regiments of the British army. Isolated snipers were vulnerable, however, and Berdan's men suffered many casualties. The units had to be combined at the end of 1864, and then members were dispersed to other regiments early in the next year.

bertha A lady's wide collar that often covered the shoulders. It was usually made of pointed lace, and a dress might have its sleeves trimmed with matching lace. The name came from Berthe, the modest mother of Emperor Charlemagne, who had worn the collar with low-cut dresses.

"Bethel Failure" A nickname for Union General Benjamin F. Butler, acquired after the failure of his attack on June 10, 1861, at Big Bethel, Virginia.

Betsy (or Bessie) A nickname used during the war for any type of gun, but especially a musket or rifle. It was derived from Brown Bessie, a nickname for a musket since the early eighteenth century.

Betty A southern nickname for a whip made out of cowhide.

Biddy The nickname given to Irish servant girls. At the time of the war, many had come to the United States, often under agreements to work off fares that had been paid by their future employers. The British at that time called an Irish servant girl a Bridget, from which the name biddy came, and they also called an Irish milkmaid biddy.

big bug A slang name for an important person, especially a general or powerful politician. The older British name, "big wig," was also used and would be the only form to survive.

The Big Ditch A nickname for the Erie Canal.

Big Drink A nickname for the Mississippi River.

big house 1. A name commonly given by slaves to the home of the plantation owner. It was sometimes called merely "the house." 2. A nickname for a federal or state pententiary; a term that survived through the twentieth century.

"big Indian war" A name given by Union Major General W.T. Sherman to his efforts to subdue Rebel forces in Georgia. This was because the fighting was informal and scattered against an enemy who could, as Sherman put it, "fight or fall back, as he pleases."

The Big Tent The nickname given to the U.S. Capitol building by some 3,000 Union soldiers assigned to barracks created within its Rotunda (which was unfinished and open to the skies), legislative chambers, and halls during the early days of the war. The men enjoyed holding mock congressional sessions, relaxing on stuffed sofas in the parlors, and penning letters home on expensive desks. The Capitol later served as a military hospital. The building's basement committee rooms were given over to ovens that produced bread for the army, and the vaults were converted to storehouses for meat and flour in case of a siege by the enemy.

"biled" shirt The usual pronunciation in Confederate camps for a BOILED SHIRT.

bilious fever Fever caused by a liver ailment. It led to the death in 1862 of WILLIE, the young son of President Abraham Lincoln.

billy A policeman's truncheon; the nickname was in common use during the war.

Billy The horse of Union Major General George H. Thomas, the ROCK OF CHICKAMAUGA. Billy was named after Major General William T. Sherman. Both horse and rider were known for their coolness under fire. *See also* Uncle Billy.

"Billy" *See* Uncle Billy.

Billy Sherman's neckties *See* Sherman's neckties.

bimbo punch A cool alcoholic drink made of cognac, lemons, sugar, and water. "Bimbo" meant a blow or punch with the fist.

bishop An informal name for a lady's BUSTLE.

"Bishop" The nickname for Confederate General Leonidas Polk, who was the first Episcopal bishop of Louisiana. He was a West Pointer who forsook military duty for the church until the war drew him back. Polk was especially beloved by his own troops and other southern soldiers. "When any position was to be held, and it was known that 'Bishop Polk' was there," recalled one of his veterans, "we knew and felt that 'all was well.'" The portly bishop was killed in 1864 by Union cannon fire at Pine Mountain, Georgia, as he walked for cover with slow dignity, hands clasped behind his back, while others ran.

bit A mostly southern name for one-eighth of a dollar, or 12.5 cents. Southerners first applied this name to a Mexican or Spanish silver real worth one-eighth of a peso. The bit is now only used in those amounts heard in the well-known football yell that begins, "Two bits, four bits, six bits, a dollar."

bite dog, bite bear A saying that expressed no interest in an outcome of something. In his famous ANDERSONVILLE diary, Union prisoner John L. Ransom noted that he had heard rumors of a Union victory, but added: "It's 'bite dog, bite bear' with most of us prisoners; we don't care which licks, what we want is to get out of this pen." The expression came from the ancient sport of bear-baiting.

biz A short, informal form for "business." It became popular during the war and was used for any business, whereas today it refers almost exclusively to show business.

Bizarre The pen name used by the drama critic of the *Sunday Chronicle* in Washington, D.C. On November 1, 1863, Bizarre called the actor (and future assassin) John Wilkes Booth "little more than a second-class actor."

blackberry A slang name for a Negro; one of several names given by whites as a humorous comparison with something black (blackbird, crow, tar baby) but derogatory because of the single criteria of color. *See also* darky.

"Black David" The nickname for Union Major General David Hunter, because he unofficially organized a black regiment. President Lincoln had to revoke an embarrassingly premature proclamation by Hunter in May 1862 that freed the slaves in Hunter's command, the Department of the South comprising Georgia, Florida, and South Carolina.

"Black Flag" A policy followed by some Confederate soldiers that any captured Yankee would be immediately shot if he had fought alongside black soldiers. "Black Flag," however, was an old term of warfare meaning death without quarter. The main advocate of the Black Flag code was Brigadier General Ben McCulloch. *See also* "fighting suit."

black fly *See* buffalo gnat.

Black Hat Brigade *See* Iron Brigade.

Black Horse Cavalry The nickname that Confederate Major General JEB STUART's cavalry earned at the first battle of Bull Run. The renowned unit was formed before the war by Major John Scott of Fauquier Country, Virginia, as he drank wine and discussed UNCLE TOM'S CABIN with dinner companions. The unit's members originally rode coal-black horses and wore jaunty plumed hats, but the war eventually reduced them to riding a variety of horses and wearing FORAGE CAPS. *See also* raid around the army.

"Black Horse Harry" The derogatory nickname for General Robert E. Lee's older half-brother, Henry Lee, Jr., because of his immoral life. The name was a reversal of "Light Horse Harry," the nickname of their father, Major General Henry Lee, a famous cavalryman with George Washington in the American Revolution. Henry Lee, Jr., had an illegitimate child with his wife's teenaged sister and embezzled money from his wife's family. However, Henry helped Robert obtain an appointment to the U.S. Military Academy.

blacking A substance used to blacken boots, shoes, and other leather items. A soldier carried it in his knapsack.

"Black Jack" The nickname for Union Major General John A. Logan. It was given by his soldiers, who would repeatedly yell "Black Jack, Black Jack, Black Jack" as they fought. Logan began as a member of "YATES' HELLIONS," Ulysses Grant's first command. A former lawyer and congressman, he led the Army of the Tennessee but disliked routine military preparations so much, he was relieved on the recommendation of Major General W.T. Sherman. Logan, however, joined Sherman for the siege of Atlanta and the March to the Sea, and then was reinstated as commander of the Army of the Tennessee.

black law The informal name for a law that restricted or even prohibited black people from moving into a state. Before the war began, black laws had been passed in the northern states of Indiana, Ohio, Oregon, and Abraham Lincoln's Illinois.

Black List A listing of soldiers who had violated camp rules, like missing roll call or avoiding work. When men were required for unpleasant or extra duties, such as burying dead horses or digging new SINKS, they would be selected from the Black List.

Black Maria A nickname for a vehicle used to carry arrested people to jail; a patrol wagon. It was supposedly named for Maria Lee, a strong black Boston woman who ran a boarding house for sailors and helped police load drunk lodgers into their van. This American name was introduced into Great Britain where it is still used for a van that takes prisoners from court to prison.

black North A derogatory southern name for the Union states because they supported freedom for blacks. The Richmond *Examiner* wrote on April 23, 1861, "It is not to be endured that this flight of abolition harpies shall come down from the black North for their roosts in the heart of the South, to defile and brutalize the land."

black Republicans The nickname given by opponents, especially in the South, to the Republican Party under Abraham Lincoln because the party supported freeing the slaves.

blacksnake The nickname for the black leather whip carried by army wagon drivers. The whips were especially needed for six-mule teams.

Black Terror The nickname for a dummy Union monitor ship sent floating with nobody aboard down the Mississippi River on February 25, 1863, during the siege of Vicksburg. Rear Admiral David D. Porter had the dummy constructed in 12 hours from an old flat coal-barge, with mud furnaces and a smokestack made of pork barrels from which black smoke bellowed. The Confederates had captured the *Indianola* and were raising it when the Black Terror appeared. Batteries from Vicksburg opened up on the ship with a furious roar, but the shots went straight through her without harm. Seeing the "turreted monster" approach, the Confederates blew up the *Indianola* to keep her from the enemy vessel and retreated in their ship, *The Queen of the West*. The Richmond *Examiner* of March 7, 1863, gave its navymen a sarcastic salute: "Well done for the *Queen of the West* and her brave officers!"

Black Thursday The South's nickname for a disasterous day—April 6, 1865—when up to 8,000 ragged and hungry Confederate soldiers led by General Robert E. Lee were captured after the battle of Sayler's Creek, Virginia. Among those captured were the commander, Major General Richard S. Ewell, and Lee's son, Major General Custis Lee. Black Thursday was the largest surrender of Americans in the nation's history; three days later Lee surrendered the rest of the Army of Northern Virginia at Appomattox Court House.

black tongue A disease that caused the deaths of many mules on both sides during the war. Horses were immune.

blacky A slang name for a Negro, then considered by whites to be more descriptive than offensive. An English woman visiting a Georgia plantation was asked "How do you like the appearance of our blackies?"

Blalock, Sam The alias used by Malinda Blalock who posed as a man to fight in the Confederate Army. Her husband, Keith Blalock, refused to enlist unless the recruiter also took his wife. The three agreed to the secret and the couple joined Company F of the 26th North Carolina Regiment. Sam (Malinda) drilled and was assigned normal military duties for two months until her husband was discharged for being physically unfit. She then confessed her true sex and was released with her husband.

blamed A milder word used for "blasted," which itself was a gentleman soldier's replacement for the commonly heard "damned."

blank book A book of blank or lined pages. Like today's notebooks, it was often used as a diary, ledger, cash book, receipt book, or record book. Henry David Thoreau used them to write his essays and poems. A large producer of blank books was Jas. B. Smith & Company of Philadelphia.

bleeder *See* fleam.

blenker A slang word meaning to "steal" and "plunder." It came from the actions of Union Brigadier General Louis Blenker's troops who looted and stole during a six-week march in 1862 in Virginia. This looting occurred because the War Department failed to provide basic food supplies, leaving the 10,000 soldiers virtually starving. Blenker was a native of Germany, and his division comprised three brigades of German-born soldiers. He was relieved of his command shortly after the infamous march. *See also* Dutchman; "I fights mit Sigel."

blister A slang name for an irritating person; the type of soldier whose unwanted appearance could ruin an evening's card game or campfire reverie.

blistering fly *See* cantharide.

blizzard A slang name for a great blast of gunfire. When Confederate Brigadier General John D. Imboden recalled the battle of New Market, Virginia, on May 15, 1864, he described Major William McLaughlin's artillery as giving the Union cavalry "a blizzard that sent them back hastily to their comrades."

block A name used, especially in the North, for a large building. They were often named for their developers, such as Buel's Block and Jones' Block, the name being placed in large letters on their fronts. A block could take up a city block and therefore face four streets. One of the vast buildings could be for a single purpose, such as a hotel, or it could be divided into stores.

blockade runner 1. A ship that ran the gauntlet of 600 Union warships blockading Confederate ports to take out cotton and bring in such desperately needed items as food, medicine, and military supplies. During the war, blockade runners are estimated to have delivered about $200 million of goods to the Confederacy, including about 400,000 rifles. Human passengers were sometimes added: Anna McNeill Whistler escaped on a blockade runner from North Carolina to London to join her son, the painter James McNeill Whistler (and later posed for the portrait known as "Whistler's Mother"). Almost 300 steamers ran the blockade from September 18, 1861, until June 23, 1865, when it was officially ended. Some were captured, destroyed, or converted into Union ships, but not enough to break this vital lifeline for the Confederacy. They operated out of such ports as Charleston, South Carolina; Mobile, Alabama; and Galveston, Texas, and were bound mostly for Havana, Cuba; Bermuda; and Nassau in the Bahamas. Well-known blockade-running ships included the *Ad-Vance*, *Old Dominion*, and *Wild Rover*. Many of them were fast, paddle-wheel Clyde Steamers converted into blockade runners by ship-

yards in Liverpool, England, and Glasgow, Scotland. 2. A captain in charge of a blockade-running ship. *See also* cotton-clad; gray ghost.

blockhead This familiar insult, for a stupid fellow, was well known in camp.

blockhouse A square defensive house used as a type of small fort (but vulnerable to artillery fire). Most were built of logs, and some were two stories high. More elaborate blockhouses were also constructed, such as the Union one that defended the Orange & Alexandria Railroad in Virginia. Built of thick logs and set on a high earthen bank, it housed a garrison of 60 men, with 12-pound howitzers for defense and a magazine below the floors.

blood disease A euphemism for syphilis.

"bloodiest day of the war" *See* America's bloodiest day.

"bloodiest region in America" The name given to the 100-mile distance between the two wartime capitals of Washington, D.C., and Richmond, Virginia, where battles raged throughout the war. Newspapers often repeated this description, which was also heard in the camps of both sides.

"The Bloody Angle" A nickname for the northwest section of the Confederates' MULE SHOE defensive line at the battle of Spotsylvania. Devastating hand-to-hand combat ensued in this cramped area, and the slaughter continued for 18 hours. After disengagement, the Rebels withdrew at midnight.

"Bloody Bill" The nickname of William Anderson, an insanely ruthless member of Quantrill's raiders. His sister had died in Union custody during the collapse of an old building used as a prison. Anderson hung scalps of dead Union soldiers from his saddle and strung them into a necklace for his horse. He once led a troop that ambushed 150 pursuing U.S. soldiers, whom they shot and bayoneted before cutting off their noses and ears. When a large union MILITIA finally killed Anderson in northwestern Missouri, they cut off his head and placed it on a telegraph pole.

bloody flux A common term for dysentery because blood is mixed with the discharge of the bowels. *See also* flux.

"Bloody Lane" A nickname given the "sunken road" that was a central area of conflict during the battle of Antietam in 1862. For more than two hours, Confederates held nearly a half-mile of the narrow wagon track. Both sides were decimated with about 5,600 killed or wounded, and a Union observer later noted that he could have walked upon the fallen bodies as far as he could see.

"Bloody Pond" (or "Bloody Pool") The nicknames given during the battle of Shiloh to a mud hole turned red by wounded and dying soldiers who tried to drink from it.

bloomers A girl's and woman's daring costume consisting of a short skirt and loose trousers buttoned at the ankles. It was usually worn with a coat and a bloomer hat that had a broad brim. Bloomers were named for the women's rights activist, Amelia Jenks Bloomer, whose followers were also called bloomers. The word was first heard about a decade before the war.

blow To boast or brag. Exaggeration was the soldier's usual way to blow about his battles, his state, his girl back home, etc.

blow down A slang term meaning "to kill with a gun"; e.g., "The Yankees tried to charge the blockhouse, but we blew down all six of them." The expression evolved in the twentieth century into "blow away."

blower (or blowhard) Slang names for a braggart or boaster. An article in *The Times* of London on Union Major General George Meade said "he is not, like his predecessor, a 'rowdy,' a profane swearer, and what is called in America a 'blower' or boaster." The derogatory name was also pinned on the Union's pompous Major General John Pope.

blow-fly A dreaded pest in camps. The blow-fly left eggs or maggots in battle wounds, which was known as "blowing a wound."

blow on someone To inform on someone, a common slang expression.

blow-out 1. A slang name, still used, for a feast, celebration, or great party. It was sometimes called a tuck-out. "Tuck" was an old British slang word for food. 2. A slang term for a loud quarrel or brawl; e.g., "Simmons was sent to the guard house after he got involved in that blow-out in town."

blow-up The informal name for losing one's temper, commonly used by soldiers during the war.

The Blue The Union forces or the United States, because of the color of the military uniform. At the war's first real battle, Bull Run, northern soldiers actually fought wearing gray uniforms, the color also worn by West Point cadets. These uniforms added to battlefield confusion, with enemy troops occasionally marching forward together before discovering their mistake. *See also* "Old Graybacks"; standard gray.

bluebacks A nickname for Confederate paper money because of its color. The term echoed the Union's GREENBACKS. When first issued in 1861, a Confederate dollar was valued at 95 cents to the U.S. dollar. At the end, it was worth about 1.7 cents. *See also* Shucks.

Confederate blueback.

blue belly (or blue-belly) A nickname for a Union soldier. The term was affectionately used by the North early in the war and Confederates were quick to turn the humorous name into a derisive one. *See also* bluebird; bluecoat; blue-skin.

bluebird A southern nickname for a Union soldier. The image was too attractive to compete with the more popular terms like BLUE BELLY, BLUECOAT, and BLUE-SKIN.

blue-blasted A mild profanity intended to have the effect of "damn." A soldier could growl about "those blue-blasted hardtack biscuits."

Blue-Book A published book that listed officeholders in the U.S. government, along with their salaries. The British had a Red-Book for their government.

bluecoat (or blue-jacket) Nicknames for a Union solider, used on both sides, because of the uniform's color. *See also* blue belly; bluebird; blue-skin.

blue devils A feeling of depression, despondency, or melancholy. The color blue has long been associated with sadness. "The blues" was used even before the war as a euphemism for the blue devils.

blue-eyed An informal name for being intoxicated or drunk. This term perhaps came from the fact that blue-eyed once meant black-eyed or having a dark ring around the eyes. See DRUNK for numerous other terms referring to intoxication.

Blue-eyed Child of Fortune The nickname given by philosopher William James to Colonel Robert Gould Shaw, who commanded the Union's first black unit. Shaw was the son of wealthy abolitionists and attended Harvard. Despite Shaw's own doubts about abolitionism and the public's general feeling that blacks would run from combat, Shaw formed and trained the 54th Massachusetts Regiment of free "persons of African descent." They were shipped to South Carolina, where their history was brief. On July 16, 1863, they repelled a Confederate attack on their camp on James Island and two days later were ordered to lead an assault on Battery Wagner, which defended Charleston harbor. Shaw told his 600 men that "The eyes of thousands will look on what you do tonight." He led the attack but was killed as the regiment suffered 272 casualties. The Confederates stripped Shaw's body and buried him in a mass grave with his dead soldiers. Although the attack failed, Sergeant William H. Carney became the first black soldier to receive the Congressional Medal of Honor, and the public realized that blacks would fight. The New York *Tribune* said their attack "made Fort Wagner such a name for the colored race as Bunker Hill has been for ninety years to the white Yankees." Within a year, the Union had created more than 50 new black regiments. On May 1, 1897, a monument to the regiment was dedicated on Boston's Beacon Street, and their story was told in the 1989 movie *Glory*.

blueing *See* browning.

blue-jacket *See* bluecoat.

The Blue Jug The nickname for the county jail in Washington, D.C., because of the dull blue color of its walls. The old, dilapidated building was north of the city hall. Serious offenders were kept in the "iron cage" but still many escaped. The prison became infamous during the war for having fugitive slaves among the inmates, giving it the more unpleasant nickname of "the Washington slave-pen." The Blue Jug was a major reason Congress passed legislation to free the slaves within the District of Columbia; President Lincoln signed the act on April 16, 1862.

blue light A slang name for a traitor. The term was especially used in the North because American traitors had used blue lights in the War of 1812 to warn British ships off New London, Connecticut, that U.S. frigates were about to leave the harbor.

blue mass (or blue powder) A mixture of mercury and chalk given by camp doctors in "blue pills" to cure constipation.

"Blue Monday" The nickname for a wartime fall of the New York Stock Market that occurred on April 15, 1864. Stock margins were wiped out and some brokers went bankrupt. However, in four days, the market began to rally.

blue plum (or blue pill or blue whistler) A bullet, because of the blue tint of the lead; e.g., "They had more men, but we gave those Johnnies a taste of blue plum."

blue ruin A slang name for bad liquor, especially a poor quality of gin.

the blues *See* blue devils.

blue-skin (or blue) 1. An insulting nickname for an especially dark black person. The name died out, however, about when the war ended. 2. A nickname sometimes heard for a Union solider, because of his uniform color. *See also* blue belly; bluebird; bluecoat.

"Blue Tail Fly" A popular minstrel song written by Daniel Decatur Emmet, who also wrote "Dixie." "Blue Tail Fly" was one of President Abraham Lincoln's favorite songs, and he often asked his young lawyer friend, the banjo-playing Ward Hill Lamon, to sing it. "Blue Tail Fly" was sometimes called "Jim Crack Corn."

blue-water sailor A true sailor who had sailed the open seas. They were dismissive of sailors who only blockaded the ports or cruised down rivers.

bluff 1. A slang name for a cheater; e.g., "He's a liar and a bluff." This usage was probably an extension of a card player's bluff to mislead his opponents. 2. The common name for poker, a popular card game among gambling soldiers. The general American enthusiasm for poker began with the soldiers, who then popularized the game with civilians.

blunderbuss An old-fashioned short gun with a large bore and flaring muzzle. It fired several balls but was accurate only at short range. Confederate Major Heros von Borcke recalled an attack on a Union troop train as follows: "The engine driver was shot down by Captain Farley, to whom I had lent my blunderbuss." The original Dutch name meant "thunder gun."

boarding-house A euphemism used by prostitutes for their houses. All areas of Washington, D.C., including respectable neighborhoods, had their "boarding-houses."

boatswain's gang On a navy ship, the company of men who made up the deck crew, maintaining such important equipment as the ropes and other riggings, anchors, and small boats. They answered to the boatswain's mate, the lively petty officer with his famously insistent pipe or whistle.

"Bob" *See* "Rob."

bobbery An argument or squabble. Soldiers could always get into a bobbery about anything from card games to military tactics.

"Bobby Lee" A nickname, always said in full, for Confederate General Lee. It was used by both sides. When staff members of General Ulysses Grant were recounting his successes in the west to officers of the Army of the Potomac, one of them noted, "That may be, but you never met Bobbie Lee and his boys."

body bag A slang name for an undershirt or shirt; e.g., "Even in a Georgia summer, the general wouldn't let us march without our body bags on."

body guard (or body companion) A humorous nickname for a louse; e.g., "I wouldn't think of going into battle without my body guards."

bogus The name of a liquor composed of rum mixed with molasses. *See also* calibogus.

Bohemian Brigade The nickname Union war correspondents gave themselves.

They composed the first U.S. press corps, often working in groups and cooperating on gathering the news. Some 350 northern reporters, some of them soldiers, covered the war.

boiled shirt (or boiler shirt) A white dress shirt with a starched front that required ironing. They were seldom seen in camp, and a soldier wearing one was subject to mischievous comments, although one private noted, it "completed the restoration of the man to decency." They were sometimes humorously called a balded-face shirt or fried shirt.

bolted Sifted, in regard to flour, corn meal, and grain. Unbolted was unsifted. The word is derived from a Latin term, *bura*, meaning "coarse cloth."

bomb-ketch A small warship that carried MORTARS that launched tremendously explosive shells. Because of the recoil of the 13-inch-caliber mortars, the ship had to be strengthened with extra timbers beneath the deck. A bomb-ketch, often just a reinforced barge, could bombard the enemy accurately at up to 4,000 yards. They were often used by the Union navy, including an attack on forts at the mouth of the Mississippi River.

bomb-proof 1. A derisive term for an able-bodied man who avoided the war. Soldiers on furlough would often seek them out. Confederate Private Carlton McCarthy recalled that "it was a delight of some of the stoutly built fellows to go home for a few days, and kick and cuff and tongue-lash the able-bodied bomb-proofs." 2. A taunting name for a soldier, even a general, who seemed to stay back from the fighting. The name was often hurled by infantrymen and artillerymen at passing cavalrymen. 3. A soldier's dugout shelter, usually covered with wood.

bone 1. To study intensely (the expression today being "bone up"). Union Gen-

Timothy O'Sullivan's photograph of a sutler's bomb-proof near Petersburg, Virginia. *Library of Congress, Prints & Photographs Division, LC-B8171-1051.*

eral Ulysses S. Grant said of Major General W.T. Sherman, who constantly studied maps and planned, "He bones all the time while he is awake, as much on horseback as in camp or in his quarters." 2. To work hard; e.g., "I'd rather bone on Sundays than sit through his sermons."

boneset The common name for a plant used for its healing properties, especially by Confederate surgeons during the blockade. Also called a thoroughwort, the plant's scientific name is *Eupatorium*

perfoliatum. Despite the optimistic folk name, it did not repair broken bones.

Bonnie Blue Flag The nickname of the secessionist flag used by South Carolina when it became the first state to secede on December 20, 1860. It was a solid blue flag with a large white star in the center.

"The Bonnie Blue Flag" A popular southern song, often sung by soldiers in camp and on the march. It was a salute to the first secessionist flag, nicknamed the BONNIE BLUE FLAG. The lyrics were supposedly written in 1861 by Irish-born Harry McCarthy, an Arkansas comedian, who used the tune from "The Irish Jaunting Car," an old Irish tune. He had seen a large version of the flag carried through the crowd at Jackson, Mississippi, at that state's secession convention. The song was first performed in New Orleans that year in the Variety Theatre by his sister, Miss Marion McCarthy. The first verse of seven went as follows:

> We are a band of brothers, and native to the soil,
> Fighting for the property we gained by honest toil;
> And when our rights are threatened, the cry rose near and far:
> "Hurrah for the Bonnie Blue Flag that bears a Single Star!"

When Union Major General Benjamin F. Butler became military governor of New Orleans in 1862, he had the song's publisher arrested, fined him $500, and destroyed the sheet music. Butler also fined anyone—man, woman, or child—$25 for singing, whistling, or playing "The Bonnie Blue Flag."

boodle A slang word for money, especially money used for a bribe or counterfeit money. *See* caboodle.

booking (oneself) Studying, especially reading books on military tactics; e.g., "Nathan can't join in cards today because he's booking himself for a promotion."

book-soldier A soldier trained by the book and who has a loyal belief that its tactics and strategies should work if followed correctly. The book-soldier was always horrified to see a battle disintegrate into mayhem, as it almost always did. David L. Thompson, a soldier with Company G of the 9th New York Volunteers, recalled that "To the book-soldier all order seems destroyed, months of drill apparently going for nothing in a few minutes."

"Boots and Saddles" The title of the bugle call for the cavalry or artillery to prepare for combat or for the former to ride out. It was originally played for battery drill in camp. The term is a corruption of a French cavalry order, *Boute selle*, meaning literally "put saddle."

Borden's milk This famous brand of condensed milk was sold by SUTLERS to Union soldiers. Another company producing condensed milk was Lewis.

Border Brigade The name of Iowa MILITIA units organized to protect the state's borders. The Southern Border Brigade was formed in 1861 with 10 companies and the Northern Border Brigade came into being the next year with 5 companies.

bore a hole in A slang expression meaning to shoot; e.g., "The picket was half asleep, which was like asking someone to bore a hole in him."

born tired An apt description for a lazy soldier.

bosh A common word during the war for "nonsense." After one Confederate read in a northern paper that the Union had won a battle, he was informed that "all accounts of an utter Rebel rout was bosh."

boss A slang word for "great" or "wonderful." A soldier receiving a letter in camp might exclaim, "That's boss!"

boudoir cabinet The nickname for southern women who had special influence in the administration of President James Buchanan, who was confronted with the secession of South Carolina in 1860. A leading member of the boudoir cabinet was the wife of former Alabama Congressman Philip Phillips. She later moved to New Orleans where her rude behavior at a Union soldier's funeral earned her a few weeks' imprisonment on Ship Island. After her release, she moved to Mobile, Alabama.

bounce A slang word meaning "to ambush"; e.g., "The Yankee courier reached the other side of the river, where we bounced him."

bounty agent A private agent in the North who recruited men for the U.S. forces by acting as a middleman for government bounties. The often disreputable agent would skim off a large part of the payment and then help their clients JUMP out of the military and re-enlist for another bounty. Agents were also known to recruit men unfit for duty.

bounty jumper See jump.

bowel complaint See diarrhea-dysentery.

"bowels yearning for battle" A manly boast around camp. "I have heard of soldiers whose 'bowels yearned' for a fight," wrote Alexander Hunter of his days in General Lee's army, "but such 'bowels' were not inside of my anatomy."

bowie knife The large hunting knife invented by the frontierman James Bowie. It was usually from 10" to 15" inches long with a blade about 2" wide. *Harper's Weekly* reported in an article on August 2, 1861, that Bowie had accidentally invented it when his sword broke while fighting Mexicans, and he continued to use it as a knife. It was most often carried early in the war by Confederate soldiers, usually worn under their belts. Bowie-type bayonets were also developed, the Union's version manufactured by Dahlgren and a thinner Confederate one made by Boyle, Gamble, and MacFee. Despite its frightening look, the bowie was more often used for camp chores than on the enemy.

"Bowie Knife Boys" The nickname assumed by Company C of the 1st Georgia Infantry. The knife was considered a prized possession in any camp, and Company C received a good supply from the state of Georgia, which had paid $4 each for 5,000 knives with 18-inch blades.

"bowlegs" A derisive but traditional nickname for a cavalryman, obviously because of the physical effect of long hours in the saddle.

bowling A zany camp version of the sport in which improvised "pins" were arranged on the ground and the players bowled with a cannon ball.

Bowman House The premier hotel in Jackson, Mississippi, during the war. Its lobby faced the Mississippi State House, and it was here on May 14, 1863, that Union generals Ulysses S. Grant, W.T. Sherman, and James B. McPherson celebrated their capture of the capital of President Jefferson Davis's home state.

boxcars The train cars often used to transport Confederate soldiers and their equipment. The arrangement was often compared to chickens in poultry wagons, because the troops would punch holes in the sides of the boxcars to improve the view and ventilation. Some brave soldiers preferred to ride on top of the cars.

boy A general southern name for a slave of any age. When Union Major General W.T. Sherman's troops descended upon Georgia, Dolly Lunt, a plantation owner, complained of their "forcing my boys from home at the point of the bayonet."

"Boy General" A nickname for Union Major General George Armstrong Custer, who in 1865 was given that rank by BREVET at the age of 25. He celebrated his promotion by designing most of his flamboyant uniform that included a red cravat and wide-brimmed hat. After the war, he became only a lieutenant colonel, his rank when he died with his men at the battle of Little Bighorn in 1876.

Boys in Blue Union soldiers, used as a fairly friendly term by both sides. Confederate Private Carlton McCarthy wrote, "The 'Boys in Blue' generally preferred to camp in the open fields."

Boys in Gray Confederate soldiers, used by both sides.

bracer A slang name for a drink of alcohol, especially one to steady the nerves or serve as a pick-me-up; e.g., "The captain had a bracer or two before he met the girl's father."

"brain, heart, and bowels of the rebellion" President Abraham Lincoln's anatomical description of the Confederate cities of Richmond, Chattanooga, and Vicksburg.

"Brains of the Confederacy" A nickname for Judah P. Benjamin, who served as the Confederate attorney general, secretary of war, and secretary of state. He was President Jefferson Davis's closest cabinet member. Benjamin was a British Jew born in the West Indies, but his parents immigrated to the U.S. and he was raised in Charleston, South Carolina. He was a lawyer in New Orleans and then elected to the U.S. Senate (1852-60). After President Davis was captured, Benjamin escaped to England and became one of that country's leading legal minds, writing *The Sale of Personal Property* (1868). He burned virtually all of his official Confederate papers, leaving only a shadowy memory of his important roles during the conflict.

brandy sour An alcoholic drink created in 1861. It contained brandy, water, sugar, lemon, and often nutmeg.

brass 1. A slang name for bravery, nerve, or impudence. 2. A slang name for money.

brass missionary A nickname for any cannon. *See also* Kingdom Come.

"A Brass-Mounted Army" A Confederate soldier's song complaining about the officers having the best food and whiskey, as well as entertaining the ladies. The final verse and chorus celebrates the end of both the war and the army:

> We'll see our loving sweethearts, and sometimes kiss them too,
> We'll eat the finest rations, and bid old buck adieu;
> There'll be no generals with orders to compel,
> Long boots and eagle buttons, forever fare ye well!
> And thus we'll leave the army,
> The brass-mounted army
> The high-falutin' army,
> Where the eagle buttons rule.

bravely An adverb meaning "excellently." One might hear in camp that a wounded soldier "is doing bravely."

breach A section of a fortification that had collapsed, usually because of artillery fire during a siege. A breach that could be entered was called a "practicable breach." Assault troops would storm the breach to widen it for a general attack. During the war, a commander of a breached fort would almost always surrender to avoid useless bloodshed.

bread During the long siege of Vicksburg, the name given by Confederate subsistence officers to field peas ground up and mixed with meal. As the desperate siege continued, this "bread" became a strange "elastic sort of concoction" consisting of only pulverized peas.

bread bag A nickname for a HAVERSACK.

breadbasket A slang term for the stomach, which is still used today.

breadbasket of the Confederacy The Shenandoah Valley of Virginia. Its fertile soil produced a vital food supply for southern soldiers and civilians. Crops were harvested and taken mostly to Richmond and Petersburg, Virginia. Confederate troops fought throughout the war to control the valley, but in 1864 it was scorched, along with more than 2,000 barns full of wheat and hay, by Union Major General Philip Sheridan's Army of the Shenandoah. Hundreds of nearly starving people fled the area. "If this war is to last another year," General Grant told Sheridan, "we want the Shenandoah Valley to remain a barren waste."

bread riot Two years into the war, the South's civilians were suffering hard economic times because of the Union's blockade and the diversion of food to the Confederate army. The desperate need to feed their families brought the women of Richmond, the Confederate capital, into the streets on April 2, 1863, to demand lower prices (flour now sold for $100 a barrel). Chanting "Bread! Bread! Bread!," they broke store windows and looted the goods. In the midst of the riot, they saw President Jefferson Davis climb onto a wagon. He accused them of demanding bread but stealing jewelry and other items. He said he understood they were hungry and without money. Reaching into his pocket, he flung bills and coins to them, saying "Here is all I have." But he also fished out his watch, held it high and informed the mob's members they would be shot by the assembled MILITIA if they did not disperse in five minutes. They did, and Davis had the ringleaders arrested.

bread sauce A sauce especially used with chicken and turkey. It was composed of bread crumbs cooked with cayenne peppers, onions, cloves, mace, and butter, with cream added before serving.

breast-to-breast fighting An alternate term for hand-to-hand fighting.

breastwork A low defense wall that was quickly built. The word was sometimes more generally used, as when a staff member of Confederate General Patrick R. Cleburne suggested at Missionary Ridge in Chattanooga, "General, here is a ditch, or gully, that will make a natural breastwork."

Photographed on April 3, 1865, these breastworks at Fort Mahone (also known as "Fort Damnation") were part of the Confederate defensive lines around Petersburg, Virginia, in 1864-65. *Library of Congress, Prints & Photographs Division, LC-B8171-3211.*

breather A slang name for something that is amazing or exceptional: "Have you seen the iron-clad *Monitor*? It's a breather."

breeching rope (or breeching) A rope used on a warship to restrain the recoil of a cannon and its carriage. The rope, as large as a man's upper arm, was threaded through the CASCABEL on the rear of the cannon and both ends were attached to the side of the ship.

breezing A slang term for being scolded or receiving an angry rebuke; e.g., "That Secesh woman gave us a breezing when we carried off her pig."

breezy A slang word for being intoxicated or drunk. See DRUNK for numerous other terms referring to intoxication.

brevet An honorary commission promoting an officer to a higher rank without an increase in pay and sometimes no more authority. Brevets were created in the U.S. army before the war when promotions took many years, and they were almost always for bravery in action. During the war, however, brevets were also given for political reasons. Some 10,000 were awarded, and of 1,950 generals in the volunteer and regular army, all but 583 were promoted with brevets.

brevet eagle A humorous name for a turkey, promoting it with an honorary military BREVET.

brevet horse A humorous term for a mule, conferring the military BREVET to upgrade its status.

Briarfield The name of Jefferson Davis's cotton plantation on the Mississippi River south of Vicksburg. It was given to him by his older brother, Joseph, and he settled there in 1835, creating a democratic system of slavery (despite the contradictory terms) that put slaves in charge of their own legal system. They would later state they were "hardly aware of slavery." After the war's end, with Davis in a federal prison, his brother secured his permission to sell Briarfield to Davis's former slave, Ben Montgomery, who had been his respected overseer. When Davis visited the property in 1867, he said he felt like "a returning ghost." In 1878, after Montgomery had died, Davis regained Briarfield through a lawsuit and, although then living at BEAUVOIR, spent much time and effort there. When he died, 13 of his former slaves and Negro workers at Briarfield wrote his wife as follows: "We, the old servants and tenants of our beloved master, Honorable Jefferson Davis, have cause to mingle our

tears over his death, who was always so kind and thoughtful of our peace and happiness."

brick A slang name for a good or fine fellow. One Union soldier on Major General W.T. Sherman's march through Georgia described a talkative southern farmer as a "jolly old brick."

brickley A southern word meaning brittle; e.g., "Mother's fudge had turned brickley by the time her package arrived in camp."

Bridge Guard Several companies of Georgia MILITIA that were formed by Governor Joseph Brown in May 1862 to guard the state's railroad bridges from attack. The Guard eventually grew into the GEORGIA STATE LINE forces.

brig An informal name for a military prison. The term, coined in the U.S., had been used about a decade before the war began. It first meant a temporary prison on a warship but was soon also applied to army guard houses.

brigade A military unit on both sides that was the largest organization of a single branch, such as infantry. It consisted of about two or three regiments, usually commanded by a brigadier general. Nicknames were popular, like the ORPHAN BRIGADE and the IRON BRIGADE, and Confederate brigades especially were often named for their commanders, such as Hood's Brigade.

Bright's disease A medical term for a group of diseases of the kidneys, in which they become inflamed and degenerate. The name is still used for a specialized disease of the kidneys involving inflammation of capillaries.

Brockenbrough house The large house purchased by the city of Richmond, Virginia, to be the home of Confederate

President Jefferson Davis. Located on a steep hill with a terraced garden, it had been built by Dr. John Brockenbrough, a former president of the Bank of Virginia. President Davis's wife, Varina, referred to it as the "old Brockenbrough house" and Mary Brockenbrough, the doctor's wife, became her frequent visitor and advisor on the rooms and garden.

brogues (or brogans) A tough shoe worn by soldiers. They had wide soles and large flat heels. Boots proved to be heavy and tiresome on a long march, with a worn heel causing the upper part to rub and twist the ankle. Brogues, on the other hand, were relatively comfortable and quicker to put on and remove. The shoes had first been worn in Ireland and Scotland, and the Gaelic-Irish name meant simply "shoe."

broma A chocolate preparation made from cocoa. It was a popular article to include in boxes sent from home to soldiers.

bronze john A slang name for yellow fever, being a word play on the original slang of YELLOW JACK.

broom-corn A variety of corn whose tufts are used to make brooms. It grew from six to eight feet tall.

"Brother Lincoln" The embarrassing name used for President Abraham Lincoln by Emilie Helm, the sister of Mrs. Lincoln, who was married to Confederate Brigadier General Benjamin H. Helm. After Helm was killed at the battle of Chickamauga on September 20, 1863, Emilie traveled from Alabama to stay at the White House where President Lincoln, calling her "Little Sister," wept as he embraced her. Her stay raised many eyebrows, however, and after nearly a week, she went to her mother's home in Kentucky.

brothers' truce The name given by western troops to special pauses in the fighting to allow friends (and sometimes brothers) to relax and converse together between the front lines.

browning A factory process that put a brown color on the barrel of a musket or rifle. In some cases, blueing was used. The Union's Springfield Armory dropped the practice in 1861 to speed up production. Soldiers then polished the barrels to a proud shine, but this was discontinued as too dangerous, since the enemy could see the glint of weapons moving into position, even by moonlight.

Brown-Roan (or The Roan) One of Confederate General Robert E. Lee's horses during the early war. He bought it in West Virginia, but the steed went blind soon after the Seven Days' battles in July 1862. *See also* Ajax; Lucy Long; Richmond; Traveller.

bruise A cooking term meaning to mash or crush, as with a mortar and pestle; also called to "jam."

bruised A slang word for being intoxicated or drunk. See DRUNK for numerous other terms referring to intoxication.

bubba A dialect form of "brother," especially used by slaves.

buck A slang name for a dollar, the term being first used about a decade before the war began.

Buck The boyhood nickname of Ulysses Grant, Jr., the second son of Union General Ulysses Grant, because he was born in Ohio, the Buckeye State. The name was given to him before the war by slaves on Grant's farm in Missouri.

buck and ball A paper cartridge for the old model .69-caliber smoothbore musket, mostly seen in Confederate hands.

This cartridge was packed with a musket ball topped with three smaller buckshot. These extra missiles created a type of shotgun fire and helped to compensate for the inaccuracy of the smoothbores.

buck and gag A harsh camp punishment for such offenses as cowardice or absence without official leave. The guilty man was made to sit with a gag in his mouth, his arms extended and hands tied, his knees pulled up between his arms, and his ankles tied. A small stick or log was then inserted under the knees and over the elbows. After 6 to 12 hours, even the hardiest victim would have to be carried back to his tent.

bucking the tiger (or fighting the tiger) A nickname for playing and gambling on the card game of FARO, because the faro table was called "the tiger." This created another slang name, "bucker," meaning a gambler. *See also* tiger den; taking a twist at the tiger.

Buckland Races The Confederate name for the route of Union forces during a cavalry battle on October 19, 1863, at Buckland Mills, Virginia. Confederate Major General Jeb Stuart's men defeated, and chased after, the troops of Brigadier General Hugh J. Kilpatrick and others, claiming to capture 250 of the enemy. The confrontation also saw Confederate Brigadier General Thomas L. Rosser in pursuit of his old friend, Brigadier General George Armstrong Custer. (The friendship was renewed after the war.) *See also* Philippi Races; Wildcat Stampede; Woodstock Races.

buckra A name used by slaves for a white man. It came from a language on the African coast where it meant a powerful spirit or being. *See also* swanga buckra.

The Bucktails The nickname of the 13th Pennsylvania Reserves, because new members had to show they were marksmen by wearing the tail or fur of a buck deer they had shot. It was often displayed on their hats.

bud (or buddy) These informal names for a friend came into use about a decade before the war. They probably evolved from "brother."

"Buffalo Bill" The nickname for William Cody, an Indian scout who served with the Union army during the war, first for the 9th Kansas Cavalry fighting against Comanche and Kiowa Indians, and then in Tennessee and Missouri against Confederate forces. He was awarded the MEDAL OF HONOR, but this was revoked after the war and then officially reinstated in 1989. Cody earned his nickname by using his Springfield rifle to kill (he said) 4,280 buffalo in 17 months under a contract to supply meat for workers building the Kansas Pacific Railway. His real and imaginary exploits became legendary through dime novels, and in 1883 he organized his famous "Wild West" show, which included such stars as Annie Oakley and Sitting Bull.

buffalo chips Dried patties of buffalo dung. It was used in the place of firewood by western troops camped in the treeless plains.

buffalo gnat A common name for the black fly, the small black gnat that was a pest in camps. One soldier said it "dives into the ear, nose, or anywhere on or under the skin."

buffalo hunt The deceptive reason given by Confederate Captain John R. Baylor in December 1860 for organizing a group of his Texas MILITIA men into a unit that became the core of the state's Confederate troops.

bug A slang name for an enthusiast, such as a hobbyist or a fan; e.g., "Most of the men in our mess were Republican bugs."

bugger A derogatory name that soldiers commonly used to describe a disliked officer; e.g., "I wouldn't march one mile for that old bugger."

buggy A light one-seat carriage or wagon that had four wheels and was pulled by one horse. *See also* gig.

buggy-nag A horse used to pull buggies and carriages.

bug-house A boarding house infested with fleas and other vermin.

bug juice A humorous name for whiskey.

bugology A comical nickname for entomology, the study of insects. It was especially used by students, beginning about a decade before the war.

the bulge The advantage a military force could acquire over the enemy. The term was often used by Confederate Lieutenant General Nathan Bedford Forrest, whose men often had the bulge on much larger forces. The expression "to have the bulge on" also meant holding an advantage over another person; e.g., "Each time I trade with Emerson, he always has the bulge on me."

bull A slang verb meaning to talk in an insincere, foolish, or exaggerated manner, especially about a subject one knows little about. A soldier might "bull about" plans for a coming battle or the weakness of an officer. The term was first used about a decade before the war began.

"Bull" The nickname for Union Brigadier General William Nelson, commander of the 4th Division of the Army of the Ohio, because of his big size, bellowing voice, and aggressive personality. He weighed 300 pounds and stood 6' 4". He was shot and killed on September 29, 1862, by one of his own officers, Brigadier General Jefferson C. Davis, after

Nelson had slapped him during an argument in a hotel lobby in Louisville, Kentucky.

bull dance *See* stag dance.

"Bull of the Woods" The nickname of Union General Edwin V. Sumner of Massachusetts, because of his roaring voice, despite being the oldest active general officer in the war. He died in 1863 of natural causes at the age of 66 while traveling to St. Louis to take command in Missouri.

bull-head A slang name for someone who acted stubborn or was stupid. The insult was first used about a decade before the war began.

bullpen A slang name for a cheap room or house used by a prostitute. *See also* clap; daughter of Eve; drab; fallen angel; fancy girl; fast house; gay young duck; "The Haystack; "Hooker's Division"; "Madam Russell's Bake Oven"; parlor house; ranch; The Wolf's Dream.

bull train A wagon train pulled by steers, the invention of Union Brigadier General James S. Wadsworth in 1863. His idea was to have bulls pull old wagons found in the area, conveying supplies to troops. He would then slaughter the animals for beef, cooking it by burning the wagons. He had his troops spend the winter and spring in Belle Plain, Virginia, breaking the steers to the yoke. When they were first used on the Gettysburg campaign, however, the bull wagons quickly fell behind the pace of those pulled by horses and mules, so Wadsworth (fearing rear attacks by Confederate raiders) abandoned his idea before the Potomac River was reached. He returned the steers to a herd, shifted supplies to normal military wagons, and burned his decrepit wagons.

bully Excellent, dashing, or jolly. A soldier would say that he had a drink of "bully whiskey" or that a companion was a "bully fighter." The interjection of "Bully!" meant "good" or "well done" and was often heard in the expression "Bully for you!" The word was later popularized by President Teddy Roosevelt.

bully soup A common hot cereal served in Union camps. It was a boiled mixture of crushed HARDTACK and cornmeal with some added ginger and wine. Eliza Harris of the SANITARY COMMISSION invented the soup, which was often called "panada" or "ginger panada."

bum To beg or to wander about in a lazy way. It also meant to go on a spree or to carouse. The verb was first used in 1863 during the war, although a lazy person was known as a bum a few years before that, and the name was applied to tramps after the war. The word was a shortening of BUMMER.

bumblebee whiskey A nickname for strong whiskey, because it gave the drinker a "sting."

bummer 1. A soldier who went FORAGING for food and other civilian items that could be taken. The most notorious examples were SHERMAN'S BUMMERS during his march through Georgia in 1864. Deserters, escaping slaves, and lawless misfits of the war were also called bummers. The name had been used before the war for idle and lazy people, and this led to the war term, HOSPITAL BUMMER. It apparently came from the German term for a lazy person, a *Bummler*. 2. A slang term used by Union sailors for a MORTAR BOAT.

bump To murder or kill someone. The slang verb was created about a decade before the war and was frequently applied to killing the enemy. The term became "bump off" in the 1920s.

bun A common name for a squirrel; e.g., "There were no Yankees to kill, but our sharpshooter brought back three buns for dinner."

bunch-of-fives A slang name for the hand or fist. The latter was often the threat to "give someone a bunch of fives." This common expression began about a decade before the war.

bungo A type of small basic boat used in the South. Some were hewn from tree trunks.

bunk it To sleep in a bunk; e.g., "Collins was raised in a fine house with a feather bed, but now he has to bunk it with common folk like us."

bunk-mates Soldiers who shared a bed in camp, usually two men to a bunk.

bunkum (or buncombe) A slang name for talk that is insincere or full of nonsense; e.g., "Instead of shoes, the Confederate Congress gave us more bunkum." The word developed from a statement made in 1821 by U.S. Congressman Felix Walker who, despite calls for him to wrap up his speech on slavery in Missouri, continued because he felt bound to "make a speech for Buncombe," a county in the North Carolina district he represented.

buoyant torpedo An underwater mine (torpedo) thrown into the water so the current would carry it to enemy ships. They contained percussion-cap firing devices and would explode on contact. They were known to blow up flowing debris.

Bureau of Exemptions The bitterly humorous nickname for the Confederate Bureau of Conscription in Richmond, Virginia, which was in charge of administering the CONSCRIPTION ACT.

Bureau of Military Justice The U.S. bureau set up by Congress in 1864 to centralize the army's legal system. It was headed by the judge-advocate general, the army's chief lawyer, who oversaw courts-martial, and also included the judges-advocate assigned to each field army.

burgle To commit a burglary or to burglarize. This short form became popular about a decade before the war began.

"Burn my skin!" An exclamation of surprise or anger; e.g., "Well, burn my skin if it ain't my old mess-mate from Alabama!"

Burns A horse ridden by Union General George McClellan, but not in the late afternoon when the horse insisted on having his meal. Burns was the namesake of the man who presented him to McClellan.

burnt brandy and peach A southern drink often used to cure diarrhea. A glass was filled with dried peaches, then cognac and sugar were ignited in a saucer and poured over the peaches.

Burnt Country The area burned in Georgia by troops of Major General W.T. Sherman on his March to the Sea in 1864. Writing on December 24, 1864, Georgia resident Eliza Andrews reported that "About three miles from Sparta we struck the 'burnt country,' as it is well named by the natives, and then I could better understand the wrath and desperation of these poor people."

Burnt District The business section of Richmond, Virginia, which was destroyed by fire when the city fell on April 2, 1865, to General Ulysses S. Grant's troops. That area of modern Richmond is still called the Burnt District.

burnt sugar coffee Coffee that is sweetened with brown sugar that has been burned black and then turned into a syrup by adding hot water. *See also* cane seed coffee; chinquapin coffee; grape coffee; okra coffee; pea coffee; potato and persimmon coffee; rye coffee; war coffee.

burst a boiler Make a supreme effort. An equivalent expression today is to "bust a gut."

burying squad A detail of men assigned to the traumatic task of burying the dead after a battle. If the defeated enemy had retreated, it meant burying friend and foe.

Bushwhacker Confederate guerrillas who operated during the war in Kansas and Missouri, and often hid in the Ozarks. Bands of bushwhackers shot or hung civilians suspected of being Union sympathizers. The most infamous bushwhacker was William Quantrill, who used the alias of Charlie Hart. "Bushwhacker" was originally a name for a backwoodsman.

the business A euphemism for combat, often used by Union General Ulysses S. Grant.

buss To kiss. The word is also a noun, along with "bussing." One Missouri soldier wrote a letter about his sweetheart, saying, "I would like to have a sweet buss from her rosy cheeks."

busser A slang name for the mouth; e.g., "Williams called me a damn Greek, so I hit him across the busser." The idea survives today with the term "kisser."

buster 1. A slang name for a strong, vigorous man. A Union soldier writing to his brother about Major General W.T. Sherman, enthused, "What a buster that man is." 2. Anything big and powerful, such as a wind. A soldier with Union Major General Ambrose E. Burnside described one of the general's surprise maneuvers as "a risky expedition but a buster." 3. A slang name for a drinking spree or a loud, wild party. The short version, "bust," remains today in the mostly college term, "beer bust."

bustle A framework of whalebone or metal worn under the skirt to support a heavy padding or cushion of dress material swept up and back. One lady living under Yankee occupation in Decatur, Georgia, used a bustle padding of northern newspapers to smuggle their military and political news to southern officers in Atlanta.

bust skull (or bust head) Humorous names for strong, cheap, distasteful alcohol that was often illegally distilled. The terms originated during the war. "Crack skull" was also used.

"Butcher" A nickname used in both northern and southern newspapers for Union General Ulysses S. Grant, because some felt (incorrectly) that his battle tactics lost more men than those of other generals.

Butlerize A slang word in the South meaning "to rob." It was derived from stories about the looting of homes by Union soldiers under Major General Benjamin F. Butler during the occupation of New Orleans. One Scottish visitor to the South heard a small boy tell his sister, "Now, don't you Butlerize all that pie." *See also* "Beast"; spoons.

butt The slang shortening of buttocks. The first known written example in the U.S. was two years before the war began.

The Butterflies A humorous nickname for the 3rd New Jersey Cavalry because they wore colorfully flamboyant uniforms with capes and jackets with extra braid across the chest. The members insisted on calling their unit the First U.S. Hussars.

Buttermilk Brigade The good-natured nickname given to soldiers from Virginia by Confederate troops from other states.

"buttermilk cavalry" (or "buttermilk rangers" or "buttermilk spies") Taunts that Confederate soldiers directed toward their cavalrymen, especially when the cavalry was ordered to the rear because the enemy's infantry was advancing. Even officers, such as Major General Jubal Early, were known to hurl the epithet at the horsemen.

"Buttermilk or cornfed?" A humorous gibe at a fat soldier or civilian.

Butternut The northern nickname for a Confederate soldier or a person who sympathized with the South. It referred to a type of Confederate uniform color of brownish-gray, the normal color of the butternut, a walnut tree. As wartime shortages grew, some Confederate uniforms were stained with dye made at home with butternut bark, walnut hulls, or a mixture of butternut oil and iron sulfate, so uniforms had a variety of shades.

Butternut Guerrillas A small volunteer reconnaissance force led by Sergeant Richard Surby that was part of the two-week (April 17 to May 2, 1863) Union cavalry raid into Mississippi by troops under Colonel Benjamin H. Grierson. The Butternut Guerrillas, nine men from the 7th Illinois Cavalry, wore Confederate uniforms and would have been hanged if captured. In one action, they seized a Southern Railroad telegraph office to keep a warning from being sent. Near the end of the raid, one of their number discovered a Confederate ambush at Union Church, allowing Grierson to circle east to safety in Union-held Baton Rouge. *See also* Quinine Brigade.

buttery A pantry or larder in a house. The name did not originally refer to a storeroom for butter, but rather for butts (large casks) of liquor.

buzzard-bait 1. A soldier who seemed fated to be killed. 2. A dead soldier that had to be left unburied. After the war, the term became "buzzard-meat." A variant name was "crow-bait."

by and again Now and then; e.g., "The general would get drunk by and again, but never in front of the men."

"By ginger!" An mild oath used to intensify a statement; e.g., "By ginger, I'll never eat another biscuit after this war is over." It was a euphemism for "by Jesus."

by (the) grapevine telegraph An expression used for a rumor; e.g., "We heard it by the grapevine telegraph," now abbreviated to "the grapevine." Early telegraph lines supposedly sagged and resembled grapevines.

"By Jukes!" A common exclamation of surprise or excitement; a euphemism for "By Jesus!" Other wartime expressions were "By jingo!," "By gravy!," "By good gravy!," and "By Joe!" All were used in the manner of "By golly!" which was a euphemism for "By God!" *See also* Jupiter.

"By lightning!" A common exclamation of surprise or anger and one often used by Union General Ulysses S. Grant, who almost never swore. *See also* "Doggone it!"

by the ears A phrase to describe a fight or quarrel; e.g., "More than once I saw a card game that brought men together by the ears." The expression came from dogs grabbing each other by the ears when fighting.

"By the gods!" An oath used to emphasize a statement or opinion; e.g., "By the gods, I'll never ask for a federal pardon."

"By the widow Perkins!" A mild oath or irritation or surprise; e.g., "By the widow Perkins, if those Rebs haven't stolen our mules!"

C

C 1. A slang name for $100, because "C," the Roman numeral for 100, was once printed on $100 bills. The term has evolved into today's "C-note." The name "century" was sometimes also used during the war. 2. The letter branded on soldiers guilty of cowardice, usually on their foreheads, cheeks, or hands. The branding was done with hot irons or, for some lucky men, indelible ink.

cab The engineer's area in a locomotive. The name was first used two years before the war began.

cabbage-head An insulting nickname for a stupid person. This meaning was created near the end of the war, having previously only been a humorous name for a person's head.

"Cabinet Car" The ironic name given to a dilapidated boxcar used by the Confederate cabinet in Greensboro, North Carolina, as they retreated from Richmond at the war's end. They conducted their dwindling business in the leaky boxcar and also slept there, foraging for flour, eggs, and coffee.

caboodle (or boodle) A slang name for all of something or a great number or amount of it. This was often heard in the expressions, "the whole caboodle" or "the whole boodle." By the 1920s, this had become "the whole kit and caboodle."

caboose The last car on a freight train. The first recorded use in this way occurred in the war's first year. The word had previously been used, and still is in Britain, for a kitchen in a ship, its original meaning in Dutch.

"Cad" The nickname for Sylvanus Cadwallader, a war correspondent for the Chicago *Times* and then the New York *Herald*. He became the favorite of Union General Ulysses S. Grant, both being quiet men who enjoyed the other's company. (The general was once described as "a man who could be silent in several languages.") Grant, who distrusted most reporters, issued Cadwallader with unlimited passes and gave orders to quartermasters to furnish him with horses and servants on demand. Cad was ultimately empowered to take possession of ships for any trip he required. For his part, the journalist was a key figure in keeping the general's heavy drinking out of the press.

cadence step The regular in-step marching of soldiers. *See also* route step.

cafeteria A coffeehouse only, not the modern idea of a cafeteria that allows selection of a variety of food. The word was American Spanish for "coffee shop," which was the other name used during the war.

Cairo war correspondent Name for a journalist who covered the war in the western theater mostly from the St. Charles Hotel near the telegraph office in Cairo, Illinois. The name was pinned on such journalists by New York *Times'* correspondent, Franc B. Wilkie, who deplored the practice.

caisson A two- or four-wheeled artillery wagon used to transport chests of ammunition. It was usually pulled by six horses.

caitiff A evil or cowardly person. Writing about the possibility of capturing Washington, D.C., the Richmond *Examiner* noted on April 23, 1861, that "many indeed will be the carcasses of dogs and caitiffs that will blacken the air upon the gallows before the great work is accomplished."

cake is all dough An expression from domestic life meaning one's hopes or chances have been dashed. When the large Union fleet of Admiral David Farragut moved up the Mississippi River on April 24, 1862, and bombarded Fort Jackson, the fort's commander, Colonel Edward Higgins, told his men, "Better go to cover, boys. Our cake is all dough!" The expression dates back to the sixteenth century.

Soldier (second from right) leaning upon a Union artillery caisson. *Library of Congress, Prints & Photographs Division, LC-B8171-7687.*

calaboose A slang name for a jail or prison. It is a Spanish word mostly used by Confederate soldiers because of influence from Mexico.

calcium light An early name for limelight. Its bright light was sometimes used during the war in devices to illuminate an area, such as approaches to a fort.

calibogus (or callibogus) The name of a liquor composed of rum mixed with spruce beer, which is made from spruce leaves and twigs or their extract. *See also* bogus.

calico A nickname for a woman or girl, because this cotton cloth was a main fabric used for feminine clothes.

California Bible (or California prayer book) Humorous nicknames for a deck of cards. The terms had originated during the California Gold Rush about a decade before the war.

The California Column Union troops that Colonel James H. Carleton took on a five-month march in 1862 from southern California to the New Mexico Territory to hold it for the Union. The soldiers had to cross mountains, deserts, and Indian country, traveling from April 13 until their arrival in Santa Fe on September 20. The California Column comprised 11 infantry and 2 cavalry companies, as well as 2 artillery batteries. It only fought skirmishes, moving south to Mesilla and forcing Confederate troops to retreat east to San Antonio, Texas.

"California Joe" The nickname for Private Truman Head, a famed marksman with the 1st U.S. Sharpshooters, known as BERDAN'S SHARPSHOOTERS. Head became a celebrity for his sniping skill with a Sharps rifle.

California Plan A heating system for hospital tents in the Union army. A fire pit was dug 2 1/2 feet deep outside one end of the tent and connected to a trench dug through the tent and covered with iron plates. The fire heated the plates to warm the tent, and the smoke escaped along the trench to a chimney (often made of barrels) outside the other end.

California toothpick *See* Arkansas toothpick.

call someone's hand To call someone's bluff or to challenge someone to carry out his threat; e.g., "Hopkins said he would trade his whiskey for my tobacco, but then shook his head when I called his hand."

call up mourners An expression used in southern religious revivals, when the preacher called up sinners to mourn for forgiveness. Confederate Private Sam Watkins, in his memoir *"Co. Aytch,"* recounted one incident when Chaplain J.G. Bolton of the 50th Tennessee Regiment called up 10 mourners to a long bench during an outside service and a burning tree fell over and killed all 10 as they knelt praying.

calomel A chloride of mercury used as a medical drug. Its overuse by Union army doctors led to it being banned, along with tartar emetic, by the U.S. Surgeon General William A. Hammond, but this ban infuriated the doctors and led to Hammond's dismissal.

calumniated Slandered or falsely accused. One Union nurse, after complaining about the wartime look of Washington, D.C., added, "It is a calumniated city in some respects. It is as bright and fresh this springtime as any town could be."

camel A large float attached to the hull below the waterline of a warship to lift it over an underwater sand bar. The IRON-CLAD CSS *Tennessee*, steaming down the Alabama River in February 1864, lost three months as several camels were attached to her so she could clear Dog River Bar for the battle of Mobile Bay in August.

camp diarrhea *See* diarrhea-dysentery.

camp fever A common name for typhoid fever. It was a special danger in Confederate camps, and a Union colonel noted, "We would rather die in battle than on a bed of fever." Union Brigadier General William H. Keim, a former congressman, died of the disease.

camp followers Civilians who moved close to military camps and sometimes followed along in the wake of moving troops. Camp followers included everyone from honest merchants to prostitutes and criminal elements. On some occasions, when an entire camp went on a day's maneuver, the soldiers would return to find their chairs, clothing, axes, pots, and other movable equipment stolen by camp followers.

camp itch (or the itch) A soldier's general problem of sore, itching skin caused by lice and other vermin, as well as irritants like dust, dirt, and filthy clothes. Serious cases were sent to general hospitals.

"Camp Misery" A nickname for any camp in which soldiers suffered from disease, unpleasant weather, or lack of supplies. The name was used for the Union encampment that was quickly set up in Alexandria, Virginia, early in the war. It became a place of filth and winter sickness leading to numerous deaths before SANITARY COMMISSION workers arrived with aid and expertise.

candy pull Another name for a taffy pull, being a sweet baked concoction of molasses or just brown sugar mixed with butter by pulling the mass into thick strings (somewhat like chewing gum).

cane seed coffee A coffee substitute in the South during the blockade. It was brewed from the seeds of sugar cane that were parched and ground. *See also* burnt sugar coffee; chinquapin coffee; grape coffee; okra coffee; pea coffee; potato and persimmon coffee; rye coffee; war coffee.

canister shot A thin 12-pound cylinder of tinplate on a heavy baseplate that was filled with from 200 to 300 small lead balls. When fired by a cannon, the tin shell would split open and the base would propel the balls and tin pieces straight at the enemy. Canister shot was especially good for short-range defense. *See also* grape shot; sand shot; spherical case shot.

canned food Food preserved in a sealed tin can. This process had been invented as early as 1812, but canned food only became common during the Civil War when it proved an excellent way of preserving food for Union soldiers braving the hot weather of the South.

cannon fever Battle fatigue or simply a desire to take leave from the exhaustion of war.

cannonade (or cannonading) Artillery fire; e.g., "At sunset there was a pause in the cannonading." Both words were also verbs: "They cannonaded our position until we were forced to retreat."

cannonier (or cannoneer) The highest rank of private in the artillery.

canoodle A slang verb meaning to kiss, cuddle, and fondle, or to pet. It came from the German word *knudeln*, to cuddle.

cantharide A Spanish fly, commonly called a blistering fly. They were used medically to irritate the skin and raise a blister to help healing.

cap An informal, short form of "captain." *See also* percussion cap.

cap box A soldier's small leather or tin box for PERCUSSION CAPS. It was attached to his belt. The infantry often discarded them as being too cumbersome, carrying the caps in their pockets instead.

capital Excellent or first rate; a popular expression during the war. People spoke of a capital speech, capital leader, capital companion, etc.

capping a gun *See* percussion cap.

captain-of-the-hole's gang On a navy ship, the company of men who were responsible for storing supplies and rotating the full and empty casks. They answered to the captain-of-the-hole.

"Captain Roberts" The alias of the British noble, the Honorable Augustus Charles Hobart Hampden, who became even more wealthy commanding the Confederate BLOCKADE RUNNER, the *Don*, which made 10 successful trips through the blockade. Hampden was the son of the Earl of Buckinghamshire. After he gave up the command, the *Don* was captured on its next sailing on March 4, 1864, by the Union ship *Pequot* off Beaufort, North Carolina, and became part of the Union navy.

cap the climax An expression meaning to surpass everything, but used ironically like "take the cake." It would be normal to say, "General Johnston failed to stop Sherman's advance and, to cap the climax, was relieved of his command."

"captured but not conquered" The slogan yelled by citizens of New Orleans to the occupying Union forces in 1862. The women of the city joined in the taunt and also wore small Confederate flags on their clothes.

"Capture or be captured." The order given on April 18, 1862, by Union Admiral David G. Farragut to his aides as their fleet battled past two forts on the Mississippi River below New Orleans. Six days later Farragut's warships defeated the makeshift fleet of riverboats defending the city.

caracol (or caracole) A horse's left or right half-turn made by the rider, often in a zig-zag pattern. The verb is also used; e.g., "Wesley found it impossible to shoot the Rebel horseman who was caracoling his steed through the thick forest."

carcass A shell covered in leather or cloth and filled with a mixture of inflammable liquids. When the carcass exploded on or near its target, it ejected the burning surface material, which stuck fast to any object. *See also* Greek fire.

card A nickname, still used, for a person who was witty, joked, clowned around, or played pranks.

carman The driver of a cart or light wagon.

Carolina potato An eastern name for the sweet potato.

Carolina racehorse A humorous nickname for a razorback hog, because they were found in abundance in North Carolina and South Carolina.

carpenter's gang On a navy ship, the company of men who maintained the planks, cabinets, and other wooden structures. They answered to the carpenter's mate, a petty officer.

carpet-bag A carrying or traveling bag made of red carpeting material. Some soldiers on both sides used them in camp and for transporting personal items. During Reconstruction, the luggage was popular with northerners going South for political and economic gains, and this spawned the derogatory name "carpet-bagger."

carriage-way An older name for a street or road, used during the war and still used in Great Britain.

Carroll Prison *See* Old Capitol Prison.

carrot-head (or carrot-top) A description of a person with red hair, often used as a true nickname; e.g., "Here comes Carrot-head Dawkins."

carry a horse to water A southern variation on the saying that you can "lead a horse to water," but you cannot make him drink.

carryall An informal name, especially in the North, for a carriage with four wheels that could carry all of a family, or several people.

carte de visite Photographs pasted on a small card. They were first produced in France in 1857, and the French name means "visiting card," because they were of that size, 2.5 by 4 inches. Their production led to the first family photo albums. A New York photographer, S.A. Holmes, advertised in 1860: "Your photo on a visiting card, London style. 25 copies for one dollar." During January 1861, America's largest photographic company, the E. and H.T. Anthony Company, produced 1,000 portraits a day of Major Robert Anderson, the Union defender of Fort Sumter (which surrendered in April). Cartes de visite of the leaders of North and South were sold in the thousands, but most treasured were family portraits. As New Orleans volunteers prepared to leave for Pensacola, Florida, when the war began, the *Daily Picayune* advised, "Every young man who goes to war ought, before starting, leave his likeness with his mother, sister, wife, or other dear parent, and every lady whose husband, or brother, or son is sent to Pensacola, ought also to give her miniature to the gallant young volunteer; for, during the

long night watch, or around the camp fire, it may be his only solace to look at the picture and kiss it."

cartel An agreement for the exchange of prisoners.

cartridge A paper tube holding a bullet and gun powder for a musket. Soldiers on both sides were each usually issued 60 ROUNDS. A round consisted of the bullet and powder for a single shot. Since the ends of a cartridge had to be bitten off before being loaded into a gun, men would have black circles around their mouths during a battle. In the heat of a conflict, they sometimes forgot to bite off the cartridge end, resulting in a misfire.

cartridge-box A soldier's leather or metal container to hold 40 ROUNDS of CARTRIDGES. The leather version had a flap and resembled a small pocketbook. The box was worn on a soldier's belt, but was heavy enough to be discarded by many men, who stuffed the cartridges in their pants or shirt pockets. Since infantrymen on both sides received 60 ROUNDS of ammunition, one-third of the cartridges were already in their pockets.

Cartridge-box. *Copyright Inge Wright 1999.*

cascabel The knob at the end of a muzzle-loading cannon. On a warship, it was much larger and had a hole through which a BREECHING ROPE could be secured. The Spanish word means a small round bell.

case 1. A slang name for a person considered to be a character, especially an odd one. "The captain is a case" was well understood on both sides. 2. A slang name for a dollar. 3. A CASKET.

casemate An armored or bombproof enclosure with EMBRASURES from which guns can be fired. The name applied to such vaulted areas in forts and the protective enclosures on ships.

cashier To remove in disgrace an officer from his command. When Union Colonel Samuel P. Heintzelman heard that he and other officers defeated at the first battle of Bull Run were to be promoted to brigadier generals, he called it a lie and added, "Every mother's son of us will be cashiered!" (They *were* promoted.)

cash in one's checks (or hand in one's checks) To die; e.g., "Before every battle, I knew I might cash in my checks." A check was a gambling chip, and the expression changed to "cash in one's chips" several years after the war.

casket A euphemism for a coffin. The name, which was established during the war, was taken from the idea of a jewelry box. In 1863, the writer Nathaniel Hawthorne called the new term "vile," saying it compelled a person to "shrink from the idea of being buried at all."

castor oil A common medicine prescribed by camp doctors for constipation.

catamaran A slang name for a person who liked to quarrel. It originally meant a disagreeable or ill-natured old woman,

and possibly came from the connection with "cat."

catarumpus A slang word for a rumpus (uproar or commotion); e.g., "When the major's pretty daughters visited him, there was a big catarumpus in camp." The first part of the word may have come from "catamount," a wildcat.

catawampus (or catawamptious) A slang word meaning fierce or destructive; e.g., "That *Alabama* was some catawampus ship." In the South and West, the expression "catawampusly (or catawamptiously) chawed up" was heard, meaning fiercely chewed up, or totally defeated.

catfish A popular food for slaves, but a fish considered unfit for a white person's palate. The journal of Frances Anne Kemble, an English woman visiting a Georgia plantation, quoted a slave's opinion of catfish as, "Good for colored folks, missis; me 'spect not good enough for white people." The fish, Kemble noted, was a "slimy beast" and "they hiss, and spit, and swear at one." Hungry Confederate soldiers, however, would happily feast on the beast.

cathead A piece of timber projecting from the bow of a ship, to hoist and secure the anchor free from the vessel's side. This was called "catting" the anchor.

cauliflower An affectionate name for a friend or fellow; e.g., "Wilkins there is a good old cauliflower."

cavalry lance An old-fashioned weapon carried early in the war by the Confederate cavalry. It was usually a 10-inch spear attached to an 8-foot ash staff that had a leather loop for the wrist. The lance proved a cumbersome weapon, and it was retired in 1863 except for ceremonial functions.

"Cease firing!" The order to stop firing, usually because the enemy had faded away or was surrendering, although the order was frequently expanded to "Cease firing. You are firing on your own men."

The Central Park During the war, the park's title included the definite article: "We spent most of the afternoon in the Central Park." The park was being designed during the war, the land having been purchased by the city in 1853. The official opening was not until 1876.

century *See* C.

cephalalgia A medical term for any type of headache.

chafe To fret or rage, or to make someone fret or rage. A soldier might say, "The captain chafes me fierce."

chain lightning A nickname for poor, cheap liquor, because it hit one like chain (zigzag) lightning.

chair A southern name for a CHAISE.

chaise A light open carriage or gig, usually for two people, having two wheels and pulled by one horse. A four-wheel version pulled by two horses also existed. Both types often had a top that folded back. *See also* buggy; chair.

chalkies A slang term for the teeth; e.g., "Murray took offense and hit him right in the chalkies."

"Chances for Travel and Promotion" Words posted in 1861 outside the U.S. army recruiting office in Massachusetts. Private Warren Lee Goss later recalled, "I must confess now, after four years of soldiering, that the 'chances for travel' were no myth; but 'promotion' was a little uncertain and slow."

change of base A euphemism for a retreat. It was first used to describe Union Major General George McClellan's retreat in the summer of 1862 to Harrison's Landing, Virginia, on the James River, following his Peninsula campaign. *See also* retrograde movement.

charcoal nigger An insulting nickname in the South for a black person who was very dark. It was sometimes an insult leveled by one black on another.

"Charge bayonets." The order given to attack a position or the individual enemy with bayonets. Although included in early drilling, the words were seldom heard in this "modern" war of firearms. Bayonets were more often used to prod prisoners or laggards back into line.

"Charge of the Mule Brigade" An anonymous poem penned by a Union soldier after a battle at Wauhatchie, Tennessee, on the night of October 28, 1863. As Union General John Geary's troops held off the Confederates of Major General James Longstreet, some 200 mules became terrified by the noisy battle and stampeded through the night into the center of Lieutenant General Wade Hampton's southerners. Deciding that this was a cavalry attack, a good number of Hampton's troops panicked and fled. This humorous escapade inspired the poem based on Alfred Tennyson's "Charge of the Light Brigade." The new version's first stanza was:

> Half a mile, half a mile,
> Half a mile onward,
> Right through the Georgia troops
> Broke the two hundred.
> "Forward the Mule Brigade!
> Charge for the Rebs!" they neighed.
> Straight for the Georgia troops
> Broke the two hundred.

Charlotte Russe (or Charlotte de Russe) A new and fashionable dessert during the war, normally custard in a type of sponge cake. The name literally meant "Russian Charlotte."

chase The barrel of a cannon between its muzzle and the TRUNNIONS attached at its middle.

chasseur A type of fancy dressed soldier or unit, named for the French chasseur forces. The chasseur cap resembled the FORAGE cap but was more decorative. Chasseur troops specialized in rapid movements, like their French counterparts.

chawed up A slang term meaning totally defeated; e.g., "Colonel Shy and his men were chawed up by the Yankees at the battle of Nashville." *See also* catawampus.

chay A name used in New England for a CHAISE.

cheap john 1. Cheap, usually poor quality, goods; e.g., "The sutler charges a high price for his cheap john." 2. A nickname for a pawnbroker; e.g., "In the last year of the war, Mother seemed to visit the cheap john more than the bank."

the checker A slang name meaning the exact thing needed or wanted; e.g., "Many things made camp life bearable, but the checker was a pipe full of Kallickanick smoking tobacco." The name derived from the ideal thing checking (blocking) other options. *See also* the ticket.

"The Checkered Game of Life" A board game popular during the war. Milton Bradley first produced it in 1860, the year South Carolina seceded. The board had alternating good and bad squares on which one could land. The labels on the squares included "wealth," "poverty," "happiness," and "suicide."

checkers The most popular board game played in camps. Backgammon was sometimes played, although chess was seldom touched. However, when Confederate General Robert E. Lee was asked about the possibility of a Union army taking Richmond while he was invading Pennsylvania, he smiled and quipped, "In that case we shall swap queens." *See also* chess.

cheek One of the two wooden side pieces that supported a cannon. The cheeks of an infantry cannon were heavy wooden blocks at the upper end of the STOCK TRAIL. They rested on the axle and had large notches at the top where the cannon's side TRUNNIONS connected. On a warship, the cheeks had solid wooden and metal sides that resembled the sides of an armchair; they were attached to a TRUCK CARRIAGE or MARSILLY CARRIAGE.

cheesebox on a raft An early humorous nickname for the Union's first IRONCLAD ship, the *Monitor*. "A Yankee cheesebox on a raft" was first used by a journalist for the Norfolk *Day Book* and became popular in the North when a Baltimore *American* article that repeated it was reprinted by the New York *Times*. The term "cheese box on a plank" was sometimes used.

Cherokee Mounted Rifles A battalion of Confederate cavalry raiders who were Cherokees, led by General Stand Watie, the highest ranking Native American in the war and the last general to surrender (on June 23, 1865, 11 weeks after Appomatox). The regiment made a name for itself in defeat at the battle of Pea Ridge, Arkansas, on March 7 and 8, 1861. The Union forces reported 30 scalped bodies, but this was never officially documented. In 1863, the Cherokee Nation switched to the Union side, but Watie's men stayed loyal to the South, strengthened by Creek, Osage, and Seminole soldiers, and continued their effective raids.

chess A board used in the flooring of a pontoon bridge supported by boats. Each chess was about 14 feet long, 12 inches wide, and 1 1/2 inches thick. A "chess party" laid them on the parallel BALKS of the bridge that spanned a river. *See also* checkers.

cheval-de-frise In fortifications, a log embedded all the way around with fire-hardened stakes whose sharpened points faced outward. The plural was *chevaux-de-frise*. The French term literally meant a "Friesland horse" because they had first been used against the Spanish cavalry by Frisians who did not have a cavalry.

chewer of the weed A person who preferred chewing tobacco. Pipes were usually the favorite "good smoke," but there was always a group of soldiers who sat around the campfire after dinner and relished the moisture of the "chaw."

chicken feed (or chicken money) Slang terms for a small amount of money, especially when one was disappointed with the amount. Only the first term survived through the twentieth century.

chicken gizzard A slang name for a coward; e.g., "The biggest chicken gizzard in our division was the general." The term was a new variation on "chicken" as a expression for cowardice, which dates back to William Shakespeare.

chicken guts A slang expression to describe epaulets and other gold trim on the uniforms of both sides. At the battle of Chickamauga in 1863, one Confederate chastised a retreating colonel with, "Take off that coat and those chicken guts."

Chevaux-de-frise that protected the main Confederate lines during the siege of Petersburg, Virginia, in 1864-65. *Library of Congress, Prints & Photographs Division, LC-B8171-3206.*

Chicken Hominy The silly nickname soldiers gave to the Chickahominy River, a tributary of the James River, in Virginia. The area saw the battles of Mechanicsville and Gaines's Mill, part of the Seven Days battles in the summer of 1862.

chicken-pie A slang southern term for funds needed to buy political or newspaper influence; e.g., "They said the senator would recommend Stephens for a commission if we could raise the chicken-pie."

chicken water A watery soup containing the essence of chicken. It was often served in Confederate hospitals by local ladies.

chief cook and bottle washer 1. A leader or superior. 2. A person capable to doing many things.

chigger The common name in camps for the redbug, a despised pest. Yankee soldiers invading the South were amazed at their size, with one Illinois private saying, "Chigres are big, and red as blood." Soldiers found that salt water bathing removed them, and some Union soldiers layered bacon on their bodies to ward off the beasts.

Chimborazo Hospital A Confederate PAVILION HOSPITAL in Richmond, Virginia, that opened in October 1861 and was called the largest hospital in North America. It had 8,000 beds in four divisions that each had 30 pavilion buildings, with patients grouped by their states. About 20 percent of the 76,000 patients treated at Chimborazo died, which was a good figure during the war. The hospital had its own farm, factory, bakery, and brewery on 40 acres. Phoebe Pember was its first matron. During the war, Chimborazo was so crowded, men who had arms amputated were sent out three days later to make room for new cases. The hospital sat on Chimborazo Heights, a hill near the James River,

which was supposedly named for a volcano in Ecuador.

Chimneyville A nickname given to Jackson, Mississippi, by the Union troops of Major General W.T. Sherman after they had burned it down, leaving a desolation of brick chimneys. General Ulysses S. Grant had ordered Sherman on May 15, 1863, to "destroy that place as a railroad center and manufacturing city of military supplies." *See also* Sherman's monuments.

chinch A bedbug. While a prisoner at Washington's Old Capitol Prison, Confederate Captain James Bosang woke up his first night "itching and burning with something crawling all over me with thousands of hot feet." Sure enough, he could "see them by the hundreds, chinches, all over me, all over my bed."

chincough A medical term for whooping cough. The "chin" did not refer to one's chin, but came from a Saxon word meaning "gasp." Chincough was generally catagorized as "an epidemic distemper."

Chinese game The military "game" of creating noise and great activity to frighten the enemy. Confederate General Robert E. Lee, writing home in February 1862 about Union Brigadier General Joseph Hooker, said: "He is playing the Chinese game, trying what frightening will do. He runs out his guns, starts wagons and troops up and down the river, and creates an excitement generally. Our men look on in wonder, give a cheer, and all again subsides . . . ." *See also* demonstration; the scare.

chin music The slang expression, still heard, meaning idle talk, gossip, or chatter.

chinquapin coffee A coffee substitute in the South during the blockade. It was made from the dried and ground nuts of the chinquapin tree, a member of the beech family, such as the dwarf chestnut. *See also* burnt sugar coffee; cane seed coffee; grape coffee; pea coffee; okra coffee; potato and persimmon coffee; rye coffee; war coffee.

chin whiskers This name for a beard was new during the war, having first been used about a decade before by gold prospectors in California.

chip in This informal term, meaning to help to pay for something, was created as the war began. It came from the language of poker, where chips were thrown into the betting "pot."

chisel To cheat someone, an informal word that predated the war. It came from the idea of chiseling off a piece of something, as a carpenter does.

chiv A slang name for a knife, now spelled shiv. It probably came from the Romany (Gypsy) word "chiv," meaning blade.

The Chivs A short form of "the Chivalry," a northern term for southern plantation owners. The term was used in the early days of the war and before it; e.g., "The Chivs won't fight."

chloride of lime A white powder used by doctors as a disinfectant. It was made by treating calcium hydroxide (slaked lime) with chlorine. After the battle of Gettysburg in 1863, it was spread over the wide streets of the town. Chloride of lime is better known today as "bleaching powder."

chloroform A general anesthetic preferred by camp doctors, although it became difficult for the Confederacy to obtain after the blockade of its ports. It was first used 14 years before the war began and was dangeorus, being poisonous if given in excess. Doctors administered it by soaking a cloth or sponge and holding it over the patient's nose until he passed

out. Union Brigadier General Charles G. Halpine died three years after the war when he took too much chloroform to cure his insomnia. *See also* ether; laudanum; morphia.

chopping An area in a woods where trees have been felled. Choppings often occurred during the war to provide timber for fortifications or winter quarters.

chow This slang word for food was used somewhat during the war, having been coined a decade earlier in California. It may have come from the Chinese word for "food," *chia*, or "to cook," *ch'ao*.

chowderhead A common insult during the war, meaning a stupid person. The name had nothing to do with the dish of chowder. It began in sixteenth-century England as "jolt head," meaning a thick or stupid head, and changed through the centuries to "jolter-head," "cholter-head," and then about 1819 to "chowderhead."

Christian Association An organization formed in many Confederate regiments to promote religious observance. Its activities included sponsoring church services, organizing prayer groups, and distributing Christian publications.

Christian Commission A Union relief society established by the YMCA to improve the morals and physical conditions of soldiers. It had about 5,000 volunteer delegates, most of them ministers, who assisted in camps and hospitals and on the battlefields. The official name was the United States Christian Commission, and it was headed by the Irish-born George H. Stuart of Philadelphia. It provided an IDENTIFIER for each soldier and sent delegates onto the fields after a battle to find the wounded and to write down final words from the dying to their families. This was also done for the Confederate enemy. The Commission was credited

An August 1863 photograph of the U.S. Christian Commission headquarters near Germantown, Virginia. *Library of Congress, Prints & Photographs Division, LC-B8171-7471.*

with having saved about 1,000 men after the battle of Gettyburg. It also distributed nearly a half million Bibles and Testaments from the AMERICAN BIBLE ASSOCIATION, ran loan libraries of 125 volumes in hospitals, and provided such items as newspapers, crutches, meat, fruits, tea, and milk. Women and children contributed gifts like bandages, shirts, socks, COMFORT-BAGS, and DAINTY FOODS. The organization also set up writing tables in camps, providing free paper, envelopes (with "Soldier's Letter" printed in one corner), and stamps. In 1864, it paid for about 100,000 letters written by soldiers. The Commission went through an estimated $6.25 million in money and supplies during the war.

Christian soldier A religious soldier who disapproved of such vices as alcohol, swearing, and gambling. Union Major-General Oliver O. Howard was such a man and often the butt of jokes by fellow officers, such as when he joined three of them in a house during the Knoxville campaign. Major General W.T. Sherman winked at Major General Jefferson C. Davis who took the hint and launched into a story littered with profanity. When puritanical Howard stalked out, Sherman and Davis roared with laughter, which upset Brigadier General Carl Schurz. "Well," defended Sherman, "that Christian-soldier business is all right in its place, but he needn't put on airs when we are among ourselves."

chuck 1. A slang term for food. The rich Texas rancher, Charles Goodnight, created the original "chuck-wagon" two years after the war from an old army wagon. 2. A slang word meaning to hit a person with one's fists, equivalent to "slugging" someone in current usage, e.g., "They argued about the hand, threw down their cards and began chucking each other."

chuck-a-luck A camp gambling game in which soldiers attempted to toss dice, rocks, or other small items into squares that contained different numbers. The squares were often scratched on the ground but sometimes chalked on the surface of a rubber PONCHO. One Confederate veteran wrote, "I always noticed that chuck won and luck always lost." *See also* "Devil's Half-Acre."

chum A special friend or, during the war, a tentmate. This is why some people are still said to be "chummy."

cicerone A guide, especially someone who shows visitors the historical and interesting places in a city or area. The name came from the joke that guides are as talkative as the Roman orator Cicero.

cider brandy *See* apple brandy.

cider cart A mobile container of cider, often just a barrel on wheels. A farmer, slave, or local person would sometimes station a cider cart along a road used by passing troops to sell the welcomed drink, and one soldier in the Army of Northern Virginia recalled that "The rapidity with which a barrel of sweet cider was consumed would astonish any one who saw it for the first time."

Cincinnati The name of General Ulysses S. Grant's favorite horse, which stood 17 1/2 hands tall. It was a gift after the battle of Chattanooga in November 1863. Grant permitted Abraham Lincoln to ride him in late March 1865 during the president's visit to his camp at City Point below Richmond. *See also* Fox; Jack; Kangaroo.

circle of fire A nickname for the heavily fortified harbor of Charleston, South Carolina, where the entrance channel led into a dead-end of water rimmed by massive firepower. When Union Rear Admiral Samuel Du Pont attacked the harbor with eight newly built ironclad ships on April 7, 1862, the circle of fire unleashed 2,209 rounds that battered the proud armada into a desperate retreat.

Cissy *See* Sis.

civilian soldier A name, often derogatory, for soldiers who had been conscripted or officers who had received political BREVET commissions. Regular army men had little positive to say about the qualities of such "civilians."

clabber (or bonny-clabber) Sour milk that has thickly curdled.

clam (or clam-shell or clamtrap) Slang names for the mouth; e.g., "When I told the captain he was wrong, the little greenhorn said, 'Shut your clam.'"

clap A common name for gonorrhea. It was seldom heard in society, but some soldiers mentioned it in letters home. The name was derived from an old English name first meaning a rabbit's warren and later a house of prostitution. *See also* daughter of Eve; drab; fallen angel; fancy girl; fast house; gay young duck; "The Haystack"; "Hooker's Division"; "Madam Russell's Bake Oven"; parlor house; ranch; The Wolf's Dream.

class A classification for the speed of mail delivery. Because of the increase in mail to Union soldiers, the U.S. created "first class," "second class," and "third class" mail in 1863.

clawbar A crowbar that had a bent, forked end used for pulling out spikes. They were one of the main tools Union Major General W.T. Sherman distributed to his men for the destruction of railroad tracks.

clawhammer coat (or clawhammer) A slang name for a formal evening coat with tails; a swallow-tailed coat. It was sometimes called a steel-pen coat.

clay-eater A southerner, especially a poor white or black, who ate clay for its nutritional value. "Dirt-eater" was sometimes used, and the names became general and derogative terms for any southerner. The practice of eating clay still exists on a limited scale.

clean thing The honorable or proper thing to do. One might say, "It isn't the clean thing to steal a friend's sweetheart."

clear the coop To leave, especially in a hurry; e.g., "When we saw the Rebel reserves coming down the hill, we decided to clear the coop."

clever Good-natured or handsome; e.g., "Luke's not smart, but he's clever."

clip One particular occasion or time; e.g., "So far, we've licked them good every clip."

clipper An informal name to describe an attractive woman or girl.

close-stool A chamber pot in a stool or box. They were used in military hospitals and were common in homes.

close up The order to march closely together. It was most often given to tired stragglers as officers rode down the line urging them to pick up their step. The men of Confederate Lieutenant General "STONE-WALL" Jackson recalled his most frequent words as being "Close up! Close up!"

"clouds of mounted men" Union Major General William S. Rosecrans's description of the gray Confederate cavalry that swept over the countryside under such leaders as Lieutenant General Nathan Bedford Forrest, Major General Jeb Stuart, Brigadier General John H. Morgan, and the GRAY GHOST, Colonel John S. Mosby.

coal-heaver A slang name for a sailor.

coal torpedo An ingenious Confederate bomb that was a blackened cast-iron device formed to look like a piece of coal and filled with 10 pounds of powder. The only recorded explosion was on November 27, 1864, when a Confederate agent planted one in the coal pile aboard the Union's steamer *Greyhound* in the James River. Major General Benjamin F. Butler, known as "BEAST" Butler in the South, was aboard at the time. The bomb created flames in the engine room, but they were quickly extinguished.

cochineal A red dye ground or powdered from the dried bodies of cochineal insects, mostly found in the West Indies or in Mexican cactuses. The dried red body fluid was used to color foods and drinks, such as the ANISE SEED cordial.

cockade A ribbon rosette worn by soldiers in their caps and hats. They were also worn by soldiers' sweethearts and by other citizens. Cockades for soldiers were made by mothers, sisters, and girlfriends, as well as by admiring girls in areas where the troops marched and camped.

cock fighting A popular sport in camp. Men bought or stole the best roosters in the area, and "trainers," often Irishmen, would conduct the fights and enforce the rules. Matches were held between regiments, with the stakes ranging from $5 to $2,000. One Confederate soldier in northern Virginia noted that "the camps sounded like a poultry show, or a mammoth farmyard."

coffee boiler 1. A soldier's small tin canister used to boil coffee over a fire. About the size of a cup, it had a lid and, above that, a wire handle. 2. The nickname for a soldier who avoided work or battles by staying out of the way. Coffee boilers often hung around camp fires together. If anything serious began to happen, like an enemy attack, they were known to fall behind and separate themselves from the units, pretending to be lost. *See also* coffee cooler.

coffee cooler The nickname for a soldier who habitually shirked his duties in camp. *See also* coffee boiler.

"coffee-grinder" The nickname for the .58 caliber Ager machine gun produced for the Union army. It was officially named the "union repeating gun." For his part, President Lincoln coined the name "coffee-mill gun." The new-fangled invention was generally rejected by officers who feared the rapid fire would overheat and explode the gun, but eventually 63 guns were purchased for the army at a cost of nearly $850 each. The "coffee-grinder" had a hopper on top (resembling contemporary coffee mills) into which were fed special cartridges. A hand crank at the side dropped single cartridges rapidly into place in sequence where their caps were struck by the hammer.

"coffee-mill gun" *See* "coffee-grinder."

coffin A witty name for a large shoe.

coffin-meat A slang word for a dead body; e.g., "When I heard those Rebel yells, I thought for sure I was coffin-meat."

cold-meat cart A slang term for a carriage that took a dead body to the graveyard; a hearse.

colic Severe abdominal pain. Since diarrhea was not a sympton, colic was one of the easiest (and most suspect) illnesses for soldiers to fake. At the battle of Shiloh, one Confederate private noted how many soldiers were "suddenly taken sick with colic."

collar To comprehend or master something; e.g., "Sherman couldn't collar why Hood was moving his troops north."

collards (or collard greens) This leafy kale vegetable was a popular item with hungry foraging Confederate soldiers because it was often readily found on farmlands.

collarette A small collar worn by ladies. It was usually of lace, linen, or fur.

"The Colonel" The nickname of Confederate General Joseph E. Johnston when he was a cadet at West Point, because of the way he strutted about with self-importance.

color The name for a flag when carried by an infantry unit. *See also* standard.

colored folk A common name used by slaves and free Negroes for their race. *See also* nigger.

color guard Noncommissioned officers, called "color-bearers," who carried the unit's COLORS. A Union regiment carried the Stars and Stripes and a blue national flag and sometimes a state one. The color guard was positioned in the middle of a battle line and drew the most fire, especially on a smoke-choked battlefield. The enemy also targeted the color guard to capture the flag. As soon as one color-bearer fell, another man would pick up the flag, and this often led to a series of deaths. At the battle of Gettysburg, the 26th North Carolina lost 14 men carrying the colors. Although life expectancy in the job was short, being a member of the color guard was considered a great honor. *See also* standard.

color line The area of a camp on which the regiment was formed for such events as roll calls and dress parades. Camp streets were at right angles to the color line, which was also called "the front."

colorphobia The fear of colored people, a word that also implied racial bigotry. The former slave, William Wells Brown, pointed out in 1854 that it existed in Philadelphia. "Colorphobia is more rampant there," he said, "than in the proslavery ... city of New York."

Colt four-pounder A nickname for the heavy (four pounds, one ounce) revolver manufactured by the Colt Company. It was also called the "Holster Pistol" and the "Dragoon." The cylinder was engraved with a battle scene showing Texas Rangers fighting Indians. The Model 1848 and Model 1851 were seen in the war's early days but were discarded as soon as possible for the new standard COLT REVOLVER.

Colt revolver The most common pistol used in the war, produced by Samuel Colt's Patent Firearms Manufactory at Hartford, Connecticut. It fired six shots and had a octagonal barrel. The pricipal Union army version was the .44 caliber Model 1860, known as the New Model Army Pistol (more than 107,000 supplied). The main Union navy weapon was the .36 caliber Model 1851 (about 215,000 made), which was the gun most copied by Confederate manufacturers. An 1861 navy version with a round barrel was less popular. *See also* Colt four-pounder.

columbarium A funeral vault with nitches for urns that contain cremated remains.

"Column forward!" The order to resume marching after a column of soldiers had halted.

comedown A person's downfall or notable reverse in business or society.

come out at the little end of the horn To accomplish little from a great effort, especially when one has bragged about it in advance; e.g., "General McClellan promised to take Richmond with his 110,000-man army (twice that of General Lee's), but came out at the little end of the horn."

comeuppance This informal and still-used word for a deserved punishment or just desserts, was first heard about two years before the war.

come up to the chalk To perform or produce as one should; e.g., "It was David's first battle, and he wondered if he would come up to the chalk."

comfort-bag The nickname for a soldier's small bag of personal items. It was usually a HOUSEWIFE containing sewing materials, with the addition of such gifts as a cake of soap and a comb. Those distributed by the CHRISTIAN COMMISSION also contained a Testament or religious tract. Comfort-bags were made and packed by women and children who often added letters; if the gifts went to unknown soldiers, the senders might enclose their own addresses for return correspondence.

comforter (or comfort) A long knitted woolen scarf worn around the neck. It was also more formally called a tippet. Alice Ready of Murfreesboro wrote as follows of a visit by Confederate General William J. Hardee on March 3, 1862: "Before the General left he took the comfort from his neck, which he had worn during the bombardment of Bowling Green and tied it around my neck, asking me to 'wear a Soldier's comfort.'"

the coming man A term used during the war, especially in the North, to describe an admired officer who seemed likely to become the strong leader the army awaited. The Union title was erroneously applied to Major General George B.

McClellan, Major General William S. Rosecrans, and several others, with few observers aware that Brigadier General Ulysses S. Grant was the coming man.

Commander-in-Chief The title of both President Abraham Lincoln and President Jefferson Davis. This title was provided for in the constitutions of the U.S. and of the Confederacy, and both presidents often issued strategic military orders. Only late in the war were generals Ulysses S. Grant and Robert E. Lee given total command of their sides' forces, Grant on March 12, 1864, and Lee on February 9, 1865 (exactly two months before his Appomattox Court House surrender).

commish A short form of "commission," the government document conferring a certain rank on an officer. The word was both a noun and a verb.

"Commissary" The Confederate soldiers' nickname for Union Major General Nathaniel P. Banks, because Rebel raiders stole so many supplies from his camps. In 1863 in Louisiana, troops of Confederate Major General Richard Taylor stole entire wagons loaded with stores from "Commissary" Banks and in a later raid made away with about $2 million of his ordnance and other supplies. *See also* Mr. Banks; "Napoleon."

common agency The early term for the government to be formed by the southern states. The name was used by delegates of the first seven seceding states meeting on February 4, 1861, in Montgomery, Alabama, to establish a joint provisional government.

"common niggers" A plantation term for slaves, also called "common field hands," who worked in the fields and lived in cabins away from the plantation home. The term was used by whites and by the slaves who were called HOUSE SERVANTS.

common road A main road used by stagecoaches, wagons and other vehicles, as well as horseriders and walkers.

common time The standard marching time for both armies, being 90 steps per minute.

commutation fee The $300 payment allowed by the United States CONSCRIPTION ACT for exemption from military service. A humorous parody popular in the North was "We Are Coming, Father Abraham, Three Hundred Dollars More," taken from James Sloane Gibbons's famous poem "WE ARE COMING, FATHER ABRAHAM" ("three hundred thousand more").

comp An informal shortening of "compliment"; e.g., "Can you believe Sergeant Hawkins finally paid me a comp?"

company A military unit on both sides, consisting of two PLATOONS or sometimes a BATTALION. Men entered the war by joining a local company. The average Union one had from 83 to 101 officers and men. Companies were designated by letters, such as Company D. The letter "J" was never used, perhaps because it resembled an "I" on a battlefield flag. Ten companies made up a REGIMENT or 12 for a cavalry regiment.

"Company" An early nickname for Ulysses Grant, earned while a cadet at WEST POINT. Because he was relatively unsocial, Grant was bullied by older cadets until he fought and defeated two of them and then challenged the entire company one by one. They declined, gave him a rousing cheer, and he became "Company Grant." The name stuck until he became a Union general, and it was replaced by "UNCONDITIONAL SURRENDER." See also "Country Sam"; "Sam"; "Uncle Sam."

company fund Money accumulated in common by a military company and used to buy extra food or items needed by everyone. The fund often came from fees charged to SUTLERS to allow them to sell goods in camp or from money paid by the government for undelivered rations, usually because the company was marching between camps. One Union soldier noted after the war, however, that he had never heard of any company receiving money "although the name of Company Fund is a familiar one to every veteran."

Company Q 1. The Confederate Army's name for soldiers on the sick list. Healthy soldiers often suspected Company Q of harboring malingers. 2. A detachment of disgraced officers of the 150th Pennsylvania Regiment. Charged with cowardice, they had been broken to the rank of private and placed in Company Q to make amends. Most fought well and became officers again.

comrade A popular name during war for a close companion or friend. The term was common until it was adopted by communists in the twentieth century. "Song of the Soldiers," a 1862 Union war song by Private Miles O'Reilly (pseudonym of Charles S. Halpine), began:

> Comrades known in marches many,
> Comrades, tried in dangers many,
> Comrades, bound by memories many,
> Brothers ever let us be.
> Wounds or sickness may divide us,
> Marching orders may divide us,
> But, whatever fate betide us,
> Brothers of the heart are we.

con To read or study something carefully. Marching into battle, a Confederate looked at his fellow soldiers and noted that "some hundred Testaments and Bibles were openly taken from pockets and conned with the same zeal that a school-boy crams for the holiday commencement."

concentrated force A military force that keeps all of its units within SUPPORTING DISTANCE, thus avoiding DEFEAT IN DETAIL by the enemy.

conductors See Underground Railroad.

Confed A short name for a Confederate. When one Rebel soldier shared his food box with a Yankee in the court house at Winsboro, South Carolina, the Union man wrote, "Thanking him kindly I took a seat beside him on the floor, and 'Yank' and 'Confed' broke bread together."

"Confederacy's best friend" A descriptive name for field peas, which later in the war helped many Rebel soldiers through days of near starvation. The expression was supposedly used and perhaps coined by General Robert E. Lee.

"Confederate beef" A nickname given to the mules killed and eaten by southern soldiers and civilians during the siege of Vicksburg. Mule meat sold for $1 a pound and was said to taste like venison. Soldiers ate the meat unofficially until July 3, 1863, the day before the surrender, when brigade commissaries finally received a directive from the chief of subsistence to butcher the animals and issue one-half pound of "mule to the ration." The *Chicago Tribune* published a humorous and inventive menu for the "Hotel de Vicksburg," that included "Mule Tail Soup," "Mule beef jerked a-la-Mexicana," and "Mule tongue cold a-la-Bray." *See also* "mule."

Confederate Bible Society See American Bible Society.

Confederate candle A name given to a candle made of a mixture of beeswax and rosin in the South. They appeared widely in camps and homes after the blockade depleted the normal supply of candles.

Confederate disease A facetious nickname for diarrhea, because of the poor food in Confederate camps, especially in the second half of the war. The joke was appreciated by Rebels as well as Yankees.

The Confederate Hospital A hospital in Petersburg, Virginia, that had been converted from a tobacco warehouse. It was a poor, dismal affair. The two-story building had a ward on each floor, a large room with six long rows of narrow beds about two feet apart. The beds were coarse cotton bags filled with corn shucks; each had a pillow and one blanket, but no sheets. Such conditions, which were not uncommon in the South, explain why more Confederate soldiers died in hospitals than on the battlefield.

Confederate oath The oath taken by soldiers volunteering for the Confederate military went as follows:

> "I, _____, do solemnly swear that I will bear true allegiance to the Confederate States of America, and that I will serve them honestly and faithfully against all their enemies or opposers whatsoever, and observe and obey the orders of the Confederate States, and the orders of the officers appointed over me, according to the rules and articles for the government of the Confederate States, so help me God."

Confederate War An early southern name for the Civil War.

"Confederate War Etchings" A series of 29 cartoon caricatures published in 1863 by Adalbert J. Volck, a Baltimore dentist who supported the Confederacy. He portrayed President Abraham Lincoln as an oriental dancer, clown, and Negro, among other humorous guises. Like the North's famous war artist Thomas Nast, Volck was born in Germany. *See also* "our best recruiting sergeant."

"Confederate white elephant" The nickname given to the disasterous *Rappahannock* by its commander, Confederate Lieutenant Charles M. Fauntleroy. It was a slow, decrepid steamer (then named *Victor*) sold by the British navy, which believed it would be used on trade routes to China. The newly named vessel blew her engines on November 24, 1863, while leaving the Thames river and drifted across the English Channel to anchor off Calais for repairs. Ship and crew remained there for more than 16 months until the end of the war, constantly watched by Union ships. After the South's surrender, Fauntleroy paid off his men and turned the *Rappahannock* over to Captain James D. Bulloch, the Confederacy's naval agent in England.

Confiscation Acts Two bills passed by the U.S. Congress in August 1861 and 1862 proclaiming that slaves should be set free in areas occupied by Union forces. The first act only allowed confiscation of slaves who had done war-related work for the Confederacy (since they were Rebel "property"), and the second act extended freedom to all slaves. However, slaves in Union states were not to be freed, a fact that President Abraham Lincoln hoped would bring southern states back into the Union. *See also* "Prayer of Twenty Millions."

conflab A slang name for an argument; e.g., "every poker game had its conflabs." The word was a humorous variation of "confab," a conversation (shortened from the fifteenth-century word "confabulation").

confess the corn *See* acknowledge the corn.

conniption (or conniptions or conniption fit) An instance of hysterical anger, like a tantrum, or of excitement. These terms were especially used of women; e.g., "When Captain Brewster forgot Laura's party, I thought she would have a conniption fit."

conquer peace (or conquer a peace) Phrases used throughout the war that meant "achieving peace," militarily or otherwise. Edward D. Baker, a U.S. senator from Oregon, said in 1861 that a war would conquer peace: "I propose to do now as we did in Mexico—conquer peace." Later in the conflict, President Jefferson Davis hoped the Confederacy could conquer peace by military victories that would wear down the will of the North, win European support, and lead to peace negotiations.

conscript A soldier drafted into service. Volunteers on both sides were in doubt about their conscripts' devotion to the war, and one Union soldier called them "the most despised class in the army."

Conscription Act The Confederate law requiring all able-bodied white men between 18 and 35 to serve three years in the military forces. It was commonly called "the Conscript Act." The first draft in American history, it was passed on April 16, 1862, nearly a year before conscription began in the North. The Act led to the first full-scale criticism in the South of their new government, because states had seceded to avoid such strong central rule. A soldier from South Carolina opined, "A more oppressive law was never enacted in the most uncivilized country or by the worst of despots." Almost half of the eligible men refused to sign up. In five months, the age limit rose to 45 and by 1864 was between 17 and 50. *See also* Enrollment Act.

conscription squad Late in the war, a squad of soldiers in the army of Confederate General John B. Hood that gathered up able-bodied men found in the countryside and forced them to join their ranks. Many had avoided conscription via the "TWENTY-NIGGER LAW."

consecrated milk A soldier's humorous nickname for concentrated milk, which was similar to condensed or evaporated milk.

consolation A euphemism for alcohol, especially whiskey; e.g., "Later in life, his mother liked a little cheese and consolation before bedtime."

consolidation A word used within the Confederacy to mean a union of their states. It was usually a negative idea expressed by those who feared states' rights would be snuffed out by a strong central government (like the U.S. government from which they had seceded).

"Constitution" The nickname for R. M. Browne, the assistant secretary of state of the Confederacy. The name was not political but referred to his previous job as editor of the Atlanta *Constitution*.

consumption The common medical name for tuberculosis, and one still occasionally used. In full, it was "pulmonary consumption," because the disease consumed the lungs. Tuberculosis that spread rapidly was called a "galloping consumption."

continued fever A camp name for a persistent fever that was usually typhoid.

contraband A former slave held by the Union army. Contrabands had either escaped, been freed, been smuggled North, or were found behind U.S. lines. The idea that they were "contrabands of war," property that could be seized during warfare, was first stated on May 24, 1861, by Union General Benjamin F. Butler. Commanding Fortress Monroe in Tidewater, Virginia, he refused to return three fugitive slaves to their owner because they were contrabands of war, or property that could aid the enemy cause. U.S. Secretary of War Simon Cameron agreed but ruled that fugitive slaves must be returned to owners in states loyal to the Union.

contract surgeon A SURGEON under contract to a Union hospital as a noncommissioned officer. As a group, contract surgeons were generally unprofessional and looked down upon by regular army surgeons in the field.

controul Another spelling of "control." It was commonly used by Confederate General Robert E. Lee.

convalescent camp The name often given to a military hospital reserved for noncritical patients recovering from wounds or illnesses. A large Union convalescent camp was located at Alexandria, Virginia.

cook-house A large, separate kitchen, as in a camp or prison.

"cook up" An order to MESS cooks to cook a certain amount of rations before a confrontation with the enemy, since long battles left little time to prepare meals. Soldiers would usually "cook up" three to five days of extra provisions before the anticipated action.

cool An informal word used to mean impudent or disrespectful. Nobody liked to receive "a cool reply" or to have another person act "rather cool."

coon 1. The nickname for a member of the Whig Party, which before the war was fatally divided on the question of slavery. After Winfield Scott was defeated in the 1852 presidential election, most southern "coons" switched to the Democratic Party and most northern ones joined the new Republican Party and helped elect its first President, Abraham Lincoln. 2. An insulting name for a black person (and still occasionally heard).

coon jigger An insulting name for a black child.

coon lover A person who respected the freedom and rights of black people. This was a general derogatory term in the South for Union soldiers and other northerners, but was also sometimes used in the North for abolitionists.

"Coonskin" The nickname for a famed Union sharpshooter, Second Lieutenant Henry C. Foster, because he wore a beloved coonskin cap. He was a member of Company B of the 23rd Indiana Volunteers. During the seige of Vicksburg in the summer of 1863, Foster built a lookout structure that became known as "Coonskin's Tower." Working under the cover of several nights, he used rails and crossties from the wrecked Vicksburg Railway to construct the high perch overlooking the Confederate parapets. From this secure position, he could pick off the enemy, whose return musket fire was buried in the crossties.

Cooper's Shop Saloon *See* Union Refreshment Saloon.

coot A nickname for a silly or stupid person, especially an old man; a simpleton.

copacetic A slang word meaning excellent, good, or fine.

copaiva (or copaiba) A balsam used to treat venereal diseases. It was an aromatic resin obtained from trees in South America.

copper (or cop) These familiar names for a policeman began about two years before the war. The terms probably came from the idea of a policeman copping (seizing) criminals.

Copperhead A northerner who sympathized with the Confederacy or was against the war. Sometimes this position led to violence. On March 28, 1864, some 100 Copperheads killed five Union soldiers on furlough in Charleston, Illinois. The leading political Copperhead was Clement L. Vallandigham, who was arrested and later failed in his campaign to become governor of Ohio. The name, coined by a Cincinnati newspaper on July 30, 1862, originally referred to radical Democrats who opposed Abraham Lincoln's Republican administration by wearing copper "liberty head" images cut from one-cent pieces (to show they defended liberty). Political cartoonists, however, were quick to depict them as copperhead snakes. *See also* "niggerhead"; Valiant Val; Vallandighammer.

copus cup An alcoholic dish. A piece of bread was toasted, cloves and a slice of lemon inserted into it, and the bread floated in a bowl filled with a mixture of brandy, ale, noyau liqueur (distilled from peach stones), lemons, cloves, and sugar. Nutmeg was grated over it, and the dish was served hot. "Copus" was an old spiced ale and spirits drink that originated in Cambridge, England. The word was a shortening of Hippocras, an aromatic medicated wine once used as a cordial and named for the straining device used to filter it, the Hippocrates' sleeve, itself named for the Greek physician Hippocrates.

corduroy road (or corduroyed road) A road covered with logs. The Union army became expert at covering poor roads in this way to protect their wagon trains, which could become mired up to their axles. Logs were placed across the road, small limbs put between them and mud spread on top. In muddy camps on both sides during the winter, soldiers laid corduroy walkways between the tents. Major General W.T. Sherman's army built the war's most impressive corduroy road through the nearly impassable Salk swamp in South Carolina, laying 12 miles a day. "If your army goes to hell," a Confederate prisoner told them, "it will corduroy the road." *See also* plank road.

cork opera A slang name for a minstrel show, because the performers' black-face makeup was made of burnt cork. The expression was popularized during the war.

corn cake A simple "cake" made by mixing corn meal with water and adding salt. It was beaten into a smooth batter, cooked in a hot oven until firm, and often turned up on its side in front of the coals so it would form a brown crust. A better tasting sweet corn cake was made with sour milk and the addition of molasses and ginger.

corncob "soda" A substitute for bicarbonate of soda, used in the South during the blockade. It was discovered that corncob ashes, especially from red cobs, possessed the alkaline needed to raise bread. After they were burned and the ashes collected in jars, water was added. A teaspoonful or tablespoonful of this mixture was then used in bread-making.

corn-cracker A poor white farmer or other poor person in the rural South. The name, used as an insult, was especially applied to natives of Georgia, Kentucky, Tennessee, and Florida. It was often shortened to "cracker."

corn dodger A common food in Confederate camps. It consisted of cornmeal fried or baked into a small, hard cake. One southern veteran recalled his days of scarce rations in Chattanooga, Tennessee, when he tried to eat a piece of fried rat on a cold corn dodger, but failed to take one bite. The name supposedly came from the cake jumping about, or dodging, while being baked.

corned A slang term meaning drunk. See DRUNK for numerous other terms referring to intoxication.

the cornerstone A descriptive name for slavery because of its place in the economy of the South. Alexander H. Stephens, vice president of the Confederacy, used the term, and George McDuffie, a governor of South Carolina, had as early as 1835 called slavery "the cornerstone of our republican edifice."

Corn Exchange Regiment A nickname for the 118th Pennsylvania Regiment, because it had been created and equipped by the Philadelphia Corn Exchange.

the cornfield An area furiously fought over during the battle of Antietam on September 17, 1862. The field was charged and countercharged, recalled Confederate Brigadier General John B. Gordon, "until the green corn that grew upon it looked as if it had been struck by a storm of bloody hail." Union troops had forced the Rebels out to the edge of the village of Sharpsburg, when Lieutenant General Ambrose Hill's "LIGHT DIVISION" arrived from a long march to come up through the cornfield and save the day for General Robert E. Lee's men.

corn fritter A small fried batter cake containing corn. Soldiers used half a canteen punched with holes to grate the corn for this popular camp dish.

corn juice A slang name for whiskey, especially among western troops.

corn pone A type of southern corn bread that is still made. Pones are small oval loafs, and the word came from the Algonquin language in Virginia.

corn, salt, and apples A Confederate soldier's well-known joke that the initials C.S.A. stood for this, their paltry basic ration.

cornstalk militia A nickname for the MILITIA. The name was a carryover from before the war, before these state organizations were virtually nonexistent in rural areas.

corps A military unit on both sides usually consisting of two or three DIVISIONS. They were designated by roman numerals, such as the XI Corps, and were usually commanded for the Union by a major general and for the Confederacy by a lieutenant general. One or more corps made up an ARMY. The Union eventually had 25 corps. The name was derived from the French *corps d'armee*.

corps badge A badge usually worn on the left side of a hat or on a cap. The Union's Army of the Potomac began the practice to boost corps spirit, and eventually placed their badges on tents, wagons, and other camp items. The U.S. western corps soon adopted the badges.

Corps d'Afrique The name given by Union Major General Benjamin Butler to a unit of free blacks and fugitive slaves that he formed in 1862 while occupying New Orleans. Banks eventually built the unit into the 1,500-man strong Louisiana Native Guards who proved their bravery during the siege of Port Hudson, Louisiana, in the summer of 1863.

corpse-reviver A slang name for a strong mixed alcoholic drink.

costiveness Another word for constipation.

cottonade A heavy fabric of coarse cotton fibers. Confederate General Robert E. Lee wore a blue cottonade uniform during his first campaign in West Virginia in 1861.

cotton-belt A general term for the southern states, from the Atlantic through Texas, where cotton was "king." The term was used before the war and is still heard.

cotton-clad The nickname for a Confederate BLOCKADE RUNNER that had cotton bales as "armor." The word was a humorous play on IRONCLAD. The bales offered a minimum of protection and proved most successful on steamers running the blockade of Galveston, Texas.

cottonocracy A nickname for the owners of cotton mills in New England, who suffered when the war curtailed southern cotton supplies. After the war, the industry began to move to the cotton states to take advantage of lower wages.

Cotton States The states of the Deep South, a term meant to describe the heart of the plantation system and its institution of slavery.

Cotton Stealing Association of the United States Navy A humorous company name given by Union soldiers to their naval counterparts occupying New Orleans. This was because the navymen were stamping local cotton bales with "CSA" to claim them as military war prizes that could be resold.

council of war A meeting held by generals and other officers to plan strategy before a battle or major move. Lincoln thought they were usually a waste of time. Trying to get his army to attack General Robert E. Lee's forces retreating from Gettysburg, Lincoln had his military adviser, Major General Henry W. Hallack, telegraph Major General George Meade the following message on July 13, 1863: "Call no council of war. It is proberbial that councils of war never fight." (Meade had already called one the previous night, and decided not to fight after being overruled by his corps commanders.)

counter-battery An artillery BATTERY put in place to fire at the enemy's battery. Counter-battery fire took place before PICKETT'S CHARGE at the battle of Gettysburg in 1863. That fatal advance occurred after the Union battery withheld

its fire, and the Confederate officers wrongly assumed that the enemy artillery had been disabled.

counter-jumper A humorous and insulting name for a shopkeeper or store clerk because it was said they would jump a counter in their eagerness to make a sale. Early in the war, Confederate cavalrymen, almost all expert horsemen, labeled their Union counterparts as "white-faced clerks and counter-jumpers."

counter-reconnaissance Special military measures taken to defeat the reconnaissance efforts of the enemy. Examples are false QUAKER GUNS and the marching of troops in a great circle to create the impression of a larger force.

countersign Another name for a password. "Halt! Advance with the countersign" was often the demand of a sentry to someone approaching.

countrified This adjective meaning "rustic" or "rural" could be an insult or compliment, depending upon the speaker. In the homemaker's book, HOME COMFORTS, the pompous Mrs. Doolittle gossips about her neighbor's children whom she saw wearing kitchen aprons: "It looks so common, and sort of countrified."

country hunk An insulting name for a soldier who came from a rural area, usually a hard-working farmer who was considered to be both innocent and dumb.

"Country Sam" A nickname given by fellow students to Ulysses S. Grant in his first year at West Point, mainly because of his awkward way of marching and walking. *See also* "Company"; "Sam"; "Uncle Sam."

coup de main A French expression often used in the war, meaning a fast, vigorous attack to surprise the enemy. The words translate as "stroke (or blow) of the hand." "Burnside hesitated for hours in front of the bridge which should have been carried at once by a *coup de main*," complained the New York *Tribune* war correspondent after the battle of Antietam in 1862.

coup d'oeil A French term used during the war to describe the ability of being able to quickly scan the countryside and form a general view of its military advantages. The French words literally translate as "stroke of the eye" and meant a quick glance.

coupe A four-wheeled closed carriage for two with a separate outside seat for the driver. When directing the early defense of Washington, D.C., in 1861, elderly General Winfield Scott rode in a coupe ahead of his marching troops.

court-martial Military justice on both sides revolved around the court-martial. The mildest forms were the Union's regimental and garrison courts-martial and the Confederacy's special court-martial. All consisted of three officers who could only hear minor cases involving enlisted men, such as petty theft. The largest fine was one month's pay, and other punishments included one month's imprisonment or such discomforts as POLICING, the WOODEN HORSE, and BUCK AND GAG. For other crimes, including ones by officers and civilians working for the military, such as SUTLERS, general courts-martials were conducted by both sides. These courts had 5 to 13 officers, and the punishments could range from a reprimand to death. Confederate courts-martial in the first year of the war were known for their leniency, even in such cases as desertion.

court plaster Cotton cloth or other fabric used as bandages for minor cuts and scratches. One side was covered with an adhesive, such as isinglass and glycerin. Court plaster was commonly made as a roll. The name evolved because ladies in royal courts once used it to create black beauty spots on their faces.

cousin A familiar form of address for anyone. When soldiers from Virginia and Tennessee regiments crowded together in the open field during PICKETT'S CHARGE at Gettysburg in 1863, someone in line complained, "Move on, cousins. You're drawing the fire our way."

cow The nickname for a third-year cadet at the U.S. Military Academy at West Point, New York.

cow juice This amusing name for milk was already well established by the war. "Cow juice" and "moo juice" are sometimes still heard today.

cowskin A slang word for a whip. It was also used as a verb; e.g., "He was known for cowskinning slaves."

cow tick A slang word for a small amount or a bit. A soldier might say, "I don't give a cow tick for the war." The term referred to a small insect that infested cows.

crab-apple A nickname for a bad-tempered or morose person; e.g., "Nobody wanted to share a tent with that crab-apple John Carlton."

Crabtown A nickname for Annapolis, Maryland, given by cadets at the U.S. Naval Academy. The city is on the Severn River near Chesapeake Bay. The nickname was first used about 15 years before the war began.

cracker *See* corn-cracker.

cracker barrel conference A crucial meeting between Confederate generals Robert E. Lee and "STONEWALL" Jackson to devise plans for the battle of Chancellorsville. They met in camp on the night of May 1, 1863, sitting on broken boxes filled with commissary biscuits. The result of the conference was a brilliant victory over General Joseph Hooker's army on May 4.

cracker box *See* hardtack box.

cracker line An amusing name for the military supply line. On October 30, 1863, when supplies finally got through to Union troops beseiged in Chattanooga, Tennessee, the shout went up: "The cracker line is open!"

cracklings A southern name for the cinders remaining from a wood fire.

crack skull *See* bust skull.

crack up To praise something or someone. Crack meant "excellent" or "first-rate," as in a "crack regiment" or a "crack hand." The idea remains today mostly in the negative phrase "not what it's cracked up to be" but also in the question "Is it all that it's cracked up to be?"

cradle of secession A nickname, especially in the North, for Charleston, South Carolina, where the war's first shots were fired at Fort Sumter in 1861.

crape The black crinkled cloth, which was the saddest symbol of the war. It was used on the front door of a home that had experienced a war death. Noted one Confederate soldier visiting Richmond, "Crape waved its sad signal from the door of house after house."

craps This gambling game with two dice was played in camps, but lacked the popularity it later acquired in the early twentieth century. A first throw of 7 or 11 provided an instant win. Craps was first played about two decades before the war;

New Orleans recorded its first game in 1843.

crash A type of coarse linen cloth with a loose, plain weave, used mainly for towels and curtains.

crawfish To back down or withdraw, either physically or from verbal promises and statements. This word came from the irregular, deceptive movements that a crawfish (crayfish) employs to escape.

crawl A slang name for a city's main street or area used for strolling and socializing; e.g., "She promised to meet me at the crawl on Saturday." It was equivalent to the modern "drag."

"Crazy" 1. The nickname given to Confederate Major R.C. Hill at West Point to distinguish him from another cadet named Hill. It really only meant that his character was often one of "suppressed excitement." The nickname worked against him and the Confederate cause after Union troops were defeated at the first battle of Bull Run. Hill reported to his generals that he had seen the Yankees in total rout. They discussed this with President Jefferson Davis, then visiting in camp, and prepared to pursue the enemy until someone mentioned Hill had been dubbed "Crazy." This revelation cast doubts on his reliability, so the remaining Union army was allowed to escape. 2. The nickname for Union Major General W.T. Sherman because of his habit of pacing and talking to himself in high-pitched tones. "Crazy" was first applied to him early in the war when he was seen doing this in a Cincinnati, Ohio, hotel.

"Crazy Bet" The nickname for Elizabeth Van Lew, a Richmond woman from an old Virginia family who became a Union spy by acting mentally slow. She was also called "Miss Lizzy." Her childlike behavior allowed her to place an informer among the servants of Confederate President Jefferson Davis. She continued to live safely at home after the war among neighbors who thought she was insane.

"Crazy Tom" An affectionate name that Confederate Lieutenant General Thomas "STONEWALL" Jackson received from his men because of his eccentric habits, such as sucking lemons. *See also* "Old Lemon-Squeezer."

the creature A nickname for alcohol, especially a strong liquor.

creeper A small iron frying pan that had three legs attached. They were especially seen in camps early in the war. Another name was a "spider."

the creevels A nickname for a nerve disorder that caused a feverish, crawling, and painful feeling.

the Cresent City The nickname of New Orleans, because the Mississippi River winds in a cresent shape around it. The nickname is still used and predominated until the latter part of the twentieth century when "the Big Easy" became more popular.

crib A short-cut aid to passing an examination, such as a literal English translation of one of the classics. A crib could amount to cheating, such as when answers to an exam were obtained.

cribbage A card game for two to four players that was often gambled on in Civil War camps. Different card combinations brought different scores, and the winner had to add up points of no more than 31. The scoring was usually kept by pegs moved on holes in a small cribbage board. The name came from the "crib," a spare hand for the dealer created by each player discarding two of his six cards.

crick A common dialect word, still used, for "creek."

cricket The English game of cricket was played in the U.S. before the war, but BASE BALL quickly replaced it in army camps because a flat smooth ground was needed for cricket. Union soldiers also discarded the English game after the North began to suspect British support for the Confederate cause.

crier The common term for a slave auctioneer who cried out the round numbers that were bid, usually followed each time by "Thank you, Sir."

crinoline accident The name commonly given when a woman's wide crinoline HOOP SKIRT was accidentally set ablaze by a candle, lamp, or open fire. The result was sometimes fatal. Crinoline, a fabric used as a lining or petticoat, was made of cotton, flax, or horsehair.

criss-cross This children's game is now known as tick-tack-toe. It was often played at school on writing slates. The English at first named the game criss-cross but now call it "noughts and crosses."

Crittenden-Johnson Resolution A U.S. congressional resolution passed on July 22, 1861, to affirm that the United States was fighting the Civil War mainly to preserve the Union, not to free the slaves. It was passed by both houses with few dissenting votes a day after the first Confederate victory at Bull Run in July 1861. The resolution was an effort to retain the loyalty of the slave-holding border states and was also an acknowledgement of racial prejudices among the northern population. The main sponsor, Senator John J. Crittenden of Kentucky, had one son fighting on each side.

critter companies The nickname that Confederate Lieutenant General Nathan Bedford Forrest gave to his beloved cavalry units which were renown for their raids.

croak A slang verb meaning to die (still used today) or to murder someone.

croaker 1. A person who grumbled in a pessimistic way, a GROWLER. 2. An insulting name for a man who stayed at home avoiding military service.

crooked as a Virginia fence Said of anything crooked or of people who were difficult to manage. Virginia fences were often made of rails running in a zigzag pattern.

crooked shoes Shoes specifically designed for right and left feet. The name was a joke in Union camps where many rural recruits had only worn straight, duplicate shoes before being issued the U.S. army's "crooked shoes."

crooked stick A person who was dishonest or not straightforward.

cross-grained A term describing a cloth whose fibers were intertwined. A Union army nurse described her hospital uniform as including "two grey cottonish cross-grained skirts."

crossroads wiseacre A simple person who professed great knowledge. President Abraham Lincoln used it as an insult, even for influencial politicians.

crow-bait *See* buzzard-bait.

crowd poisoning The spead of disease through crowded conditions and poor ventilation. Civil War doctors considered it a major problem in overcrowded military hospitals.

crusher A slang name for a crowded event, such as a party. One of Mrs. Lincoln's LEVEES was described as a crusher by Major B.B. French, a prominent Republican who was commissioner of public buildings.

CS or C.S. Initials for the "Confederate States," which were used on belt buckles and other accouterments in the same manner as CSA OR C.S.A. The initials were also used in writing, such as "it happened in the C.S."

CSA or C.S.A. Besides the "Confederate States of America," soldiers of the South joked that the initials stood for "CORN, SALT, AND APPLES," their basic ration.

cuffie, cuffee, or cuffy A nickname for a black person. The word has an African origin. President Abraham Lincoln once used it in the White House and offended members of the Committee for Recruiting Colored Troops. He apologized by saying that "you know I am by birth a Southerner and in our section that term is applied without any idea of an offensive nature." The expression "proud as cuffie" referred to someone as proud as a Negro dressed up in his finest clothes.

cul-de-sac A common name for a dead end. A Union naval staff officer used this term to describe the harbor of Charleston, South Carolina. It is still the normal name used in Great Britain. The French term, first used in anatomy, literally means "bottom of a sack."

"Cump" A nickname for Union Major General W.T. Sherman, which was a short form of his middle name Tecumseh. Confederate General Joseph E. Johnston, Sherman's old friend, used it when he surrendered the Army of Tennessee to Sherman on April 26, 1865, at Greensboro, North Carolina. "Cump" was a family nickname (as well as "Cumpy") when Sherman was a boy, and it became a popular nickname for the general among his troops.

cumshaw A gratuity, especially a bribe. The original Chinese words meant "grateful thanks."

cunning Neat and pretty, a compliment often heard in New England; e.g., "She's a cunning little girl."

cupboard A nickname for the stomach; e.g., "I couldn't eat another bite. My cupboard's full."

Cupid's Own Library A series of erotic stories published in the North and especially prized by many Union soldiers. The different-sized volumes cost 25 cents, 50 cents, and a dollar. See also *The Rakish Rhymer*.

"Curly" A nickname for Union Major General George Armstrong Custer, because of his long curly hair.

curlyhead An insulting nickname for a Negro.

cush A dubious dish in Confederate camps. Chucks of meat, hopefully bacon, were fried in grease and water and vegetables were added to create a stew that was then turned into a mush by crumbling cornbread into it. This concoction, eaten after the water had boiled off, helped disguise the maggots that usually infested the meat.

cut and run To depart quickly; to drop everything and run. The expression began during the war, and troops winning a battle would often say the enemy had "cut and run."

cut a wide swath or cut a swath To swagger around making a great display; e.g., "General Magruder was called 'Prince John' because he knew how to cut a wide swath." The word was derived from the swinging motion of a scythe that cut a swath.

cut dirt To run fast enough to kick up dirt. It was a popular description of an enemy's retreat. To "cut gravel" was also sometimes said. *See also* scratch gravel.

cutlery A slang name for a knife or knives; e.g., "He always had a bowie knife and some smaller cutlery."

cut stick or cut one's stick To leave, especially immediately and quickly. An encampment could "cut stick, double quick."

cut up extras To behave in a loud or bad way; e.g., "Midshipman Haynes was a decent man but cut up extras after consuming the grog ration he had saved up all week."

cut up jack To act wildly or cause a commotion. This phrase often referred to angry or abusive behavior. One Confederate soldier recorded such an incident when a deserter went before a firing squad: "He was then carried to the death post, and there he began to cut up jack generally. He began to curse Bragg, Jeff Davis, and the Southern Confederacy, and all the rebels at a terrible rate."

cyclopean Gigantic or enormous. The *New York Herald* used the word to describe Union Major General W.T. Sherman's bombardment of Atlanta. The name is derived from the Cyclops, the race of one-eyed giants in Greek mythology.

Cyprian A euphemistic nickname for prostitutes. Nashville, Tennessee, was a center for the trade after 1862 because of the large number of occupying Union forces. The military expelled and shipped 150 of the Cyprian ladies north in a boat in 1863 but had to sail them back into Nashville after official complaints from Cincinnati and Louisville.

"Czar of Pennsylvania" The nickname for U.S. Secretary of War Simon

Cameron, because of his powerful political machine and manipulations. After being appointed to Abraham Lincoln's cabinet in 1861 as a result of an election deal, Cameron was often accused of corruption involving military appointments and war contracts.

Because of the political clout he wielded in his home state, Simon Cameron, President Lincoln's first secretary of war, was known as the "Czar of Pennsylvania." *Library of Congress, Prints & Photographs Division, LC-B8172-1599.*

D

D The letter branded with hot irons on soldiers guilty of desertion, usually on their foreheads, cheeks, or hands. Compassionate officers used indelible ink.

dab (or dabster) An expert or person skilled in something. The British still use the word "dab hand" in this way.

daguerreotype An early form of photography in which the image is fixed on a coat of silver that covers a sheet of copper. People who view daguerreotypes also see their own image. Practitioners of the art were known variously as daguerrian artists, daguerreotypists, or daguerreans. Although this system began to be replaced in the mid-1850s by AMBROTYPES, Civil War homes still displayed daguerreotypes, and many soldiers carried those images of their family members and sweethearts into the war.

Dahlgren papers Documents found on March 2, 1864, on the body of Union Colonel Ulric Dahlgren. These documents detailed plans to burn Richmond, Virginia, and assassinate Confederate President Jefferson Davis and his cabinet. These plans were part of a speech intended for Dahlgren's troops. Dahlgren and 92 of his men were killed by Confederates as they approached Richmond; the

papers were discovered by a 13-year-old boy, William Littlepage.

Daily Rebel Banner A Confederate camp newspaper published by soldiers of General Braxton Bragg.

dainty A delicacy; the choice food or drink. On August 20, 1862, a Georgia woman named Ludy Smith wrote a letter to Confederate President Jefferson Davis complaining about "big generals" stealing wines and food she had sent to soldiers in hospitals who "rarely get sight of the dainties that are sent them . . . the head ones eats the dainties sent to the sick themselves."

damaged A coy name for being drunk. It was first used two years before the war. See DRUNK for numerous other terms referring to intoxication.

damned old goggle-eyed snapping turtle A common description given by his troops to Union Major General George Meade, whose ill temper was legendary. Meade, who was not popular, took command of the Army of the Potomac on June 28, 1863, and had to rush it immediately to the important battle at Gettysburg, Pennsylvania. A fourth of his men were killed or injured, and Meade's weak pursuit of the retreating Confederates caused President Abraham Lincoln to moan that his general was like "an old woman shooing her geese across the creek." His later hesitations to engage in battle prompted Lincoln to give overall control of the U.S. armies to General Ulysses S. Grant.

"Damn your eyes!" A curse used during the war. Lieutenant Arthur Sinclair of the Confederate commerce raider *ALABAMA* recalled that Rear Admiral Raphael Semmes rarely displayed temper, but if a captain of a captured merchantman tried to lie to Semmes about the ownership of the cargo, "Then, there's many a 'd___n your eyes.'"

D and D The popular abbreviation for drunk and disorderly. See DRUNK for numerous other terms referring to intoxication.

dandyfunk A sailor's name for a stew often served in the U.S. Navy. It consisted of HARDTACK soaked in water and then baked with molasses and salt pork.

"Dang it to hell!" A well-known curse, used both in sorrow and joy. It was unusual in that a euphemism was used for "damn" but not for "hell." After winning the battle of Nashville on December 16, 1864, Union Major General George H. Thomas greeted his cavalry commander in a booming voice, "Dang it to hell, Wilson, didn't I tell you we could lick 'em?"

Daniel Webster The name of Union General George McClellan's favorite horse, a bay, that he called "devil Dan."

Daniel XI The chapter of the Bible that Confederate Lieutenant General "STONEWALL" Jackson often mentioned to his men to show that the South would defeat the North. The chapter, however, is ambiguous in predicting the future and also recounts victories by the North. Jackson emphasized verse 7 which says the king-

dom of the south "shall come with an army, and shall enter into the fortress of the king of the north, and shall deal against them, and shall prevail." However, verse 15 reads as follows: "So the king of the north shall come, and cast up a mount, and take most fenced cities, and the arms of the south shall not withstand."

darbies A slang name for handcuffs. It began in England where handcuffs to keep two prisoners together were called "darbies and joans," because Darby and Joan was an expression, still used in Great Britain, for an older, loving couple.

dark as hell's cellar A simile meaning terribly dark.

dark wagon A covered wagon used as a photographer's darkroom. It was mostly seen by Union forces photographed by Matthew Brady, Sam A. Cooley, and others.

darky, darkey, or darkie A slang name for a Negro, used in the South and North by whites who, in those times, considered it to be inoffensive. The same term was used in Great Britain. *See also* blackberry.

daubing the chinks Filling in gaps in a log cabin with clay mixed with water. Done by soldiers building winter quarters, this final touch of sealing the cracks and crevices in the house and its chimney might be done by a whole MESS.

daughter of Eve A euphemism for a prostitute. *See also* clap; drab; fallen angel; fancy girl; fast house; gay young duck; "The Haystack"; "Hooker's Division"; "Madam Russell's Bake Oven"; parlor house; ranch; The Wolf's Dream.

"Daughter of the Confederacy" The nickname for Confederate President Jefferson Davis's daughter, Varina Ann, born in late June 1864. The family also called her "WINNIE" and "Pie-Cake," which was soon shortened to "Pie."

David The common name for a Confederate "semisubmersible" (submarine) boat with a torpedo projecting from the bow. Several were built for crews ranging from 2 to 12 men and called Davids because their role was to sink "Goliath" Union ships. On Febraury 17, 1864, the eight-man CSA *Hunley* made a successful suicide attack that sank the USS *Housatonic* in Charleston Harbor, the first submarine in history to sink an enemy ship in combat. Five previous crews had already died testing the *Hunley*. The Union's only submarine, the *Alligator*, sank in April 1863 while being towed off Cape Hatteras, North Carolina. It had accomplished nothing during its 17-month life. The *Hunley* was raised on August 8, 2000, still virtually intact, to be placed in the old Charleston navy base.

Davis boot An army boot worn by both sides. It was named for Jefferson Davis, because it was introduced when Davis was U.S. Secretary of War from 1853 to 1861. It was produced in only a few standard sizes that were supposed to fit any soldier.

day-dawn Another term for daybreak. Confederate General Braxton Bragg ordered his troops to attack at "day-dawn" on September 20, 1863, at the battle of Chickamauga.

"Day of National Humiliation, Fasting, and Prayer" A special day proclaimed by President Abraham Lincoln for Thursday, April 30, 1863. The initiative had come from Congress. The proclamation noted that the people had forgotten God and become "too proud to pray." This day was an echo of President James Buchanan's "Day of Special Humiliation, Fasting, and Prayer" proclaimed on January 4, 1861, as the newly seceded state of South Carolina began to put pressure on Fort Sumter.

D.B. The initials for a "deadbeat," meaning any able-bodied soldier or civilian male who was not required to fight during the war. Just before the war, Ulysses S. Grant was even described as a "deadbeat military man" because he had been discharged from the OLD ARMY.

dead-alive A term describing a dull, depressed, or inactive person. A "dead-alive" soldier was actively avoided in camp.

deadbeat *See* D.B.

dead card A slang name for someone or something that is finished or ruined, such as a card that cannot be played in a card game. The term had the same meaning as a "dead duck." President Abraham Lincoln was incorrectly called a dead card, even by members of his own party, before he was renominated and reelected in 1864.

dead cart The common pessimistic nickname given by Union soldiers to military ambulances.

dead cock in the pit An informal description of someone or something that was either dead or considered as good as dead. Union Major General W.T. Sherman, writing about the last year of the war, recalled, "Of course Charleston, ever arrogant, felt secure; but it was regarded by us as a 'dead cock in the pit' and fell of itself when its inland communications were cut."

dead house A house next to a military hospital or prison, in which dead bodies were kept to await burial.

dead line 1. One of the lines of a large square drawn on the ground for prisoners of a battle. They were put into the square and told that anyone crossing a line would be immediately shot. "It was simply a line drawn upon the ground," marveled one Confederate prisoner, "a step beyond which was death." 2. A light railing in the Confederacy's ANDERSONVILLE prison that ran parallel to the prison fence and 20 feet away from it. Anyone crossing this line was to be shot dead. The prison commander, Major Henry Wirz, was accused of luring men over the line. One prisoner recalled seeing guards kill inmates who reached under the dead line to scoop up water in one case and moldy bread in another.

"Dead March" A slow, melancholy march played by military bands for funerals, with emphasis on the fife and muffled drum. Union nurse James Kendall Hosmer wrote in 1863, "I have the heard the wail of the fife, but never made it real to myself until then, when across the parade-ground, down the street, then from the distance, came the notes of the Dead March."

"Deaf Burke" The nickname of a Confederate spy from Texas who was famous for his many disguises and accents. Burke was variously a Quaker, old farmer, sophisticated gentleman in Washington, D.C., and Yankee tent-mate. He once smuggled messages in logs driven over Union lines. He eventually went back to the West where he was killed in combat with his Texans.

death post (or death stake) A common name for the post at which soldiers, convicted of desertion and other serious crimes, were tied in camp to be excuted by a rifle squad. A soldier would sometimes have to wait two hours while the detail dug his grave and planted the post. "Men were being led to the death stake every day," recalled one Confederate serving under the unpopular General Braxton Bragg.

"death without benefit of the clergy" A dire penalty for treason against the state of South Carolina, passed after the state seceded. The idea of a condemned man

not being attended by a clergyman, however, was a misreading of an ancient legal phrase, "death without benefit of clergy." The Catholic Church originally had the right to try clergymen at its own tribunal, so many condemned men professed to be Catholic priests. The phrase, misused in the South Carolina proclamation, meant these claims of being priests would be ignored.

the debility A common name for a camp disease whose symptoms were a general weakness and diarrhea. Epidemics occurred in prison camps and often led to deaths.

debt of honor A gentleman's promise, often signed, to pay back a debt or loan at a later date. When the Confederate commerce raider *ALABAMA* captured Union merchant ships, those captured vessels were usually burned, but sometimes Rear Admiral Raphael Semmes would allow the vessel to leave on the captain's promise to pay a certain amount to the Confederate government when the war was over. "I have some of these debts of honor in my possesion, now," Semmes humorously wrote after the Confederacy had collapsed, "which I will sell cheap."

deck 1. This name for a set of playing cards only came into usage about eight years before the war began. It replaced "pack of cards," which is still the British term. 2. The roof of a railroad passenger car.

declension The declining of a political nomination; e.g., "I decided not to vote at all following my candidate's declension."

decoction of stump water A humorous slang name for alcohol, especially whiskey.

"Dedicatory Remarks" The official program listing for President Abraham Lincoln's speech of less than three min-

utes on November 19, 1863, at the conse-
cration ceremony for the Gettysburg military cemetery. His few famous words have
since been known as the Gettysburg Address. Lincoln had been asked to say "a
few appropriate remarks" and was not
the main speaker at the event; he followed
a two-hour oration by Edward Everett, a
former secretary of state and Massachusetts governor. When Lincoln sat down,
he noted, "I failed, I failed, and that is
about all that can be said about it." The
Chicago Times agreed, calling his speech
"silly, flat and dishwatery utterances."
His wife, Mary Todd Lincoln, had tried
to have Lincoln back out of the event because their son, TAD, was ill.

deep game A complex and usually clever
plan or maneuver. After Confederate
General Robert E. Lee had tricked Major
General George Meade into moving his
troops 60 miles backwards, Meade wrote
his wife on October 21, 1863, that his op-
ponent had played "a deep game, and I
am free to admit that in the playing of it
he has got the advantage of me."

defeat in detail A military term meaning
to defeat an enemy's separated troops one
part at a time.

"Defender of Vicksburg" The nickname
given to Confederate Lieutenant General
John C. Pemberton, whose troops held
the city of Vicksburg, Mississippi, against
General Ulysses S. Grant's seven-week
seige before starvation forced their surrender on July 4, 1863. Pemberton was a
Pennsylvanian who had served alongside
Grant in the U.S. army, but then married
a Virginia girl and sided with the South.
His army at Vicksburg was effectively
eliminated by Grant, who allowed the
troops to leave on their promise (lavishly
unfulfilled) that they would sit out the rest
of the war. After the surrender, the embarrassed Pemberton reduced himself in
rank to a lieutenant colonel of artillery.
See also "Gibraltar of the West."

delegate A representative to the U.S. Congress from a territory. Such a person
could not vote but was allowed speak on
the issues under discussuion.

Delmonico's New York's fashionable restaurant was a meeting place for both the
political elite and the wealthy. It was located on the northeast corner of Fifth
Avenue and 14th Street.

Demand Notes *See* greenbacks.

dementia A standard diagnosis by military surgeons for a number of mental and
nervous problems encountered in soldiers. Many men with "dementia" (often
battle fatigue) were discharged and sent
home without supervision.

demonstration The open movement of a
military unit, with great activity and
noise, to suggest more strength and size
than it actually had, or to give a false picture of the direction it (or the battle)
would take. Confederate Major General
John B. Magruder was a master of dem-
onstrations. See also the Chinese game;
the scare.

"Deo Vindice" The motto of the Confed-
eracy, meaning "God as Our Defender."
The Latin words were approved by the
Confederate Congress to appear on the
Great Seal of the Confederate States.

department The large TERRITORIAL organizations used by both sides during the
war. The names of the field ARMIES were
taken from those of the departments,
which the Union named for rivers and the
Confederacy named for states. Examples
include the Union's Department of the
Potomac, which covered northeastern
Virginia and all of Maryland and Delaware, and the Confederacy's Department
of South Carolina, Georgia, and Florida.
Several departments were organized into
a territorial MILITARY DIVISION.

depredating A common word for the illegal foraging and plundering of civilian food and property. Confederate Private Sam R. Watkins recalled that "General Bragg issued an order authorizing citizens to defend themselves against the depredations of soldiers—to shoot them down if caught depredating."

Derby An annual horse-racing event held on St. Patrick's Day, March 17, by the Union's Army of the Potomac. Some of the races had hurdles. The stands were filled with officers, dignitaries, and ladies. General Thomas F. Meagher, the Irish-born commander of the Irish Brigade, usually presided as the race's patron in the costume of an old Irish gentleman. Music was added by several regimental bands combined for the occasion.

derringer This small handgun, which is still popular, was used by John Wilkes Booth to assassinate President Abraham Lincoln in April 1865. It was named after Henry Deringer (one "r" only), the Philadelphia gunsmith who invented it in 1835. He also supplied rifles to the Union army. Deringer died three years after his pocket pistol was used in Booth's grievous crime.

desecrated vegetables The irreverent name given by Union soldiers and sailors to dessicated (dehydrated) vegetables issued as supplements to their daily diet to prevent scurvy. Their official name was "desiccated compressed mixed vegetables." The dry, distasteful shredded vegetables were pressed into hard, tight cakes that were put into boiling water to soften and expand them. Mischievous warnings told of men who ate the cakes dry and nearly exploded when they expanded in their stomachs. *See also* desiccated potatoes.

"deserter" The name was sometimes bogus in regard to Confederate "deserters" because southern troops had a habit of sending phony deserters into Union lines to give them misleading information about troop positions and strengths. Victory or defeat could depend upon judging if a Rebel was a true deserter or not.

desiccated potatoes Dehydrated potatoes that were part of a Union soldier's rations because the army believed (incorrectly) that they prevented scurvy. The finely cut potatoes were fried as cakes and added to soup but remained unpopular. *See also* desecrated vegetables.

the detail The list of military duties assigned to men in camp. It was read out each day by the orderly. Groups of soldiers doing one task were also termed a detail.

devil fish The nickname given by Union troops to Confederate torpedoes discovered guarding Charleston in 1863. The slender four-foot-long torpedoes were shaped like a fish and strung together by wire that detonated their fuses if struck by a ship's bow.

"The devil is loose, the devil is loose" The words given by some soldiers to the REVEILLE bugle call.

devil-may-care The adjective, popularized during the war, which still means being reckless, rash, or careless.

Devil's Den An area of ferocious fighting during the battle of Gettysburg in 1863. It was the local name for an outcropping of rock near the foot of LITTLE ROUND TOP and, at the time of the battle, next to a wheatfield.

devil's dye A nickname for whiskey. By the twentieth century, this term had been replaced by "devil's brew."

"Devil's Half-Acre" A gambling den near Fredericksburg, Virginia, where Confederate soldiers, despite raids by officers, operated CHUCK-A-LUCK boards off and on during the winter of 1862 and 1863.

Alexander Gardner took this photograph of a dead Confederate lying among the rocks of the Devil's Den, the scene of furious fighting at the battle of Gettysburg, Pennsylvania, on July 2, 1863. *Library of Congress, Prints & Photographs Division, LC-B8171-7942.*

D.G. Initials for Davis Guards, a mostly Irish regiment in the Confederate Army. The initials were inscribed on the only Confederate medals ever awarded for bravery. The Davis Guards, under the command of Lieutenant Richard W. Dowling, took part in an amazing 45-minute action on September 8, 1863, in Texas, defending tiny Fort Grisby, which guarded the mouth of the Sabine River at the Gulf of Mexico. With his garrison of 43 men and 6 cannons, Dowling repulsed a naval force of 4 gunboats and several transports carrying 4,000 men. The Davis Guards captured 2 Union gunboats and 340 prisoners without suffering a single injury. The medals they received had "D.G." on one side and

"Sabine Pass, September 8, 1863" on the other. The Confederate Congress also accorded the garrison an official vote of thanks.

D.H. The abbreviation for "dead head," written on U.S. telegrams that were sent free. Telegrams addressed to the CHRISTIAN COMMISSION, for instance, were always carried without charge.

dial-plate The face of a clock.

diarrhea-dysentery The double term used by Union doctors to describe any illness or disease leading to the symptom of loose bowels. Common general names included "camp diarrhea" and "bowel complaint." It was usually blamed on poorly cooked food. "Diarrhea-dysentery" officially killed about 50,000 northern soldiers and a larger number of southern troops. It is estimated that only 5 out of every 1,000 men in the Union army completely avoided some form of diarrhea-dysentery. Hot tea was a trusted home cure in camps. Some soldiers found, surprisingly, that the heat of battle cured the problem. Confederate Private W.A. Fletcher wrote that "the excitement or something else, had effected a cure. I inquired of some of the others and they reported a cure."

dick A slang name for the penis. The term first became common during the war.

"Dickens take it all!" An exclamation of anger or frustration; e.g., "We need more supports. Where are the Georgians, Dickens take it all!"

dickey 1. In a carriage, the driver's seat or the servant's seat at the rear. The driver's seat was sometimes called a "dickey box." 2. A man's false shirt front or shirt collar that could be detached, one type being the "paper dickey."

"The Dictator" The nickname for a famous 13-inch, 8.5-ton MORTAR used by the Union army during its long siege of Petersburg, Virginia, in 1864-65. The Dictator fired 200-pound missiles from a railroad flatcar and a wooden ground platform. During the siege, which ended in its tenth month on April 2, 1865, the mortar was also nicknamed the "Petersburg Express."

diet kitchen (or special diet kitchen) The common name for a kitchen in a military hospital, especially a Union one. These facilities were often designated as "low diet" or "extra diet" kitchens.

dig A student who studied hard, a slang name that was carried over into military camps to mean a diligent soldier. The verb was also used; "to dig" meant to study hard, and one could "dig a lesson."

digging A southern slang word meaning "costly." Soldiers would talk about a SUTLER's "digging prices."

dig up the hatchet To start a war or battle, the opposite of burying the hatchet; e.g., "Once this rebellion is over, the South won't be digging up the hatchet again for a while." It was also used figuratively in regard to any controversy; e.g., "If the two factions of the Democratic Party dig up the hatchet, the election is lost."

diked out Dressed in fancy clothes.

dime novel A popular type of fiction found in camps on both sides. Published on cheap wood-pulp paper and printed in two columns, they were sensational adventure tales that usually featured American frontier heroes. One of the first was Ann Sophia Stephens's *Maleska: The Indian Wife of the White Hunter*, published in 1860. The most popular series was Beadle's Dime Novels, published in a pocket size specifically for Union troops.

din To repeat something in an insistent or persistent way, such as an idea, request, or criticism; e.g., "The little sergeant was known for dinning rebukes at us all."

ding or dinged A southern slang term for "very," as in "ding cold" or "a dinged long march."

dingbat A slang name for a strong alcoholic drink.

dingy An adjective meaning black and often used to describe a slave or free Negro, such as "a dingy woman" or "dingy house servants." Pronounced to rhyme with "singe."

dinner The normal name in both armies for lunch. The bugle dinner call was at noon, and soldiers received some free time after the meal.

dip 1. A candle made by dipping a wick in tallow. Henri Lovie, a war artist for *Frank Leslie's Illustrated Newspaper,* bemoaned on May 17, 1862, the "working until midnight by the dim light of an attenuated tallow 'dip.'" 2. A slang name for a pickpocket. "Genteel dips" were known to operate among the chaotic wartime crowds on the streets of Washington, D.C.

diplomatist A common alternative form of "diplomat."

dipping snuff or dipping The practice of dipping a small wooden stick into snuff in a snuff box and then chewing on the wood or rubbing it over the teeth. The stick was first split like a brush and wet. An old wives' tale said it kept the teeth white, and some women, especially in the rural South, were avid dippers. They often carried the stick tucked away in their glove or under their garter string.

dirk A long, straight dagger. The verb, "to dirk," was used symbolically and often by politicians during the war, in the manner of "to stab someone in the back." Ohio's Congressman S.S. Cox wrote on June 20, 1864, that he feared that peace supporters would try to "dirk" the proposed Democratic presidential candidate, General George McClellan.

dirt-digger A derogatory name for an officer who advocated the digging of entrenchments and other field works. Especially early in the war, some military minds thought it was beneath the dignity of soldiers to be digging ditches instead of concentrating on traditional military tactics. An exception was Union Major General W.T. Sherman, who felt that this new idea of defensive earthworks would be used in future wars because it allowed a relatively small number of troops to hold off or slow down larger forces. Another advocate was Confederate General Robert E. Lee, who became known as the "ACE OF SPADES."

dirt-eater *See* clay-eater.

"Dirt Eating papers" A term used for northern newspapers that sensationalized the news and criticized the government and military. Union Brigadier General Joseph Hooker banned such papers from his camps, calling them "disloyal." They included the New York *World* and the New York *Express.*

dirty niggers The insulting name hurled at Republicans by Democrats during Abraham Lincoln's second presidential race in 1864. A more formal rendition was "negro abolition traitors."

discombobulate To upset or disturb someone; e.g., "Our foragers were told they could steal crops in the field but not to discombobulate the ladies in the houses." The word was probably a humorous extension of "discomfort."

disremember A southern term meaning to forget.

Disunionist A person who wished to break up the Union. On July 22, 1861, the day after the first battle of Bull Run, the U.S. House of Representatives, to refute a northern war of conquest, passed a resolution resolving "That the present deplorable civil war has been forced upon the country by the Disunionists of the Southern states." An amendment changing this to "Disunionists of the Southern and Northern states" was rejected.

ditch The common name used by soldiers for a trench, although the latter term was also used, especially in formal reports.

ditching Digging trenches. "Ditching all the time," wrote one complaining Confederate soldier at work on protective earthworks. "My plan would be to quit ditching and go to fighting."

ditty-bag A sailor's bag for small items, such as razors, toothbrush, and sewing materials. The name, still used, was first heard in England and America about the time the war began.

division A military unit on both sides, consisting of about two to four BRIGADES. Artillery batteries or battalions were also part of a division, and sometimes cavalrymen serving as provost gurads. Usually two or three divisions made up a CORPS.

"Dixie" The South's battle song, with words and music by an Ohio minstrel composer, Daniel Decatur Emmet, who also wrote "BLUE TAIL FLY" (sometimes known as "Jim Crack Corn"). "Dixie's Land" was composed for Bryant's Minstrels in a New York boarding house one cold and rainy Sunday. Emmet said he used the melody of "Come Philander," a song his grandmother had sung to him as a child, and chose the theme "I wish I was in Dixie" because his wife was complaining about the freezing winter. (A black family in Knox County, Ohio—Thomas and Ellen Snowden—claimed they taught the song to Emmet.) The song, which begins with the same three bugle notes as "The Star-Spangled Banner," was introduced April 4, 1859. It was an instant hit and skyrocketed to fame in the South in the spring of 1861 when presented in New Orleans in a burlesque drama entitled "Pocahontas." It became a patriotic classic on February 18, 1861, when it was played at the inauguration of Confederate President Jefferson Davis in Montgomery, Alabama. Emmet was horrified and northern newspapers charged him with treason. "If I had known to what use they were going to put my song," he answered, "I will be damned

if I'd had written it." He tried new words for the North ("Oh, we're marching on to Victory! Hurrah! Hurrah!"), but they never caught on. "Dixie" was played during Confederate General George Pickett's famous fatal charge at Gettysburg and by a Union band during the surrender at Appomattox Court House. It was the last song requested by President Abraham Lincoln, who had used the melody for his 1860 presidential campaign ("At Chicago they selected, Lincoln who will be elected, Abraham, Abraham, Abraham, Abraham.") At a White House reception on April 10, 1865, Lincoln called it "one of the best tunes I have ever heard" and added, "Since we've conquered the rebel army, we've also conquered 'Dixie.'" For his part, Emmet ended up touring the South after the war at the age of 80, raising many ex-Confederate roofs with his weak-voice rendition.

Dix's American Flag Dispatch A dispatch message sent on January 29, 1861, by U.S. Secretary of the Treasury (later Major General) John A. Dix to his government in New Orleans, ordering that "If anyone attempts to haul down the American flag, shoot him on the spot." This was in response to the revenue cutter *McClelland* refusing to surrender the vessel to the U.S. government. The order infuriated southerners but inspired northerners. Warren Lee Goss of Massachusetts, who became a Union private, recalled, "Before I reached the point of enlisting, I had read and been 'enthused' by General Dix's famous 'shoot him on the spot' dispatch."

doc This shortened nickname for a doctor first became popular about six years before the war began.

"Doc" The nickname of Cullen B. Aubrey, a young boy at Gettysburg who rode among the armies during lulls in the shooting on July 3, 1863, to sell a newspaper account of the first day of the battle on July 1. This was the first time in history when troops read about a battle while they were still fighting it. "Doc" had met a train and picked up copies of the Philadelphia *Inquirer* that carried telegraphed dispatches from its correspondent on the scene, Uriah Painter.

doctor The tongue-in-cheek complimentary nickname given by sailors to their ship's cook.

doctoress A common name for a female doctor.

doctor woman A female slave in charge of nursing ill slaves. Also called the "sick nurse," she was generally one of the most intelligent slaves on the plantation and was given great authority in her position.

dodger A soldier who dodged his duties; also a BEAT or SHIRK.

do don't A complicated southern way of saying "do not" or simply "don't." It originated in Georgia, and produced such statements as "Do don't fire until the enemy advances."

dodunk A slang name for a simple person or fool; e.g., "We talked with the Rebel prisoners and discovered they were not dodunks."

do execution on (or upon) To make an impression on someone. You could therefore "do great execution upon the ladies."

dog-cart A small civilian two-wheel carriage. It was open and had two back-to-back seats. The name came from its original sporting use when a hunting dog was transported in a box under the seats.

dog cheap A very cheap price; e.g., "Compared to Richmond, the goods in Washington were dog cheap."

dog collar The nickname given by Union soldiers to the regulation army issue of an uncomfortable, stiff leather cravat to be buckled around the neck. They became camp jokes that were almost never worn.

dog fall An inconclusive battle. The name came from a wrestling term. One Confederate soldier explained it as "Both sides claim the victory—both whipped."

"Doggone it!" One of the favorite exclamations of Union General Ulysses S. Grant, who avoided profanity. *See also* "By lightning!"

dog-hungry An informal adjective meaning very hungry or ravenous.

dog leg A twist of cheap tobacco, because it resembled a dog's leg.

dog-poor Especially poor, such as a "dog-poor family."

dog robber A humorous name for a soldier assigned as an officer's servant or for one who cooked for his mess. In both cases, it was assumed he took scraps that might have gone to a camp dog.

dogs A slang name for andirons (metal supports for firewood in a hearth); e.g., "The remaining logs were so small, we nearly had to push the dogs together.

dogs' bodies (or dog's body) A camp dish of dried peas boiled in a cloth. It was especially (and boringly) served to sailors in both navies.

dog tent Nickname for the small two-man shelter tent that began to replace the cumbersome SIBLEY TENT in the war's second year. Soldiers first bitterly complained about losing the warm social space of the large Sibley, but quickly appreciated the ease of moving the light dog tent. Two soldiers each carried half, and at night the two thick, unbleached muslin pieces were buttoned together over a pole. The space was 6 x 7 feet, and a Massachusetts artilleryman, John D. Billings, noted, "It would only accommodate a dog, and a small one at that." The shelter was breezy, being open at both ends. When Union General William S. Rosecrans rode by the newly installed tents in his camp, he smiled at the signs displayed there, such as "Sons of Bitches Within" and "Bull Pups Here." When his soldiers appeared at the entrances on all fours and began barking and baying, Rosecrans laughed out loud. The dog tent, of course, was later called the pup tent.

doings Decorations and trimmings, especially on a dress; e.g., "Her wedding dress had more doings than a general's uniform."

do-little A slang name for a person who was lazy or inactive; e.g., "The General said President Davis was surrounded by a bunch of do-littles."

doll baby A slang name for a beautiful or attractive young woman; e.g., "Paul's mother was a fearful dragon, but his sister was a doll baby."

domestic institution *See* peculiar institution.

domestic sentimentalists The term used to describe the group of women writers who dominated romantic fiction during the war. The stories all had female heroines who struggled to become more moral and to find their true roles in life, usually ending in marriage and domestic happiness. The domestic sentimentalists had been dominant since the 1820s, and one of the most popular during the war was Maria Sussanna Cummins, who had written the immensely successful *The Lamplighter* in 1854. The popularity of the women novelists caused Nathaniel Hawthorne to complain to his publisher

that "America is now wholly given over to a d____d mob of scribbling women, and I should have no chance of success while the public taste is occupied with their trash."

domestics Cotton goods made in America, a term established before the war.

done brown A slang term meaning completely cheated or tricked; e.g., "One lady was done brown by foragers who asked for water and stole both her pigs while she fetched it."

done for To be cheated, especially out of money. A new recruit lured into a shady card game could complain that "I was done for, to the tune of $15."

done gone A nonstandard southern and southwestern expression meaning destroyed or missing; e.g., "I hurried home after the surrender and found the house still standing but everything else done gone."

done up To be ruined by something, such as by spending too much money, by gambling, or by drinking; e.g., "Grant will end this war in a year if he's not done up by whiskey."

don't care a hang An common expression of disdain; e.g., "I don't care a hang if you believe me or not."

don't care whether school keeps or not An expression for not caring if something happens or continues. A Union soldier, writing about discontent in the army in 1863, noted, that "A great many say that they 'don't care whether school keeps or not,' for they think there is a destructive fate hovering over our army."

"don't swap horses while crossing the river" A phrase that became popular during the war after President Abraham Lincoln used the idea when accepting his renomination in 1864. He told Republicans that the honor had not come because he was the best man but rather because they had concluded that "it is not best to swap horses while crossing the river." Lincoln added that the Republicans had decided "I am not so poor a horse that they might not make a botch of it in trying to swap." The expression had been around earlier in the century, and it eventually evolved into today's "don't change horses in midstream."

Doodle A southern name for a Yankee soldier. It came, obviously, from Yankee Doodle. A popular verse with the soldiers, "Call All," first printed in the Rockingham *Register* in Virginia, advised Confederate soldiers on how to overcome the shortage of weapons: "Want a weapon? Why capture one! Every Doodle has got a gun, Belt and bayonet, bright and new; Kill a Doodle, and capture two!"

dornick A slang name for a stone or small rock.

dot A marriage dowry. After Yankee soldiers had stripped her Baton Rouge home, Sarah Morgan wrote on August 28, 1862, that nothing remained of "the cut-glass celery and preserve dishes that were to be part of my 'dot,' as mother always said."

do the big job A slang expression meaning to kill; e.g., "I'd never even seen the enemy, and as the distant guns grew louder I wondered if I could do the big job."

double harness A slang term for marriage; e.g., "MacDonald went home on his furlough and took on a double harness."

double shot Two loads of CANISTER SHOT or GRAPE SHOT fired together from a cannon, usually in emergency situations. The order would be to "double shot" a cannon, and soldiers spoke of "double-shotting" and a "double-shotted" gun. Sometimes, even a triple shot was ordered. ("Double-shotted" was also a slang term to describe someone who was drunk.)

double team To overcome a person or group by doubling up against them; e.g., "We used supporting troops to double team the Alabama regiment." The term originally referred to a farmer using two teams of horses or mules to pull a heavy load. It survives today as sports jargon.

double time (or double quick) A soldier's fast advance at from 165 to 180 steps a minute. Units were often ordered into battle this way, and the exertion could wear out the attackers before the enemy was reached. "We started in double quick from our entrenchments," wrote a Confederate who charged with the 19th Virginia at the first battle of Bull Run, "and went until we were near broke down."

dough This slang term for money was first heard about a decade before the war.

doughboy A nickname for the Union INFANTRYMAN. Many suggestions have been made about the word's history, including the resemblance of infantry uniform buttons to dough, the fact that U.S. soldiers ate a baked mixture of flour and rice during the Mexican War, and the idea that western troops were once covered in adobe dust. The term existed years before the war and was popular during World War I, often being incorrectly attributed to that conflict.

dough-face An insulting nickname in the North for anyone in the Union, especially a politician, who supported slavery. Southerners later used the name in a reverse way for any southerner who did not support slavery. The term pre-dated the war, with the *New York Tribune* stating in

1848 that "while Southerners need and are willing to pay for the services of the *dough-faces*, they dislike their persons and despise their discourse." The idea of pliable politicians could explain the "dough" label, and the name was eventually expanded to include any politician who could be easily influenced.

Dover's powder A medical preparation of opium and IPECACUANHA used by military doctors to treat pain and induce perspiration. It was sometimes prescribed with other medicines for malaria.

down-easter A nickname for a person from New England, especially Maine.

down to the ground An expression describing something done completely or in a perfect way; e.g., "We had memorized the drill manual down to the ground."

the dozens A lively game of insults and taunts among slaves and free blacks during the war. Two people hurled witty but rough verbal abuse back and forth until one lost his temper and thereby lost the competition. Some blacks have kept alive the tradition of the dozens.

drab A nickname for a prostitute. *See also* clap; daughter of Eve; fallen angel; fancy girl; fast house; gay young duck; "The Haystack"; "Hooker's Division"; "Madam Russell's Bake Oven"; parlor house; ranch; The Wolf's Dream.

draft riots Riots that killed at least 105 people in New York City after names were first drawn on July 11, 1863, for conscription. Trouble began on July 13 (10 days after the victory at Gettysburg) with an attack on the draft office by a mob of mostly Irish protesters, who burned the building. A mob estimated at up to 50,000 people, some chanting "Hurrah for Jeff Davis," rioted for three days, killing at least a dozen people. Blacks were tar-

geted as a major cause of the war, with one crippled coachman hanged, his fingers and toes hacked off, and his body burned. The mob also burned down a black church and orphanage. Soldiers of the Army of the Potomac, some just back from Gettysburg, joined police to fight the rioters in running battles through the streets and even over rooftops. Peace was maintained by circling the city with 43 regiments. The draft selections began again on August 19. *See also* "the left wing of Lee's army."

dragged out To be worn out or exhausted; e.g., "That spade work really dragged me out."

"Dragon Dix" The nickname for Dorothea Lynde Dix, who at 60 became superintendent of the Union army's more than 3,000 nurses. She received no pay during her four years of service. Only five feet tall, her fearsome nickname alluded to her autocratic personality and relentless insistence that women belonged in military hospitals. Dix insisted, however, that "all nurses are required to be very plain-looking women," could not be under the age of 30, and had to wear brown or black dresses with no adornments. "No hoop skirts," added Dix, who even turned down nuns.

dragoon A cavalryman or mounted infantrymen who dismounts to join a battle.

Dragoon *See* Colt four-pounder.

drat This affable British oath of the early nineteenth century was mostly heard in the South, as in the exclamations "Drat him!" and "Drat it!" and also such usages as "Drat his infernal orders." The adjective, equally southern, was "dratted," often applied to the "dratted war."

draughts The game of checkers; the term is still used in Great Britain.

drawing room An elegant SITTING ROOM in a house, in which guests were received and entertained. It could be more intimate and less formal than a PARLOR. The name was originally a "withdrawing room" to which ladies withdrew after dinner.

"Draw it easy!" An expression of disbelief, telling the speaker to stop exaggerating; e.g., "Your regiment marched 100 miles in a day? Please, chum, draw it easy!"

draw your furrow straighter Tell the truth. Because the U.S. in the nineteenth century was a largely agrarian society, this farm metaphor drew a clear picture for most men of the time.

dray A low, flat, strong, and heavy cart with detachable sides for carrying heavy goods. The driver was called a drayman.

"Dr. Bull Run Russell" An abusive northern nickname for William Howard Russell, correspondent for the London *Times*, because of his detailed report of how the Union forces panicked and ran after the battle of Bull Run in July 1861. His newspaper accounts of the battle were also printed as a pamphlet.

dresser A medical assistant who dressed wounds. In Union hospitals, dressing was often done by a medical student or volunteer in the MEDICAL CORPS.

dressing station or advance station An area used by doctors to immediately dress the wounds of soldiers taken from the battlefield. Sometimes called an "aid station," it was located just beyond the range of enemy fire. An assistant surgeon would give the victims liquor or drugs while he tried to stop the bleeding, remove bits of metal or other foreign bodies, pack the wound with lint, and bandage it. The wounded were then taken or had to walk to the regimental or divisional hospital tent, commonly called the FIELD HOSPITAL, which was usually several miles away.

dress the line Straightening a military line by having each soldier look to his right or to the center. Although usually done during dress parades, it was also done during PICKETT'S CHARGE at Gettysburg when Confederates amazingly stopped to dress their line under fire in the middle of the field because so many fallen comrades had created holes in it. "My God," shouted one Yankee, "they are dressing the line!" *See also* guide right.

Dr. Green A slang name for a young naive person, such as a new soldier, because green was associated with being fresh or unripe; e.g., "Welcome to the war, Dr. Green!"

drilling A type of stout twilled linen or cotton cloth. A SHELTER TENT was often made of cotton drilling. The material was also used for pants and other clothes. The name came from the German word *Drillich* taken from the Latin *trilix* meaning three-threaded.

drinky An adjective describing someone who was slightly drunk or tipsy; e.g., "The sergeant could say nothing, because he was drinky too." See DRUNK for numerous other terms referring to intoxication.

driver On a southern plantation, a slave directly in charge of supervising, controlling, and disciplining the slaves working in the fields or on gangs. He answered to the HEAD DRIVER. On the Butler plantation on the Georgia coast, the driver was allowed to administer one dozen lashes to a misbehaving worker. If this failed, the head driver could inflict three dozen or the OVERSEER could administer up to 50 lashes.

drive well A southern expression meaning to supervise or keep people in order.

It was originally applied to a plantation OVERSEER, HEAD DRIVER, or DRIVER, but was soon used in other contexts. Both an officer leading his men and a college teacher controlling his students were said to "drive well."

driving in the pickets An expression that meant an approaching enemy was forcing PICKETS back into camp to give the warning. This usually happened in a cavalry raid or with the arrival of a skirmish line in advance of a large enemy force. If the attackers moved with stealth to delay the pickets at their posts, the camp would have little defense. The pickets had been driven in," wrote Union nurse Eliza Howland on June 23, 1862, "and ["STONEWALL"] Jackson was supposed to be close at hand."

droger or drogher A slow-moving ship built to transport a particular commodity. Cotton drogers were common in the South. The name was borrowed from a slow type of West Indian ship.

dropsy Edema, a swelling in the leg or other part of the body caused by fluid retention. Union Chaplain F.F. Kiner, joining Yankee prisoners at Macon, Georgia, wrote, "Many were afflicted with swelled feet and legs, having the appearance of dropsy, caused by weakness and diseased constitutions."

drum-head court-martial A summary court-martial held in the field for offenses during a battle. The sentence was usually carried out immediately. On November 25, 1861, the Confederate Secretary of War Judah P. Benjamin issued official orders concerning "traitors of East Tennessee," who had been burning bridges, saying they were "to be tried summarily by drum-head court-martial, and, if found guilty, executed on the spot by hanging." This type of court-martial was originally held around an upturned drum-head.

"Drummer Boy of Chickamauga" The nickname given to Johnny Clem, age 12, a member of the 22nd Massachusetts, because he killed a Confederate colonel who tried to capture him at the battle of Chickamauga in Tennessee on September 20, 1863. Born John Klem, he had run away from home at 9 to join the war and was adopted as a mascot and drummer by the 22nd before he was allowed to enlist as a regular soldier in May 1863. He was also earlier called "Johnny Shiloh" because his drum was supposedly destroyed by an artillery shell at the battle of Shiloh, an incident that was turned into a popular song, "THE DRUMMER BOY OF SHILOH." After the war, Clem resumed his military career in 1871, retiring as a major general in 1915, the last Union veteran still in the army.

"The Drummer Boy of Marblehead" A Union poem about a drummer boy from Marblehead, Massachusetts, killed during a battle near Roanoke, Virginia. The final verse is as follows:

> Once more we'll have our good old air,
> Tis fitting on this glorious field,
> Twill quell the traitors in their lair,
> And teach them how to yield!
> It swelled, to stir our hearts like flame;
> Then back a hostile bullet sped,
> And Death delivered up to Fame,
> The drummer boy of Marblehead.

"The Drummer Boy of Shiloh" A song about Johnny Clem, who was known as Johnny Shiloh and later famed as the DRUMMER BOY OF CHICKAMAUGA. This song was popular in both the North and South because it did not mention on which side the boy served. Although the real Johnny survived the battle, he died in the typically sentimental song.

> "Oh, Mother!" said the dying boy,
> "Look down from Heav'n on me,
> Receive me to thy fond embrace,
> Oh take me home to thee.
> I've loved my country as my God,

To serve them both I've tried."
He smiled, shook hands.
Death seized the boy who prayed before
    he died.

drumming-out The degrading but sel-dom used ceremony of expelling a soldier from the army in front of the entire camp. In an instance in General Robert E. Lee's army, two deserters were marched up and down the ranks behind a drummer and fifer playing "THE ROGUE'S MARCH"; their heads were then shaven and they took the march again before being released with a dishonorable discharge. It was soon decided that drumming-out would send a bad (and probably lucky) fellow into society or, worse, into the enemy's army, so other punishments were substituted, from humiliations to firing squads.

drunk This name for an intoxicated per-son ("a party of drunks") came into use about a decade before the war began. It had already been a name for a spree ("go on a drunk.") and an adjective for being intoxicated ("a drunk person"). *See also* balmy; bamboozled; blue-eyed; breezy; bruised; corned; D and D; damaged; drinky; drunk as a fool; drunky; frazzled; fuddled; gin barrel; half-shot; have a brick in one's hat; how-come-you-so; jug-steamed; mellow; over the bay; rocky; rummy; rum-sucker; shot in the neck; slewed; snapped; squiffed; sucker; turkey on one's back.

drunk as a fool A popular simile during the war, and one of dozens used to de-scribe a high level of intoxication. See DRUNK for numerous other terms referring to intoxication.

drunky or drunkie An adjective mean-ing drunk, and often used before a name; e.g., "We met drunky Wilson on the road." See DRUNK for numerous other terms re-ferring to intoxication.

"Dry Land *Merrimac*" or "Land *Merrimac*" The nickname given by Rich-mond newspapers to a Confederate ar-mored railroad freight car, also called the "Railroad *Merrimac*." It was invented by Lieutenant James Barry of the Norfolk United Artillery and built in 1862. A long floor was laid over two cars and an ar-mored CASEMATE was then constructed like that on the Confederate IRONCLAD ships—Barry had served on the *Virginia* (*Merrimac*). Inside, behind 18-inch-thick timber, was placed a 32-pound Brooke RIFLED GUN adapted to fire shot or shell. The 60-ton train moved slowly, and the engineer was protected by walls of cot-ton bales. The traveling gun saw action near Fair Oaks and Savage's Station, but was useless if the enemy did not approach the York River Railroad line.

dry-land sailor An infantryman or other combatant transferred to a warship with little knowledge of shipboard warfare. Naval enlistments were never high, and on some ships, more than half the crew were dry-land sailors.

dry nursery The humorous nickname for the training facility established in Wash-ington, D.C., for regiments recently formed. Brigadier General Silas Casey, who had fought Indians and in the Mexi-can War, was in charge of shaping up about 100,000 recruits and forming them into provisional brigades and divisions.

dry seaman A sober sailer. This Union term was heard on July 14, 1862, when Congress had the Navy Department re-place the daily GROG ration with a daily payment of five cents. The Bureau of Medicine and Surgery was bold enough to suggest ice tea as a replacement. How-ever, near mutiny resulted in the rein-statement of the daily rum ration.

dry wash A way of "cleaning" shirts es-pecially among Confederate soldiers and even officers, who sometimes had only one or two. The shirts were removed and beaten against an object, such as a saddle, to shake out the vermin.

duck trousers White cotton bell-bottom trousers worn by sailors on both sides. The light trousers were normal for seamen. The name came from *doek*, the Dutch term for cloth.

"Dudy" The pet name given to Union General Ulysses S. Grant by his wife Julia Grant.

duff A boiled pudding dish popular with Union troops. It was simply flour and water with dried fruit or nuts added and molasses for sweetness.

dull music Anything that was monotonous or tedious. The long Union shelling of Vicksburg was "dull music" to the besieged residents.

dumpish In the dumps; sad and melancholy. A Massachusetts soldier invading the South said, "This climate is making me terribly lazy. I lose all my strength here, and feel dumpish continually."

dunderhead A slang name for a stupid person or a dunce. The term was popular during the war, and even U.S. Navy Secretary Gideon Welles wrote in his diary about the "dunderheads" at the War Office.

dundrearies or dundreary whiskers Long side-whiskers that became fashionable during the war, being made popular by the character of Lord Dundreary in the comedy OUR AMERICAN COUSIN. *See also* dundreary.

dundreary A person who postured as a dandy, being meticulous about his clothes and appearance. The name came from the simpleton character of Lord Dundreary in the 1858 British comedy OUR AMERICAN COUSIN, which President Abraham Lincoln was watching when he was assassinated in April 1865. *See also* dundrearies.

dust 1. A slang word for money. It supposedly came from "gold dust," which had been called "dust" during the California Gold Rush. But the term had also been applied to money in England in the eighteenth century. 2. A verb meaning "to leave quickly"; e.g., "Each time her mother returned, I had to dust."

Dutch fit A slang name for an angry outburst or an uncontrolled rage; e.g., "When the captain saw us running from the Rebels, he had one of his Dutch fits." The term came from the stereotypical belief that the Dutch were overly serious and prone to intense anger.

Dutchman The common name for a German. Rebel soldiers were upset at the many "mercenary Dutchmen" who fought for the Union, and even Yankees on occasion called them "dumb Dutchmen." More than 200,000 fought in Union ranks, and the 9th Wisconsin was composed entirely of Germans. After the battle of Bull Run, one immigrant "Dutchman" from Missouri wrote that he was fighting against traitors who wanted to "destroy the best and noblest government on earth." Many died for the cause, particularly at the battle of Chancellorsville in May 1863, when Confederate Lieutenant General "STONEWALL" Jackson's flanking march routed the German troops comprising a large part of the Union 11th Corps. *See also* blenker; "I fights mit Sigel."

dwelling-house A home where someone lived. The name was often used to designate the large house among other buildings on a plantation, which also had cabins or quarters for slaves.

dyspepsia The medical word for indigestion. It was considered serious, being due to a "functional derangement of the stomach," and was said to cause weakness, loss of appetite, and even depression. Confederate Lieutenant General "STONEWALL" Jackson compained of dyspepsia and treated it by sucking lemons and wrapping cold towels around his stomach. The latter was done by Jackson's servant after the general had been shot in May 1863, and may have hastened Jackson's death.

dyspnea A severe shortness of breath caused by wounds to the chest, a common occurrence on the battlefield. Dyspnea could be relieved if a doctor sealed the wound with collodion, a solution of pyroxylin (nitrocellulose), ether, and alcohol, which quickly dried into a tough, resilient film. However, this process also sealed in any infections.

E

---

eagle The name of a U.S. gold coin worth $10. Modern gold coins called eagles are still authorized by Congress.

the earlier Revolution A southern term for the American Revolution.

ebonic A humorous slang name for a black person, used in both the North and South.

echelon attack A type of attack, used especially by Confederates, that sent one flank against the enemy and withheld the other flank to reinforce the attack. When the attacked part of the enemy position collapsed, the rest of his line could be rolled back. The technique did not have a good success rate. For instance, at Gettysburg in 1863, the Confederates attacked "in echelon" with unfortunate results. The maneuver was also called the oblique order of attack and the progressive order of attack.

Eddie The nickname of Edward Baker Lincoln, the second of President Abraham Lincoln's four sons. He was named for Union Colonel Edward D. Baker, a close family friend and former congressman, who was killed in 1861 at Balls Bluff, Virginia. Eddie Lincoln died when he was nearly four, 11 years before Lincoln became president in 1861. The boy's death brought his parents closer together and Mrs. Lincoln joined the Presbyterian Church, although her husband never became a member of any church.

educated soldier A soldier, usually a career officer, trained in military tactics.

effective A soldier or sailor fit enough for combat. In June 1863, near the end of the Union siege of Vicksburg, Mississippi, fewer than half of the defending Confederate troops were listed as "effectives."

effective range The range of fire that best reached enemy troops. Some soldiers, especially new ones, tended to fire too high at a long distance or too soon as the enemy advanced. Officers recommended that they hold their fire until their more experienced comrades began firing.

egg-nog This thick drink, already a tradition during the war, consisted of beaten eggs, milk or cream, sugar, nutmeg, and alcohol ("nog" was strong ale). The festive drink was served on southern plantations, with a former slave, Josiah Henson, recalling "dances before old massa's door for the first drink of egg-nog."

egg-sucker An insulting slang name for a worthless person, such as one who avoids work; e.g., "The general has surrounded himself with a staff of egg-suckers." Someone or something that was worthless was called "egg-sucking," such as "the egg-sucking marines" or "egg-sucking fatigue duty."

elbow-crooking A slang expression for the act of drinking alcohol. Soldiers might say they were going into town for some "cooking and elbow-crooking." By the twentieth century, the term had become "elbow-bending."

elder wine or elderberry wine An alcoholic drink composed of elderberries, brandy, sugar, raisins, cloves, ground ginger, and brewer's yeast.

Elements of Military Art and Science The influencial manual on military strategy written by Major General Henry W. Halleck and published in 1846. It was used throughout the Civil War. Halleck, the Union general-in-chief of the Western theater, was jealous of General Ulysses S. Grant and in 1862 called him an alcoholic and demoted him.

the elephant *See* see the elephant.

"The Elephant" The nickname for Thomas W. Knox, the burly war correspondent for the New York *Herald*. After the defeat of Union Major General W.T. Sherman's forces at Vicksburg, Mississippi, on December 29, 1862, Knox wrote about the general's "mismangement." Sherman, already paranoid about press reports that might aid the enemy, had him arrested and tried as a spy by a court martial. The court expelled the reporter from Sherman's army. The case was eventually appealed by the press fraternity to President Abraham Lincoln, who sided with the journalists. Although Sherman continued to ban Knox, he became less aggressive toward other journalists.

elevating screw A large screw attached to a cannon's STOCK TRAIL underneath the rear of the cannon barrel. It was used to elevate the cannon's muzzle (by lowering the screw) or to lower it (by raising the screw).

Ellsworth's Avengers The nickname of the 44th New York Regiment, a volunteer unit formed after U.S. Colonel Elmer Ellsworth was murdered on May 23, 1861, the day after Virginia's voters approved their state's ordinance of secession. Ellsworth was shot by the proprietor of a hotel in Alexandria, Virginia, after the colonel removed a Confederate flag from the hotel roof. Ellsworth's aide killed the assassin. To join Ellsworth's Avengers, a man had to be at least 30 years old, 5'8" tall, unmarried, and of good moral character.

"Emancipation!" The slogan and cry of abolitionists, beginning in the 1850s and gaining strength throughout the war.

Emancipation Proclamation Issued by President Abraham Lincoln on January 1, 1863, the Emancipation Proclamation declared the freedom of slaves in the Confederacy, but not in states that remained within the Union. The President had published a preliminary version on September 24, 1862, shortly after the battle of Antietam. The proclamation legally freed no slaves, but it encouraged them to escape to the North and assured them that they would be free if the Union won the war. Besides being a humanitarian gesture, the proclamation was designed to wreck the economy of the South and win British support. Lincoln was morally opposed to slavery, but as a pre-war politician he had promised not to interfere with it. Many of his military officers and soldiers did not support emancipation. Major General George B. McClellan had written to the President on July 7, 1862, warning that a declaration of radical views on slavery "will rapidly disintegrate our present armies." *See also* "the Emancipator."

"the Emancipator" or "the Great Emancipator" Northern nicknames for President Abraham Lincoln, even before he officially issued the EMANCIPATION PROCLAMATION on January 1, 1863.

embalmed beef A derogatory nickname given by Union soldiers for canned beef, an unusual item issued as rations. It was canned in Chicago under a government contract.

embalming surgeon An embalmer who, during the war, set up business behind the lines. Bodies thus preserved could be shipped home for proper burial. The embalming process intrigued war photographer Matthew Brady, who wrote that the corpse's veins "were pumped full of some liquid which possesses the power to arrest and prevent decay."

embrasure An opening built into a fort's PARAPET (wall) so that a cannon can be fired at the enemy.

Emerald Guards The nickname for Company I of the 8th Alabama Regiment because 104 of the 109 men were born in Ireland. The company began the war wearing dark green uniforms and carrying a flag that depicted a shamrock wreath around an Irish harp and the

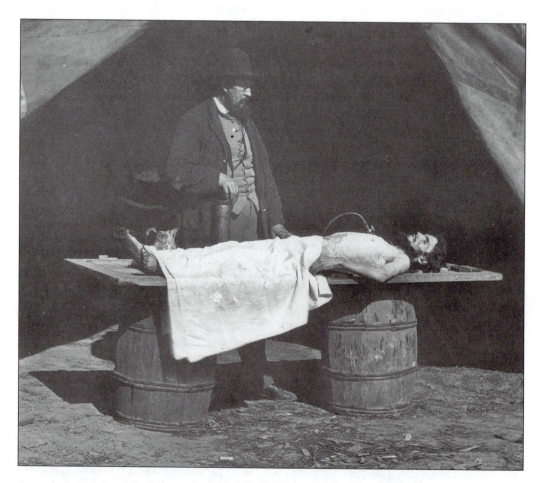

An embalming surgeon prepares to work on a soldier's body. *Library of Congress, Prints & Photographs Division, LC-B8171-2531.*

words "Erin-go-Bragh" ("Ireland Forever").

emotional instability An general illness category that could allow soldiers to be discharged, especially early in the war. Clay Allison left the Confederate army in this way but returned to scout for Lieutenant General Nathan Bedford Forrest and then become a notorious gunfighter in the West.

en barbette A term, taken from the French, describing a cannon placed on a platform so that its barrel projects over a wall.

encounter battle A battle that begins when the opposing armies encounter each other unexpectedly. Both sides are usually caught by surprise and quickly attempt to bring together their often scattered forces. The battle of Gettysburg supposedly began this way when a Confederate division led by Major General Henry Heth sought supplies from a shoe factory near Gettysburg and ran into the Union cavalry of U.S. General John Buford. (Heth had asked his commander, Lieutenant General Ambrose P. Hill, if there was any reason he should not go pick up the shoes, and Hill answered "None in the world.")

en echelon A military attack with units slightly to the left or right of the one charging before it, so each has a clear view of the enemy. This French expression was commonly used in the war.

en embrasure A term, from the French, describing a cannon placed in an EMBRASURE (opening) of a fortification.

energize To activate or invigorate or to give energy or strength to someone; e.g., "Halfway through the battle, I saw General Drayton riding up to the artillery to energize the men."

enfilade Sweeping gunfire directed at the enemy from the length of a column of troops; the position of the soldiers under fire was also called an enfilade. A verb also existed—an officer of the 14th New Jersey Infantry Regiment fighting Confederate troops in July 1864 near Washington, D.C., wrote, "Their batteries enfiladed us and did excellent execution."

the English A name given by the Amish religious sect to all Americans who were not Amish. They considered the Civil War to be an English war that did not concern their people. The peace-loving Amish would not fight on either side or even resist when foragers stole or appropriated their food and equipment. Their humble life today without modern conveniences is still a mirror of the Amish communities during the war.

"Eno's folly" The nickname for the Fifth Avenue Hotel in New York, built by Amos R. Eno. It was called a folly because of his extravagance in building a six-story "white marble palace." The lobby contained a massive white marble staircase, and the hotel had the first elevator in the U.S. The building also fronted Broadway, 23rd Street, and 24th Street. It opened in 1860 just before the beginning of the war, which threw it into financial difficulties, but the Fifth Avenue Hotel survived to earn the title of "the best house in the city."

Enrollment Act The United States conscription law passed on March 3, 1863, which required men aged 20 to 45 to enroll to be selected for three years of military service. Substitutes could be hired (as President Abraham Lincoln did, although he was too old to fight) or exemptions bought by paying the government $300. Major General Henry W. Halleck complained of the act, "It takes more soldiers to enforce it than we get from its enforcement." The first drawing of names in New York City led to DRAFT RI-OTS on July 13, 1863. Other violent but smaller protests occurred in several cities, including Boston; Portsmouth, New Hampshire; Wooster, Ohio; Troy, New York; and Rutland, Vermont. *See also* three-hundred-dollar clause.

ensign This lowest commissioned rank in the Union navy was created in 1862 during the war. It was derived from the British ensign, the lowest grade of commissioned army officer, who had carried the ensign (banner or flag) as far back as the sixteenth century.

environ To surround, encircle, or envelop. During the war, on September 24, 1862, President Lincoln said he was "environed with difficulties." A day after capturing Vicksburg, Mississippi, Union Major General W.T. Sherman wrote his wife on July 5, 1863, that he looked forward to a quiet home where they could prepare their children "for the dangers which may environ their later life."

epaulment A defensive work on the sides of a BATTERY to protect it from flanking fire. It was usually made up of bags of earth, GABIONS, or FASCINES.

equipage 1. The arms and equipment of a soldier. "Camp equipage" included camp furniture, tents, utensils, and other items. 2. A carriage with its horses and liveried servants.

Ericsson's folly A northern nickname for the Union's first IRONCLAD ship, the *Monitor*, designed by John Ericsson. It was also called "Ericsson's Iron Pot." Ericsson was a Swedish engineer who had lived in the U.S. since 1839. Many thought his heavy vessel would immediately sink when launched.

erysipelas A localized rash or inflammation of the skin or mucous membranes,

accompanied by fever, a common result of battlefield wounds. It is caused by a streptococcus, but doctors during the war believed it was an airborne infection and isolated such patients. The only treatment known was to dab iodine around the wound because this halted its expansion.

esplanade An open space of ground in a fort that is used to drill or exercise troops.

the Essayons A dramatic group formed by Union soliders of the 50th New York Engineers. As engineers, they had little trouble building stages, such as the fine timbered one they constructed in 1864 while in camp in Petersburg, Virginia.

essence of coffee A type of coffee in the Union army, composed of coffee, Borden's condensed milk, and sugar. The concentrated mixture was described as resembling grease and tasted too vile for most soldiers. It was soon removed as a ration item.

essence pedler A humorous name for a skunk.

ether A general anesthetic used by camp doctors. The supply was limited or nonexistent for Confederate patients because of the Union blockade. Ether had first been used successfully in surgery in 1846 in Boston and was safer than the more powerful (and preferred) CHLOROFORM. It later was the most used anesthetic in the twentieth century. *See also* laudanum; morphia.

Ethiopian A nickname for any black person; the term persisted through the first half of the twentieth century.

euchre A popular card game in camp, with two to four players who often gambled on the results. Only the sevens to aces were used, with each player receiving five cards. The winner was the player or side who named the trumps and successfully took three tricks. When one player or side was prevented from doing this, he or his side was "euchred" and received a score of two. (The verb was also used to mean "to cheat," as in "Those two crooks euchred me.")

European Legion An organization that policed New Orleans in the spring of 1862 after Confederate troops evacuated the city and before Union ones took possession. Union Major General Benjamin F. Butler, commanding the occupying army, invited the European Legion to work with his soldiers because it was "not in arms against the United States, but organized to protect the lives and property of the citizens."

"Evacuating Lee" *See* "Granny Lee."

eventuate To end or terminate; e.g., "This situation has to eventuate."

everybody and his cousin An expression of exaggeration for a lot of people; e.g., "The day we visited the fair, everybody and his cousin were there."

every mother's son A common expression that, from the military standpoint, meant every soldier. Confederate prisoners captured at the battle of Chancellorsville were told by one of their captors that "We'll have every mother's son of you before we go away."

everywheres A incorrect substitute for "everywhere," as in "We looked everywheres for your horse."

every which way This expression, for being or going in all directions, originated with slaves in Virginia.

evil genius The nickname given by RADICAL REPUBLICANS to U.S. Secretary of State William H. Seward because he urged President Abraham Lincoln to resist the Radicals' early calls to free the slaves. He

successfully advised Lincoln to wait until the Union had major military victories before issuing the EMANCIPATION PROCLAMATION. Although he contemplated war with Great Britain, Seward negotiated the TRENT AFFAIR and was instrumental in keeping the British neutral. He was nearly killed in the conspiracy that assassinated Lincoln, but his wife and daughter never recovered from the shock of the attack and both died within the year. Seward recovered to again annoy the Radicals by supporting President Andrew Johnson's conciliatory Reconstruction. After the war, he negotiated the purchase of Alaska, which was known as "Seward's Folly."

evolution Charles Darwin's startling theory of evolution was sprung upon the world two years before the war began and was continually argued about and discussed in military camps and on the home front. Americans on both sides ridiculed the theory because it conflicted with the historical accuracy of the Bible.

Excelsior hat *See* whipple hat.

exchange A newspaper sent to another newspaper office in exchange for one of its issues. This was a common practice during the war to allow journalists to share as much information as possible. An editor usually kept the information in a large "Exchanges" file.

excurt To make an excursion; e.g., "Many of the richest women in New York continued to excurt to Europe during the war."

exempt A name, usually derogatory, for a man who was exempt from military service. It was also applied by regular soldiers to members of the HOME GUARD who avoided combat duty. Confederate Major General Daniel H. Hill lambasted them in 1863: "When our independence is won, the most trifling soldier in the ranks will be more respected, as he is now more respectable, than an army of these skulking exempts."

expectorate A fancy name meaning to spit, especially tobacco juice. When Scotland's Reverend David Macrae visited the United States just after the war, he found his train ticket printed with the following: "Those who *expect-to-rate* as Gentlemen, will not *expectorate* on the floor!"

extacy A early correct (but now obsolete) spelling of "ecstacy." It was used by Robert E. Lee in his letter quoted below in the PERSONATE entry: "Roony has personated your extacies at the sight of the moonlight dancing on the water."

"Extinguish lights" The camp order to put out lamps and candles and go to bed.

"Extra Billy" Nickname of Governor William Smith of Virginia. He was the first to seriously propose, in the war's last year, that the South arm its slaves to fight the Yankees. His nickname came after he had once ordered an extra stagecoach for a journey.

Extra Press Edition A special, extra edition of a newspaper printed to rush out important news and hawked loudly on the street by NEWSIES. "War Extras" were expected following major battles and crowds gathered outside New York newspaper offices to await them and the latest military news released in Washington, D.C. Condensed war bulletins were also posted outside newspaper buildings. After moving from New York to Washington, D.C., Eliza Howland wrote, "One longs now and then for a real living and lying 'Extra' boy, with his mouth full of fearful statements, all disproved by his paper which you imprudently buy." During World War II, "Extras" were still hawked by newsboys with the familiar cry of "Extra, extra, read all about it!"

"The Eye" The nickname for Allan Pinkerson, who headed the Union's SECRET SERVICE. This name later evolved into all private investigators being called "private eyes."

eye-opener A slang name, still used, for the first alcoholic drink taken early in the day.

"eyes and ears of my army" The nickname given by Confederate General Robert E. Lee to Major General JEB STUART, whom Lee said "never brought me a piece of false information." *See also* "Gay Cavalier"; raid around the army

"eyes of the army" A nickname for the U.S. cavalry, given by Major General Joseph Hooker after he took charge of the Army of the Potomac on January 26, 1863. He expanded, and gave special recognition to, the cavalry, which had been virtually ignored by one of his predecessors, General George McClellan.

F

Faber No. 2 A popular brand of pencil, especially favored by northern journalists covering the war.

face the music This expression, still meaning to face up to unpleasant consequences or punishment, was coined in the U.S. about a decade before the war. It has been associated with "THE ROGUE'S MARCH," which was used to drum a soldier out of the service.

facing Trimming on a uniform, as on the collar and cuffs. The style was prescribed, but officers were often inventive, especially in the war's early days.

fagged out A slang term for being fatigued or worn out; e.g., "How could Old Pap march us all night and not expect everyone to be fagged out?"

falderal or folderol 1. Complete nonsense, especially foolish talk or ideas; e.g., "The war was lost, but President Davis was still full of falderal about saving the cause." 2. A trinket or trifle; e.g., "His sister gave paper flowers and other folderols to soldiers at the hospital."

fallen angel A euphemism for a prostitute. In 1863, the Washington *Star* estimated that central Washington, D.C., had about 5,000 prostitutes, with half as many more in Georgetown and Alexandria. *See also* clap; daughter of Eve; drab; fancy girl; fast house; gay young duck; "The Haystack"; "Hooker's Division"; "Madam Russell's Bake Oven"; parlor house; ranch; The Wolf's Dream.

fallen into his last sleep A romantic euphemism for "died." *See also* gone home; gone up.

Falls City The nickname for Louisville, Kentucky, which was a major Union army headquarters and supply depot throughout the war. The name refers to the city's location by the waterfall of the Ohio River.

fancy A special photograph that was not the usual picture of a family member. These included photos of beautiful women, actors, outdoor scenes, and biblical and allegorical poses. Fancies were usually put on the last pages of photo albums.

fancy girl A euphemism for a prostitute. *See also* fallen angel. *See also* clap; daughter of Eve; drab; fallen angel; fast house; gay young duck; "The Haystack"; "Hooker's Division"; "Madam Russell's Bake Oven"; parlor house; ranch; The Wolf's Dream.

fanny A slang name for the bottom. The name, which was derived from the feminine name Fanny (perhaps from the novel *Fanny Hill*), became established during the war.

"Fanny" A nickname for Union Major General George Armstrong Custer, because of his beautiful long yellow hair.

farmer A mocking name for anyone from a rural area, whether a farmer or not. It was also used in direct address; e.g., "Hey, Farmer, missing your pigs?"

faro A popular card game for gambling in camp. Players bet on the order of cards to be revealed when the dealer removed them singly from the top of the deck. The name came from the picture of a pharaoh used for the king on the original French cards used for the game. *See also* bucking the tiger; tiger den.

Far South A name used during the war for the Southwest.

fascine Bundles of small sticks used to reinforce earthworks. Normally sandbags or cotton bales would be used, but facines were the best substitute on a field. The sticks were tied together at the ends and one or two more times along their lengths. They were also used to fill or strengthen the sides of ditches. This French word meant, simply, a bundle of sticks. A fascine looked like an ABATIS.

fast house A slang name for a house of prostitution. *See also* clap; daughter of Eve; drab; fallen angel; fancy girl; gay young duck; "The Haystack"; "Hooker's Division"; "Madam Russell's Bake Oven"; parlor house; ranch; The Wolf's Dream.

fast trick A nickname for a woman of easy virtue; e.g., "I knew Hattie was sweet, but her sister was a fast trick."

"Father Abraham" A popular nickname among Union soldiers and civilians for President Abraham Lincoln.

"Father Neptune" The nickname given by U.S. President Abraham Lincoln to Gideon Welles, his secretary of the navy, who had a white Neptune-like beard. Others also called Welles "Old Father Neptune." Welles took over a 90-ship navy, oversaw the construction of 136 ships in the first year of the war, and eventually increased its strength to 670 ships. His daily diary, the only complete one kept by a Union cabinet member, is one of the most important accounts of the war. *See also* Uncle Gideon.

"Father of Annapolis" The nickname of Confederate Admiral Franklin Buchanan, because he had helped plan the U.S. Naval Academy and was its first superintendent. A native of Maryland, Buchanan commanded the *Virginia* (*Merrimac*) in its famous IRONCLAD confrontation with the *Monitor*. He was later defeated at the battle of Mobile Bay by Admiral David Farragut.

"Father of Waters" A nickname for the Mississippi River. After Union Major General Nathaniel P. Banks captured Port Hudson, the last Confederate stronghold on the river, on July 9, 1863, President Lincoln told the nation that "The Father of Waters goes again unvexed to the sea."

fatigue duty Any work around camp that is not associated with strict military drilling, instruction, or other training. Fatigue duty would include such unpleasant jobs as POLICING, digging the SINKS, and feeding or burying horses.

"Faugh!" An explosive exclamation of disgust or contempt; e.g., "Faugh! Smell the pork they are sending us now."

"Fed and Cornfed" A joke among Confederate soldiers near the end of the war, because they often survived on parched corn. It was a shortening of "Federal and Confederate."

Federalists, Federals, or Feds Names for Union troops. At the first battle of Bull Run in 1861, Frank Vizetelly, an artist with the *Illustrated London News*, told a British journalist that "the action had been commenced in splendid style by the Federalists." Confederate Lieutenant General "STONEWALL" Jackson, out of respect, always referred to the enemy as Federals and never as Yankees.

federal principle A system adopted by some northern charity organizations, such as the Woman's Central Relief Association, that boxes of medical supplies, clothing, and food donated by the public could not be designated for a particular regiment or individual.

feeler Artillery fire aimed in the supposed direction of the enemy to see if they were there or were strong enough to respond. Before the battle of Jonesboro, Georgia, on August 31, 1864, one southern soldier watched his guns "feeling for the Yankees" and joked that "it is impossible to tell of the movements of the enemy, because our cannon balls had not come back and reported any movements to us."

"feeling above his fellows" A common expression used by soldiers to describe a friend who had become a line officer and, they believed, was feeling too superior to them; e.g., "Davis has had straps on his shoulders for two months and is already feeling above his fellows."

feel streaked or feel streaky To feel alarmed or confused; e.g., "When the Rebels charged us at Gettysburg, I believe every man felt a little streaked."

Fenian Brotherhood A revolutionary, armed Irish-American society active during the war. It was founded by John O'Mahony in 1858 and was especially intent on attacking British Canada. When Confederates began using Canada as a base for incursions into Union states, the Fenians offered President Lincoln their services to prevent such invasions, but the president turned them down. During the war, Fenians on the Union and Confederate sides met secretly in the winter of 1862-63 near Falmouth, Virginia, to plot post-war attacks against England. After the war, the organization conducted terrorist raids into Canada to avenge and discourage Britain's occupation of Ireland. The raids ended in 1877, when O'Mahony died and the Fenian Brotherhood broke up.

fetch up To come to a quick stop; e.g., "There was movement in the cornfield, and we saw our advance guard fetch up." The phrase "fetch up all standing" was also used, having evolved from a sailor's term for a ship that halts suddenly while her sails are still set.

F.F.V. The abbreviation for First Families of Virginia, a proud social distinction in that state.

fiddle-de-dee! or fiddle-dee-dee! An expression of exasperation that was equivalent to "Nonsense!" It was popular during the war (as Margaret Mitchell demonstrated through Scarlett O'Hara in her novel *Gone With the Wind*) but was at least 200 years older.

field-artillery Light artillery, such as cannons and mortars, used on the field of battle.

field-gun *See* field-piece.

field hand The general term for a slave who worked the land. Field hands were the lowest class of slaves who were not trained to join a GANG of skilled workers.

field hospital The military hospital that handled casualties from the battlefield after the victims had received emergency treatment at the ADVANCE STATION. A field hospital, usually five miles or more from the battle scene, was often a church, school, or house. Union hospitals were marked by a green "H" in the center of a yellow flag having a green border and, if time permitted, small flags marked the path from battlefield to hospital. Wounds were often treated by placing patients under the influence of strong whiskey and drugs like opium and morphine. Because speed was important during large battles, arms and legs were quickly amputated in preference to an uncertain longer-term treatment. During the first year of the war, a field hospital was most often a wall tent, officially called the regi-ment hospital tent. The hospital corps usually consisted of a surgeon, assistant surgeon, steward, ward-master, four nurses, two cooks, and a man who did general work, such as cut wood and carry water. "God pity the world," wrote Union nurse James Kendall Hosmer in 1863, "if it has sights in it more melancholy than a military hospital!"

field officer An army officer with the rank of colonel, lieutenant colonel, or major.

field-piece or field-gun A small cannon transported on a light carriage and used on the field of battle. *See also* piece.

fieldwork or work Any temporary protection thrown up by infantry soldiers, such as a trench or earth barrier. Fieldworks

James Gibson photographed this field hospital at Savage Station, Virginia, in late June 1862. The men pictured here were wounded during the series of battles around Richmond that became known as the Seven Days. *Library of Congress, Prints & Photographs Division, LC-B8171-0491.*

were either defensive positions or protective ones used during an assault on an enemy's fort or other defenses.

fife A small flute used in the bands of both armies. It usually had six holes, and the sharp whistling sound provided a sweet balance to the rhythmic rattle of the drums. The Union fifes were made of fine rosewood; Confederate ones came in three different sizes.

fifth wheel A derogatory description of the SANITARY COMMISSION when it was first planned. Skeptics felt that it would be a useless "fifth wheel to the coach" to have extra civilian personnel running about trying to improve the conditions of soldiers.

fig Something worthless or of little consequence. Modern usage is negative—"I don't care a fig" or "it's not worth a fig"—but during the Civil War people spoke insultingly of giving a fig about someone or something. During the Union occupation of Fredericksburg, Virginia, Betty Maury began making clothes at home and exclaimed in her diary on August 18, 1862, "Hurrah for domestic manufactures, and a fig for the Yankees. We can do without them."

"fighting editor" An editor kept on a newspaper staff, especially in the South, to fight or duel with furious readers who threatened to assault the owner, editors, or writers over articles. After his 1886 travels through the South and visits with editors, the Scotsman David Macrae wrote that if a member of the public went to the "writing editor" to demand satisfaction for being branded a liar, "he handed you over politely to the fighting editor,—the gentleman who managed the pistolling department."

"Fighting Joe" A nickname for Union Major General Joseph Hooker, who claimed he disliked it because the public would think he was "a hot-headed, furious young fellow, accustomed to making furious and needless dashes at the enemy." The name was acquired by accident when the ASSOCIATED PRESS used the slug (label) "Fighting—Joe Hooker" on a routine story, and some newspaper changed it into the headline, "Fighting Joe Hooker." On January 21, 1863, Hooker confided to a journalist that President Lincoln was an imbecile and the country needed a military dictator. Four days later, by coincidence, Lincoln asked him to command the Army of the Potomac. Hooker efficiently reorganized it but was relieved in May after being badly defeated by General Robert E. Lee at the battle of Chancellorsville. On November 24, Hooker commanded two corps of his old army to victory in the "BATTLE ABOVE THE CLOUDS." *See also* Lookout.

"Fighting McCooks" An Ohio family that sent 17 men to the war as officers, including six who became generals. They included three brothers, Major General Alexander McCook, Brigadier General Daniel McCook and Brigadier General Robert L. McCook (the latter two were killed), and their cousin, Brigadier General Edward M. McCook, who was with Major General W.T. Sherman on his March through Georgia in 1864.

"Fighting Parson" 1. The nickname for Union Colonel John Milton Chivington, because he had been the presiding elder of the Rocky Mountain Methodist District. Chivington's Christian fellowship was not extended to Indians. He took a break from the war to massacre 600 Cheyennes and Arapahoes, including women and children, at Sand Creek in Colorado in 1864. Asked why he killed children, the Fighting Parson explained, "Nits make lice." 2. The nickname for William Gannaway Brownlow, a Tennessee Methodist preacher who left the church to found and edit a newspaper, the *Knoxville Whig*, in which he espoused his pro-Union and anti-war opinions (although he supported slavery). His presses were destroyed, and he was imprisoned and then banished to the North where he wrote a best-seller, *Sketches of the Rise, Progress, and Decline of Secession*. When Knoxville was occupied by Union troops, Brownlow returned to edit his paper. He was later elected as governor of Tennessee (1865-69), succeeding Andrew Johnson, and then as U.S. senator. *See also* "Parson."

"Fighting Phil" A nickname given by his men to Union Major General Philip Sheridan, whom most called "LITTLE PHIL." Known for his bad temper, he was usually victorious when he ordered his troops into battle. See also "Smash 'em up! Smash 'em up!"

"fighting suit" A special black velvet suit that Confederate Brigadier General Ben McCulloch wore instead of a uniform. Black was a symbolic color for McCulloch, who followed the "BLACK FLAG" policy toward Yankee prisoners. A native of Tennessee, he was a former hunter, trapper, and Indian fighter who had served under Sam Houston during the war for Texas independence and who had led a company of Texas Rangers. McCulloch was killed on March 7, 1862, leading his brigade in the confused fighting at Pea Ridge in Arkansas.

fighting the tiger *See* bucking the tiger.

"Fight it out on this line" Words that became a household phrase in the North in 1864 to indicate Union General Ulysses Grant's determination to stick to an original plan of action. It usually meant meeting the enemy's forces head-on and staying there as long as it took to outfight or outlast them. The phrase derived from suggestions by Grant's officers that he try a different approach to Richmond after the Union failure on May 5 and 6, 1864, to push back General Robert E. Lee's army at the battle of the Wilderness. Grant replied, "No, I propose to fight it

out on this line if it takes all summer." He had shown the same attitude a year earlier when a Confederate woman asked him when he intended to capture Vicksburg, Mississippi. "I don't know when," said Grant, "but I shall take it, if I stay here 30 years."

fight like fun To fight furiously; e.g., "The Texans were cornered, but they fought like fun." A similar expression was to "fight like sin."

"fight man fashion" A saying often heard on both sides early in the war, meaning a soldier should bravely face up to enemy fire. This West Point saying was based on the idea that you would reveal your fear to the enemy if you dug trenches and hid behind breastworks. The reality of battle soon disproved this old theory.

file closer During a forward-moving attack, a soldier assigned to a detail that moved laggards up into the line, even by the use of a bayonet.

fillip Something that stimulates or incites. After the South won the first battle of Bull Run in 1861, the Confederate diarist Mary Chesnut warned that "the shameful farce of their [the Yankees'] flight will wake every inch of their manhood. It was the very fillip they needed."

"finest army on the planet" The Union nickname for its Army of the Potomac.

finif, finnif, or finiff A slang name for a five-dollar note or a total of five dollars. The name came from the Yiddish language.

"fire and brimstone!" A popular exclamation, usually of anger. It was a eupemistic way of saying "Hell!" One Confederate private recalled leaving his place during a march to collect a newer rifle at the roadside, only to draw the wrath of his colonel: "Fire and brimstone! What are you doing out of ranks?"

"Fire at will." The order given to soldiers, usually in defensive positions, to shoot when they feel it is necessary, rather than to wait until the enemy advances within a certain distance.

fire away To begin or continue, especially in speaking. Borrowed from the military, this term existed before the war. Audience members would tell a speaker to fire away, and an auctioneer might use the expression to ask buyers to begin bidding.

fireball A coal substitute used in southern houses when the coal supply dwindled during the war. Fireballs were hard clumps of sawdust and coal dust stuck together with clay and sand.

fireboard A decorative panel used in a home to hide the fireplace during the summer.

fire-eater An ardent defender of slavery and the South. The nickname was first given to extremist southern senators before the war, but once the Confederacy was established, both men and women in the South proudly called themselves fire-eaters. In April 1862, General Albert Sidney Johnston was killed by a MINIÉ BALL at the battle of Shiloh while riding a bay horse named Fire-eater.

"fire in the rear" Criticism from your own side. President Abraham Lincoln used it in 1863 to refer to northern Democrats, especially those who opposed conscription and emancipation.

fire laddie An informal name for a fireman. Members of volunteer fire companies were known for their courage and often became local heroes.

fire raft A raft set ablaze and sent drifting toward a warship. The intention was to set the enemy ship's rigging and hull on fire. When the fleet of Union Captain David Farragut approached the Missis-sippi channel below New Orleans, Confederate Captain George N. Hollins had nearly 50 unmanned fire rafts constructed to ride the current into the enemy. The rafts were piled with pine knots soaked in turpentine and with barrels of resin and tar. They were then sent downriver toward MORTAR boats, but, as one Yankee wrote, "we would tow them ashore as soon as they would come round the point." However, Farragut's flagship, *Hartford*, was set ablaze by one raft; the *Hartford* survived only because its crew quickly extinguished the fire. *See also* fire ship; powder boat.

fire-room The boiler room of a warship or other steamship. The power was provided by coal. After Union General Benjamin F. Butler's POWDER BOAT attack on Fort Fisher in North Carolina went awry, the rapid retreat of his flagship caused one Union sailor to remark that it "spoke well for the energy of her fire-room force!"

fire-sheet lightning A term used to describe the flash of a cannon at night. Soldiers who were the target could become experts at timing the arrival of the shell.

fire ship A wooden ship set afire and drifted toward the enemy fleet in the manner of a FIRE RAFT (ships were used less frequently than rafts). The most lethal fire ship was one filled with explosives, if the timing of the explosion was correctly estimated. *See also* powder boat.

fire-step A step in a trench that allowed soldiers to fire over the parapet at the enemy.

first classman A fourth-year cadet at the U.S. Military Academy at West Point, New York. He was thus in the class to graduate that year.

"First in Vicksburg" The motto Union Major General W.T. Sherman authorized his men to add to their colors, for leading an attack on the Mississippi city on May 19, 1863. Unfortunately, they were also the first out of Vicksburg, being repelled by the enemy and losing 43 percent of their force as casualties. During the attack, the 13th Infantry flag was riddled by 55 bullet holes.

first luff A nickname for a first lieutenant in the navy. It was first used in the U.S. navy about a decade before the war began.

First National *See* Stars and Bars.

fish trap A slang name for the mouth; e.g., "Shut your ugly fish trap."

fit to be tied A common expression during the war that described, as it still does today, someone who was angry, frustrated, or annoyed; e.g., "When General Lee saw President Davis ride up during the skirmish, he was fit to be tied."

Fitz The nickname for Confederate Major General Fitzhugh Lee, a nephew of General Robert E. Lee (being the son of his brother, Sydney Smith Lee). Fitz fought Indians before the war, and led his cavalry brigade at Antietam, Gettysburg, and Spotsylvania. After the war, he was governor of Virginia from 1885 to 1889 and then fought in the Spanish-American War.

fixed fact A true or well-established fact. Often the term was overused and unreliable; e.g., "That the Yankees won't fight is a fixed fact."

fixings Secondary dishes at a meal or garnishings for a particular dish; e.g., "Anna served potatoes as fixings for the fish."

fix-up An alcoholic drink, such as whiskey; e.g., "No grog was allowed on ship, but Andrews knew where we could acquire a fix-up."

fizz An alcoholic drink that was a SOUR made with soda water.

flag officer A naval officer in command of a squadron or fleet. President Abraham Lincoln had the authority to appoint any naval captain or commander to the position, rank, and title of flag officer.

flam A lie or false story. It was also used as a verb meaning to deceive someone with a false story. The word was taken from "flim-flam." Robert E. Lee once wrote of a friend that "the rumour of his marriage is all flam."

flank The common word for outflanking someone or something, used in the two following ways: 1. To go around the flank of the enemy, thereby avoiding them. This idea was often used creatively, as when one hungry Confederate suffering from a shortage of food in General Joseph E. Johnston's army wrote in his diary that he had "flanked" his dinner. 2. To outwit or thwart someone. A soldier often talked of flanking a sentinel, guard, or officer.

flankers Soldiers formed into a single line to march parallel to the main column. If enemy troops were close by, flankers were put out on both sides. On a road, each column of flankers was a few feet from the main troops. This distance increased to about 30 yards in woods and about 60 yards in open country. If an attack was made on one side, those flankers became the skirmish line, defending until the main column went into action.

flapdoodle A slang word for foolish talk or nonsense. Also used as an interjection, the term is related to an older word, fadoodle, which also means nonsense or something ridiculous.

flat A flatboat or river barge. When Yankee gunboats approached Baton Rouge, Louisiana, on April 26, 1862, plantation owners and their slaves piled bales of cotton onto flats, doused them with alcohol, and set them on fire to drift down the Mississippi, denying the enemy this valuable product.

flatfoot A nickname for a slave or free Negro, because most of their work was done standing.

fleam A small surgical knife or a type of lancet also called a "bleeder." It was used by surgeons for bloodletting, which was still a common practice during the war. Fleams were often spring activated.

flicker A slang name for a coward, usually repeated several times. Private Sam Watkins of the 1st Tennessee Regiment recalled these taunts hurled by enlisted men at a colonel retreating during the battle of Chickamauga: "baa, baa, black sheep; flicker, flicker; ain't you ashamed of yourself? flicker, flicker." The name came from the yellow streak on a yellowhammer (woodpecker). The bird was especially found in Alabama, which has been nicknamed the "Yellowhammer State," so Alabama troops often had to endure a good-natured round of "flicker, flicker, flicker" as they marched by their compatriots.

flimsy A slang name for a thin piece of paper. During the war, such paper was often used to send insults or bad news to the other side, with the flimsy wrapped around a rock or other heavy object and tossed into the enemy lines. The name was also often applied to telegrams and banknotes.

flounce A piece of ruffled cloth sewn as a decorative strip or border to a lady's skirt or sleeves. Flounces were much in evidence at dances, such as at President Abraham Lincoln's inaugural balls.

flub dubs A slang term for insignificant odds and ends. President Abraham Lincoln complained to Major B. B. French,

the commissioner of public buildings, about the excessive amount of money that Mrs. Lincoln had spent on the White House by "over-running an appropriation of $20,000 for flub dubs."

flummox A slang word for a failure; e.g., "The cavalry raid was one great flummox." The verb was also used; e.g., "It looked simple, but we flummoxed the mission."

flunk out To back out or retreat, especially through fear; e.g., "As soon as our regiment charged, we could see the Rebels flunking out."

flux Diarrhea, one of the more medically related names used by soldiers, with flux being the bowel discharge caused by the disease. *See also* bloody flux.

fly-away A person who is flighty or runs away. One Union woman nurse early in the war wrote what people at home were saying about her decision: "Goodness me! A nurse! All nonsense! Such a fly-away!"

flying artillery or horse artillery The swiftest branch of the artillery, because each CANNONEER rode his own horse. Normally in the light artillery, they would either ride on the gun carriage or march beside it. The flying artillery, usually equipped with 10-pounder rifled guns, was so mobile it could easily accompany the cavalry.

"Flying Cloud" The nickname given by Confederate soldiers to the Mohawk chief, Konshattountzchette, a member of the South's 1st Kentucky Brigade. Few people could pronounce or spell his real name. He had a frightening face, created by a Union bullet that had removed part of his upper jaw, but his fellow soldiers found this to be an advantage when foraging. They would send Flying Cloud into yards and slave cabins to terrify the occupants with war yells before he requested a donation of food. When it arrived, usually in a few minutes, the chief would give a kindly smile and add his assurance, "Me no hurt you."

flying telegraph train A Union train that transported two BEARDSLEE TELEGRAPH instruments and their accompanying equipment. About 30 trains were used, with each telegraph having its own wagon.

flying torch *See* talking torch.

fly-up-the-creek A nickname for a person from Florida, because the small green heron seen throughout the state was commonly called this.

F.M.C. or F.W.C. Initials for "Free Man of Color" and "Free Woman of Color." The initials were used even before the war, and many free blacks and freed slaves who could write would attach the initials after their names.

fogeyism The policy in the U.S. army up until the Civil War that allowed senior officers to remain in commanding positions for years. The U.S. Commissary General George Gibson held his post from 1818 until 1861. Fogeyism meant that new officers often had to wait decades for promotion.

food for powder A term that meant something like "target for a gun." One Union soldier, released from LIBBY PRISON in Richmond on PAROLE to his own home, was notified three weeks later by his company that he had been officially exchanged, which, he wrote "meant that I was again, legally and technically, food for powder."

"Fool Tom Jackson" A derisive nickname given by some of his men to Confederate Lieutenant General Thomas "STONEWALL" Jackson. The name was a play on Jackson's earlier nickname of "Tom

Fool," which was given to him by the cadets he taught at the Virginia Military Institute. On one forced march in 1862, as they struggled through the mountains of Virginia in snow, sleet, wind, and rain, a few of Jackson's soldiers spoke the name as he rode by, loud enough for him to hear.

foot torch *See* talking torch.

forage cap A soft, woolen cap with a visor that was preferred by soldiers on both sides. It was comfortable and informal, being worn for fatigue duty or with casual dress. The cap, basically a floppy version of the SHAKO, was sometimes called a McDowell cap, named for Union Major General Irvin McDowell, who had taught at the U.S. Military Academy before the war. *See also* Hardee hat.

Forage cap. *Copyright Inge Wright 1999.*

foraging The act of scouring the land for food. Both sides became experts at this, with the poorer Confederate troops often relying on foraging to eat, and Union soldiers eventually considering it as a just form of retribution on southern civilians. Early in the war, Union generals believed that taking crops and animals from enemy farms would unite the South even more, so troops were forbidden to take personal property. Later, however, it was decided that these food items might be sent to Rebel soldiers. Union Major General W.T. Sherman was at first horrified to see civilian property taken by his troops, who it was said could "catch, scrape, and skin a hog without a soldier leaving the ranks." On July 7, 1862, Sherman issued orders that said "Stealing, robbery and pillage have become so common in this army that it is a disgrace to any civilized people. This demoralizing and disgraceful practice of pillage must cease, else the country will rise on us and justly shoot us down like dogs and wild beasts." By 1865, however, he was encouraging the worst examples of foragers, known as *SHERMAN'S BUMMERS, during his march through Georgia. However, many religious and conscience-stricken Union and Confederate soldiers refused throughout the war to steal the property of civilians.

fore-handed An adjective to describe someone who is comfortably off, especially financially; e.g., "By the time the poker games ended, I had become a fore-handed man."

"Foreign News" After South Carolina seceded from the Union, the *Charleston Mercury* gave this title to its column of news from the northern states.

"Form square!" The order to infrantrymen to form a HOLLOW SQUARE for defense. This command might be followed by orders of "Platoons right and left wheel!" and "Kneel and fire!"

"Fort Damnation" *See* "Fort Hell."

"Fort Greenhow" The nickname for the home of Mrs. Rose O'Neal Greenhow, a Confederate spy who was sentenced to house arrest in Washington, D.C., on August 23, 1861, by Alan Pinkerton, who headed the Union's SECRET SERVICE. The federals also confined other Confederate women spies in her home. Mrs. Greenhow, a widow, continued to direct spying from "Fort Greenhow" until she was banished to the South on June 2,

1862. She published a book, *My Imprisonment*, in 1863 in London. *See also* "my little bird"; trust bearer.

"Fort Hell" The nickname used by both sides for the Union's Fort Sedgwick, because of the deadly artillery fire that issued from it each dawn and dusk during the siege of Peterburg, Virginia (June 19, 1864, to April 2, 1865). The fort was located east of Petersburg on the south end of the Union entrenchments. Fort Mahone, the Confederate fort opposing it, was dubbed "Fort Damnation."

fortified town A city or town in which war materials were stored. The enemy considered such a place fair game for bombardment. Union Major General W.T. Sherman justified his shelling of Atlanta by saying, "I was not bound by the laws of war to give notice of the shelling of Atlanta, a 'fortified town' with magazines, arsenals, foundries and public stores."

"Fort Pillow Butcher" *See* "Wizard of the Saddle."

Fort Pillow massacre A northern name for the "indiscriminate slaughter" of black Union soldiers on April 12, 1864, during the recapture of Fort Pillow, Tennessee, 40 miles north of Memphis. The attackers were the troops of Lieutenant General Nathan Bedford Forrest, who became known in the North as "the Fort Pillow Butcher." His 1,500 men surrounded the fort and demanded its surrender. Union Major William F. Bradford requested an hour to decide because he was awaiting reinforcments. Forrest gave him 20 minutes, then attacked, forcing the Union soldiers out of the fort and down the bank of the Mississippi River. Many tried to surrender, but the Rebels supposedly shot them, especially the men of the 11th UNITED STATES COLORED TROOPS. Confederate reports said the enemy had continued to fight. The Union suffered 221 men killed and 100 wounded, the Confederates 14 killed and 86 wounded. Only 20 percent of the black soldiers were taken prisoner, but nearly 60 percent of the whites. Forrest reported after the battle that "The river was dyed with the blood of the slaughtered for 200 yards. It is hoped that these facts will demonstrate to the northern people that negro soldiers cannot cope with Southerners." The U.S. Congressional Committee on the Conduct of the War concluded that the Union men had been murdered while trying to surrender and some black soldiers had been buried alive.

Fort Sumter Medal A bronze disk-shaped memorial medal (not to be worn) awarded to each of the Union defenders of Fort Sumter by the New York Chamber of Commerce. It was approved on June 6, 1861, eight weeks after the Charleston fort surrendered, and personally awarded in a ceremony in May 1862.

forty The nickname for a 40-acre farm; e.g., "I wouldn't have one of those small forties if they gave it to me." Other farms had similar designations, such as a "sixty."

"forty acres and a mule" The slogan supposedly used by the FREEDMEN'S BUREAU for distributing confiscated and abandoned land after the war, but less than 1 percent of the former slaves received land from the government.

forty dead men An soldier's optimistic nickname for a CARTRIDGE-BOX, because it held 40 rounds.

"forty-rod" A nickname for strong alcohol, because it supposedly could kill a person from 40 rods (220 yards) away.

"Forty Thieves" The nickname for a gang of youthful robbers who operated in Washington, D.C., during the war.

"For Your Eyes Only" A classification used during the war for secret or sensitive documents and letters. When President-elect Abraham Lincoln wrote Confederate Vice President Alexander H. Stephens in December 1860, promising he would not interfere with the institution of slavery, he marked the letter "For Your Eyes Only."

fougasse A land mine placed in the path of advancing troops. It was usually an artillery shell or mortar bomb buried 6 to 12 inches under the ground. The explosion was set off by a percussion fuse activated when the enemy marched over the hidden weapon.

four corners A name for any small or rural place, because of the four corners created by a crossroads; e.g., "What four corners does Abraham Lincoln come from?"

"four-finger drinker" The term used to describe the drinking habits of Union General Ulysses S. Grant. He would hold a glass with his little finger even with the bottom, rest three fingers above the little one, fill the glass with whiskey up to the top finger and drink it without adding water.

"four old friends" Confederate General Robert E. Lee's nickname for the four fountain pens he carried through the war. When his cousin Martha Custis Williams sent him new pens just after the war ended, Lee wrote her on June 24, 1865, that "you have forced me to give my four old friends, that have continued with me in heat & cold, care & danger, to wounded rebels, & replace them by new ones. It gives me acute pain to part with old friends, though as in this case, I may be the gainer."

Fourth of July America's Independence Day was still treasured by many Confederates. Unlike the U.S. flag, which was banned as an enemy banner, the Fourth of July was generally respected because it was the day of independence from Great Britain (won by the Virginian, George Washington). Betty Maury, a Virginian, noted in her diary on July 4, 1861 that "Not a gun was heard this morning. I hope our old National holidays will not be dropped by the Southern Confederacy."

fox To repair the upper part of a boot with new leather.

Fox Union General Ulysses S. Grant's roan horse at the battle of Shiloh. *See also* Cincinnati; Jack; Kangaroo.

fox and geese A popular board game in camps. It was played somewhat like checkers with pieces called the geese moved over the board to try and surround or corner one piece called the fox.

"Fox of Kinderhook" A nickname for former President Martin Van Buren, an antislavery supporter, in recognition of his cunning political maneuvers and because he was from Kinderhook, New York. *See also* "Little Magician."

"Fox of the White House" A nickname for U.S. Secretary of State William S. Seward, because of his subtle diplomatic skills. The name was popularized by the North's famed female orator Anne E. Dickinson, who disliked Seward's moderate views.

Franklin stove An open cast-iron stove used to heat a room. It resembled a fireplace, but some versions could be closed by doors in front. The stove was named for Benjamin Franklin, who invented it.

frazzled or frazzled out A slang term for being drunk; e.g., "Jim was frazzled out before we met the girls." See DRUNK for numerous other terms referring to intoxication.

free delivery The U.S. system of free mail delivery within a city, inaugurated to help communications during the war.

Freedmen's Bureau The common name for a bureau formed by the U.S. Congress to help former slaves. It was established on March 4, 1865, five weeks before General Robert E. Lee's surrender, with the official title of the Bureau of Refugees, Freedmen, and Abandoned Lands. Headed by Major General Oliver O. Howard, it had little funding or personnel and was hurt by corruption among its agents who took advantage of the former slaves. Still, the bureau distributed clothes and food to more than four million new citizens, gave them confiscated and abandoned land, and built "Freemen's Villages," schools, colleges, and hospitals. The organization made some small progress concerning civil rights before it was dissolved in 1872. Howard founded Howard College for Negroes in 1867 in Washington, D.C., and was its first president.

Fremont's proclamation A proclamation issued on August 30, 1861, by Union Major General John C. Fremont, commander of the Western Department. Declaring martial law in Missouri, the proclamation said anyone in the northern portion of the state with arms would be court-martialed and shot if found guilty of bearing arms. It added that slaves would be freed if their owners took up arms against the Union or supported such an action. President Abraham Lincoln, however, informed Fremont that nobody should be shot without the president's authorization because the Confederates would "shoot our best man in their hands in retaliation; and so, man for man, indefinitely." Lincoln also requested that the statement liberating slaves be modified because it was "objectionable in its nonconformity" to a congressional act and "will alarm our Southern Union friends and turn them against us." The president later told Fremont's wife that "It was a war for a great national idea, the Union, and that General Fremont should not have dragged the negro into it." On November 2, 1861, Lincoln removed Fremont from his command. In 1864, Fremont ran unsuccessfully against Lincoln as a presidential candidate for the new Radical Democracy Party. *See also* "New Orleans, and home again by summer!"

French fever A euphemism for syphilis, because sexual activity was supposedly rampant in France.

French leave A euphemism for desertion or being A.W.O.L. During the war, one out of seven Union soldiers deserted and one out of nine Confederates. The expression came from eighteenth-century France, where guests would leave a reception without informing the host or hostess.

freshet A river flood caused by rain or melting snow. Union Major General George Stoneman, halted from crossing the Rappahannock River on April 15, 1863, reported that "The railroad bridge has been partly carried away by the freshet."

fresh fish A humorous name for new recuits or new prisoners. When a new man or regiment arrived for training, the veterans filled the air with laughter and calls of "fresh fish."

fried shirt *See* boiled shirt.

frock coat A close-fitting and often double-breasted military or civilian coat that reached to the knees.

frog 1. A slang name for a policeman, because he jumped people. 2. A slang name for a worthless or despicable person.

frogging On a uniform, the braided or corded trimming in the form of loops,

Frock coat. *Copyright Inge Wright 1999.*

sometimes resembling a three-leaf clover. The trimming was decorative but also often used to fasten a coat. Frogging was usually gold, but other colors were seen, including black worn on the gray uniforms at West Point during the war. Zouave frogging included red on blue uniforms and yellow on red ones.

frolic A happy or wild time or party or an event marked by frivolity. A member of the 12th Georgia Regiment recalled a battle on August 9, 1862, at Cedar Mountain, Virginia, in which his fellow Georgians talked and laughed throughout the fight, acting "as if we had been invited to a frolic."

from A to Izzard A variation of the phrase "from A to Z." "Izzard" was a dialectic word for "Z" and was derived from "zed," which is still used in Great Britain.

the front *See* color line.

front-door yard The front yard of a house.

fuddled A slang name for being drunk. See DRUNK for numerous other terms referring to intoxication.

full chisel At great speed or quickly, used in the same way as LICKETY-SPLIT or lickerty-cut.

full drive A common term meaning full speed; e.g., "The cassions lumbered down the plank road at full drive." The expression goes back to the fourteenth century, being used by Geoffrey Chaucer in the *Canterbury Tales*.

full split Done in a furious rush and with great violence; e.g., "The first line of Ohioans charged the Rebel guns at full split, yelling and firing as they came."

full swing Full sway or control over a situation; e.g., "From the time they left Atlanta, Sherman's troops had full swing over the countryside."

"the fun" A light-hearted name that war correspondents used for any battle; e.g., "Let's stay with the brigade or we'll miss the fun."

furlough Official temporary military leave. Some officers offered them as prizes for bravery, and cowardly soldiers sometimes tried to be slightly wounded to receive one. (A popular Confederate story said an officer asked a soldier why he was standing behind a tree during a battle and waving his hands out on both sides. "I'm feeling for a furlough," he replied.) When Confederate Private Sam R. Watkins was granted one, he discovered that "Everywhere I went someone wanted to see my furlough." Worst, almost everyone seemed to have a false one: "Men who I knew had never been in the army in their lives, all had furloughs." He concluded that "It has a sickening sound in the ring of it—'furlough!'" When Rebel soldiers were asked for their furloughs as they deserted home after the battle of Gettysburg, many were allowed to proceed after they patted their guns and said "This is my furlough."

further West A general term usually applied to the area beyond the Mississippi River, known also as the TRANS-MISSISSIPPI. President Jefferson Davis often spoke of "the further West" when he voiced his concern for the welfare of southerners in that region.

F.W.C. *See* F.M.C.

G

gabion Large hollow rolls of wicker filled with earth and stones and used by a besieging force. Gabions were protective devices rolled in front of soldiers who were digging trenches closer and closer to the enemy's fortifications. They were also used to fortify field positions. When Union IRONCLAD WARSHIPS attacked stonewall forts, such as Fort Sumter, the Confederate defenders found that the soft gabions were the best reinforcement, but they had to be constantly renewed.

gaff In COCK FIGHTING, a needle-sharp steel spur fitted over the spur of a gamecock.

gal-boy Another name, especially in New England, for a tom-boy.

"Gallant Hood" The nickname for Confederate General John B. Hood, who was known for his bravery and bold fighting abilities. As a leader of men, however, he acquired a reputation for bad judgment. Hood's arm was crippled at Gettysburg, and he lost a leg after being wounded at Chickamauga, forcing him to be strapped to his horse when he went into battle thereafter. He was given command of the Army of Tennessee and soon wrecked it. He lost 15,000 men hopelessly trying to save Atlanta from Major General W.T. Sherman. Deciding on the bold strategy of invading Tennessee, he quickly marched his men northward for senseless attacks against larger Union forces, and was badly defeated at the battles of Franklin and Nashville. In the latter, where about 1,500 of his men were killed or wounded and another 4,500 captured, Hood was seen pulling his hair and sobbing. After the war, he moved to New Orleans, married, had 11 children in 10 years, and died with his wife and a daughter in a yellow fever epidemic. See also "Old Wooden Head"; "Yellow Rose of Texas."

gallanting Courting a woman, although the word often had more sinister meanings, as when the Washington *Star* complained about soldiers "gallanting the painted Jezebels with which the city is stocked."

"Gallant Pelham" The nickname given to Confederate Major John Pelham of Alabama by General Robert E. Lee, after seeing him fight at the battle of Fredericksburg in December 1862. "It is glorious to see such courage in one so young!" enthused Lee of the 23-year-old artillery commander under Major General Jeb Stuart. Pelham, also called "the boy major," was a handsome but modest man known for flirting with females throughout the South. When he was killed at Kelly's Ford, Virginia, Stuart wept and said "Our loss is irreparable." (Three young women in the vicinity donned mourning dress.) At Lee's appeal to President Jefferson Davis, Pelham was promoted lieutenant colonel posthumously.

gallinippers A nickname given, especially by Confederate soldiers, to large mosquitoes.

galloping consumption *See* consumption.

gallowses Another name for a pair of suspenders for pants.

"Gal on the Log" A tune used for square dances in the South. Diaries show that women visitors to camps had danced to it, but soldiers more often did so by pairing off in a STAG DANCE.

galoot or geeloot A recruit or awkward soldier. Originally applied to marines by sailors, the name was a good-natured slight. It quickly entered the American language to describe any clumsy, ill-mannered person, especially from a rural area.

galop A fast round dance in 2/4 time in which the dancers moved in a circle. It came from Germany.

galoshes Overshoes worn to protect everyday shoes from water, mud, dirt, etc. The name was common in the nineteenth century.

galvanized Yankee A Union soldier who fought in the Confederate army, often to gain release from a Confederate prison. "To galvanize" meant to confer a false vitality upon something, and this meaning came from the process of galvanizing that used an electric current to coat iron with zinc as a protection. "Galvanized

Confederates" also existed in smaller numbers.

gam A slang word for a chat or social call; e.g., "During the night, pickets from both sides got together for a 30-minute gam." The noun "gamming" was also used.

gambado A sprightly leap or antic. One woman, writing about the flourishing caper of a slave stepping off a path to let her pass, described the movement as "so sudden, grotesque, uncouth, and yet dexterous a gambado."

"Gamecock of the South" The nickname of Jefferson Davis when he served in the U.S. Senate and as U.S. secretary of war before becoming the Confederacy's president.

gander dance *See* stag dance.

gander-pulling A cruel but popular gambling sport in which cavalrymen or other horsemen tried at full gallop to wrench off the head of a live gander hung by his legs. The task was extremely difficult because of the erratic dodging of the frantic bird's head and because the soldiers usually plucked and greased the head and neck. Gander-pullings were often held at dress parades. Some birds survived the contest for up to three hours before tiring and being beheaded. One writer said Ulysses Grant took part in the sport before the war in 1844 while a lieutenant stationed at Camp Salubrity near Natchitoches, Louisiana.

gang A respectable name for a group of workers in the same trade. On a plantation, trained slaves were organized into gangs of blacksmiths, bricklayers, coopers, carpenters, and other skilled workers. *See also* field hand.

garibaldi A woman's or girl's loose blouse that had a high neck and full sleeves. It was named for and imitated the red shirts worn by Italy's General Giuseppe Garibaldi and his followers. The first blouse versions were red, but later any color was used.

Garibaldi Guard The nickname of the 39th New York Infantry Regiment made up mostly of Italian-Americans from New York City. Many had fought in Italy under Giuseppe Garibaldi in his republican uprising and continued to wear the distinctive Garibaldi red shirt during the Civil War. However, many other nationalities were represented in the unit, including soldiers with German, Hungarian, Spanish, and Swiss backgrounds.

garret The common name for an attic. Southern women used it as a popular but usually futile hiding place to keep valuables from Yankee soldiers. One lady was overjoyed when the invaders overlooked her whole gilt-edged china set stored there. Another had less luck, recording that the Yankees had laughed at seeing the meager supplies in the pantry, "but their laughter was immense when on ascending to the garret they saw the hens and chickens running over the floor."

"Gath" The pen named used by George Alfred Townsend, the *New York Herald*'s war correspondent (though "correspondent," not "war correspondent," was the only term then used). He covered the war from the Seven Days' battles in 1862 to the fall of Richmond in 1865.

Gatling gun A famous early machine gun invented by Dr. Richard J. Gatling. Mounted on wheels, it had up to 10 barrels rotated by a hand crank. The gun could fire up to 350 rounds a minute with an effective range of 2,000 yards. Twelve .577-caliber guns of the original basic design were sold at $1,000 each to Union General Benjamin Butler, who used them during the long siege of Petersburg, Virginia, which ended on April 2, 1865. That same year, the Union army tested an ad-

vanced design and asked Gatling to build a one-inch caliber gun that could fire balls for long-range warfare or buckshot for close engagements. As he eagerly worked on the task, the war ended. The gun was adopted by the army the following year.

"Gay Cavalier" A nickname for Confederate Major General JEB STUART. The name came from his dashing gallantry when leading his famed cavalry. He wore a yellow sash and black plume, as well as golden spurs. Stuart also had a happy devil-may-care personality and played the BANJO. See also "Beauty"; "eyes of the army"; "Jeb"; raid around the army.

gay young duck A humorous euphemism for a prostitute. *See also* clap; daughter of Eve; drab; fallen angel; fancy girl; fast house; "The Haystack"; "Hooker's Division"; "Madam Russell's Bake Oven"; parlor house; ranch; The Wolf's Dream.

G.D. or G.d. Initials for "God-damned," as in "On Saturday, our G.D. captain refused to allow any man to leave the ship."

"Gee rod!" An exclamation of excitement; e.g., "Gee rod! How those Johnnies skedaddled!"

"Gee whillikins!" or "Gee whillikers!" A mild exclamation of surprise, being a euphemism for "Jesus." By the end of the nineteenth century, it had become "Gee whizz!"

gelt A nickname for money. It was derived from the German word, *Geld*, which was pronounced "gelt." The Union army had numerous Germans in the ranks.

"General" A Confederate train engine stolen on April 12, 1862, on the railroad line between Atlanta, Georgia, and Chattanooga, Tennessee, by Captain James J. Andrews, a Union spy, and by 21 Union soldiers dressed in civilian clothes. Their plan was to tear up the track, but they were pursued by Captain W.A. Fuller, a conductor on the Western & Atlantic Railroad, and Anthony Murphy, a roundhouse foreman. The two men ran on foot until meeting a handcar and its crew. They later encountered and switched to two different engines, changing because Andrews's men had destroyed some track, which eventually forced the Confederates on foot again. With luck, they met a train pulled by the "Texas" engine and, filling a car with volunteers, ran it backward in pursuit. As the pursuers closed in on the "General," Andrews delayed them with a number of obstacles, including two released cars, crossties thrown onto the track, and a burning boxcar. The "Texas" overhauled the "General" at the Georgia-Tennessee line. Andrews and his men dashed into the woods, but most were captured.

"The General" A bugle call used by the Union infantry and, in a different arrangement, by the artillery. It instructed soldiers to strike their tents to be packed in the wagon train. "The General" was seldom used after the first two years of the war because the DOG TENT came into use and was carried on soldiers' backs.

general government Another name for the U.S. federal government. The Massachusetts writer Nathaniel Hawthorn, in an article in the July 1862 issue of *Atlantic Monthly*, said that allegiance to "the State comes nearest home to a man's feelings, and includes the altar and the hearth, while the General Government claims his devotion only to an airy mode of law, and has no symbol but a flag."

"General Horace" A nickname for Horace Greeley, the owner of the New York *Tribune*, for his constant advice on how the war should be run, including his newspaper's "ON TO RICHMOND" campaign. He was given credit for the advice, "GO WEST, YOUNG MAN, GO WEST."

general hospital A large military hospital that took any type of patient requiring long-term medical care. This freed beds in FIELD HOSPITALS for newly wounded soldiers.

general-in-chief The Union title for a general in charge of large armies. In the early days of the war, Major General George McClellan was appointed General-in-Chief of the Army of the Potomac. General Ulysses S. Grant was given full control of the war on March 12, 1864, when he was made General-in-Chief of the Armies of the United States, giving him overall command of all Union forces in both the Eastern and Western Theaters.

general officer An army officer above the rank of colonel, which would be a brigadier general, major general, lieutenant general, and general.

General Orders No. 11 *See* "Grant's Jew Order."

General Orders No. 28 The infamous orders issued on May 15, 1862, by Union Major General Benjamin F. Butler, commanding the troops that occupied New Orleans. It compared disrespectful ladies in the city with prostitutes and was the main reason the South nicknamed him "BEAST" Butler. The order read as follows:

> As the Officers and Soldiers of the United States have been subject to repeated insults from the women calling themselves ladies of New Orleans, in return for the most scrupulous non-interference and courtesy on our part, it is ordered that hereafter when any Female shall, by word, gesture, or movement, insult or show contempt for any officer of the United States, she shall be regarded and held liable to be treated as a woman of the town plying her avocation.

The humiliating order was read by Confederate General P.G.T. Beauregard (from Louisiana) to his men, after which he gave the following plea:

Men of the South! Shall our mothers, our wives, our daughters and our sisters, be thus outraged by the ruffianly soldiers of the North, to whom is given the right to treat, at their pleasure, the ladies of the South as common harlots? Arouse friends, and drive back from our soil, those infamous invaders of our homes and disturbers of our family ties.

The outrage spread across the Atlantic, with the London press repeating the "Beast" epitath and British prime minister, Lord Palmerston, saying, "Any Englishman must blush to think that such an act has been committed by one belonging to the Anglo-Saxon race." Butler, however, said he had copied the order from London statutes: "I changed 'London' into 'New Orleans'; that was all. The rest I copied *verbatim et literatim*."

"General Starvation" A Union gibe yelled at Confederate soldiers during the siege of Vicksburg. A typical taunt would be something like, "Have you got your new general yet, Johnny? General Starvation?"

"General Tom Thumb" The stage name of the dwarf Charles S. Stratton, who was presented by the showman P.T. Barnum during the war. When appearing with Barnum's circus in Washington, D.C., Tom Thumb was said to be the most admired general in the nation's capital. He was then 25 and stood 32 inches high. He had been with Barnum's show since the age of 4 when he was only 24 inches. In 1863, Stratton married Lavinia Warren, 22, another dwarf, and they were entertained at a private reception given in the White House by Mrs. Lincoln.

general treat A round of drinks bought by a person for everyone in a saloon, tavern, or other drinking establishment, the same as today's "drinks on the house."

"General Tubman" The nickname given by the abolitionist John Brown to Harriet Tubman, who was also called "Moses." A former slave, Tubman helped some 300 slaves escape to the North. Brown said she was "one of the best and bravest persons on this continent."

"Gentle Annie" or "Gentle Anna" See "Michigan Annie."

gentleman of color A respectful or facetious name for a black man.

"Gentleman's Agreement" The term chosen by Union Major General George B. McClellan to describe his official agreement with newspaper correspondents: They would publish nothing to aid or comfort the enemy, and he would provide them with suitable military information and the telegraph service to transmit their reports immediately. The agreement was signed on August 2, 1861, with 12 correspondents serving as representatives for all northern newspapers.

gentlemen A polite form of address among officers, even when ordering men into battle. A typical example occurred when Confederate Major General Jeb Stuart woke his officers at 2 o'clock one morning with the words, "Gentlemen, in ten minutes every man must be in his saddle!"

Georgia State Line A MILITIA organization in Georgia that evolved from the BRIDGE GUARD. Established on December 13, 1863, the State Line forces grew to two infantry regiments and a cavalry company, all members being exempt from serving in the regular Confederate army. The State Line also opened its own hospital in Savannah in 1864. *See also* Virginia State Line.

the German A common name for the German cotillion, a type of QUADRILLE dance with an elaborate set of steps and figures. The dance leader devised the figures and the other dancers were obliged to follow them. The German became fashionable during and after the war, although critics complained about the "liberties" taken by the couples as they danced.

Gervais Street A street in Columbia, South Carolina, well known to soldiers as the brothel district. When Union troops occupied and burned the city on February 17, 1865, one of the first fires was set in the low wooden houses of Gervais Street.

get a beat on A slang expression meaning to get the jump on someone or to have an advantage over someone; e.g., "Before Hooker knew it, Lee had got a beat on his right wing." A similar expression was "to get the run on."

get it A slang expression, first heard during the war, meaning to be wounded or killed by gunfire; e.g., "I saw O'Ryan raise the colors just before he got it."

get the mitten To be jilted by a sweetheart or rejected as a suitor. This was a common fear among soldiers, although they could also give someone the mitten. The equivalent in World War II was to get a Dear John letter.

get the run on *See* get a beat on.

get the wrong pig by the tail or get the wrong sow by the ear To accuse the wrong person; e.g., "If you think I would steal your old mess kettle," Davis said, "you've got the wrong pig by the tail."

getting the starch out of one's shirt Working hard. The expression was a favorite of the artillerymen commanded by Confederate Lieutenant Colonel William T. Poague.

get up and dust *See* get up and get.

get up and get An expression meaning to move quickly. A Confederate soldier having his morning coffee and listening to the braying of the enemy's mules in the distance, remarked, "It's time to git up and git. There are Sherman's trumpeters!" A similar expression was "get up and dust."

gewgaw A showy but inexpensive ornament, like a bauble or trinket. It often meant a child's toy. In his 1857 book, THE IMPENDING CRISIS OF THE SOUTH, the southerner Hinton Rowan Helper warned that almost all the South's products came from the North, including "in childhood" when "we are humored with Northern gewgaws."

ghost A slang name for a DAGUERREOTYPE photograph because of its ghost-like image. *See also* shadow.

G.I. The abbreviation in both armies for "galvanized iron." Some sources believe the nickname for a World War II soldier came from this term instead of from "Government Issue."

Giant of Battles A large, brilliant rose variety, especially popular in the South.

"Gibraltar of the West" A southern nickname for Vicksburg, Mississippi, whose location on heights over the Mississippi River seemed virtually impregnable. The name was popularized by Confederate President Jefferson Davis. To take the city, Union General Ulysses Grant had to conduct a 14-month campaign, ending with a 6-week seige that forced the starved city to surrender on July 4, 1863. Vicksburg refused to celebrate the Fourth of July until 1945. *See also* "Defender of Vicksburg"; "the nailhead."

gig A light, open, two-wheeled carriage drawn by one horse; a chaise. The name was especially used in New York. *See also* buggy; chair.

gig or gigi A slave and southern word for a toy or other object to which a child is especially attached. The words come from "gri-gri" or "gris-gris," the name of a voodoo fetish.

gill A measurement of four ounces used for spirits. Union sailors were given a daily ration of one gill of rum mixed with water.

Gillmore Medal of Honor A medal created by Union Major General Quincy A. Gillmore, commander of the Department of the South, who awarded it to soldiers who had served with distinction during the siege of the Charleston area from July 10 to September 6, 1863. One side of the medal depicted the destroyed Fort Sumter with the date "Aug. 23d 1863" (when the fort was recaptured), and the other side had "For Gallant and Meritorius Conduct" along with an inscription of the general's signature.

gimp A slang name for courage or vitality; e.g., "After McClellan took command, all the boys had gimp or thought they had."

gin barrel A nickname for a drunk person; e.g., "They said that Grant was just a blue gin barrel." See DRUNK for numerous other terms referring to intoxication.

ginger beer A fermented drink that often replaced liquor in the South during the blockade. Made of ginger, molasses, and water, it was heated for fermentation.

ginger cake A sweet cake beloved by soldiers and overpriced by SUTLERS.

ginger panada *See* bully soup.

"ginned cotton" A nickname among Confederate soldiers for bread made of a poor quality of flour. It was often part of their rations, and also went by the name of "leather."

"Gipsies" *See* Iowa Grey Hounds.

give someone goss To beat or kill someone, often in revenge. In the battle of Shiloh, a badly wounded colonel of the 23rd Tennessee Regiment recognized newly arrived troops from his state and yelled: "Give 'em goss, boys!" That's right, my brave First Tennessee. Give 'em Hail Columbia!"

glanders A contagious and fatal disease that killed many horses and mules in both armies. The bacteria caused swollen lymph glands, inflamed mucous membranes in the nose, skin ulcers, and fever. Soldiers spoke of a "glandered horse."

glass A common name for a field glass or binocular telescope. A southern lady in Vicksburg recalled searching for Yankees on the opposite side of the Mississippi River in 1863, saying "we ranged the shore with the glass, seeing what the gentlemen believed to be a battery."

Glorious Cause A descriptive southern name for the Civil War.

gloze Flattery. When Varina Davis, the wife of Confederate President Jefferson Davis, was introduced to the ladies of Richmond in July 1861, she wrote that she was impressed with their simplicity and sincerity and "the absence of the gloze acquired by association in the merely 'fashionable society.'"

goatee or goaty This name for a pointed beard on the chin, meaning "little goat," became popular during the war, having first appeared about two decades before.

"Go boil your shirt!" A soldier's irritable dismissal of someone. It was equivalent to "Go fly a kite!"

go by To visit. This southern expression originated among people on plantations, who were separated by miles from their neighbors. They often rode across the countryside, and neighbors would invite them to "go by" their house, meaning to stop in. The invitation was often to "go by and dine with us."

go callyhooting A slang expression meaning to move in a quick and loud way; e.g., "It seemed like the whole camp went callyhooting toward the new sutler's wagon."

"God Save the South" The title of a song published in 1863, with words by George H. Miles and music by C.T. DeCoeniel. It was optimistically sold as "Our National Confederate Anthem."

going down the line A euphemism for visiting prostitutes.

go it bald-headed or go at something bald-headed To rush to do something; e.g., "Carson first saw the rabbit and went at it bald-headed." The image is of hurrying eagerly without taking time to put on a hat.

go it blind To agree to something without considering it carefully; e.g., "Once you have your orders, you simply go it blind and suffer the consequences."

go it strong To do something with great energy and enthusiasm; e.g., "Randall was no fighter, but he could go it strong in a poker game."

Gold Hoax The greatest journalism hoax of the war. On May 18, 1864, Joseph Howard, Jr., an editor, and Francis A. Mallison, a reporter, both on the *Brooklyn Eagle*, created a false ASSOCIATED PRESS report of a document from President Abraham Lincoln (with his forged signature) saying General Ulysses Grant's campaign in Virginia had failed, a draft of 400,000 men was required, and the president had designated May 26 as a day of

"fasting, humiliation and prayer." The opening of "Fellow Citizens of the United States" was not a phrase used by Lincoln in proclamations, and editors were suspicious. The story was only printed by two newspapers, the *New York World* and the *Journal of Commerce*. Lincoln was furious and had to postpone his planned call for 300,000 volunteers. The hoaxers and the two duped editors were imprisoned for a few months. The phony story had been created to raise the value of gold (by lowering confidence in greenbacks) so the men could make a profit. Howard, who later became a successful journalist, also wanted to embarrass editors who had refused to employ him.

gone above An expression meaning "died," a variation on GONE UP. *See also* gone goose; gone home; goner.

gone goose Someone too wounded or ill to recover. The name was often used before the preposition "with," as in "The bullet missed his heart, but it looks like a gone goose with him." Variations included "gone gander," "gone gosling," "gone chicken," "gone beaver," and "gone coon." *See also* gone above; gone home; goner; gone up.

gone home A common euphemism for "died." Also popular was "gone to his reward." *See also* gone above; gone goose; goner; gone up.

goner Someone who is dead or about to die. The term, still common, was popular during the war. An Iowa soldier wrote that "when a man gives up and lies down he is a goner." *See also* gone above; gone goose; gone home; gone up.

"Gone to the War" A sentimental poem published in the North by Horatio Alger, Jr., and published in 1861. It takes the viewpoint of a mother and the first two verses set the tone:

My Charlie has gone to the war,
My Charlie so brave and tall;
He left his plough in the furrow
And flew at his country's call.
May God in safety keep him,
My precious boy—my all.

My heart is pining to see him,
I miss him every day;
My heart is weary with waiting,
And sick of the long delay.
But I know his country needs him,
And I could not bid him stay.

gone up or gone up the spout 1. Be killed. Confederate Private Sam Watkins recalled his first thought when he was surprised by a line of Union soldiers: "I'm gone up now, sure." (They turned out to be prisoners.) A Georgia soldier home on a sick FURLOUGH decided there was no need to fight again for the Confederacy "for we are done gone up the Spout." The expression was also used if something went awry or was bungled. A soldier would describe a failed military maneuver as "gone up." 2. To be destroyed or ruined. People said "Richmond's gone up" when it was captured and "the Confederacy has gone up" when General Robert E. Lee surrendered in 1865. *See also* gone above; gone goose; gone home; goner.

gone with A southern term meaning "become of," used for people or things; e.g., "What's gone with gentlemen officers and chivalry?"

goniff or gonif A slang name for a thief or swindler. The word was also a verb; e.g., "He was trying to goniff me out of five dollars."

goober or goober pea A name for a peanut, heard mostly in the Deep South. It evolved from the Bantu word, *nguba*. A comic song in southern camps told of a Confederate general who feared the Yankees were attacking when he heard cracking and popping, only to discover that it was "the whole Georgia MILITIA, eating

goober peas." One Louisiana soldier with a spelling problem recorded that his unit received 12 "gobers pease" in lieu of four days of sugar. Confederates also brewed a coffee substitute from parched peanuts.

goober grabber A nickname in southern camps for a soldier from Georgia, because of the popularity of peanuts in that state. It was also applied to men from Arkansas and North Carolina.

good egg An informal name for a good person or a fine fellow. The expression is still used in Great Britain. When a Pennsylvania delegation asked President Abraham Lincoln to promote Brigadier General Samuel P. Heintzelman to major general, he refused, joking that Heintzelman was "a good egg" and therefore would soldier on if promotion was delayed.

good fellow Sometimes a stealthy way of calling a person stupid or a fool. This meaning was derived from the context and a condescending voice; e.g., "The corporal won't know you're gone. He's a good fellow."

goose A clothes iron with a handle curved like a goose's neck. The handle was sometimes called the goose. A new volunteer in Massachusetts leaving with his unit for Washington, D.C., in 1861, later recalled that the town's young ladies gave almost every recruit "an embryo tailor's shop, with the goose outside."

gooseberry vinegar A vinegar substitute made by fermenting mashed gooseberries, sugar, water, and yeast.

goose egg Zero, especially in a game's score; nothing. This comparison with a goose's large egg was first used about a decade before the war began.

goose squad A group of new recruits being trained in the basics of marching.

goosestep A basic military drill for balance practiced at West Point and elsewhere. The cadet or recruit stood on one leg and swung the other one forward and backward; he then alternated the exercise from one leg to the other.

gopher chase A soldier's slang expression for digging an entrenchment, or a GOPHER HOLE, while under fire; e.g., "Murray was wounded while on a gopher chase."

gopher hole A dug-out shelter. Soldiers in winter quarters would sometimes dig gopher holes in the side of a ravine and create a makeshift room with the addition of logs and earth. Confederate soldiers used the name for the small cellars dug by civilians to hide in while the enemy occupied or passed through their area. Women and children hid in gopher holes they dug under Atlanta homes when the city was shelled by Major General W.T. Sherman's troops.

gorm A slang word meaning to eat voraciously like a glutton. It was a shortened form of "gormandize."

"Gorry!" A mild oath, being a euphemism for "God." A soldier might exclaim, "Gorry! I thought we were goners that time."

"Gosh almighty!" A mild oath, being a euphemism for "God almighty!" Another version was "Gosh all!"

"Gosh darn" or "Gosh dern!" A mild oath, being a euphemism for "God damn." Variations included "Gosh-dang," "Gosh-danged!," and "Gosh-ding!"

go sparking To go courting, an expression used mostly in the North; e.g., "When Jim returned from Boston, you could see he had been sparking."

go the entire animal *See* go the whole hog.

go the whole critter *See* go the whole hog.

go the whole figure or go the big figure To go the whole way, or to the fullest extent, to achieve something; e.g., "Our regiment always goes the whole figure for victory."

go the whole hog To do something completely or boldly, an expression commonly used before and during the war, and still popular. Also used was "go the whole critter" and a refined version suitable for parlor conversations, "go the entire animal."

gov This short form for "governor" existed during the war; e.g., "The gov says we can send 4,000 more men if needed."

government suit A slang term for a military uniform.

"Go west, young man, go west" A popular expression before and during the war, attributed to Horace Greeley, owner of the New York *Tribune*. He had used the thought in an 1851 editorial, advising "Go west, young man, and grow with the country." Although Greeley said John Soul had created it earlier in the year in the *Terre Haute Express* in Indiana, the public continued to associate him with the catch phrase.

grab a root To eat dinner, especially to eat potatoes.

graft To repair a boot with new soles and to FOX the upper part.

grafter 1. A swindler or cheat; e.g., "He said many of the companies producing military equipment were run by grafters." 2. A thief, such as a pickpocket.

graham bread Bread made with unsifted wheat. It was considered to be easier to digest and was often served to invalids. The name derived from Sylvester Graham, a famous nineteenth-century vegetarian. *See also* Graham system.

Graham system A popular vegetarian health diet advocated by Sylvester Graham, a temperance lecturer who was active several years before the war. "Grahamites" who followed his strict diet could not even drink tea or coffee. He especially recommended the use of whole-wheat flour that was coarsely ground and not sifted, which gave the name to graham crackers, graham wafers, graham flour, and GRAHAM BREAD. Civilians who had attempted the diet found it impossible to maintain after becoming soldiers.

grand division A giant military unit that existed briefly in the Union's Army of the Potomac. For a few months in 1862, Major General Ambrose Burnside combined his several CORPS into a Center Grand Division, a Right Grand Division, and a Left Grand Division. After the defeat at Fredericksburg and Burnside's dismissal, the grand divisions were broken up.

"Granny Lee" A derisive nickname that southern newspapers gave Confederate General Robert E. Lee in March 1861 when he retreated South before the Union army of General George McClellan as it advanced through what would soon become West Virginia. Some reports called the Confederate commander "Evacuating Lee."

Grant, U.H. The signature used by Ulysses Grant on personal letters until he left West Point. Grant had been named Hiram Ulysses Grant, but his parents called him by his middle name, so he simply reversed his first two names. Officials at West Point mistakenly recorded him as U. S. Grant, and he began to use this after graduating, but always informed others that the "S" stood for nothing.

"Grant's Jew Order" An informal name for General Orders No. 11 issued by Union General Ulysses Grant on December 17, 1862, ordering Jews to be removed from his area of operations. In a case of bad judgment and worse prejudice, Grant ordered that "The Jews, as a class violating every regulation of trade established by the Treasury Department and also Department orders, are hereby expelled from the department within twenty-four hours from receipt of this order." The previous month, he had denied trading permits to the "Israelites." Grant was reacting to news of corruption among northern merchants who were permitted to trade with southern cotton planters in occupied areas. After official Jewish complaints, President Abraham Lincoln decided on January 1, 1863, to have the order repealed, noting that the government could not blame a whole class, "some of whom are fighting in our ranks."

grape coffee A southern coffee substitute used during the Union blockade. The seeds of grapes were boiled to produce the drink, an idea borrowed from German-Americans. *See also* burnt sugar coffee; cane seed coffee; chinquapin coffee; okra coffee; pea coffee; potato and persimmon coffee; rye coffee; war coffee.

grape shot or grape A type of cannon ammunition used for a range extending to about 400 yards. Similar to CANISTER SHOT, it consisted of SAND SHOT packed in a canvas bag attached to a wooden base. This package was tightly tied with twine causing the small balls to protrude in a grape-like shape. When fired, the sand shot would scatter. Grape shot added little to the better coverage of CANISTER SHOT and SPHERICAL CASE SHOT, and it disappeared before the war ended.

grapevine A personal, unofficial means of passing along news or rumors. The term, short for the "grapevine telegraph," was created in 1862 after soldiers saw telegraph wires that had collapsed and lay twisted on the ground like grapevines, an obviously unreliable system of information.

grapey A slang word to describe someone who was grumpy or bad tempered, as in "our grapey captain."

grass An informal name for asparagus, because a dialect version was "sparrow-grass." Some people wrongly thought "asparagus" had been derived from "sparrow-grass."

graveyard coughing The gloomy name given by soldiers to the fits of coughing heard around camps at night. The coughs often resulted from pneumonia, influenza, or other serious ailments.

The Gray The Confederate forces or the Confederacy, because of the color of the military uniform.

grayback or graycoat A Confederate soldier, because of the color of his uniform.

graybacks A humorous name for lice. Both sides found it impossible to rid camps of the creatures, and even took up the sport of racing them. One soldier said he had stopped killing graybacks because "I believe 40 of them comes to every one's funeral." Another who watched a soldier busy "cracking graybacks" said that "it reminded me of an old woman knitting." A Confederate private gave up trying to remove them from his uniform, saying it was useless to "scald, scour, scrub, clean, rub, purify, or bury the raiment under ground" because "they only seemed to enjoy it and multiplied under the process."

Graybeard Regiment The 37th Iowa Volunteer Infantry, because it was restricted to men over the age of 45. The War Department established it to prove that older men who could avoid the draft ("draft-proof") were able to fight for the Union.

graycoat *See* grayback.

"Gray Fox" *See* "Uncle George."

gray ghost The nickname given to a Confederate BLOCKADE RUNNER, because such ships feathered their propellers for relatively quiet passages and burned smokeless coal to help hide their positions.

"Gray Ghost" A nickname for Confederate Colonel John S. Mosby, because he always slipped away from his pursuers. Mosby was a lawyer who led his PARTISAN RANGERS, the 43rd Battalion of Virginia Cavalry, on raids behind Union lines in Maryland and Virginia. When Major General Philip Sheridan sent a contingent of 100 soldiers to capture him in 1864, Mosby's men killed or captured 98 of them. During the war, he captured two Union generals and claimed to have just missed General Grant. Grant ordered that Mosby be immediately hanged if captured, but after the war the two men became close friends, and the former Gray Ghost, to the horror of his southern friends, supported Grant's successful campaign for president.

grease A slang name for money, because it caused things to go easily.

greased pig contest A competition staged in some camps, although Confederate soldiers were normally too hungry to play with their food beforehand. In the winter of 1863, Union Major General George Meade's troops had time to engage in both greased pig and greased pole contests.

greaser This insulting nickname for a Mexican was coined about 25 years before the war and was well known throughout the Southwest.

"Great Bear of Wall Street" The nickname for Jacob Little, one of the most famous brokers on the New York Stock Exchange prior to the war, and said to be able to sway the market at will. The war's effect on the market, however, produced disasterous losses for Little, and he died in poverty in 1861.

great-coat A large heavy overcoat. The name has been used since the seventeenth century. During the war, they were often of flannel, double-breasted, and with capes.

"greatest crime of the ages" The title given to the Civil War by the *New York Times* on May 1, 1865. The paper called the war "a crime costing the lives of more than half a milllion men, and aimed at the overthrow of the best government the world ever saw."

"Great Hammerer" A nickname given by northern newspapers to Union General Ulysses Grant after his successes at Vicksburg and Chattanooga in 1863.

"Great Jerusalem!" An mild exclamation of surprise or anger, although it was a euphemism for "Great Jesus!"

"Great Rebellion" *See* War of Rebellion.

Great Scott! A popular exclamation of surprise during the war. A euphemism for "Great God," it was derived from the name pinned on Winfield Scott for his pompous attitude as a (losing) presidential candidate in 1852.

Great Seal of the Confederacy This seal consisted of George Washington on his horse encircled by a wreath showing the South's main agricultural products: cotton, tobacco, corn, wheat, sugar cane, and rice. The margin contained the motto, "Deo Vindice" and the words "The Confederate States of America, 22 February 1862." The date, Washington's birthday, was chosen for the inauguration of the permanent Confederate government. The seal was authorized on April 30, 1863, by House Joint Resolution No. 13.

Great Skedaddle The Union army's nickname for its defeat and hasty retreat at the first battle of Bull Run on July 21, 1861. The North, however, usually used the verb SKEDADDLE to describe retreating Rebel soldiers.

"Great snakes!" An exclamation of surprise, considered to be a mild oath; e.g., "Great snakes! Look at that damn flood."

Great Snowball Battle A famous snowball fight among Confederate soldiers of the Army of Tennessee. Snowball battles, called "snow balling," often occurred on both sides, but none equalled this wild warfare, which took place in March 1864 in winter quarters at Dalton, Georgia. The casual tossing of snowballs among the lower ranks escalated until regimental battles began and even generals rushed to lead the icy attacks. During the "fun," a number of soldiers had their eyes put out by the missiles.

Greek A humorous and common slang name for an Irishman. Some sources suggest the connection arose because both races were considered to be happy and roisterous. Writers, as far back as William Shakespeare, had often commented on the "merry Greeks."

Greek fire The mixture of inflammable liquids (usually tar, turpentine, and resin) placed in a CARCASS shell. Sometimes called a "carcass mixture," the sticky concoction stuck to anything when the shell exploded. Greek fire also appeared in other forms: eight Confederate agents set 19 fires in New York City hotels on November 25, 1864, using four-ounce bottles filled with the mixture.

greenbacks This name was invented by Union soldiers for paper money, officially known as Demand Notes. U.S. Secretary of the Treasury Salmon Chase printed the green bills in 1862 as the first federal paper money. The name was sometimes shortened to "greens." The troops were among the first to receive them. Chase included his own picture on them because he hoped to run for president. They also carried the new notice: "This note is a legal tender." *See also* bluebacks.

greenhorn The insulting name for an inexperienced person. Soldiers used it with special venom to describe unpopular or unskilled officers.

greens *See* greenbacks.

green sickness A common name for chlorosis, an iron-deficiency anemia, because the skin turns greenish.

"grinding up the seed corn" A metaphor for the war killing good young men. It was a favorite expression of Confederate President Jefferson Davis, who said the South could not afford to grind up the seed corn.

grit A slang word for courage, fortitude, perserverance, etc. It has today been replaced by "guts."

groggery A slang name for a saloon, which was also sometimes called a "grog-hole" or "grog-shanty." *See also* rum-hole.

grog-hole *See* groggery.

grog ration The daily portion of rum diluted with water that was given to sailors in both navies. Union sailors received one GILL (four ounces) of grog a day; Confederates received their ration sporadically due to a restricted supply. On both sides, the grog ration was only enough to create a craving for more, and many sailors

hoarded it until they had enough to get drunk. One navy officer said the rum was the cause of "all insubordination, all misery, every deviltry." Congress eliminated the ration on September 1, 1862, creating the DRY SEAMAN, who was given five cents daily as a replacement. The ration was reinstated, however, after mutinies were threatened. Rum had been called grog since 1745 when a British admiral, Edward Vernon, began the practice of diluting rum on his ships. He wore a cloak of grogram (coarse fabric made of silk, mohair, and worsted) and was called "Old Grog." *See also* "Splice the main brace"; "warrant officers' champagne."

grog-shanty *See* groggery.

ground pea A name for a peanut, especially heard in South Carolina.

grouse A woman as a sexual object, comparing her to a plump game bird. After visiting prostitutes in Petersburg, Virginia, a Confederate soldier wrote in 1864 that "You can get plenty of Grouse here, but you will get wounded [venereal disease] nine times out of ten."

growler A grumbler and usually a general pessimist. This term was similar to a CROCKER.

grub scout A derogatory name devised by the infantry and artillery for a cavalryman.

grubstake Money or provisions obtained by a gold prospector who agreed, in return, to share part of his findings or profits. The name originated in 1863 after recent gold rushes in California (the "fifty-niners"), Nevada, and Arizona. Many soldiers on both sides vowed to get a grubstake after the war and find their fortune.

grub time A slang expression for mealtime. One Confederate soldier wrote that "it was an uphill business for me to wash up 'the things' after 'grub time' in our mess." Food has been called "grub" since the seventeenth century in England.

"Grumble" The nickname for Confederate Brigadier General William E. Jones, because of his nature. He began the war as a colonel in the 1st Virginia Cavalry, and one of his privates was John Mosby, later famous as the GRAY GHOST. Jones was impressed with Mosby as soon as he entered the camp and offered him the position of adjutant. "I was as much astonished," recalled Mosby, "as I had been the night before to be asked to sit at the table with generals." In 1862, Jones commanded the 1st and 7th regiments. He fought at the battle of Gettysburg and was killed on June 5, 1864, when Union forces routed his men at Piedmont, Virginia.

guard-house A military jail. Soldiers would be sentenced there for various periods, from a few hours to more than a month, and many considered the room and board a welcome rest from normal duties. The camp guard-house was usually filled with sentries who had fallen asleep on duty, deserters, and those who had gone A.W.O.L., as well as soldiers who defied orders or engaged in BACK TALK to officers and more minor offenders. Many in the guard-house were awaiting a COURT-MARTIAL. The guard-house at the Confederacy's Fort Clifton (on the Appomattox River about two miles below Petersburg, Virginia) was a two-story wooden building about 12-feet square, one room above the other. Its guard detail was required to remain in the building with the prisoners. Sometimes, when an army was on the move, the "guard-house" was merely a field marked off with ropes and patrolled by sentries.

guerrilla or guerilla A person who fights a war in a small, irregular group, or fights alone. Cordelia Scales, while guarding her home—"Oakland"—in Mississippi

from invading Yankees, wrote as follows to a friend on October 29, 1862: "I know you would take me for a Guerrilla. I never ride now or walk without my pistol. Quite warlike, you see." The name, surviving through the twentieth century, was first used in the early nineteenth century.

guide center to the colors or guide to the colors An order to a long advancing line of troops to watch their flag so a relatively straight line can be maintained. If a man is dropped by gunfire, the man next to him would close up toward the flag to keep the line intact.

guide right An order to an advancing line of troops, telling each soldier to look at the person to his right to keep the line straight. The person farthest right, on the end of the line, is called the "guide." The command is also given to marching and parading soldiers. *See also* dress the line.

guidon 1. The flag carried to identify a military unit. The first guidons were small forked silk standards carried by cavalry guides. 2. The color-bearer who carried a guidon. When General Robert E. Lee surrendered at Appomatox Court House in 1865, the guidon of the 2nd Company Howitzers of the Army of Northern Virginia cut their silk battle flag into 4" x 6" pieces that were given as momentos to each man present.

Gullah 1. A Creole dialect spoken by slaves along the coastal regions of Georgia and South Carolina and the Sea Islands. Still spoken, it is a mixture of several West African languages, probably from the area of Angola, blended with seventeenth- and eighteenth-century English. 2. The slaves who spoke this dialect. After being freed, they continued in communities along the coast where their descendants still live.

gump A stupid or foolish person. The name has survived in humorous popular-culture names, such as Andy Gump (comic strip) and Forrest Gump (book and movie).

gunboats A humorous slang name for large boots or GALOSHES.

gunner's gang On a navy ship, the company of men who inspected the guns, ammunition, gunpower, and various other items, such as signal flares. They answered to the gunner's mate, a petty officer.

gunning A northern word for hunting game; e.g., "Fairfax was our best forager. He has been gunning since he was a baby."

gutta-percha A hardened gum resembling rubber or plastic and used for uniform buttons. Today it is used for temporary dental fillings and to make golf balls and electrical insulation. The Malaysian name means "gum from the percha tree."

gut-winder A slang term for a gun-shot wound in the abdomen; e.g., "Whitman went down with a gut-winder and died the next morning." A "winder" was something that took a person's breath away.

guy To mock, tease, or ridicule. Union Major General W.T. Sherman recalled that a woman surgeon assigned to his army had "complained that my men had guyed her" about wearing a surgeon's uniform. (His advice was to get rid of the uniform because it was "damned unfeminine!")

H

H An abbreviation for "hell." A preacher might say, "Bless your enemies in church, boys, but give them H on the battlefield."

hack 1. The common name for a hired hackney carriage, taken in cities and across the countryside. When the war began, Betty Maury left Washington, D.C., for her native Virginia and recorded the $25 paid to take a hack from Alexandria to Manassas Junction, Virginia. Hackneys were named for the English village of Hakeney (now Hackney, part of London) where they were first built. Taxicabs are still called hacks. 2. A slang name for a try or attempt; e.g., "Someone had to eliminate the sharpshooter, and Sloane decided to take a hack at it." Today's equivalent would be "whack."

hacked Worn out and dispirited. It was often used to describe soldiers after a battle, particularly a defeat.

hail Columbia A euphemism for hell. Officers urged their troops to "Give 'em hail Columbia!" before and during a battle. A soldier could also get "hail Columbia" during a severe scolding or punishment.

hail fellow well met A common expression during the war, and still used, to describe a person who is friendly to everyone, mostly in a superficial way; e.g., "Our new lieutenant was hail fellow well met with all the men, but discipline suffered."

"Hail to the Chief" The official music, still played, for the entrance of the U.S. president. The music was written in 1812 by an Englishman, James Sanderson, and first used in 1815 during James Madison's administration. It was constantly performed for Abraham Lincoln's official and informal duties. When he arrived late at Ford's Theater the evening he was assassinated, the play was interrupted while the band struck up "Hail to the Chief." The music was sometimes played as a tribute to others. When Union Major Robert Anderson surrendered Fort Sumter on April 13, 1861, and emerged from its gate to board a steamer, his band changed from playing "Yankee Doodle" to "Hail to the Chief." At Gettysburg, a Union band similarly honored Major General George G. Meade during an evening lull in the fighting, causing a war correspondent to tease, "Ah, General Meade, you are in very great danger of being President of the United States." By 1864, bands played the music for General Ulysses S. Grant "at every stopping place."

"Haines!" or "Hanes!" A shout to warn someone of danger; e.g., "Haines! There's a sharpshooter ahead!" The name was derived from the expression "MY NAME IS HAINES."

hair of the dog This expression, meaning an alcoholic drink to ease a hangover, was coined a few years before the war. It was a short version of "the hair of the dog that bit you" which, itself, was a variation of "the hair of the same wolf that bit you," dating back to the seventeenh century. During the war, such a drink was sometimes called a "hair."

half-and-half A slang term for a person who had a mixed racial background, such as a "half-breed."

half-shot Half intoxicated, which is an expression that still survives today. Soldiers also used "half-slewed," "half-sprung," and "half-snapped." See DRUNK for numerous other terms referring to intoxication.

Hamite A slave. The name was sometimes used, especially in the South, to give Biblical backing to the institution of slavery, because God decreed that the sons of Ham should become the slaves of Shem and Japheth. Samuel Davies Baldwin's book *Dominion*, released in 1858 by the Southern Methodist Publishing House in Nashville, Tennessee, also used the terms "Hamitic slavery" and "Hamitic bondage." He noted that "Hamitic service does result in direct obedience to God's law" and that "Providence has kept the negro race in a state of singular satisfaction with its lot in the South."

hammer and tongs With great noise and violence. This slang expression, which came from a blacksmith's work, was popular during the war and survives today. A fierce battle was often described as the two armies "going at it hammer and tongs."

Hampton's Cattle Raid The name given to the Confederate capture of Union cattle six miles from General Ulysses Grant's headquarters in Virginia on September 16, 1864. General Robert E. Lee's cavalry commander, Major General Wade Hampton, took three brigades to Coggins Point and rustled nearly 2,500 U.S. army cattle (along with more than 300 Yankees). He lost fewer than 60 of this own men. This audacious raid provoked Grant on December 28 to attack and take Fort Harrison on the outer defenses of Richmond.

"Hancock the Superb" The nickname given by Union Major General George McClellan to Major General Winfield S. Hancock, because of his excellent military record, integrity, and his handsome and distinguished bearing. Soldiers were amazed that Hancock constantly wore a clean, white shirt and kept his linen in the same pristine condition. A Pennsylvanian who graduated from West Point, Hancock had previously fought in the Mexican War and Seminole War. He acquired the nickname during the Peninsula campaign in 1862 and subsequently fought at Antietam, Fredericksburg, and Chancellorsville. He led the entire 2nd Corps at Gettysburg, where his troops met the full assault of PICKETT'S CHARGE, with Hancock badly wounded after galloping along the front lines and saying "These are times when a corps commander's life does not count." (He was one of 15 at that battle later honored by the "Thanks of Congress.") He later saw action at the Wilderness and Spotsylvania and in the Petersburg campaign, where his forces were crushed on August 25, 1864, at Reams's Station. Hancock was then assigned to Washington, D.C., to recruit a veterans' corps. After the war, he was sent South to help direct Reconstruction in Texas and Louisiana but was granted a transfer North in 1868 after he enraged RADICAL REPUBLICANS by resisting their instructions to replace civilian control with military authority. In 1880, Hancock was the Democratic candidate for president, losing by a narrow margin to James A. Garfield. Five years later, he was in charge of the funeral of his former commander and president, Ulysses S. Grant.

hand-grenade Steel cylinders packed with powder that was exploded by an attached fuse. They were in short supply in the Confederate army and were mostly a Union weapon. Rebels became adept at throwing back enemy hand-grenades before they went off, and they also devised their own heavy versions, filling large artillery shells with powder, attaching fuses, and rolling them down hills at Union positions. The Ketcham hand-grenade was an experimental Union device shaped like a heavy dart. *See also* Ketcham's grenade.

hand in (one's) checks An informal expression meaning to die. Checks were counters used in card games.

handspike The heavy bar at the end of a cannon's STOCK TRAIL. It was used as a lever to maneuver and point the cannon.

hanger-on In the war, this name was usually a soldier's sneering description of a noncombatant in camp, such as a courier and even staff officer.

hang up one's fiddle To stop working or retire. This term was sometimes shortened to "hang up," as in "The sun went down, so we had to hang up for the day." The full expression is echoed today when an athlete "hangs up his spikes."

hansom or hansom cab A one-horse, two-wheeled covered cab for two people with the cab driver sitting elevated in the rear looking over the carriage top. It was supposedly designed by Joseph A. Hansom in London, England, and first appeared in 1834 as the "Patent Safety Cab," which later became popular in the United States.

happy as clams at high water A popular simile among soldiers, especially from New England. When Union General George McClellan became commander of the Army of the Potomac in 1861 and visited his troops, a Massachusetts artilleryman wrote that "The boys are happy as clams at high water." The expression was sometimes shortened to "happy as a clam."

hard-baked Uncompromising or unrelenting, the equivalent of "hard-headed." A soldier might complain about his "hard-baked sergeant."

hard cash Gold or silver coins. They were also called "hard money."

Hardee hat The popular name for a dashing army hat, usually of black felt, worn by both the Union and Confederate armies, and also called the Jeff Davis hat. It was officially the 1858 dress pattern for the U.S. Army hat of the OLD ARMY, and the names were derived before the war from Major William J. Hardee, who wrote the training manual, HARDEE'S TACTICS, and from Jefferson Davis, the future Confederate president who was then U.S. secretary of war. The hat had a high crown with colorful piping lying on the brim, and one side folded up against the crown. Up

Hardee hat. *Copyright Inge Wright 1999.*

to three ostrich feathers were often seen attached to the other side. Brass badges were worn in front as the insignia of the branch of service, such as two crossed cannons for artillerymen. The U.S. version had a brass eagle fastening the side to the crown. The Hardee was stiff and could not be crumpled, so marching soldiers preferred the informal FORAGE CAP.

Hardee's Tactics The common name for *Rifle and Light Infantry Tactics*, the standard military instruction manual written by Lieutenant General William J. Hardee and published for the OLD ARMY in 1855. It was therefore used by both sides. The manual introduced updated maneuvers, such as soldiers moving more quickly because of the new faster-firing rifled muskets. Special versions of the book were published for MILITIA, black troops, and other regiments, but by 1862 Hardee's Tactics was being replaced in the North and sometimes the South by the SYSTEM OF INFANTRY TACTICS written by Union Brigadier General Silas Casey. Hardee was a Georgian who led Confederate troops at Shiloh and other major battles, ending the war by being driven from Savannah, Georgia, and through the Carolinas by Major General W.T. Sherman's forces.

hardhead An insulting nickname for a rural dweller of Tennessee or Kentucky.

hard lot A slang name for an unyielding, tough, or aggressive person; e.g., "Sherman and his men knew that Bedford Forrest was a daring horseman and a hard lot."

hard row to hoe An expression for something difficult to do, still used but new during the war.

hard run To be hard up for something, especially money; e.g., "Our whole mess was hard run, and we could barely afford a sutler's pie."

hardscrabble A name for any land that was barren or poorly producing. In 1855, when Ulysses Grant tried farming in Missouri on 60 acres given to him by his father-in-law, he named his newly built two-story log farmhouse "Hardscrabble" before giving up the difficult life (even with three house slaves).

hardtack The hard military cracker served with most meals. A normal ration usually contained nine or ten pieces of this unleavened bread, a baked mixture of flour and water. It was tasteless, tough, often worm-infested, and the butt of many camp jokes. It was about 3 inches by 3 inches with a thickness of about 1/2 inch. John D. Billings, an artilleryman in the Army of the Potomac, described it in his wartime memoir, *Hardtack and Coffee*, as "a piece of petrified bread honeycombed with bugs and maggots." Many men crumbled hardtack into their coffee, only to find weevils swimming out of the fragments, but, as Billings added, "they were easily skimmed off, and left no distinctive flavor behind." Before eating their biscuits, soldiers developed the habit of beating them on a hard surface to frighten the creatures out. Yet, one southern soldier recalled soaking hardtack well and frying it in bacon grease to create "a dish which no Confederate had the weakness or the strength to refuse." Rebels were amused early in the war to hear Union prisoners use the name "hard crackers" and "hard bread" for hardtack. *See also* soft-tack.

hardtack box or cracker box A small wooden box in which HARDTACK biscuits were stored. Soldiers and officers, including generals like the Union's W.T. Sherman, sat on them, even for meals. Creative men also turned the empty boxes into writing tables resting on their laps, general tables (with legs added), and "dish closets" (with shelves inserted).

hardware A slang name for hard liquor or whiskey.

Harper's Weekly A popular and influencial magazine in the North, which declared in December 1861 that President Lincoln was not a great leader. The magazine was especially noted for its sketches of battle scenes and camp life, many done by their artist Thomas Nash. Other art was provided by Winslow Homer, who at the age of 25 provided a two-page sketch of Lincoln's first inauguration and became the magazine's war correspondent. Homer became famous after the war for his seascapes. *See also* "our best recruiting sergeant."

Harrison's Landing letter A letter handed by Union Major General George McClellan to President Abraham Lincoln during the president's visit on July 9, 1862, to his camp at Harrison's Landing, Virginia, on the James River. McClellan's letter, which referred to Lincoln as "YOUR EXCELLENCY," gave detailed instructions on how the President should be running the war. Two days later in Washington, Lincoln replaced McClellan as general-in-chief with Major General Henry Halleck.

Hart, Charlie An alias sometimes used by Confederate Captain William C. Quantrill, who led the murderous gang called Quantrill's Raiders on the Missouri-Kansas border. Members included such outlaws as Jesse and Frank James and the psychotic "BLOODY BILL." Quantrill, born in Dover, Ohio, had been a schoolteacher and gambler who first fought with JAYHAWKERS against the South before switching sides. Quantrill's BUSH-WHACKERS killed civilians as easily as soldiers, his raids culminating in the massacre on August 21, 1863, at Lawrence, Kansas, when his men murdered some 150 men and boys in front of their families and destroyed nearly 200 buildings. Quantrill, called "the bloodiest man in the Annals of America," was eventually shot in 1865 by a Union patrol in Kentucky; he died in a U.S. prison infirmary.

Harvey's Oyster Saloon A popular wartime restaurant in Washington, D.C. When Confederate forces blockaded the Potomac in the early days of the conflict, Harvey's boasted that its fishing boats daily ran the blockade and Rebel batteries.

hash driver A nickname for a cook.

hasty entrenchment The name given by soldiers to a defensive earthwork, especially a FIELDWORK like a trench, that was quickly dug before and during an engagement with the enemy. Engineering troops became expert at this task as the war proceeded.

hasty pudding A dish of mush made from cornmeal that was popular on both sides. The thick boiled batter was eaten with butter, milk, and molasses or sugar. The name came from the fact that it was quickly made (and, some noted, quickly served and eaten).

hat on a shingle A early northern nickname for the *Monitor*, the Union's first IRONCLAD ship. The name derived from the ship's lonely round turret rising above the flat deck.

have a brick in one's hat To be intoxicated; e.g., "The only time I saw the general laugh was when he had a brick in his hat." See DRUNK for numerous other terms referring to intoxication.

havelock A protective cover attached to a soldier's cap and hanging as a flap over the back of his head and neck to protect from the sun. It was usually an OIL-CLOTH made of cotton or linen. Before the first battle of the war, the Ladies Havelock Association of New York sent the 7th New York Regiment 1,000 white linen havelocks. During the war, however, havelocks proved to be bulky and irritating (as well as a bright target for enemy sharpshooters), so most were quickly abandoned. The item was named for Sir Henry Havelock, a British general who wore it in India.

havelock cap *See* whipple hat.

have (one's) return innings To get revenge. After taking insults and jokes from Union troops passing along a road, a Confederate prisoner wrote, "We were a motley crowd enough, certainly, and it *did* look as if our friends in blue were having their return innings."

haversack A soldier's bag for carrying his rations, although it often was used to replace the KNAPSACK. It had a strap and was worn on the right shoulder, hanging on the left hip. Although the haversack was made of strong canvas, bacon grease could ooze out, so Union bags were waterproofed with tar. One starving Confederate was seen to boil his haversack to create his own soup. Some individually made haversacks were fancy and expensive, such as those made of chamois. Other soldiers did without the item and traveled light, carrying only a few articles in their pockets.

Haversack. *Copyright Inge Wright 1999.*

have the staff in one's own hand To own property, with the implication of being in charge and deserving respect; e.g., "Af-

ter the war, it was difficult for a Southron to have the staff in his own hand."

hawing and geeing A slang expression to describe going back and forth or in all directions. After being marched and countermarched around the streets of Boston in 1861, a rural Massachusetts recruit complained about all the "hawing and geeing." Both words relate to driving horses, especially without reins: "haw" being a command to turn to the left and "gee" to the right.

hay foot, straw foot The humorous system used in camps on both sides for soldiers who did not know "left" from "right" during marching drills. Drill sergeants would have them tie a small bundle of hay on the left foot and straw on the right, and then call out "hay foot" or "straw foot" during drill maneuvers. A new recruit during the war was called a "straw foot."

"The Haystack" A popular house of prostitution in Washington, D.C., whose madam was a Mrs. Hay. *See also* clap; daughter of Eve; drab; fallen angel; fancy girl; fast house; gay young duck; "Hooker's Division"; "Madam Russell's Bake Oven"; parlor house; ranch; The Wolf's Dream.

Hayti A spelling of Haiti used during the war. President Abraham Lincoln's administration shipped free blacks to that West Indian country in 1862 in an effort to establish a small colony there. Although only volunteers were sent, the colony failed. This effort stemmed from a Congressional Act that authorized "transportation, colonization, and settlement in some tropical country, beyond the limits of the United Staes, of persons of African descent."

head driver On a southern plantation, the highest ranking slave supervising the slaves working in the fields or on gangs. Also called the "head man," he answered directly to the OVERSEER and was in charge of every DRIVER. The position was given to a trustworthy and intelligent man and carried great responsibility because the head driver was in charge of the plantation work when the white overseer was absent. He often handled provisions for the workers, decided on punishments, and gave permission for slaves to be off the estate.

head-log A large log placed on top of an earthen parapet and just in front of a trench to protect soldiers in the trench from incoming fire. Space was usually left beneath the log to allow the entrenched soldiers to shoot at the enemy. One Confederate private recalled a Yankee attack that nothing stopped "but the hot shot and cold steel that we poured into their faces from under our head-logs."

head man *See* head driver.

headsplitter A strong whiskey, especially moonshine.

healing by first intention The expression used by doctors when a wound healed without producing LAUDABLE PUS. No one was certain why this happened.

heap *See* sight.

hearty as a buck A vigorous statement of good health, borrowed from hunters and in common use; e.g., "I was hearty as a buck when this war started, but look at me now."

heavy or heavy infantryman A name for a heavy ARTILLERYMAN who was ordered by Union General Ulysses Grant to fight as an infantryman. Grant forced these special artillerymen to leave their easier jobs in fortifications to form new regiments and swell the ranks of the fighting riflemen. The shocked heavies were often welcomed with jeers by battlefield veterans.

hedge To hide or protect oneself. Confederate Major General Evander M. Law once traded missed shots with a Yankee who had popped up behind a pile of earth. "This time my friend didn't 'hedge,'" Law later wrote, "but commenced reloading rapidly, thinking, I suppose, that I would have to do the same." The general, however, had another musket at hand and wounded the enemy.

heifer A slang name for a pretty young woman; a rather dubious compliment.

hellabaloo A great, wild confusion or riotous noise; e.g., "The battle had turned into one big hellabaloo."

"the Hell-Cat" The nickname given by John Nicolay, Abraham Lincoln's private secretary, to the president's wife, Mary Todd Lincoln. Nicolay and his assistant, John Hay, slept in the White House and were virtually members of the Lincoln family, an arrangement that created friction with Mrs. Lincoln. *See also* Mrs. President; "the She Wolf."

"the Hell Hole" The nickname given by Union soldiers to New Hope Church, Georgia, after the battle there on May 25-27, 1864. Confederate General Joseph E. Johnston repulsed the advance of Major General Joseph Hooker's troops, causing Union Major General W.T. Sherman to move his army east around the position. "Hell Hole" mostly described three hours of furious fighting on May 25 that ended in a drenching thunder storm. In that short time, Hooker had 1,665 men killed or wounded, while Johnston, whose troops had better cover, lost half that number.

"Hellmira" A nickname given by Confederate prisoners to the brutal Union prison outside Elmira, New York, where an average of 10 men died every day. Overall, it held 12,123 prisoners and about a fourth, 2,963, died there. This death rate was nearly that of the South's infamous ANDERSONVILLE prison. To supplement the meager food, prisoners traded tobacco for rats. Elmira had been designed for 5,000 prisoners, so most had to sleep outside in tents. When soldiers' families sent them coats and clothes for the bitter New York winters, prison officials withheld them and hundreds froze to death after they were given only one stove for every 100 men. Even the barracks began to fall apart because of the cheap wood that had been used.

Hell's Half-Acre A name given to the Round Forest, where fighting was concentrated during the battle of Stones River, Tennessee, from December 31, 1862, to January 2, 1863. It has also been called "the Mississippi Half-Acre" because of the extensive casualties taken by the 2nd Mississippi Brigade led by Brigadier General James R. Chalmers. The forest, held by the Union troops of Major General William S. Rosecrans, became a magnet for a series of Rebel charges directed by Major General Braxton Bragg and resulting in heavy loses for short gains. The inconclusive battle killed 1,730 Union soldiers and 1,294 Confederates.

helmet As used during the Civil War, the term simply referred to any soldier's cap or hat, such as the WHIPPLE HAT with a HAVELOCK. It no doubt was a light-hearted comparison to a knight's more protective armored headgear.

help A domestic servant or hired worker, considered as an individual. One gentleman in New York, for example, engaged "three Irish helps."

hen-fruit A witty name for an egg.

"Here's your mule!" A slang Confederate catchword that had little meaning beyond being a humorous insiders' joke. It supposedly related to a man entering a Rebel camp looking for his lost gray mule.

Some soldiers, impressed by one of their number who had large ears and was sleeping on straw in his tent, yelled to the man, "Here's your mule!" The call then came from other parts of the camp, and the story was soon passed to other units until "Here's your mule!" became a mischievous phrase shouted at fellow soldiers and puzzled civilians.

hern A substitution for "her," especially in the dialect of poorly educated southerners and slaves, although the word was correct English in the fourteenth century. Similar terms are HISN, OURN, YOURN, and THEIRN.

Heroes of America *See* Red Strings.

"hero of the *Trent*" The informal title given by Union newspapers and the public to Captain Charles Wilkes, captain of the *San Jacinto*, which was involved in the controversial TRENT AFFAIR with the British ship of that name, on November 7, 1861.

hickory shirt A coarse, durable shirt made of heavy twilled cotton that was popular with Confederate troops in the early days of the war. It had a pattern of checks or narrow blue stripes.

highfalutin An informal word to describe someone who was pretentious, pompous, or snobbish; e.g., "General Lee got the job done without the usual highfalutin talk associated with officers."

high feather A slang expression for being greatly elated or in high spirits. It was a favorite expression of Union Major General W.T. Sherman, who informed General Ulysses Grant after Shiloh, "Now I am in high feather." *See also* in full feather.

Highfly One of Confederate Major General JEB STUART's best horses. Stuart escaped on the fleet Highfly when Union troops nearly captured him and his command group on August 18, 1862, at Verdiersville, Virginia. *See also* Virginia.

high-number regiment A Union regiment that was formed later in the war and therefore had a higher number. The higher number indicated the regiment comprised relatively inexperienced troops—young men or older ones finally caught by conscription. Such regiments were looked down upon by older low-number regiments.

high tide of the Confederacy or high tide of the Rebellion A nickname for the greatest penetration of the Confederate forces in PICKETT'S CHARGE, which on July 3, 1863, the third day of the battle of Gettysburg, briefly reached the Union lines.

high-toned An informal description of dignified or upper-class officers or men. One hard-working Union soldier complained that "some of the 'high-toned' commanders had the picket [outpost] paved with cobblestones."

"The Hirling and the Slave" A popular southern poem that defended the institution of slavery. William J. Grayson wrote it in 1854 using the form of heroic couplets.

hisn or his'n A substitution for "his," especially in the dialect of poorly educated southerners and slaves, although the word was correct English usage in the fourteenth century. Similar terms are HERN, OURN, YOURN, and THEIRN.

hissing An object of great dislike, such as something one would hiss at. A Union prisoner in Richmond's LIBBY PRISON in 1862, later recalled: "We were not treated with special severity, for Libby was not at that time the hissing it afterward became."

hoe-cake A thin bread made of baked cornmeal. The name came from the rural habit of baking it on a hoe over the fire. On his way home after his surrender at Appomatox Court House, General Robert E. Lee stopped at a private house along the way for a meal that included Virginia hoe-cakes.

hoe-down In military camps, a hoe-down was normally a musical gathering, either sung or played by individual soldiers or more formal groups, like the minstrel bands of some units. The wide range of instruments might include harmonicas, flutes, fiddles, and drums, as well as homemade mongrel devices. The term "hoe-down" was first used at the start of the war.

hog path A small meandering path; e.g., "The Yankee guards had no chance of capturing me again. I knew every hog path in the Appalachians."

hog race A popular sport in camps with soldier "jockeys" riding large hogs, although the "steeds" were inevitably eaten. In one Confederate hog race in Vicksburg, Mississippi, in 1862, one hog fell over a cliff and killed its rider. The surviving hog was killed and eaten that same evening by the man's grieving friends.

"hog-skin cravat" A camp punishment devised by the 27th Mississippi Infantry for pig thieves. A hole was punched into the skin of the slain pig, and the guilty soldier had his head shoved through and was ordered to wear the covering all day long in sight of the provost guard.

"Hold the fort" The misquote of a WIG-WAG MESSAGE sent by Union Major General W.T. Sherman, who sent two messages from Kennesaw Mountain, Georgia, to General John M. Corse during the battle of Allatoona Pass on October 5, 1864. The first message advised,

"Sherman is moving in force. Hold out." It was followed four hours later by "General Sherman says hold fast. We are coming." This was later quoted as "Hold the fort, for I am coming" and became the basis of a famous revival hymn, "Hold the Fort" by Philip Paul Bliss. During the battle, Corse lost 706 of almost 2,000 men and Confederate General Samuel J. French lost 799 of more than 3,000. French retired with his army after his men sighted Sherman's messages.

holiday soldier A soldier who regarded the war as a holiday from usual tasks and behaved accordingly. After a young Confederate woman, Constance Cary, watched veteran soldiers of New Orleans' Washington Artillery march past her house in Richmond, Virginia, in March 1862, she wrote: "These were no holiday soldiers. Their gold was tarnished and their scarlet faded by sun and wind and gallant service."

hollow square l. An infantry formation in which the soldiers formed a large defensive square. It proved a success when attacked on all sides by the enemy's cavalry because horses usually did not withstand or survive direct fire. The first line of men in a hollow square would kneel and place the butt of their guns against their knees, pointing bayonets at the advancing cavalry, while a second line would fire at the enemy over the heads of the first line. When Union forces were retreating in disarray from the first battle of Bull Run in 1861, the troops of Colonel W.T. Sherman slowed the Rebels by forming a hollow square, covering the federal retreat, and leaving the battlefield last. 2. Any soldiers' formation that resembles a hollow square, such as an alignment of men for a military funeral or at the hanging of a deserter. *See also* "Form square!"

Holster Pistol *See* Colt four-pounder.

holydays An alternate spelling of "holidays" preferred by some, including Confederate General Robert E. Lee. It is a reminder of the religious origin of many of the days of rest.

holystone The large, flat block of soft sandstone used by sailors to scrub their ship's wooden decks, usually once a week. Sailors probably originated the name (humorously or profanely) because the decks were cleaned for Sundays or because they did the work on their knees. The decks were said to be "holystoned."

home Another name for a home run in base ball; e.g., "He made a home and won the game." Both terms were first used about five years before the war.

Home Comforts A popular wartime book of household hints, first published in 1855 under the pen name of Lillie Savery (real name unknown). It described the perfect family of Mrs. Savery, an economic, ingenious, and industrious homemaker. The family of four seems to have survived on pennies, with Mrs. Savery baking a cake for 3 cents and fashioning her shoes out of old soles and pantaloons. The book was known in the South, where it should have been welcomed during the blockade.

home guard or home guards A volunteer military company formed to defend a city, town, or area. It was essentially another name for a MILITIA.

home-made Yankees A term used in west Tennessee, north Alabama, and other southern areas for Unionists who supported the North. Some even fought for the invading Union forces.

"The Homespun Dress" A sentimental southern song honoring the Confederate women who had to sew their own clothes during the wartime blockade. It ended as follows:

Hurrah, hurrah,
For the sunny south so dear,
Three cheers for the homespun dress
The southern ladies wear.

Note that the southern-British pronunciation of "dear" ("de-ah") made it rhyme with "wear." The song was sometimes titled "I Am a Southern Girl."

homesteader President Abraham Lincoln signed the Homestead Act on May 20, 1862. It provided free or cheap western land (up to 160 acres at $1.25 an acre) to homesteaders who would settle there for five years and cultivate the land. The act was an effort to populate the West with Union citizens. The first known homesteader was a former Union soldier, Daniel Freeman, who settled in the Nebraska Territory. *See also* quarter section.

"Home Sweet Home" The old nostalgic Victorian song that was popular on both sides, especially its line, "There's no place like home." The song was composed by Sir Henry Rowley Bishop, an Englishman, for the 1823 London play, *Clari*, written by an American, John Howard Payne. The song was so melancholy, the U.S. army banned it in camps during the winter of 1862-63 after the Union defeat at Fredericksburg on December 13. After the first day of fighting at the Battle of Murfreesboro (or Stones River) on December 31, 1862, one side's band began to play "Home Sweet Home" in the cold night, and the opposing side's band joined in to express the common sentiments of the two homesick armies. Other joint concerts of the song, including singing, were recorded during the war.

"Honest Abe" The nickname of Abraham Lincoln, especially promoted by his Republican Party. This name was often expanded, as in northern newspapers, to "Honest Abe Lincoln."

"Honest George" A nickname for George Adams, the Washington correspondent for the New York *World*, because he wrote candidly about the war, including reports about the prostitutes and gambling in the nation's capital.

"Honeybun" The affectionate nickname for Confederate Lieutenant Walter Hullihen, a popular member of Major General JEB STUART's staff. When Stuart was fatally wounded on May 11, 1864, at Yellow Tavern, Virginia, he turned to Hullihen and asked, "Honeybun, how do I look in the face?" Hullihen's untruthful reply was, "You are looking all right, General."

Hood's Minstrels A performing troupe of regular soldiers in General John B. Hood's Confederate army. One of their best shows occurred on April 15, 1864, while in camp in east Tennessee. The stage was built of planks used to ship horses by train, the back scenery was tent material, and the footlights were candles screened by a board that served as a reflector. Soldiers gathered in "standing seats" and Hood's Minstrels performed their black-faced show, which included the farce "Lucy Long," the song "Fine Arkansas Gentleman," and a skit, "P. T. Barnum's Ball."

Hood's Second Sortie The official Confederate name for the stalemated battle of Atlanta fought on July 22, 1864, between the troops of Confederate General John B. Hood and Union Major General James B. McPherson. "Hood's First Sortie" was the inconclusive battle of Peach Tree Creek, fought two days earlier against Brigadier General George H. Thomas.

hoofing it A term for marching that is now a slang expression for walking.

"Hooker's Division" A section of Washington, D.C., that had numerous houses of prostitution, obviously named for its military clientele. One popular place on

Pennsylvania Avenue was boldly named Hooker's Headquarters, probably because Union Brigadier General Joseph Hooker had placed the area off limits.

hoop skirt A wide skirt worn over flexible steel hoops that could be sewn into a petticoat or worn as a separate piece. The name was first heard in 1857 and became common during the war. The dress was a revival of an eighteenth-century fashion but now used a crinoline petticoat that sometimes caused the tragic CRINOLINE ACCIDENT. Southern women secured precious articles on the inside hoops to hide them from Union soldiers occupying their area, and daring female smugglers were known to tie boots underneath to take through enemy lines.

hoosier A country bumpkin; the term was not restricted to natives of Indiana. Southern soldiers joked about hoosiers from Arkansas and other states.

hop A slang name for a dance. During the war, large city hotels, such as those in Washington, D.C., held hops. Although it is usually considered to be a modern American word ("high school hop"), the term began in eighteenth-century England, deriving from a humorous sixteenth-century description of a dance step or leap.

"Hope and hang on when you are wrecked." An old saying in the navy that was used by sailors on both sides during the war.

hop scotch This children's game was often played in camps on both sides.

hop the twig A slang expression meaning to get married; e.g., "The sergeant said he had a nightmare about hopping the twig."

horehound candy A brittle candy made from the juice of horehound, an herb with a bitter taste. Horehound cough medicine was also sold and used in military hospitals.

horizontal refreshment A humorous euphemism for sexual intercourse.

hornet A bullet, because of the buzzing sound made by a close miss. *See also* "Hornet's Nest."

"Hornet's Nest" The nickname given by soldiers to a small sunken lane that was the center of the battle of Shiloh on April 6-7, 1862. The descriptive name referred to the noise of bullets, often called HORNETS.

hornswoggle A slang verb, still used, meaning to cheat, trick, or deceive.

hornwork A defensive fortification built with angular points, or horns.

hors de combat A French term (literally "out of combat") used for soldiers who were wounded or otherwise could not fight.

horse artillery *See* flying artillery.

horse-car *See* street-car.

horse collar A slang name for a type of blanket roll, or BEDROLL, that had straps. When worn around the neck, it reminded soldiers of a horse collar, like the harness put around the neck and shoulders of an ARTILLERY HORSE.

horse sense A popular term for common sense. It supposedly began in the American West.

horse sergeant The common name for the sergeant in charge of the well-being of horses and mules in camp, including their shelter, food and water, currying and cleaning, and exercise and burial.

hospital bummer or hospital rat A soldier who faked an injury or overstated one so he could avoid combat and relax in a military hospital.

Hospital Directory A publication of the Union's SANITARY COMMISSION that listed soldiers confined to hospitals. It was continually updated and constantly checked by the family members of soldiers missing in action.

Hospital Sketches A book published in 1863 and containing letters written home by Louisa May Alcott about her experiences as a nurse in Union Hospital in the Georgetown section of Washington, D.C. Within weeks of arriving in December 1862, she had fallen ill, was diagnosed as having "typhoid pneumonia," and was sent home with the expectation that she would not survive. She did, and in 1868 published her famous novel, *Little Women*.

hospital steward An assistant in a military hospital. His branch of service was denoted only by medical chevrons on his sleeves. A hospital steward acted as a clerk, was in charge of medicines, and carried a gun to guard the drug supplies. He received basic medical instructions and could attend to slightly wounded patients. Some stewards pulled bad teeth. A more important job was to help during operations, and the best hospital stewards could be promoted to assistant surgeons. Later in the war, female nurses took over many of the stewards' functions in the large military hospitals.

Hospital Transport System An organization of hospital boats run by the Union's SANITARY COMMISSION early in the war. It was allowed possession of large steamers not used by the military or government and outfitted them as hospital vessels with beds and medical supplies, as well as surgeons, nurses, WARD-MASTERS, APOTHECARIES, and other personnel, all without

cost to the government. Some of the ships were the *Knickerbocker, Vanderbilt, Daniel Webster,* and *Wilson Small.* The floating hospitals won praise for conveying wounded and sick soldiers to regular hospitals in an efficient and relatively comfortable way, saving lives in the process. The system was eventually copied by the government and the charity Hospital Transport System was disbanded.

Hospital Visitor Member of an organization of women volunteers who visited Union military hospitals to comfort patients and generally serve as hospital aides.

hoss A western and southern nickname for a strong, courageous man. The southern journalist Edward Albert Pollard recorded a conversation between two slaves in 1858 in which one called the other "big hoss." The word, a corruption of "horse," was also used in place of a first name; e.g., "Hoss Davis was our cook."

hostler or ostler A person who takes care of horses, whether on a plantation or at a stable or inn (the word coming from "hosteler," an innkeeper).

hot as the hinges of Hades An alliterative simile that avoided the more shocking "hot as hell."

Hotchkiss maps Confederate military maps drawn by Jedediah Hotchkiss, the topographical engineer on Lieutenant General "STONEWALL" Jackson's staff. The general was weak in reading terrain, so Hotchkiss had sessions with him to explain the maps. Hotchkiss's skill at mapping major points of offense and defense led to many southern successes, including Jackson's Shenandoah Valley campaign in 1862. Hotchkiss was later on the staffs of Lieutenant General Ambrose P. Hill, Lieutenant General Richard S. Ewell, and Major General Jubal A. Early. Born in New York, he had been a schoolmaster in the Shenandoah Valley before becoming the war's premier mapmaker. He drew about half the Confederate maps that survive today.

Hot Cockles A party game in which a man knelt down before a lady, "concealing his face in her lap," and put his open hand behind his back to be slapped by the other players. If he guessed correctly, that person took his place. If not, the slaps usually became worse.

hot jackets A "sport" among Confederate soldiers that involved duels with limber hickory switches.

hot shot Solid iron shot heated in a furnace before being fired. The red, hissing weapon was especially used in attacks on wooden ships and forts, where it caused devastating fires and explosions of gunpowder. Special hot-shot furnaces were maintained, several of them abroad warships. Part of the bombardment of Fort Sumter by Fort Moultrie was hot shot that set the officers' quarters ablaze. One personal account noted, "the red balls continued to drop, until every portion was in flames."

"Hot work!" An explanation of approval for a job well done; e.g., "Your last shot brought down the sharpshooter. Hot work, Jason!"

house A short name for a house surgeon in a hospital. Georgeanna Woolsey, training to be nurse in a Union hospital, recalled: "I remember it gave me a little shock that first day in the ward to hear the young 'house' say peremptorily: 'Nurse, basin!'"

the house See the big house.

houseless A word commonly used for "homeless." In 1862, Elizabeth Hyde Botume, a teacher of freed slaves, wrote that "There was still a great throng houseless, with no resting-place."

house niggers See house servants.

house servants A name for slaves who worked in a plantation home, such as girls who assisted the MAMMY, and such workers as waiters, chambermaids, and the seamstress. Whites and other slaves sometimes called them "house niggers." They were almost considered part of the household, and they looked down upon the so-called "common field hands" or "COMMON NIGGERS."

housewife The nickname for a soldier's small sewing kit containing items like a needle, thread, buttons, a thimble, and scissors. Each soldier was required to repair his own uniform, but this became a useless order later in the war, especially among ragged Confederate units. Many soldiers were not skillful at the work and preferred, for instance, to tie a string around an open toe of a sock. The housewife was normally supplied by the soldier's family, a girlfriend, or, sometimes, in the case of the Union army, by organizations like the CHRISTIAN COMMISSION or the SOLDIER'S AID SOCIETY. A housewife was often expanded into a COMFORTBAG.

Hovey's Babies A nickname for the 10,000 soldiers recruited by Union Brigadier General Alvin P. Hovey, because he would only take unmarried men. Hovey was an associate justice of the Indiana Supreme Court before the war and a U.S. congressman and governor of Indiana after it.

"How!" Union Major General Philip Sheridan's usual toast, which he had learned from the Indians. At the BATTLE ABOVE THE CLOUDS at Chattanooga, Tennessee, Sheridan made the loud toast to his men as he took a drink from a flask of whiskey before storming up the mountainside with them.

"How are you, Sanitary?" The common greeting given by Union soldiers in the field to the nurses and agents of the SANITARY COMMISSION.

how-come-you-so or how-come-ye-so Humorous combinations meaning slightly drunk; e.g., "Howard spent the evening in Montgomery and looked how-come-you-so when he got back into camp." Whiskey itself was sometimes called this. The words were a corruption of a Biblical quotation. See DRUNK for numerous other terms referring to intoxication.

"How does your corporosity sagaciate?" A humorous Latinized question meaning "How are you doing?" or "How do you feel?"

howker A slang name for a sailor who had two (or more) girl friends. The name came from a Dutch fishing ship with two masts, also called a "hooker."

the Hub A common nickname for Boston.

huckleberry A slang word used to describe something that was small in size or degree. In the first days of the war, an officer of a Missouri unit for the Confederacy noted that "The foot soldiers were preceded by the 'huckleberry' cavalry."

huguenot A slang name, especially heard among Kentucky soldiers, for a peanut.

humbug Common wartime slang for a fraud or hoax, or for a deceptive person. Before the Union's *Monitor* was built, U.S. Assistant Scretary of the Navy Benjamin Isherwood said he "thought ironclads a humbug." When Union Major General John Pope took charge of the new Army of Virginia, the correspondent for the New York *Tribune* wrote his editor that "My opinion of the man is that he is a humbug." The term dates back to the mid-eighteenth century, and perhaps came from the idea that some people might hum as they deceived others.

hundred-gun salute A traditional Union victory salute. General Ulysses Grant was so delighted when the battle of Nashville was won on December 16, 1864, he ordered the salute to be fired twice.

hunk A slang word describing someone or something that is all right or in great condition. A soldier might say he felt hunk after a battle. "Hunk" was a Dutch word meaning "home," and was used in a New Amsterdam (later New York) children's game of tag where a player was safe by reaching the designated "hunk" or goal. "Hunky" meant great, good, or okay. When asked how he was able to cook, a Union prisoner in ANDERSONVILLE told his fellow inmates, "Oh, I'm hunky on the oven," meaning he could borrow one. *See also* hunky-dory.

hunky-dory A slang term that described something that was great, fine, or all right; e.g., "Simpson wrote home every week and always lied that military life was hunky-dory." *See also* hunk.

Hurrah for hell! A profane cheer heard in camps, especially from a soldier emboldened by alcohol.

hurra's nest A jumble of things or a state of confusion; e.g., "She had braved the wind, but her hair looked like a hurra's nest."

hurryment A southern variant of "hurry." A Confederate soldier might note, "The Yankees even left the camp fires burning in their hurryment to escape."

hurry up the cakes An expression meaning to hurry or look alive; e.g., "Let's get those horse shelters up. Hurry up the cakes!" The order supposedly originated in cheap New York eating establishments where waiters would impatiently yell at the cooks.

Hutchinson Family Singers A famed New Hampshire singing group during the war. Union Major General George McClellan banned them from camps because they sang abolitionist songs, but President Abraham Lincoln had them reinstated, saying "It is just the character of song that I desire the soldiers to hear." One of their renown songs was the "Hymn of Liberty," which set the words of John Greenleaf Whittier to the music of "Ein' feste Burg ist unser Gott" by Martin Luther. The original Hutchinson family singers, the 16 children of Jesse and Mary Hutchison, had sung abolitionist songs two decades before the war.

huzzaher A person who gives loud shouts of joy or support, such as enthusiastic delegates to a political convention. A loud shout of "huzza!" was an early form of "hurrah!"

"Hymn of Freedom" A poem by Ralph Waldo Emerson published in the North in 1863. Supposedly a long speech by God, it had 21 stanzas of 4 lines each, including the following one:

> I break your bonds and masterships,
> And I unchain the slave:
> Free by his heart and hand henceforth,
> As wind and wandering wave.

"the hypo" President Abraham Lincoln's name for the bouts of depression that he suffered throughout his life. It was short for "hypochondria."

I

i The small "i" was sometimes used in letters by southern women as a sign of modesty.

"I Am a Southern Girl" See "The Homespun Dress."

I.C. Inspected Condemned. This was stamped on Union military equipment, including horses and mules, that a government inspector had examined and condemned for further use. The initials were often written by soldiers on various personal and camp articles as a joke.

I dad! An exclamation of surprise or excitement, used in the western states; e.g., "I dad! We whipped them."

identifier A piece of parchment worn by Union soldiers to identify them if killed in battle. It was supplied to every soldier by the CHRISTIAN COMMISSION. One side contained blank lines for the soldier's name, company, regiment, brigade, division, and corps, and a line to add the name of the relative to be notified. On the back were the following directions: "Suspend from the neck by a cord, and wear *over* the shirt: in battle, *under*." Many soldiers also wore an IDENTITY DISC.

identity disc A small metal disc worn by soldiers to identify them if they were killed. Soldiers had to buy these themselves because the dog tag did not yet exist. Besides circular types, the discs came in the shape of crosses, stars, and shields. A typical one listed the soldier's name, rank, company, and regiment. Silver ones were sold for one dollar by Drowne & Moore jewelers of New York, but poorer soldiers made do with wooden labels. Despite these efforts, 55 percent of Civil War soldiers buried in national cemeteries are unknown. When discs were not available, many soldiers wrote their names and units on a piece of paper or wood chip and placed it in their pocket or attached it to their uniforms. Some added "Killed in action" and the date.

"I fights mit Sigel" A boast, often amusingly quoted during the war, of thousands of German-born Union soldiers led by Major General Franz Sigel, who was also German-born. His units included the German XI Corps of the Army of the Potomac. Although he had graduated from Germany's military academy, Sigel was a weak leader who had the habit of snapping his fingers at shellbursts and shouting orders in his native language to his amazed non-German troops. After being defeated on May 15, 1864, by Major General John Breckinridge at New Market, Virginia, Sigel was relieved of his command. *See also* blenker; Dutchman.

I.F.W. The initials for "In for the War," which some soldiers printed on their knapsacks. Wits in camp claimed to have seen lice wearing the initials.

"If you see a head, hit it." A habitual battlefield saying of Union Brigadier General Michael K. Lawler, who used it in regard to the enemy. Born in Ireland, Lawler weighed more than 250 pounds, which forced him to wear his sword belt over his shoulder. He had also served in the Mexican War. Lawler distinguished himself at the capture of Fort Donelson in 1862 and during the Vicksburg campaign the following year.

Ik. Marvel The pen name of Donald G. Mitchell, a popular northern essayist and social satirist during the war. A native of Connecticut, Mitchell became a household name with such works as *Fudge Doings* (1855) and *My Farm at Edgewood* (1863).

illumination or grand illumination A special lighting up of a town or city as a commemoration or celebration. Washington, D.C., had a grand illumination on April 13, 1865, to celebrate General Robert E. Lee's surrender four days before. The city's Patent Office alone burned nearly 6,000 candles in its windows and the humblest shanty window flickered with a single flame. Gas jets illuminated City Hall and other buildings, and the citizens strolled aimlessly through the bedazzling streets, watching fireworks explode overhead.

illuminator A person in Virginia who burned candles in windows to celebrate the state joining the Confederacy. Local people looked upon nonilluminators with suspicion.

"The Immortal Regiment" The U.S. 4th Artillery, because of the old age of its officers, including many "new" junior officers.

"The Immortal Six Hundred" The name given in the South to 600 Confederate prisoners held for 45 days by Union Major General John G. Foster on Morris Island off Charleston to put them in the line of fire from Confederate guns. Amazingly, all survived without even a serious injury. Foster, whose forces were besieging Charleston, was responding to news that 600 Union prisoners were being held in the city.

The Impending Crisis of the South A book written in 1857 by a southerner, Hinton Rowan Helper, in support of the abolition of slavery. President Abraham Lincoln had a copy in which he had marked passages, including "Let the oppressed go free—Proclaim liberty throughout all the land unto all the inhabitants thereof." The book was thought to have given Lincoln moral support for issuing the EMANCIPATION PROCLAMATION.

imperial A small tuft of hair on the lower lip and chin, which was a style made fashionable by Napoleon III. Many imperials were blackened with burnt cork.

improvement A slave's word for a correction of something said, usually by another slave. "The improvement" of statements was especially important to slaves seeking betterment and education.

in a box An informal expression meaning in trouble or in a dilemma. It came into use toward the end of the war.

in a freeze A slang expression meaning in a state of excitement; e.g., "By the time we approached Chattanooga, our whole regiment was in a freeze."

"In battery" The command to artillerymen to line up their cannons and assume their positions for battle. A cannon was "in battery" when it was in a field position ready to fire.

incapable A soldier who could not do well in battle, either from fear or poor military training; e.g., "There was a large class of incapables among our officers when the war began."

income tax The first U.S. income tax in history was passed by Congress and signed into law by President Lincoln on August 5, 1861, to help fund the war. A person earning more than $800 annually had to pay the government 3 percent. In 1864, it was increased to 10 percent for those earning more than $10,000 a year.

indeedy A happily informal way to say "indeed." It evolved in the twentieth century to the set expression, "yes, indeedy."

Indiana Legion The organization of Indiana state MILITIA established on September 10, 1861 and organized by Major General John Love. Its two divisions were needed during the war to resist Confederate raids.

Indian Home Guard A brigade of Native Americans formed to fight for the Union in the western Indian Territory. They proved to be ferocious fighters but had the chronic problem of being absent without leave. The regiment was made up of Creeks, Cherokees, Seminoles, Osages, and other groups. Members of the brigade included Captain Spring Frog, Private Big Mush Dirt Eater, Pot Falling, Alex Scarce Water, Bone Eater, and Camp Chicken.

indigo mud An informal name for homemade indigo dye. During the South's hard war years, indigo plants were cut and packed into a vat, then covered with water to ferment for eight or nine days. To extract the dye, women had "indigo churnings" in which the water was churned up and down with a basket. Weak lye was added to separate the indigo "mud" to the bottom of the vat. The water was poured off, and the mud was put into a sack and hung up to dry into a clear, bright blue.

infantry parapet A FIELDWORK wall that is about chest-high, like a fort's parapet. By March 1862, Confederate General P.G.T. Beauregard had infantry parapets built between 13 forts in the area of Manassas and Centreville, Virginia.

infare A dialectic word for a reception and feast following a wedding. When Abraham Lincoln was snubbed as a young man by not being invited to an infare after a double wedding, he paid a neighbor to exchange the bridal beds of the couples, causing a near comedy consummation. He then wrote *The First Chronicles of Reuben*, a satire on the incident that was widely read in Indiana.

infernal machine The common name given to unusual weapons, especially those hidden as boobytraps, such as landmines and the topedo underwater mines.

in full feather In the best condition or feeling great; e.g., "Our regiment was formed the first month of the war and marched off for Washington in full feather." The older term "full feather" meant a person's best clothes. *See also* high feather.

"In God We Trust" The United States motto was first added to coins during the war by order of an act of Congress passed on April 22, 1864. The motto was first seen on a two-cent coin. The legislation was pushed through by Secretary of the Treasury Salmon P. Chase, who had received a letter in 1861 from the Rev. M.R. Watkinson of Ridleyville, Pennsylvania, which urged that the Creator be somehow included on coinage because of "our national shame in disowning God." Congress did not make the words the official national motto until July 30, 1956.

Innominata Embalming fluid used by Thomas Holmes during the war. He became wealthy by charging $100 for each of the more than 4,000 dead Union soldiers he embalmed. Innominata, which used arsenic as one ingredient, was "guaranteed to contain no poison."

the inside track President Abraham Lincoln's name for keeping the Union army between the Confederate army and Washington, D.C. When Union Brigadier General Joseph Hooker began to follow General Robert E. Lee into Pennsylvania in 1863 (the campaign ended with the battle at Gettysburg), Lincoln instructed him to carefully keep to the inside track.

Inspector General's Department The U.S. department that overlooked all military units to see that affairs were conducted according to regulations. By 1862, an assistant inspector general, with the rank of lieutenant colonel, was appointed to every unit, beginning at the corps level.

insurrectionist A northern name early in the war for a Rebel. President Abraham Lincoln commonly used it, as in his message to Congress on July 5, 1861, when he noted that "the insurrectionists announced their purpose to enter upon the practice of privateering."

intaglio A ring with a figure or design cut into the stone. It was the prized possession of many a lady.

interior lines A military situation in which one side can deploy troops faster than its enemy can respond with troops. In 1863, Confederate Lieutenant General James Longstreet declared that "the only hope of reviving the waning cause was through the advantage of interior lines."

intermittant fever or simple intermittant fever A surgeon's name for the dreaded camp disease of malaria.

in the air The common description of a unit's flank that has become separated from the main fighting line and therefore is vulnerable to attack. A key to the Confederate victory at Chancellorsville in 1863 was the discovery that the Union right flank was in the air and could be attacked by "STONEWALL" Jackson's troops.

"In the Hospital" A famous northern war poem by Mrs. Robert S. Howland, the wife of a Union hospital clergyman. The last four lines are as follows:

> My half-day's work is done, and this is all
> my part—
> I give a patient God my patient heart;
> And grasp His banner still, though all the
> blue be dim;
> These stripes, as well as stars, lead after
> Him.

Invalid Corps *See* Veteran Reserve Corps.

"invincible in peace and invisible in war" A popular comic description of bad soldiers during the war. It was used, for instance, by Georgia's Senator Hill to describe a SHIRK. Other forms were used, such as "in peace invincible; in war invisible," a description of Missouri troops by Union Colonel James E. Mulligan, commander of the 23rd Illinois.

involuntary labor A euphemism for slavery.

"Iowa Grey Hounds" The nickname given by Union Brigadier General Nathaniel Lyon to his 1st Regiment of Iowa Volunteers, because of their long legs and marching ability. He had first called them "Gipsies" because of their ragged appearance. The regiment, composed of a variety of eastern Iowa volunteers, from laborers to lawyers, operated in southwest Missouri to keep that state in the Union. In one notable 24-hour stretch, the Grey Hounds covered more than 48 miles. When two regular Missouri regiments tried to keep pace and their men began dropping out, a Missouri surgeon galloped up to warn Lyon to halt or he would kill all the Missourians. The regiment only existed for about three months; Lyon was killed on August 10, 1861, at the battle at Wilson's Creek, Missouri, and the Grey Hounds disbanded 11 days later and joined other units.

ipecacuanha A preparation used by camp doctors to treat diarrhea. It was made from the dried roots of a South American plant and contained emetine, which causes vomiting.

"Irish Bridget" or "Irish Biddy" The nicknames given to Union army nurse Bridget Divers, who followed her husband in the 1st Michigan Cavalry throughout the war. Also known as "Michigan Bridget," she stood picket day and night, had several horses shot from under her, and is credited with rallying the troops during battles. Confederate troops once allowed her to ride 12 miles through their ranks to retrieve the body of a captain. After the war, the couple stayed with the army for the Indian wars, with Irish Bridget working as a military laundress.

Irisher A person born in Ireland or of Irish extraction.

iron See ironclad.

Iron Brigade l. The only "all-Western" brigade in the Union's Army of the Potomac, although "Western" meant frontiersmen from 2nd, 6th, and 7th Wisconsin and the 19th Indiana brigades. The 24th Michigan was added in 1862. Also called the "Black Hat Brigade" because of their black felt hats, they were com-

manded by Brigadier General John Gibbon of North Carolina. The origin of the tough brigade's nickname is uncertain, but was probably given by General George McClellan when a third of its members were lost stopping an assault by Major General "STONEWALL" Jackson's troops on August 28, 1862, near Centerville, Virginia. The name was popularized at the battle of Antietam by a war correspondent. The brigade also fought bravely at Fredericksburg, Chancellorsville, and then Gettysburg, where 65 percent of its men were lost. After that, the Iron Brigade lost its esprit de corps because eastern soldiers were transferred in as replacements. 2. A brigade in the same division as the western Iron Brigade, but bearing the name earlier. It was composed of four New York regiments, the 22nd, 24th, 30th, and 84th, and the 2nd U.S. Sharpshooters. This less-known Iron Brigade was disbanded in May 1863.

ironclad The general name for a warship covered in thick iron plates, the war's first being the Union's *Monitor* and the Confederacy's *Virginia* (the former Union ship *Merrimac* with iron bolted on). After their famous battle on March 9, 1862, at Hampton Roads, Virginia, both sides developed MONITOR FEVER—the North turned out duplicate designs of its flat-decked ship and the South replicated its slanted version. "Ironclad" was sometimes informally shortened to "iron." Great Britain and France had been the first countries to build (unused) ironclads.

iron-clad battery *See* iron-clad steam-battery.

Ironclad Oath The oath of allegiance to the United States required by legislation passed by Congress on July 2, 1862. Every military officer or government official had to swear allegiance to the Constitution and declare that he had never borne arms against the Union or aided the rebellion.

The former Confederate ironclad *Stonewall* rests at anchor off Washington, D.C., in June 1865. *Library of Congress, Prints & Photographs Division, LC-B8171-7912.*

iron-clad steam-battery or iron-clad battery The original name for a proposed ship that became the *Monitor*, the Union's first IRONCLAD warship. The name was devised in 1854 by its designer, John Ericsson. On January 20, 1862, he chose the name "Monitor" (something that warns) because, he wrote, it would serve as a "severe monitor" to southern leaders that their rivers were no longer barriers to the Union navy and also be a monitor to the British who were planning to build four expensive, but poorly designed steel-clad warships.

iron coffin A grim northern nickname for the *Monitor*, the Union's first IRONCLAD ship.

iron column A nickname for the strongest element of an army or military unit. Union General Winfield Scott planned to organize an entire grand army of volunteers around his iron column of regular soldiers.

iron devil A nickname for any locomotive engine.

iron neckties *See* Sherman's neckties.

"I swan!" An exclamation of surprise or other emotion, still heard today. "Well, I swan!" was often heard during the war.

"I take pen in hand" A traditional way to begin a letter; e.g., "Dear Mother, I take my pen in hand to write you a few lines." Another popular introductory phrase was "I seat myself down."

the itch *See* camp itch.

"It is an order" President Abraham Lincoln's warm traditional saying to parting guests after he had invited them to visit him again.

"It takes a man's weight in lead for every soldier killed in battle." A well-known saying during the war, meaning

160 • "It takes a man's weight in lead for every soldier killed in battle."

that much ammunition had to be produced for each of the enemy killed. It reflected the belief that most shots hit trees, horses, or nothing.

J

jack A slang name for money. The word had described certain types of money since about 1700, but this general sense was first heard two years before the war.

Jack 1. The nickname for a sailor, which derived from "jack tar." Confederate Admiral Raphael Semmes recalled issuing his *ALABAMA* crew two daily servings of GROG: "I was quite willing that Jack should drink, but I undertook to be the judge of how much he should drink." 2. Union General Ulysses S. Grant's first horse during the war. He purchased the light tan horse in Galena, Illinois, where he kept the accounts in his father's leather and hardware store. Grant rode Jack until the end of summer in 1863. *See also* Cincinnati; Fox; Kangaroo.

jackass rabbit The original name that has now been shortened to "jackrabbit." Westerners said the animal's long ears resembled those of a male donkey.

Jack's Alive A party game in which a piece of paper was twisted, lighted, and the flame blown out. The paper was then passed from player to player, and the one holding it when the last spark went out was the loser who had to pay a forfeit. Each time the paper was handed along, the player announced "Jack's alive." The most daring would try to trap the next person by holding on until the last ember was dying before making the pass.

Jackson Hospital A large Confederate PAVILION hospital in Richmond, Virginia, which had 6,000 beds.

Jackson's foot cavalry or Stonewall's foot cavalry The whole CORPS of Confederate Lieutenant General "STONEWALL" Jackson's troops. They received the proud name because of the amazing speed of their marches.

jackstraws A popular game in camp and prisons, still played today. The small wooden "straws" were often handcarved by the soldiers into different shapes with hooked ends to require more skill in removing them from the pile. A player's turn ended when he disturbed the other jackstraws in picking up one. The player who retrieved the most was the winner.

Jacob's-ladder A flexible ship ladder with rope sides and wooden rungs. Union Admiral David G. Farragut kept them aboard his warships so carpenters could climb down with "inch-board, lined with felt, and ordinary nails" to repair holes made by enemy cannon shots.

jail fever A common name for a virulent form of typhus, because it spread quickly in jails and other crowded places, which also gave it the name of "ship's fever."

jam *See* bruise.

jam-up An adjective meaning excellent or first-rate; e.g., "a jam-up victory."

janizary A loyal or submissive soldier or follower. After South Carolina seceded in 1860, southern U.S. senators in Washington, D.C., complained about (General Winfield) "Scott's janizaries" stationed around the nervous city. A janizary was originally a member of the Turkish sultan's foot-guards.

Jayhawker A Union guerrilla in Kansas and Missouri during the war. "Jayhawking" was a slang word for stealing. General James H. Lane, a former U.S. senator from Kansas, led a wild band of Jawhawkers who ravaged entire towns suspected of aiding Confederates. The 7th Kansas Cavalry was known as "Jennison's Jayhawkers" and one of its members was John Brown, Jr. They stole everything from horses to silver from Confederate sympathizers, murdering several along the way.

jeans This famous American name meant any type of trousers during the Civil War. Levi Strauss, the first manufacturer of denim jeans, did not begin producing them until several years after the war. The name "jene" was first used in England in the sixteenth century for a type of twilled cotton cloth.

"Jeb" The nickname of Confederate Major General James Ewell Brown Stuart, the famous cavalry leader. Derived from Stuart's initials, the nickname was created by his friends when he served in the OLD ARMY. He fought at both battles of Bull Run, helping to win the second by a 60-mile, 26-hour raid on Union Major General John Pope's headquarters that netted a notebook detailing the federal troops. Stuart's other major battles included Chancellorsville and Gettysburg. A week before the latter, he conducted a raid that captured more than 400 prisoners and 125 wagons. He was wounded at Yellow Tavern on May 11, 1864, and died the next day. *See also* "Beauty"; "eyes of the army"; "Gay Cavalier"; raid around the army.

Jeff Davis hat *See* Hardee hat.

Jeff Davis muddlehead A nickname for C. Godfrey Gunther, elected New York's mayor in 1863, because he was sympathetic to the South. He was an anti-war Democrat, supported states' rights, and was in favor of letting the South secede. Gunther had also been a founder of the Anti-Abolition State Rights Association.

Jeff Davis neckties *See* Sherman's neckties.

Jefferson Davis The name of one of General Ulysses S. Grant's horses.

Jefferson Hospital A large Union military hospital at Jeffersonville, Indiana, across the river from Louisville, Kentucky. Completed in 1864, it eventually had 2,600 beds on 24 pavilion buildings that were each 175 feet long.

"Jeffn" An abbreviation for his first name that Confederate President Jefferson Davis often used in his letters and messages.

jerked beef Beef dried in the open air without using salt. Other jerked meat included venison.

Jersey lightning A comical name for applejack, brandy that was distilled from fermented cider.

jigger A slang name for a device, contraption, or gadget.

jiggermaree A slang name for a fanciful contraption considered to be worthless, ridiculous, or both.

Jim Crow 1. A name for an average, common man, especially a poor one. 2. An insulting name for a black person.

jimhickey A excellent or exceptionable person or thing; e.g., "I always knew that President Lincoln was a jimhickey." The name was equivalent to "jim-dandy," which was also common during the war.

jim-jams Nervousness or the delirium tremens.

Job's turkey Anyone or anything having a look of destitution or starvation. Union Hospital Steward Solon Hyde of the 17th Ohio Volunteer Infantry, who was captured and held in LIBBY PRISON, noted: "Our squad seemed to be of the 'Job's turkey' order, completely poverty-stricken." The expression came from the Old Testament account of the patriarch Job.

joe or Joe A nickname for a privy or toilet, a variation on the older JOHN OR JOHN.

Joe Brown Pike A pike (lance) ordered by Georgia Governor Joseph E. Brown for Confederate troops from his state. They were each a 12-inch blade on about a 6-foot pole. Some were equipped with ingenious devices, such as a trigger that would shoot a hidden point out of the staff, or a "bridle cutter," a hook to grab and cut an enemy cavalryman's reins. Thousands of Brown's weapons were produced for $5 each and a few were carried around camp, but apparently none was ever launched at a Yankee.

Joe Brown's Pets A nickname for the Georgia MILITIA of Governor Joseph E. Brown. They fought bravely when their state was invaded, being defeated in 1864 at Macon but days later routing the enemy at Honey Hill, having only 8 men killed and 42 wounded to the Union's 88 deaths and 623 wounded.

john or John This nickname for a privy or toilet dates back to the eighteenth century and was commonly used during the war, as was the variant, JOE OR JOE.

John Barleycorn The humorous personification of liquor, especially malt liquor made of barley. One southern soldier remembered a Christmas celebration in camp when "Our generals, and colonels, and captains, had kissed John a little too much."

"John Brown's Body" The stirring, repetitive song that has been called the most popular marching song of Union soldiers, and enjoyed equal popularity with northern civilians. Commemorating the hanging of the abolitionist John Brown in 1859, it appeared in the first year of the war. The author of the song is unknown, but the lyrics of the seven stanzas added to the original one were written by Charles S. Hall of Charlestown, Massachusetts. The first stanza and verse are as follows:

> John Brown's body lies a-mouldering in the grave;
> John Brown's body lies a-mouldering in the grave;
> John Brown's body lies a-mouldering in the grave;
> His soul is marching on.
> Glory, halle—hallelujah!
> Glory, halle—hallelujah!
> Glory, halle—hallelujah!
> His soul is marching on!

Julia Ward Howe later wrote new lyrics to the same tune for her equally popular "THE BATTLE HYMN OF THE REPUBLIC." *See also* "We'll Hang Jeff Davis from a Sour Apple Tree."

Johnny or Johnny Reb The Union nickname for a Confederate soldier. Union Major Clifford Thomson recalled his dash from an enemy attack as follows: "Lying down on my horse's neck, I gave him the spur, and the yells of the 'Johnnies' behind further stimulated him, so that we got over the ground in a lively manner." The name was used as a rude familiarity but also in a friendly way when troops fraternized.

"The Johnny Reb's Epistle to the Ladies" A Confederate poem written in 1862 by "W. E. M." to thank southern women for sending socks to the troops. The final verse went as follows:

> For all the socks the maids have made,
> My thanks, for all the brave;
> And honored be your pious trade,
> The soldier's sole to save.

Johnny Shiloh *See* Drummer Boy of Chickamauga; "The Drummer Boy of Shiloh."

jollification A happy celebration or gathering. When Abraham Lincoln was elected president in 1860, Ulysses S. Grant recalled having "a jollification" in his father's store in Galena, Illinois, in which liquor and oysters were served to the townspeople.

"Jonah" The nickname for a soldier who supposedly was accident prone and brought bad luck to a camp. John D. Billings, a Union ARTILLERYMAN in the Army of the Potomac, recalled Jonahs who spilled soup on companions and kicked over coffee pots and one who accidentally cut his toes off with an ax. Billings added that "The profuseness of the Jonah's apologies—and they always were profuse and undoubtedly sincere—was utterly inadequate as a balm for the wounds he made."

joy juice A slang name for alcohol.

Juba A traditional African dance (originally spelled "Giouba") popular with plantation slaves who developed their own jig dancing style. The slaves were often asked to perform for guests of the plantation owner. One or two performed at the same time inside a large drawn circle in which other slaves sang out a rhythmic song. The dancers improvised the movements and slapped out the same rhythm on the ground with their feet, such as follows:

> Juba jump an' Juba sing.
> Juba cut dat Pigeon's Wing.
> Juba! Juba!

"Jubilee" *See* "Old Jube."

jug To imprison. In his book *Captive of War* (1900), Solon Hyde, a hospital steward of the 17th Regiment of Ohio Volunteer Infantry, wrote about his recapture by Confederates, in a chapter titled "'Jugged' Once More."

jug-steamed A slang name for being intoxicated or drunk. See DRUNK for numerous other terms referring to intoxication.

julep *See* mint julep.

jump In the Union army, a change of name and regiment to collect a bonus for enlisting. New York paid a bounty of $677 to a new recruit. Disreputable drifters, often aided by BOUNTY AGENTS, would receive a bonus for joining a unit, then desert and use an assumed name to join a distant one for another payment. One New York "bounty jumper" was jailed after 32 jumps. A New Englander recalled that after his regiment had ended a long trip down the Rappahannock River in Virginia, half of the newly recruited bounty jumpers had forgotten their aliases and were unable to answer roll call.

junk A derisive nickname used by sailors on both sides for a hard piece of salted beef. A sizable portion of this tough meat was usually served at breakfast with a pint of strong coffee.

Jupiter! A mild curse or expression of surprise, often heard as "By Jupiter!" It was the name of the Roman god of thunder, but also served as a euphemism for "Jesus."

K

Kanawha The name originally proposed for the new loyalist state to be taken from the western counties of Confederate Virginia. More practical minds opted to retain a name connection with the historically famous state, replacing Kanawha with West Virginia.

Kangaroo The name of the horse used by General Ulysses S. Grant during the Vicksburg campaign. It was a Confederate steed found on the field at Shiloh in April 1862 and was described as being large and ugly, with a habit of rearing and charging off when mounted. This happened on June 7, 1863, when a drunken Grant mounted Kangaroo and jammed his spurs into the horse. The war correspondent "CAD" CADWALLADER, recalled the horse's reaction: "Grant literally tore through and over everything in his way. The air was full of dust, ashes and embers from camp fires; and shouts and curses of those he rode down in his race." Cadwallader tried to catch up with the general "as fast as I could go, but my horse was no match for Kangaroo." *See also* Cincinnati; Fox; Jack.

Kearny Cross A bronze cross of valor awarded in posthumous honor of Union Major General Philip Kearny to enlisted personnel in his former command who distinguished themselves during battle. Kearny had been killed on September 1, 1862, and his successor, Brigadier General David B. Birney, instituted the award on March 13, 1863. Those who had been awarded the KEARNY MEDAL could not receive the Cross. One of the first people selected for the Cross was nurse Anna Etheridge, who was known as "MICHIGAN ANNIE."

Kearny Medal A gold medal awarded in posthumous honor of Union Major General Philip Kearny to officers in his former command who had served with distinction in battle under him. The medal was a cross with a circle containing the words *"Dulce et decorum est pro patria mori"* ["It is sweet and meet to die for one's country"] and the name "Kearny" in the center. It was instituted by the officers on November 29, 1862, three months after Kearny's death in battle, and a few months before the KEARNY CROSS was awarded.

Kearny patch A piece of scarlet cloth worn on the front of the caps of officers and men commanded by Union Major General Philip Kearny, who supposedly had his own red flannel blanket cut up for this purpose. The patches were worn so Kearny could identify his own soldiers. That decision came after he had cursed out a group of officers from another command whom he had mistakenly identified as stragglers from his division. His troops became known as the Red Diamond Divison, and the Kearny patch was worn with such pride that Major General Joseph Hooker issued an order on March 21, 1863, commanding other army corps to wear badges as well. This order led to the shoulder patches that have been worn ever since by U.S. soldiers. The Confederate troops had no badges.

keep a stiff upper lip This American expression (often thought to be British) was current during the war. It could be employed on the battlefield to urge a man not to panic and used in camp to persuade a mess mate to be unmoved by a sweetheart's fickleness.

keep company To court or to be a romantic couple; e.g., "The sergeant and that Miss Arnold in town seem to be keeping company a lot this summer."

keep tavern To be in control, especially through good organization. This was a favorite expression of President Abraham Lincoln, who once said of Brigadier General Joseph Hooker that he could fight, but "whether he can 'keep tavern' for a large army is not so sure."

keg torpedo An underwater mine ("torpedo") invented by Confederate Brigadier General Gabriel J. Rains, head of the Topedo Bureau. Made from beer barrels, the torpedoes were shaped like thin (modern) footballs and resembled lanterns peering from the water. A combustible substance was ignited by friction and a wick in a tube led down to a can packed with from 35 to 120 pounds of powder. Kegs were the most successful torpedoes of the war, sinking six ships around Mo-

bile in 1865, but also two Confederate steamers in Charleston harbor when the devices drifted away from their moorings.

kelter A slang name for money.

keno A game like bingo that was popular with gamblers in camp.

Keokuk A Union IRONCLAD warship that, after being fired upon by the guns of Fort Sumter on April 7, 1862, was described by an eyewitness as "the most severely mauled ship one ever saw." The *Keokuk* took 90 direct hits from Sumter's cannons during the engagement in which the fort devastated eight new ironclad ships under Rear Admiral Samuel Du Pont. Returning "riddled like a colander," the *Keokuk* sank within hours. The other monitors were also badly crippled, taking more than 200 hits between them.

kepi A soldier's wool cap with a low crown, tipped slightly forward, and a straight leather visor. It was based on a French style of FORAGE CAP, with "kepi" meaning "cap." Officers could add gold piping and braid on the crown, but enlisted men wore them plain. A popular copy of the kepi was the MCCLELLAN CAP.

kersey A coarse woolen cloth, often ribbed, that was used for blankets, especially for enlisted men, and for some uniforms, such as the sky-blue ones worn by the VETERAN RESERVE CORPS. The name came from Kersey, England, which had a woolen trade.

Ketcham's grenade The most popular HAND-GRENADE used by the Union army, with more than 93,000 produced for the war. Resembling a large fat dart, it was a cast-iron device filled with gunpowder and steadied in flight by a rear wooden rod with pasteboard fins. On impact, a flat-nosed metal rod in the grenade's oval head would be thrust back to set off a percussion cap and explode the powder.

kick A southern word meaning to break off with a male sweetheart or suitor or to jilt someone; e.g. "That Tennessee girl kicked the sergeant last weekend."

kick and cuff To fight or scuffle by kicking and hitting.

kick the bucket The familiar euphemism, meaning to die, has continued in fashion since the eighteenth century and was a familiar phrase during the war. It possibly referred to a hanging suicide in which the person died by kicking away from bucket on which he stood. Also, a slaughtered pig in England was hung from a piece of wood called a bucket. Earlier slang terms in England for dying, included "kick," "kick up," "kick it" and "kick up (one's) heels."

kick up a dust To start a big argument or cause a disturbance or commotion; e.g., "Every time Pender loses at cards, he kicks up a dust."

kid-glove boy An insulting name for a soldier, especially one who was fastidious in camp.

kidnapping Stealing free black children and adults to sell them to plantations. The term originated in the slave system in the

Ketcham's grenade. *Copyright Inge Wright 1999.*

seventeenth century, and by the time of the war meant stealing blacks from free states to sell in the South. Kidnapping before and during the war was illegal and also disapproved by most slave holders. *See also* sold South.

Kilkenny-cat affair A rough and tumble fight or argument. A running feud between the Union's Major General Benjamin Butler and Admiral David Porter was described as "a regular Kilkenny-cat affair." A Kilkenny cat was a simile for a wild, desperate animal or person. This image came from an old story in the Irish county of Kilkenny of two cats that once fought so ferociously that only a small piece of the tail of one of them remained.

kill To drink every drop or eat every bite. "I can kill a watermelon" would be an understood boast in camp.

"Kill Cavalry" A nickname given to Union Brigadier General Judson Kilpatrick after his March 1864 cavalry raid to rescue prisoners in Richmond was repulsed by a HOME GUARD of youths and old men, and Kilpatrick's 3,500 men were routed back to Union lines by regular Confederate soldiers. As used by his troops, the nickname was ambiguous, suggesting he was either an aggressive leader or one who killed off his own cavalry. Also called "Little Kil," Kilpatrick had been the first regular army officer to be wounded in the war (on June 10, 1861) and ended it leading the cavalry of Major General W.T. Sherman on his march through Georgia.

killick or kellick A small anchor. Sometimes a killick for a rowboat was merely a stone or other weight secured by a rope or chain.

kindlers Kindling wood for starting a fire.

Kingdom Come The Kingdom of Heaven, the name coming directly from the Lord's

General Judson Kilpatrick, a Union cavalry officer, was nicknamed "Kill Cavalry" by his men. *Library of Congress, Prints & Photographs Division, LC-B8172-1391.*

Prayer. In 1862, Union artillerymen at the battle of Shiloh fired their BRASS MISSIONARY CANNONS and vowed to "convert the Rebels or send 'em to Kingdom Come."

"Kingdom Coming" A Union marching song celebrating the freedom of the slaves. It was written in 1861 by the abolitionist songwriter Henry Clay Work, who chose the Negro dialect for the lyrics. The song was sung by Union troops as they marched into Richmond after General Robert E. Lee's surrender in 1865. The chorus began as follows:

De massa run? ha, ha!
De darkey stay? ho, ho!
It mus' be now de kingdom comin',
An' de year ob Jubilo!

"King of Spades" *See* "Ace of Spades."

Kirby Smith-dom The TRANS-MISSISSIPPI (west of the Mississippi) Department of the Confederacy. It was named for General E. Kirby Smith who ruled the area (one-third the size of the whole Confederacy) like a king. He was a tough leader who adopted the policy of executing any black U.S. soldier whom he captured. Smith was one of the last officers to surrender, doing so at Galveston, Texas, on May 28, 1865, seven weeks after General Lee's surrender in Virginia. *See also* "Seminole."

kissing cousin A southern name for a distant relative whom one could legally marry.

kiss-me-quick The delightful, informal name for a lady's quilted bonnet worn to important social occasions or the theater. The bonnets, usually homemade, did not extend beyond the face as sun-bonnets did.

"Kiss my arse" or "Kiss my ass" This timeless insult was one of the most common during the war, and often said by bold enlisted men to officers. "Arse" is the traditional British spelling and pronunciation, still used in that country.

"Kit" The nickname of Christopher Carson, a Union brigadier general by BREVET. Born in Kentucky, he was well known as an Indian agent, guide, trapper, and hunter. Although he married an Arapahoe woman, Carson led Union volunteers against Indian groups that supported the Confederacy.

Klapperschlangenflagge The nickname given to the Confederate flag by Germans in the Union army. It meant "Rattlesnake Flag."

knapsack A bag holding a soldier's necessities, such as his pipe, underwear, paper and pens, soap, towels, toothbrush, eating utensils, comb, cotton strips for wounds, a HOUSEWIFE with sewing items, and anything else a man felt he needed.

Knapsack. *Copyright Inge Wright 1999.*

Wrapped around the knapsack were usually two blankets and a rubber blanket. All this could weigh up to 25 pounds, and Eisha Rhodes of the 2nd Rhode Island Volunteers wrote, "My knapsack was so heavy that I could scarcely stagger under the load." Many soldiers discarded them as the conflict wore on, stuffing the items into their smaller HAVERSACK. Knapsacks, however, could also easily serve as makeshift pillows during short breaks on the march.

knapsack drill A punishment in the Union army for minor violations of camp rules. The offender would have to wear his KNAPSACK filled with bricks or rocks as he walked a beat under the eye of a guardsman, usually for two hours on and two or four hours off.

knee-high to a splinter Very young, because the height mentioned is always in a sentence similar to, "I knew him when he was knee-high to a splinter." Also popular during the war was "knee-high to a toad."

Knights of the Golden Circle A secret organization of southern sympathizers in the North. They called for an end to the war, its members becoming PEACE DEMOCRATS and being labeled COPPERHEADS. In his 1863 book, *Our Stars*, Norman Gunnison of the 2nd New Hampshire Volunteers, addressed the organization, asking, "are you so lost to all sense of honor, to the common dictates of humanity, as to dip your hands in the blood of your fathers, brothers and sons, as you are now doing, and hold them, reeking with kindred gore, to the world?" By 1863, the Knights had become the Order of American Knights and a year later were renamed the Sons of Liberty.

knocked into a cocked hat An expression meaning knocked out of shape or ruined, because an old-fashioned cocked hat had three corners. "Beauregard has knocked them into a cocked hat," said one secessionist shopkeeper in Washington, D.C., after the two sides skirmished a day before the battle of Bull Run in 1861.

knock off This familiar expression, meaning to quit work for the day or a shorter period, was first heard about a decade before the war began.

knock someone into the middle of next week To defeat or beat someone badly. After the Union defeat at the second battle of Bull Run in 1862, President Abraham Lincoln quoted the phrase and, recalling the first battle of Bull Run in 1861, added that "the Rebels have knocked us into the middle of last year."

knock up To tire out with fatigue; e.g., "We marched all day through mountain roads until the whole brigade was knocked up."

know B from a bull's foot A delightful insult was that a person "doesn't know B from a bull's foot," meaning he was stupid. Sometimes this became "doesn't know B from a broomstick." Both terms meant nothing in themselves, other than the alliteration of the "b" sound.

know on To know about. This form was common in the speech of slaves.

Konshattountzchette *See* Flying Cloud.

L

"la belle Rebelle" "The beautiful rebel," the French nickname given in the U.S. to the Confederate spy, Belle Boyd. After being caught and imprisoned twice in northern jails, she fled to London, England, where on August 25, 1864, she married a Confederate BLOCKADE RUNNER who had followed her. She became an actress and published her memoir, *Belle Boyd: In Camp and Prison*. After the war, Belle returned to the U.S. to act and give public talks about her spying days.

Ladies Defense Association An organization formed in March 1862 by women in Williamsburg, Virginia, to raise money to build an IRONCLAD warship that would patrol the James River and defend Richmond. Women throughout Virginia raised money by selling their personal jewelry, silver plate, and other heirlooms. They also helped collect the iron by donating iron railings, broken plows, and scrap iron. Within four months, the *Richmond* was completed, modeled on the *Virginia*. It served actively in the James River squadron, and was burned with the other ships of the squadron on April 3, 1865, as the Confederate government was vacating the city. *See also "Merrimac No. 2."*

lager Beer was considered the poor relation of stronger spirits during the war, and soldiers were strangely unimpressed with lager. Confederate soldier Allen C. Redwood of Virginia recalled after the war that "Whisky was, of course, at a high premium, but a keg of 'lager'—a drink less popular then than now—went begging in our company."

lamp-post 1. A nickname for a gunboat's elongated shell, such as the 10-inch shell. The term was especially used by Confederates. 2. A nickname for an artillery shell in flight, because the eye preceived it as a hazy pole-like blur that reminded soldiers of a lamppost. 3. A Confederate nickname for a stand that held grape shot. It was a cylinder attached to a cast-iron base, resembling a lampstick in a bowl. The Union ship *Brooklyn* even fired them at Fort St. Philip on the lower Mississippi River. After surrendering, the Confederates complained that the fort was full of "infernal lamp-posts," which were worse than the grape shot.

The Lancers A fashionable dance that was a type of QUADRILLE in which four couples danced different figures from a square formation.

"Land of Legree and the Home of the Slave" The New York *Tribune*'s description of the southern states. This rewording of the *Star-Spangled Banner* worked in Simon Legree, the cruel overseer in Harriett Beecher Stowe's UNCLE TOM'S CABIN.

"Landsakes!" An exclamation of surprise or irritation; e.g., "Landsakes, private! Can't you calm that horse?" The form "For landsakes!" was often used, clearly showing that the euphemism replaced "For the Lord's sake!"

landsman A derogatory nickname for a naval recruit who had never gone to sea.

lanyard The braided cord that a gunner pulled to fire a cannon. The lanyard was attached to the primer and was jerked to ignite the primer and send a flash of fire at the cartridge. The name came from short ropes used on ships.

larrup An informal or dialect word meaning to whip, thrash, beat, or defeat.

the last ditch A symbolic term used for the grave of the Confederacy, based on the many ditches (trenches) dug during the war. John Wilkes Booth, in a letter left with J.S. Clarke, his brother-in-law, before the assassination of President Abraham Lincoln, said of the South: "They say she had found that 'last ditch' which the North has so long derided and been endeavoring to force her in, forgetting they are our brothers, and that it is impolitic to goad an enemy to madness. Should I reach her in safety, and find it true, I will proudly beg permission to triumph or die in that same 'ditch' by her side."

laudable pus A military doctor's common term for the pus excreted by an infected wound, usually three to four days after it was incurred on the battlefield. The pus was called "laudable" because surgeons believed the liquid matter was the wound's lining and that the excretion was a cleasing process to allow the growth of new, healing tissue.

laudanum An opium and wine mixture; a tincture of opium. In addition to its use by military doctors during the war, this drug was made and used at home. Parthenia Hague, on a plantation near Eufaula, Alabama, described how ladies would grow poppies in their gardens for opium to make laudanum. ("This at times was very needful.") The women would pierce the opium capsules with large sewing needles to extract the opium gum. Hague proudly noted that "The soporific influence of this drug was not excelled by that of the imported articles." *See also* chloroform; ether; morphia.

lavender water A sweet-smelling toilet water or perfume made from lavender flowers. It was used by nurses in military hospitals, who dabbed the area, as well as themselves, to overcome bad odors.

law or laws A dialectal exclamation of astonishment. In Harriett Beecher Stowe's UNCLE TOM'S CABIN, the slave girl Topsy usually resorted to "Laws, Missis!" when accused by her mistress of stealing.

lay it on heavy over An especially informal southern expression that meant to surpass or be better. After Confederate soldier Sam Watkins heard the prayer of a local preacher, he said "it lays it on heavy over any prayer I ever heard."

lead pills A witty and flippant name for bullets.

leadsman A ship's sailor in charge of taking depth soundings with a lead line. They were especially needed when warships negotiated rivers. *See also* "No bottom."

leaseways The dialect form of "leasewise," meaning "anyway." It was much more commonly said during the war than today.

"leather" *See* "ginned cotton."

leatherhead A nickname for someone from Pennsylvania.

leather medal A slang name for a lash used as punishment in camp. The term was also used for the scar caused by such a lashing.

"Lee's Miserables" The nickname Confederate soldiers gave themselves late in the war. It was a pun on Victor Hugo's popular novel, LES MISERABLES, which was published during the war.

left wheel or right wheel A military movement to outflank an enemy. A left wheel was accomplished when troops on the right swung forward and around like a wheel moving counterclockwise, while a right wheel had troops of the left swinging forward and around clockwise.

"left wing of Lee's army" A derogatory nickname given by northerners to the street mobs of the New York City DRAFT RIOTS, which terrorized the city from July 13-15, 1863.

leg case The humorous description used by President Abraham Lincoln for a normally brave man who ran from a battle because, the president said, he had cowardly legs.

leghorn A hat or bonnet made of plaited Italian straw that has been bleached. A northern female observer at the first battle of Bull Run in 1861 was described as "looking brave as possible, with her narrow-brimmed leghorn hat." The hats were traditionally made in Leghorn, a seaport in Tuscany, Italy.

legion A nonregulation military unit popular early in the war, especially in the South. Usually commanded by a colonel, and about the size of a REGIMENT or BRIGADE, it brought together all the arms of the infantry, artillery, and cavalry. Most were later broken up, such as Hampton's South Carolina Legion, which was separated into an infantry regiment and artillery battalion, with the cavalrymen sent to a larger cavalry unit. Today's equivalent to a legion is the combat team. *See also* Indiana Legion.

Les Miserables Victor Hugo's novel, first published in 1862, that became a sensation in both North and South during the war. One southern woman known only as Agnes sent a copy to her friend, Mrs. Roger Pryor, saying, "You'll go wild over that book—I did—and everybody does." She noted that all the soldiers were reading it, adding, "They calmly walk into the bookstores, poor dear fellows, and ask for 'LEE'S MISERABLES faintin'!'—the first volume being 'Fantine'."

Let her rip! This well-known slang expression was coined in the United States a few years before the war and was popular among soldiers on both sides. It generally meant "let her go," as when firing a cannon.

Letterman Ambulance Plan The first professional-style ambulance system in the Civil War. It was formed by Jonathan Letterman, medical director of the U.S. Army of the Potomac, before the battle of Antietam in 1862. Each division had an organized ambulance system that worked together under a line sergeant, and each ambulance was assigned a regular driver and two stretcher-bearers to take the wounded from the battlefield to a DRESSING STATION and then to a FIELD HOSPITAL. Prior to Letterman's plan, the Union used members of the army band to drive ambulances. The U.S. Ambulance Corps bill of 1864 put this type of system into operation in all Union armies.

letters of marque Official documents issued by the Confederacy to ships allowing them to arm and seize Union merchant vessels. The common northern word for this agreement was "piracy."

levee Tradionally, a morning reception, although some were held in the afternoon. They were important social events in Washington, D.C., with famous ones being given by the wife of Illinois Democratic Senator Stephen A. Douglas. When the Lincolns hosted their first levee after arriving in Washington, it was so disorganized, the Washington *Star* estimated that only one in ten guests left with their own coats and hats. Confederate President Jefferson Davis also held frequent levees in Richmond, Virginia, where officers, politicians, and fashionable citizens could mingle and socialize. This French word for "raising" was used in the sense of having a reception soon after people had risen in the morning.

"Level Eye" A nickname for Brigadier General Grenville M. Dodge, a civil engineer, given to him by Indians before the war as they watched him engaged in railroad surveying.

The Libby Chronicle A handwritten newspaper published by Union prisoners held in LIBBY PRISON in Richmond, Virginia. *See also* "Libby Lyceum."

"Libby Lyceum" A debating society organized by Union officers held prisoner in LIBBY PRISON in Richmond, Virginia. The ongoing debates were said to be spirited. *See also The Libby Chronicle.*

Libby Prison A three-story Confederate prison on the James River in Richmond, Virginia, often called "The Libby." The building was formerly the warehouse of Libby and Sons, ship chandlers (suppliers of ship equipment). It was next to two other prisons, Pemberton and Smith, sometimes incorrectly considered to be part of Libby because all had a central administration. Libby was restricted to

An 1865 photograph of Libby Prison in Richmond, Virginia. *Library of Congress, Prints & Photographs Division, LC-B8171-2726.*

Union officers, held in the west wing, but the prison, whose commandant was Thomas P. Turner, had a "hell hole" reputation. On February 9, 1864, Colonel Thomas E. Rose of Pennsylvania led 107 other Yankee officers in a famous escape, tunneling down to the basement and 50 feet into the James River Towing Company next door. A total of 58 escapees successfully reached their own lines, Rose and 47 others were captured, and two drowned crossing the James. By May 1864, all of Libby's inmates were transferred to a new prison in Macon, Georgia, mainly because of Union raids. *See also The Libby Chronicle*; "Libby Lyceum."

"Libeler of the Press" The sign pinned by Union General George Meade on Edward Crapsey, the *Philadelphia Inquirer*'s war correspondent. Crapsey had filed an unfavorable story on the general, so Meade had his men affix the sign and place the reporter backward on a mule to be ridden out of camp. Meade's name was thereafter dropped from influential northern newspapers except in stories of Union defeats in which he was involved.

liberate To steal, a soldier's euphemism. Foraging troops might "liberate a hen" for a special evening meal.

The Liberator The Boston abolitionist newspaper established and edited by William Lloyd Garrison, who was also one of the founders of the AMERICAN ANTISLAVERY SOCIETY. The paper, published from 1831 through the war, had great influence in the North, especially New England. Its masthead showed Jesus standing over a manacled slave and a frightened slaveowner, surrounded by the words "I come to break the bonds of the oppressor." Below were the words "Thou shalt love thy neighbor" and the paper's motto, "Our Country is the World, Our Countrymen are all Mankind."

"Liberty Hall" The home of Confederate Vice President Alexander H. Stephens at Crawfordsville, Georgia.

lick 1. A physical hit or mental blow. When Senator Charles Sumner of Massachusetts asked President Abraham Lincoln to issue a general decree of emancipation on July 4, 1862, Lincoln replied that it would be "too big a lick." 2. A tiny amount or small portion or a bit. This Scottish word was used then and now in such sentences as, "He can't fight a lick."

lickety-split or lickety-cut These expressions, meaning at a great speed or quickly, were created about a year before the war began. "Lickety liner" was sometimes heard. The first of the three still survives.

lickspittal A slang name for a servile person who is dependent on someone.

lief Willingly or gladly, always used in the phrases "had as lief" and "would as lief." It was said of Charles A. Page, war correspondent for the New York *Tribune* that

"He had just as lief go under fire as go into an oyster house." The word is related to the German "lieb" ("beloved").

lier-out The nickname for a Confederate soldier who deserted or was a fugitive from conscription. They often hid out in the moutains.

life everlasting A common name for the cudweed. It was sometimes called a herb and was used by Southern women to make a substitute for yeast, having a similar property of hops.

light ball A CARCASS shell filled with magnesium that would flare into a brilliant light when exploded. Such shells were used at night to illuminate enemy positions and were sometimes exploded behind enemy lines to silhouette the defenses.

light cornbread A spongy cornbread made by southern soldiers (and often by their northern prisoners). The soft part of the cornbread was soaked overnight, making it sour. This was whipped into a light, sweet batter by adding soda. New extra meal was then added to provide more body before the bread was baked.

The Light Division The nickname for the division of Confederate Lieutenant General Ambrose Hill, because of its members' rapid marching. He led them at Mechanicsville and Gaines' Mill in 1862 before the DIVISION was transferred to Major General "STONEWALL" Jackson. They later fought at the second battle of Bull Run, Fredericksburg, and at Antietam, where they marched 17 miles in eight hours on a hot September day to arrive at the last minute and save the endangered Army of Northern Virginia.

lighthouse A slang name for any saloon.

Lightning Brigade The nickname given to the mounted infantry brigade of Union

Brigadier General John T. Wilder, who insisted his foot soldiers be given horses and repeating Spencer rifles. The brigade was later commanded by Brigadier General Abram O. Miller.

like a duck hit on the head One of President Abraham Lincoln's favorite expressions to describe someone who was baffled or dumbfounded. After Union Major General William S. Rosecrans was defeated at Chickamauga on September 20, 1863, Lincoln complained that his general was acting "confused and stunned, like a duck hit on the head."

like a thousand of brick A simile that was an adverb meaning "heavily" or "vigorously." After a battle, a soldier might brag, "We were on them like a thousand of brick."

like shoveling flies across a barnyard A humorous expression describing something that was difficult or useless to do. It was popular with President Abraham Lincoln, who employed it when explaining the futility of sending reinforcements to the Union's hesitant Major General George B. McClellan. *See also* shovel fleas.

limber The two-wheeled front section of a gun carriage. The limber was attached to the horses (usually six) by a shaft, and the cannon was attached behind the limber. Upon arriving at a battlefield, the cannon was "unlimbered" (detached) and moved into firing position. The limber was then taken to the rear; the recommended distance was six yards, but this was usually increased because of the danger of an explosion. A BATTERY would "limber up" or "limber the guns" after a battle or if retreating. A LIMBER CHEST (ammunition chest) was usually carried on the limber. The word is related to "limb" because limbers were once only boughs of trees. *See also* "Limber to the rear!"

limber chest An wood and iron ammunition chest for cannons carried onto the battlefield on a LIMBER that was unhooked during a battle. In the routine of artillery firing, gunners Number 6 and Number 7 manned the ammunition chest and passed cartridges to Number 5. Extra ammunition chests were carried on CAISSONS.

Limber chest. *Copyright Inge Wright 1999.*

"Limber to the rear!" The order to a BATTERY to move a cannon's LIMBER to the rear out of danger during a battle. This was immediately after the gun had been "unlimbered."

limner A formal and somewhat pompous name for an artist, especially one who painted portraits; e.g., "*Harper's Weekly* is known for the quality of its limners." The word, which dates back to the fourteenth century, orginally referred to illuminators of manuscripts.

Lincoln boys A nickname, especially in the South, for Union soldiers.

Lincoln gimlets *See* Sherman's neckties.

Lincoln pies or McClellan pies Nicknames given by Union soldiers to HARDTACK biscuits.

"Lincoln's life or a Tiger's death" *See* "Tiger Rifles."

Lincoln's soldiers A common name given by slaves to Union troops.

links of one sausage, made out of the same dog The evocative description of like things or groups that have different names. A Judge Miller of Ohio used the simile in regard to the WAR DEMOCRATS and abolitionists. Miller was quoted by New York's Governor Horatio Seymour during the National Democratic Convention that assembled in Chicago on August 29, 1864.

lip A slang word, still used today, for disrespectful or insolent talk.

liquor up To drink liquor, especially to become drunk.

litter corps A detail of soldiers who carried wounded men from the battlefield, usually on litters (stretchers). When done during a battle, litter bearers would sometimes drop their charges in their haste and even be shot themselves. Some of the bearers even made a habit out of robbing the seriously wounded.

"Little Aleck" The nickname for Georgia's highly intelligent Alexander Stephens, the Confederate vice president, because he was small and frail, weighing only about 90 pounds, and had a high-pitched, weak voice. He was a former friend of Abraham Lincoln, who nevertheless described him as a "little, slim, pale-faced consumptive man." Stephens voted against his state seceding but then embraced the Confederacy to such an extent that he ran for the presidency, losing to Jefferson Davis. The two men often disagreed about the war and the government. Stephens was one of three Confederates who officially met with Lincoln on February 3, 1865, to try (unsuccessfully) to negotiate an end to the war that would preserve the Confederacy. See also "Smart Aleck."

"Little Billy" 1. The nickname for Confederate Major General William Mahone, a short Virginian. He was so thin that his wife, when told he had received a flesh wound, remarked that it was serious because "William has no flesh whatever." A gray slouch hat always shaded his blue eyes. Mahone, who fought in key battles from Bull Run to Gettysburg, was on the spot promoted to major general by General Robert E. Lee on July 30, 1864, after Mahone's victorious action at the PETERSBURG CRATER. Lee's surrender in 1865 came after Mahone sent a request to Union Major General Andrew A. Humphreys for an hour's truce to treat the wounded. With agreement to the truce came General Ulysses Grant's letter to Lee asking for surrender. After the war, Mahone, despite his piping voice, became a U.S. senator. 2. The nickname of Confederate Major General William H. Chase who was beloved by his troops. Below average height, he fought at such battles as first Bull Run and Seven Pines, finally defending Fort Fisher, North Carolina, where he was wounded and captured on January 15, 1865. He died two months later in prison.

"the Little Creole" A nickname for Confederate General P.G.T. Beauregard, because he was a Creole of short stature from Louisiana. See also "Little Napoleon"; "Man of Sumter"; Peter; "Old Bory."

"Little Kil" See "Kill Cavalry."

"Little Mac" The nickname given by his men to Union Major General George McClellan of the Army of the Potomac, because of his short height. He was also called YOUNG NAPOLEON. He graduated second in his class at West Point in 1846 and during the war proved an inspiring officer and wonderful organizer, but hesitant in the field. (He had ironically called General Robert E. Lee "cautious and

Union Major General George B. McClellan, shown here with his wife Ellen Mary Marcy, was nicknamed "Little Mac." *Library of Congress, Prints & Photographs Division, LC-B8172-1765.*

weak.") In November 1862, after failing to follow up his success at Antietam, McClellan was relieved of his command by President Lincoln. Little Mac's revenge in 1864 was to run as the Democratic candidate for president, claiming the war was a failure. Lincoln defeated him for a second term. *See also* "McClellan's Bodyguard"; "Our George."

"Little Magician" A nickname for former President Martin Van Buren, because of his political skills and his ability to manage the press. The diminutive man was also called "Little Van." Having been the presidential candidate in 1848 for the antislavery Free-Soil Party, he later supported Abraham Lincoln's successful bid

for the White House and continued to promote his antislavery views until his death in 1862. Washington, D.C., honored his death by lowering flags to half-mast, giving gun salutes, and hanging CRAPE (black crepe paper) around the city. *See also* "the Fox of Kinderhook."

"Little Napoleon" A nickname for Confederate General P.G.T. Beauregard, because of his French heritage, short height, and commanding presence. *See also* "Little Creole"; "Man of Sumter"; Peter; "Old Bory."

"Little Phil" The nickname of Union Major General Philip Sheridan, who was 5'5" tall and weighed 115 pounds. When group photographs were being arranged, Little Phil would quickly sit in an available chair. Size meant nothing, however, when Sheridan took to the battlefield. He became head of the cavalry corps of the Army of the Potomac in April 1864. He was successful at the BATTLE ABOVE THE CLOUDS at Chattanooga, the Wilderness, and the battle of Five Forks, but suffered a costly defeat at Chickamauga in 1863. Sheridan is perhaps best known for his famous 1864 Richmond raid, riding completely around General Robert E. Lee's army and, at the battle of Yellow Tavern, leading his 12,000 men to victory over the 4,500 troops of General Jeb Stuart, who was mortally wounded. Sheridan is also remembered for his ruthless "scorched earth" devastation of the Shenandoah Valley in 1864 and 1865. His last success was cutting off General Lee's retreat from Appomattox Court House to end the war. After the war, in 1884, he was made commander of the entire army. *See also* "Fighting Phil"; "Smash 'em up! Smash 'em up!"

Little Round Top A small rocky hill that was successfully occupied by Union forces at the battle of Gettysburg. From its height, artillery pounded the Confederate lines, and Rebel troops made a great effort to capture the position, which would have laid the entire Union position open to ENFILADE. The attack, however, was beaten back by troops led by Brigadier General Gouverneur K. Warren, who had recognized the hill's strategic position. A monument to Warren now rests on Little Round Top.

Little Sorrel *See* Old Sorrel.

"Little 'Un" The nickname given by his men to diminutive Confederate Brigadier General James R. Chalmers, an infantryman who transferred to the cavalry. As a colonel, he fought under Lieutenant General Nathan Bedford Forrest before assuming command of all cavalry in Mississippi and West Tennessee on February 18, 1865. Chalmers fought at Shiloh and Stones River. He once pursued the troops of A.J. Smith so vigorously in Mississippi that the Union general abandoned some 100 miles of telegraph wire. After the war, Chalmers became a Democratic congressman.

"Little Van" *See* "Little Magician."

living within oneself Being self-sufficient. It was a common expression on plantations, as Mary Boykin Chestnut of South Carolina recorded in her diary on May 24, 1862: "And then the planters live 'within themselves,' as they call it. From the plantations come mutton, beef, poultry, cream, butter, eggs, fruits, and vegetables."

"Lo" The nickname given by his men to Confederate Brigadier General Lewis A. Armistead. It stood for Shakespeare's character, the seducer Lothario, a joke on the shy and quiet-spoken widower who was known to admire the ladies. He was also known for his temper, however, having been dismissed from West Point for breaking a plate over the head of Jubal Early. Armistead participated in the campaigns of General Robert E. Lee and was killed in 1863 leading part of PICKETT'S CHARGE at Gettysburg, dying over the muzzle of a Union cannon.

loblolly A dialect word for a thick gruel or mudhole. "The dirt road would soon be worked into a loblolly of sticky yellow mud," wrote one of the soldiers on Union Major General W.T. Sherman's march through Mississippi in July 1863.

lobscouse A Union stew or soup seasoned with salt meat, usually pork, and thickened with vegetables and HARDTACK biscuits. It was a traditional meal of sailors but also enjoyed by the army. It originally was "lob's course," with lob being an old word for "boiling."

lobster back A Union sailor's insulting nickname for a marine. The marines were disliked by navymen because they were not assigned drudgery work on ships. A Union sailor, Alval Hunter, wrote, "One of the first things taught me was that a marine was the natural enemy of every sailor, and that all sailors were in duty bound to get ahead of the marines whenever possible."

Loco-foco The Democractic Party or a member of it. The name dates back to 1835 during a dispute between New York's Democrats in Tammany Hall. One group extinguished the gas lights to end the loud, confused debate, but the Equal Rights group had anticipated this and lit candles from friction matches called loco-focos. The name was soon applied to the faction and then to the party or any Democrat.

locomotive An alcoholic drink made of burgundy, curacao liqueur, and egg yolks and flavored with the essence of cloves. It was whisked and served hot.

lodgment A lodging house or similar accomodation; e.g., "We found a lodgment when we arrived in Richmond."

logicize A formal word meaning to reason; e.g., "One of God's highest gifts to man is the ability to logicize."

"Lone Star flag" Although now associated only with Texas, the Lone Star flag was the nickname for the flags of several Confederate states, especially Louisiana, South Carolina, and Virginia. The Louisiana state flag, adopted in 1861 after the state seceded, had 13 stripes (for the expected Confederate states) that were colored (from the top) four blue, six white and three red. The square design was red with one pale yellow five-pointed star in its center. When Union troops entered New Orleans and hauled the flag down from the City Hall, the mayor warned them that anyone lowering it might be shot by "the indignant populace," but the large crowd only looked on in sullen silence.

Long Bridge The wooden bridge over the Potomac River at Washington, D.C. During the war, the planks were removed at night to protect the capital from Confederate cavalry across the river. After the first battle of Bull Run in 1861, the defeated and devastated Union soldiers flooded over Long Bridge to fill the streets of Washington.

long chalk A long way or great amount. A soldier might say, "We marched a long chalk further than they did." The expression "by a long chalk" is still common in Great Britain, coming from the chalk used to score games, such as darts.

long roll A long snare-drum roll to wake sleeping soldiers for quick action. It often was given between 2 a.m. and 4 a.m. on the day of a battle, or for early marches to a battle.

a long summer day A southern expression meaning a long time. Union General Ulysses Grant told the visiting President Abraham Lincoln in June 1864 about his certainty on reaching Richmond and added, "It may take a long summer day, as they say in the Rebel papers, but I will do it."

long sweetening A nickname for molasses; e.g., "Our mess had not seen sugar for a month and not much long sweetening."

"Long Tom" The nickname for a 30-pounder PARROTT cannon. The name was originally used for a Union cannon that was captured at the first battle of Bull Run 1861, and then applied to any Parrott.

loo A card game in which players had to contribute stakes into a pool and pay a forfeit ("loo") for not taking a trick or for breaking a rule of the game. A player having to pay was "looed." Versions included three-card loo and five-card loo. The game, first played in seventeenth-century Europe, was a favorite of Union General Ulysses S. Grant.

looking-glass A common wartime name for a mirror.

looking out for number one This well-know modern expression about protecting one's own self-interest was common during the war; e.g., "The army wants you to volunteer for this and that, but I'm looking out for number one."

Lookout The name of Union Brigadier General Joseph Hooker's horse, which he named after the BATTLE ABOVE THE CLOUDS on Lookout Mountain at Chattanooga, Tennessee. The chestnut horse stood almost 17 hands and was noted for its rapid trot.

"loose bowels" An irreverent nickname for an army doctor.

looseness An informal name used in the West for freedom and candidness; e.g., "General Butler always spoke with a natural looseness."

"Lorena" A beautiful, melancholy southern song composed by the Rev. D.H. Webster, a Trappist monk in Kentucky, with words by J.P. Webster. It has been called the song closest to the Confederate soldier's heart and the "ANNIE LAURIE" of the Confederate trenches. When the troops of Confederate General John B. Hood left Atlanta after burning ordnance stores before Major General W.T. Sherman's army arrived, they marched out to the strains of "Lorena." The last of the six stanzas is as follows:

> It matters little now, Lorena,
> The past is in the eternal past;
> Our heads will soon lie low, Lorena,
> Life's tide is ebbing out so fast.
> But there's a future, oh! thank God—
> Of life this is so small a part.
> 'Tis dust to dust beneath the sod;
> But there, up there, 'tis heart to heart.

the lost army The nickname given by the northern press to the army of Union Major General W.T. Sherman as it went out of contact for 33 days during its march through Georgia. Even President Abraham Lincoln admitted: "I know the hole he went in at, but I can't tell you what hole he will come out of."

"Lost Order" or "Lost Dispatch" Special Order No. 191 by Confederate General Robert E. Lee that detailed his plans to invade Maryland in September 1862. It was accidentally left behind on September 12, 1862, at Frederick, Maryland, and discovered the next day by a Union soldier, Private B.W. Mitchell of Company F of the 27th Indiana Volunteers. The order, found wrapped around three cigars, was quickly sent to Major General George B. McClellan, who used the information to stop the advance of Lee's army at the battle of Antietam.

"Lost tribes of Israel" The nickname Union General A.J. Smith gave to his troops, because they had been shifted continuously from one commander to another. He first called them this in December 1864 after the battle of Nashville.

louse fight A dubious sport in which soldiers bet on a combat between two lice. The creatures were often placed within a circle drawn with charcoal on the side of a canteen. The losing louse was the one that seemed to retire disabled.

louse race A race between lice found in camp. The lice were placed on different plates and the first one to crawl off was the winner. One Confederate soldier named Dornin was a frequent winner until the other lice owners discovered that he heated his plate.

lousy Having lice. An Alabama wife, Amie Kelly, wrote on July 8, 1862, to her husband serving in a regiment with the Army of Northern Virginia, "I heard before that some of the Reg. were lousy. Is it the case? Do try to keep them off you. I would hate it so bad for you to get lousy." The word's modern definition of feeling bad—"I feel lousy"—comes from this original meaning.

lousy with A slang expression meaning "full of," "having many of," or "amply provided with," such as someone who is "lousy with money."

lover A person in love with another. The name, even used by soldiers, was an innocent description, without today's suggestion of sexual activity.

low diet A light diet fed to Union soldiers in a military hospital. It usually consisted of milk and water, wine whey, and rice gruel. Small red flags were attached to the foot of the beds of those receiving a low diet.

low-down An adjective, still used, meaning contemptible, vile, or despicable.

Loyalty Oath The oath President Abraham Lincoln required rebellious southerners to take to be pardoned and become U.S. citizens again. Announced in his message to Congress on December 1, 1863, it read as follows:

"I _____ _____, do solemnly swear, in presence of Almighty God, that I will henceforth faithfully support, protect, and defend the Constitution of the United States and the Union of the states thereunder; and that I will, in like manner, abide by and faithfully support all acts of Congress passed during the existing rebellion with reference to slaves, so long and so far as not repealed, modified, or held void by Congress, or by decision of the Supreme Court; and that I will, in like manner, abide by, and faithfully support all proclamations of the President made during the existing rebellion, having reference to slaves, so long and so far as not modified or declared void by decision of the Supreme Court. So help me God."

lucifer A friction match, because the Latin word originally mean "light-bringing." Union soldiers were issued matches with blue ends that left a streak wherever they were struck.

Lucy Long One of Confederate General Robert E. Lee's horses, given to him in 1862 after the second battle of Bull Run by his famed cavalry leader Major General "JEB" Stuart. Lee called Lucy Long a quiet horse and stopped riding her because she had "failed." *See also* Ajax; Brown-Road; Richmond; Traveller.

lunch room or lunch An establishment selling quick, cheap lunches, an early name for a snack bar.

lunch stand An outside booth on the sidewalk that offered a quick lunch.

lunette 1. A small defensive field fortification with two or sometimes three sides. These were mostly used early in the war. 2. A ring on the end of a cannon's STOCK TRAIL that could be connected to the LIMBER that towed the cannon. The lunette fit over the limber's PINTLE.

lung fever A common name for pneumonia.

lunk-head A common insult, still used, for a stupid person or a blockhead; e.g., "This regiment is led by a lot of lunk-heads."

lush A slang name for alcohol or liquor. The term dates back to the eighteenth century.

lush Betty A slang name for a whiskey bottle.

lyceum Local and professional groups that organized adult educational series, usually to hear debates and outstanding speakers. Among those who traveled the lyceum circuit were abolitionists like Henry Ward Beecher. Thousands of the organizations existed before the war, but they languished until the conflict ended, then returned in a more commercial form. The name came from the Lyceum in ancient Greece where Aristotle lectured.

Lyss or Lyssus Boyhood names for Ulysses S. Grant, who was then named Hiram Ulysses Grant.

M

"Mac" The nickname of Union Brigadier General James Birdseye McPherson, the chief engineer of Major General W.T. Sherman's army. (Also the nickname for most officers and soldiers having last names beginning with the Scottish "Mc" or "Mac.") *See also* "Little Mac."

Macaria, or Altars of Sacrifice A patriotic and melodramatic southern novel that was popular in Confederate camps but banned in Union ones by the U.S. government. Written in 1864 by Augusta Evans Wilson, an Alabama author, it revolved around a war episode.

machicoulis gallery A open balcony projecting out from the parapet of a fort, which allowed the defenders to drop fire and heavy objects like bricks onto the attacking force. Fort Sumter had three wooden machicoulis galleries, useless additions in the age of long-range shelling.

Mackinaw blanket A thick woolen blanket often carried by Union soldiers. The item, usually brightly colored, took its name from Michigan's Mackinac Island where it was popular with Indians and lumbermen. When a fellow soldier lost Union Major Henry Hitchcock's blanket during Major General W.T. Sherman's march through Georgia, the major wrote in his diary on November 24, 1864, that "The fool seems so distressed. I can't scold. But a good double Mackinaw blanket is a bad loss."

Mackrelville The nickname during the war for the poor Irish section of New York City on Manhattan's lower East Side. The name was the usual stereotypical association of Catholics eating fish on Fridays.

Madam Russell's Bake Oven The name of a house of prostitution on Pennsylvania Avenue in Washington, D.C., that was frequented by soldiers during the war. Competition was provided by Madam Wilton's Private Residence for Ladies.

mad as a wet hen A simile for extreme anger, popular during the war years and still heard today.

magnetic telegraph A scientific-sounding name for the telegraph. News reports in the New York *Tribune* carried a standing headline in each edition: THE LATEST NEWS RECEIVED BY MAGNETIC TELEGRAPH.

mail carrier A common name for a spy, especially one delivering written messages.

"The Mail Must Get Through" Supposedly the informal slogan of the Pony Express. It operated until October 1861, three months after the first battle of Bull Run.

mail ship A Union ship that carried mail destined for soldiers in the field. One, the *Arago*, commanded by Captain Gadsden, shuttled mail back and forth between New York City and Savannah, Georgia, for Major General W.T. Sherman's troops near the end of the war. To use the ship's army mail system, a family in St. Louis could address a letter to their son at "Maj. Gen. Sherman's Headquarters in the Field" and simply put "via New York" in the envelope's corner.

mail train A train officially designated to carry the mail. The name was first heard six years before the war, and mail trains were particularly important to Union soldiers during their southern campaigns.

Main Street The sadly humorous name given by Union prisoners to the main meandering path through the poor outdoor shelters of infamous ANDERSONVILLE prison.

"make a good ready" An expression used by Union Major General W.T. Sherman for preparing his troops fully before striking quickly at the enemy.

make a spoon or spoil a horn An expression for a situation that would be either a full success or a total failure, with nothing in between. An example early in the war was when nervous northerners said their generals would either capture Richmond or lose Washington, D.C., to Rebel forces.

make one's toilet An expression describing a woman's process of dressing, fixing her hair, and applying cosmetics. "Toilet" was used as a name for the dressing-room table, the covering on it, and the articles used. After several days in a Confederate military hospital, a nurse wrote, ". . . as to making our toilet, that was out of the question. I have not undressed since I came here."

make small potatoes of someone To deflate the self-importance of someone, such as a boaster; e.g., "My first duty is to make small potatoes of the sergeant."

make the fur fly To wound someone badly; e.g., "We had an old sharpshooter who made the fur fly every time a bluebelly approached the creek."

make your better acquaintance An expression, common among slaves and other blacks, meaning "get to know you better." It was often a friendly greeting to a stranger; e.g., "I hope to make your better acquaintance."

malison A curse or malediction (the opposite of a blessing or benediction). "Malisons on him," wrote Union nurse Abby Woolsey on July 5, 1865, upon finding that a surgeon had ordered weak men back to their units.

Mammy The traditional southern name for a slave who cared for white children. She was an elderly, respected person who raised the plantation's white children and referred to them as "my babies." Even when they became young adults, they went to Mammy for cuddling and sympathy, but were still in danger of being scolded by her. "Mammy" is a secondary name, then considered inferior, for mother. Some plantation owners refused to allow slave children to use the word "mother" for their own mothers. An ex-slave in New Orleans recalled being whipped for telling her mistress, "My mother sent me." She reasoned that "It made it come too near the way of the white folks."

mania A medical condition often diagnosed by military surgeons for mental problems brought on by the war, including combat fatigue and shell-shock.

manifest destiny This well-known term, meaning Americans had a divine right to occupy the land across the continent to the Pacific Ocean, was coined in 1845 by John L. O'Sullivan, editor of the *United States Magazine and Democratic Review*. The belief in manifest destiny aggravated the political debate between North and South over whether the new territories won from Mexico in 1846 should be slave or free.

manikin During the war, a manikin was only a model of the human body used by doctors to demonstrate the parts and organs of the body and surgical techniques.

"man of Sumter" A nickname for Confederate General P.G.T. Beauregard, because he commanded the assault on Fort Sumter in Charleston harbor, initiating the war. *See also* "Little Creole"; "Little Napoleon"; "Old Bory."

Mansion House Hospital A Union military hospital in Alexandria, Virginia. Its grand name derived from the building having been a famous hotel before the war. The street in front ran down to the Potomac River where many battle casualties arrived by boat.

A Manual of Military Surgery The manual for Confederate surgeons written by J.J. Chislom and published in 1863. Many of Chislom's prescribed drugs became unavailable during the blockade. Others of his health suggestions were dubious, such as the advice to prevent foot sores by soaking one's socks in soapy water each morning before putting them on. Chislom also encouraged soldiers to eat raw bacon while on the march when there was a lack of time or convenience for proper cooking. He added this reassur-

ance: "Our soldiers, who are very fond of the alternative, have not, apparently, suffered from its very frequent repetition."

manumission The formal term for the freeing or emancipation of a slave. The word dates back to the fifteenth century.

manure spreaders A humorous name for the cavalry.

"marble" The label placed on boxes of ammunition and field guns shipped from Baton Rouge, Louisiana, by the Confederate government to Missouri Governor Claiborne F. Jackson, who had requested it. The shipment, which arrived on May 8, 1861, was stored at a MILITIA camp, but two days later federal troops surrounded the camp and hauled all the "marble" to the U.S. arsenal.

The Marble Heart A play in which John Wilkes Booth made his first appearance at Ford's Theatre in Washington, D.C., in October 1863. In the audience watching his future assassin's performance was President Abraham Lincoln.

"the Marble Man" A nickname for General Robert E. Lee. This association with the strength of marble reminded soldiers of "STONEWALL" Jackson's nickname, but Lee had been called the "Marble Model" by classmates at West Point because of his perfect four-year record (no demerits).

marbles A popular game on both sides in camps and prisons, especially among younger soldiers. They would draw circles on the ground and often gamble on the outcome. Marbles were used as a weapon in one incident of the war, when the USS *Essex* fired them at the CSS *Arkansas* during an encounter on July 22, 1862, on the Mississippi River at Vicksburg. An amazed Lieutenant George W. Gift on the Confederate ship, reported that "We picked up a hundred

Confederate General Robert E. Lee, shown here in an 1863 photo, was known as "the Marble Man." *Library of Congress, Prints & Photographs Division, LC-B8172-0001.*

unbroken ones on our forecastle. There were 'white-allies,' 'chinas,' and some glass marbles." *See also* alley.

"March" A Union war poem written by Bayard Taylor and published in 1862. One verse reads as follows:

> Say to the picket, chilled and numb,
> Say to the camp's impatient hum,
> Say to the trumpet and the drum:
> Lift up your hearts, I come, I come! March!

"Marching Song of the First Arkansas" A song written for the First Arkansas Colored Regiment of the Union Army and eventually popular with all black troops. It was written in 1863 by the regiment's commander, Captain Lindley Miller, who set the words to the tune of "JOHN BROWN'S BODY." One verse and chorus went as follows:

> We have done with hoeing cotton, we have done with hoeing corn,
> We are colored Yankee soldiers, now, as sure as you are born;
> When the masters hear us yelling, they'll think it's Gabriel's horn,
> As we go marchin on.
> Glory, glory, hallelujah, Glory, glory, hallelujah, Glory, glory, hallelujah,
> As we go marching on.

"Marching Through Georgia" The Union song late in the war that celebrated Major General W.T. Sherman's march through the state to the sea. It was written by Henry C. Work, a native of Connecticut, who was also an inventor of everything from a walking doll to a rotary engine. His song was the only great one of the war not written in its first year. Part of it went as follows:

> How the darkies shouted when they heard the joyful sound!
> How the turkeys gobbled which our commissary found!
> How the sweet potatoes even started from the ground!
> While we were marching through Georgia.
> *Chorus:* "Hurrah! Hurrah! we bring the jubilee!
> Hurrah! Hurrah the flag that makes you free!"
> So we sang the chorus from Atlanta to the sea,
> While we were marching through Georgia.

marooning A southern name for a long picnic. A "marooning party" usually stayed for several days on the beach or in the countryside.

marquee The canopy of an officer's tent. The name came from the French word, *marquise*, with the "s" dropped because it was incorrectly thought to be plural. (During the war, a tent-shaped chicken coop was sold as a "marquee coop.")

marriage abroad The marriage of one slave to another belonging to a different owner. Such marriages were discouraged or forbidden by plantation owners but were necessary on small farms. Husbands generally spent the weekend with their wives and children.

"Marse Robert" A nickname for Confederate General Robert E. Lee. "Marse" was an imitation of a slave's pronunciation of "master."

Marsilly carriage A naval cannon carriage invented during the war. It was like a TRUCK carriage without the two rear wheels, so the rear carriage rested on the ship's deck and restricted the gun's recoil, although some sand had to be scattered on the deck. After the gun was reloaded, two men used a lever on small wheels to lift the rear slightly and push it back into firing position.

Martinez The name used during the war (and until 1894) for a martini, the famous alcoholic drink. It was supposedly invented about 1861 by a bartender in San Francisco's Occidental Hotel for a guest traveling to Martinez, California.

"Mary Had a Little Lamb" A humorous version of "THE BATTLE-CRY OF FREEDOM," which became popular with Union soldiers on the march. It went as follows:

> Mary had a little lamb,
> Its fleece was white as snow,
> Shouting the battle cry of Freedom.
> And everywhere that Mary went,
> The lamb was sure to go,
> Shouting the battle cry of Freedom.

"Maryland" The nickname for Confederate cavalry leader Brigadier General George H. Steuart, who was a native of Maryland. He was a West Pointer who had been an Indian fighter before the war. He saw action at first Bull Run, Gettysburg, the Wilderness, and Spotsylvania, being captured at the last but exchanged in time to fight again at Petersburg.

"Maryland, My Maryland" *See* "My Maryland."

Mason and Dixon's Line An early and still used form of the Mason-Dixon Line.

"Massa Jeff" A nickname given by Confederate soldiers to President Jefferson Davis. It was affectionate but had the bitter recognition that soldiers were little better than slaves. This was vividly brought home when they cried "Give us something to eat, Massa Jeff," as he passed by hungry troops camped on Missionary Ridge at Chattanooga, Tennessee, in November 1864.

master-at-arm's gang The policemen on a navy ship. They enforced regulations, kept order, were in charge of prisoners, and carried out punishments. They answered to the master-at-arms, a petty officer.

match safe A small box or round container for matches.

"Matthew," "Mark," "Luke," and "John" The names given to four of his cannons by Confederate Brigadier General William Nelson Pendleton, who was an Episcopalian minister. He continued to preach during the war while holding the post of Chief of the Artillery of the Army. *See also* Twelve Apostles.

maulie A slang name for the hand or fist. It was sometimes spelled "mauly" or "mauley."

Maxims of War A book of military knowledge written by Napoleon Bonaparte. It was a valued possession of many officers during the war, and one of only three volumes in the haversack of Confederate General "STONEWALL" Jackson (the other two being the Bible and Webster's AN AMERICAN DICTIONARY OF THE ENGLISH LANGUAGE).

Maynard Tape Priming A primer device system for carbine rifles invented and patented in 1848 by Dr. Edward Maynard, a dentist in Washington, D.C. The paper or linen tapes had 60 detonating pellets of fulminate of mercury spaced in them. The tape was coiled in the weapon's stock and when the gun was cocked a racket device moved one pellet up to be exploded by the hammer. This form of this idea is still used in a child's cap gun. Maynard later also produced an accurate carbine, and 20,002 were bought for Union forces during the war, along with more than 2 million metal cartridges he invented for the breech-loading weapon.

McClellan cap A copy of the KEPI cap. Named for Union Major General George McClellan, it was especially popular with Union officers.

McClellan pies *See* Lincoln pies.

"McClellan's bodyguard" The nickname President Abraham Lincoln gave to the Army of the Potomac under Major General George McClellan, who hesitated to engage the enemy. On April 9, 1862, Lincoln used the term in a letter he wrote to McClellan, in which he asked if he could borrow the army for a while if McClellan did not intend to use it. Lincoln never mailed the letter.

McDowell cap *See* forage cap.

McGuffey's Electic Reader Any of a series of six school reading books that were popular during the war, especially in the Midwest and South. The first four were written by William H. McGuffey, president of Cincinnati College. He laced his reading lessons with moral proverbs and selections from the best English literature, such as Shelley and Shakespeare. The last of the series was published in 1857, and *McGuffey's Electic Readers* were used in the twentieth century.

M.D. The abbreviation for the Medical Department of the Union forces. Naval surgeons wore the "M.D." in Old English letters on their epaulettes and within an oak leaf wreath on their caps.

m.d. The abbreviation for an army MULE driver.

m.e. The abbreviation for "managing editor." Charles A. Dana was the first to hold this title in American journalism; he was the managing editor for the New York *Tribune* from 1849 until 1862. He described a managing editor as "a being to whom the sentiment of remorse is unknown." From 1864 until after the war ended in 1865, he was an assistant at the U.S. War Department.

mean 1. A singular version of "means," the way that something is done or obtained; e.g., "We tried to figure out the best mean to secure our safety." 2. An adjective describing someone who was stingy; e.g., "We asked for a donation but he was too mean." This usage still exists in Great Britain.

mean whiskey Strong or terrible whiskey, often created in camp from bad alcohol and strange local ingredients, such as pine branches.

mean white *See* poor white trash.

meat bag An unappealing slang name for the stomach.

Medal of Honor The highest U.S. medal for military bravery, established by a Joint Resolution of Congress on July 12, 1862. About 1,200 were awarded during the war. The army version, with a large star attached to an eagle under a cloth of red, white, and blue, was first awarded to Union soldiers on March 25, 1863. The navy version, with an anchor replacing the eagle, first went to U.S. sailors and marines on April 3, 1863. Lieutenant Thomas Custer, the brother of Major General George Armstrong Custer, was the only person to receive two (for capturing two enemy flags). The medal was somewhat devalued when it was offered to volunteer infantrymen as an inducement to re-enlist, and the army later removed 911 names of soldiers and a few others. Dr. Mary Walker, an assistant surgeon, was awarded the medal in 1865 and refused to return it when it was revoked in 1917. It was posthumously restored to her in 1977 and to eight Indian scouts, including William BUFFALO BILL Cody in 1989. The Confederate government never created a medal.

Medical Corps A Union organization made up of medical student volunteers who worked in hospitals as DRESSERS and general assistants.

medic or med A shortened name for a medical student. "Medic" did not become a term for a military doctor until after the war.

meeting engagement An accidental confrontation between Union and Confederate troops, when neither was prepared for action. The battle of Gettysburg evolved out of a meeting engagement when a few Confederate troops from the Army of Northern Virginia went to that small Pennsylvania town looking for shoes at the local shoe factory and ran into the surprised 8th Illinois Cavalry.

melainotype *See* tintype.

mellow An informal name, still used, for being intoxicated or drunk. See DRUNK for numerous other terms referring to intoxication.

merino shirt A woolen shirt made of the fine fleece from a merino sheep, originally a Spanish variety. Soldiers wore these early in the war but soon found that cotton shirts were easier to wash and offered better protection from vermin.

"Merrimac No. 2" A Union nickname for the Confederate IRONCLAD *Richmond*. The name was based on reports given by Union prisoners released from Richmond who had briefly seen it being constructed in the summer of 1862, but their descriptions exaggerated its size. *See also* Ladies Defense Association.

mess A military group cooking and eating together. Soldiers on both sides often took turns cooking for their squad or even "messed" with friends, usually 5 to 10 men in the Union army and 4 to 8 Confederates. They often collected a mess fund to supplement rations. Early in the war, officers tended to eat with enlisted men, but soon withdrew to form officers' messes. The Union Army switched to professional cooks for companies in 1863, while Confederate companies later in the war often had to share one frying pan. The food consumed usually went by such names as "mess-pork" and "mess-beef." Some Confederate soldiers brought along a slave as their own cook because mess cooks were notoriously bad. Sailors on both sides usually ate on a table in messes of 8 to 14 men who did the same type of duty, such as gun crews or engineers. They were also assigned a one-week mess duty or cook detail about every 8 to 14 weeks.

"The Mess" The name of the home of General Robert E. Lee and his wife at 707 East Franklin Street in Richmond, Virginia, from January 1, 1864, to June 1865. The name was chosen because the house was previously occupied by staff officers. *See also* Arlington House.

mess gear Military cooking implements, such as a MESS KETTLE, mess pan, tin dipper, and eating utensils. Soldiers each received a knife, fork, tin plate, and tin cup, and Union troops, after 1863, were issued a spoon. These utensils often folded for storage and some, like today's Swiss knife, folded out of the same handle. Especially early in the war, men eating together in a MESS often conveyed their mess gear in a chest filled with such items as a frying pan, skillet, ladle, lard bucket, coffee boiler, and boxes or "mess tins" of coffee, flour, sugar, and salt, along with the various utensils. Up to 10 of the heavy chests were carried on one wagon. In the navy, each mess had its own mess chest.

mess kettle The beloved metal container used by soldiers to boil their coffee and tea and cook their meat, potatoes, soup, sauces, and other foods. They also used it between meals to boil their clothes clean.

mess-mate A soldier in a group that forms a MESS together; e.g., "I lost two of my mess-mates at Shiloh."

metallic coffin An type of airtight coffin used to transport bodies of soldiers home, especially when embalming was delayed or impossible. One Gettysburg salesman advertised them as follows: "Can be placed in the Parlor without fear of any odor escaping therefrom."

metheglin A cordial made with honey boiled (preferably in a barrel of spring water) and skimmed. Ginger, cloves, mace, and yeast were added and, after fermentation for six months, the liquid was drawn off and bottled. This drink is a type of mead, and the original Welsh name "meddyglyn" means "mead juice."

miasma The medical name for a poison vapor carried in the air. Doctors suspected that it arose from decaying corpses and was the cause of malaria and other diseases. The only general prevention was ample ventilation in hospitals and barracks.

"Miasma" The crew's nickname for the *USS Miami*, a Union sidewheel steamer, because of the boring military duty it of-

fered. The name was a humorous adoption of the medical term, MIASMA.

"Michigan Annie" The nickname of Anna Etheridge, a famous Union nurse also known by her patients as "Gentle Annie." She served through the war with the 3rd and 5th Michigan regiments. Her bullet riddled dresses attested to her service under fire, but Annie only received one superficial graze on her hand. Union Major General David B. Birney awarded her the Kearny Cross for bravery.

"Michigan Bridget" *See* "Irish Bridget."

Middle States The term preferred by many in the North for the border states because the latter term might emphasize the border between two countries. President Abraham Lincoln was careful with the usage, and even in his message to Congress on July 5, 1861, noted: "In the border states, so-called—in fact, the Middle States. . . . "

middling A description of meat that had a medium length of cooking, between "rare" and "well-done."

middy A nickname for midshipmen at the U.S. Naval Academy. Still used, the term was first heard on ships during the War of 1812.

midwife A woman skilled in delivering babies. Southern plantations had one of the older slave women trained as a midwife for the other slaves, and she was held in great esteem by the plantation owner.

mile The singular version of "miles" was often heard during the war; e.g., "We marched 40 mile and then went straight into fighting."

mileage Traveling expenses paid to government employees, such as U.S. congressmen.

Military Bill A Reconstruction bill passed by the 39th Congress that divided the former Confederate states (except Tennessee) into five military districts. President Andrew Johnson was to appoint a commander of each district, not below the rank of brigadier general. The districts were: (I) Virginia; (II) North Carolina and South Carolina; (III) Georgia, Alabama, and Florida; (IV) Mississippi and Arkansas; and (V) Louisiana and Texas.

military commission A Union military tribunal equivalent to a general COURT-MARTIAL. The commission was used for occupied areas in enemy territory or for any place under martial law, and it could also try sutlers and other civilians working for the army. Soldiers charged with crimes against civilians were often tried before a military commission. *See also* military court.

military court A Confederate military tribunal acting in the manner of a COURT-MARTIAL. Military courts were created on October 9, 1862, by the Confederate Congress to handle offenses committed beyond military jurisdictions, such as crimes by stragglers and deserters. Such trials would otherwise be time-consuming and detrimental to army discipline. *See also* military commission.

military division A territorial unit on both sides that was the largest organized military area, usually consisting of more than one DEPARTMENT. The Confederacy, for example, had a Military Division of the West made up of the Departments of Tennessee, Georgia, Alabama, Mississippi, and East Louisiana. *See also* grand division.

Military Medical and Surgical Essays A medical instruction book published during the war by the SANITARY COMMISSION. The essays were mostly written by doctors at Bellevue Hospital in New York and included such subjects as "Pain and Anaesthesia" and rules for "preserving the Health of the Soldier."

military murder A term heard when the military purposely killed prisoners or civilians. Confederate officers cried "military murder" when General Ambrose Burnside's troops in Kentucky captured Rebels wearing civilian clothes (because their uniforms were tattered) and hanged them as spies. Confederates later captured and hanged uniformed soldiers from Burnside's army in retaliation, and these tit-for-tat "military murders" continued for some time.

militia A state's own soldiers, equivalent to today's National Guard. The name of HOME GUARD was sometimes used. Militia in U.S. states could be called into national duty by the president, which was Abraham Lincoln's first act in response to the capture of Fort Sumter. This move created the THREE-MONTH MAN. Officers often made sure militia members were combined with regular soldiers. The Army of Northern Virginia sometimes used two militia men and one veteran soldier for picket duty. Many militia units, especially in the South, included youths and old men.

milk punch A drink made of milk, rum or whiskey, sugar, and usually nutmeg. It was often a treat served in military hospitals. Charlotte E. McKay, a Union nurse, complained on May 3, 1863, about a wild ride given by her ambulance driver: "Perhaps he indulged a little too freely in the milk punch he had been helping to administer to the wounded."

Milledgeville myth The name given to a rumor that the Union officers of Major General W.T. Sherman had held a lascivious ball with young black women in Milledgeville, then the capital of Georgia. The story was printed in southern and northern newspapers until Confederate General P.G.T. Beauregard visited

Milledgeville after the invaders had left and found that the report was untrue.

Milroy's weary boys The nickname known on both side for a Union brigade commanded by Brigadier General Robert H. Milroy. They acquired the dubious name in 1862 after Major General "STONEWALL" Jackson's troops had run circles around them in the Shenandoah Valley. Two years later, under Brigadier General Truman Seymour (but stuck with the Milroy name), they were still showing signs of weary confusion and panic during engagements.

Minié ball or minnie ball The most famous and most common projectile in the war. It was not a ball, but a lead bullet with an elongated shape. It had a hollow base that expanded when fired, pushing the sides against the grooved barrel to give the bullet spin, which meant better accuracy and longer range. The Union army bought 46 million Minié balls of .58 caliber. Union soldiers at the siege of Vicksburg in 1863 were delighted to discover that the new ammunition penetrated alligator hides. Before the bullet arrived in the spring of 1863, the old round projectiles fit loosely in barrels and allowed gunpowder to seep in front. The Minié, so-called by both sides, was named for the French army's Captain Claude Minié, who invented it and the Minié rifle.

minim A medical measurement of about a drop. It was the smallest prescribed amount of liquid and was officially 1/60th of a fluid dram. *See also* morphia.

mint julep or julep A popular southern drink consisting of bourbon or brandy, sugar, and mint leaves. It was usually served in a tall glass with crushed ice. As Confederate General Joseph Johnston's army retreated through North Carolina at the end of the war, his staff accepted a local doctor's offer "to partake of a mint-julep." One of the generals told the host

that the younger staff members never touch alcohol. Recalled Lieutenant Bromfield Ridley, "We just had to look at that julep and sigh."

"Minute Men" 1. The nickname for the 2nd Regiment of State Guard Infantry organized in February 1861 in St. Louis, Missouri, by pro-slavery men. The 700 members were surrounded and captured on May 10, 1861, by about 7,000 troops commanded by Union Brigadier General Nathaniel Lyon (who had spied on the enemy camp by walking through it disguised as a woman). When the prisoners were being marched through the streets of St. Louis, riots broke out between Union and Confederate sympathizers and lasted for two days with 36 people killed. (Two innocent bystanders in the crowd were the former U.S. Army officers, Ulysses Grant and W.T. Sherman.) 2. The name of the HOME GUARD created in several other states, such as Arkansas, when that state left the Union, or Indiana, which created such a force in July 1863 to defend against Rebel raiders.

The Mississippi Half-Acre *See* Hell's Half-Acre.

Mississippi punch A strong alcoholic drink of the South composed of rum, brandy, bourbon, lemons, and sugar, topped with decorative berries and orange slices.

Mississippi Rifle A common nickname for the .58 caliber United States Rifle, Model 1841, because it had been issued in the OLD ARMY to the 1st Mississippi Regiment commanded by Colonel Jefferson Davis. The regiment made it famous in 1847 during the Mexican War. The rifle was the army's first general issue weapon to have a percussion cap and was .54 caliber until the Minié ball became common in 1863. The weapon was so reliable, it was preferred to newer models; as one North Carolina soldier wrote, "Our choice was the Mississippi Rifles." As late as 1865, a Confederate copy of the gun was being manufactured by the Dickson, Nelson Company of Dawson, Georgia.

Miss Lizzy *See* "Crazy Bet."

"Miss Nancy" A derogatory name given to an effeminate man.

Mister The title humorously given to inanimate objects by slaves. This created such names as "Mister Cotton," "Mister Rifle," and "Mister Whiskey."

mixologist A humorous name for a bartender. It was first used about five years before the war began.

mizzle A slang word meaning to abscond or run away; e.g., "He borrowed five dollars and then mizzled."

mock funeral A ceremony of dismal humor held in several camps during the war, in which men would conduct the imaginary death and funeral of a company officer they despised. The victim would be hanged in effigy and the dummy placed in an ornate coffin that had a list of his offenses pinned to it. Many officers reformed, transferred, or resigned after such a warning, and a few were actually killed later by their own men.

"The Mocking Bird" This well-known song was popular during the war. During the siege of Vicksburg, Mississippi, southern soldiers sang a revised version that included the following lines:

> Listen to the Parrott shells,
> Listen to the Parrott shells:
> The Parrott shells are whistling through
> the air.

Model 1840 A Union cavalryman's heavy saber. Nearly 190,000 were ordered for the war. It was virtually the same saber as the MODEL 1860, but was a quarter-inch wider. The Confederate cavalry used copies of the 1840.

Model 1860 A Union cavalryman's light saber. More than 203,000 were ordered during the war. It had a slightly curved blade 41 inches long with a one-inch width at the hilt. The grip was covered in black leather secured with brass wire, and the guard protecting the hand was made of brass. The pommel (knob on the hilt's end) was shaped like a helmet. The wrought-iron scabbard had two rings to hook it to the belt. Confederates copied the 1860 for cavalry use, but the quality was poorer.

modiste A person who made or dealt in fashionable dresses, hats, and other articles of clothing for women.

moke An insulting name for a black person, especially one portrayed in a minstrel show. The term, which came from the black color of Mocha coffee, was first used about five years before the war.

Molly Cotton Tail The popular name given to any rabbit or hare. Soldiers virtually considered them a delicacy for the pot, and an entire unit would often go in pursuit when a Molly was spied. Confederate Private Carlton McCarthy recalled the commotion, adding that "often it was said, when the rolling shout arose: 'There goes old General Lee or a Molly Cotton Tail!'"

Molly Mcguires A secret labor union of mostly Irish workers in the coal mines of Pennsylvania and West Virginia. They organized in 1862 and held violent protests to oppose military conscription. After the war, their violent labor disputes in the 1870s led to their leaders being imprisoned or hanged and the union destroyed. Their name came from an Irish organization that had opposed landlords.

monitor fever The rush in the Union navy to build a fleet of ironclad gunboats, based on the impressive U.S.S. *Monitor*, the first of the breed in the North. Later refinements produced the POOK TURTLE.

monkey jacket A nickname for a close-fitting jacket usually made from coarse, thick cloth. It resembled the small jackets worn by trained monkeys.

monkeyshines This familiar name, still used, meant pranks, jokes, and mischievous or foolish acts. It was popular during the war, having first been used about a decade before it began.

monkey show *See* see the elephant.

monogahela An informal word for whiskey. The name was generalized from the rye whiskey called monogohela because it was produced near the Monogahela River in Pennsylvania.

Monroe Guard The name taken by a group of men in New Orleans during the Union occupation who unsuccessfully attempted to break out and join Confederate troops. Included were six soldiers who had received PAROLES when Fort Jackson (guarding the city) was captured. Because they had violated their pledge, the soldiers were sentenced to hang. New Orleans citizens strongly petitioned for their lives—one condemned man claimed he had not known what "parole" meant—and Union General Benjamin Butler commuted the sentence to confinement on Ship Island.

monte A popular card game in the camps of both sides. It is played with a deck of 40 cards. Players turn up two cards from the top or bottom of the deck and bet a "banker" that a suit will be matched by the next card drawn.

The Montgomery Issue The first Confederate paper money printed, in denominations of $50, $100, $500, and $1,000. They were produced, surprisingly, in New York (where the city's commercial interests produced much sympathy for the South) and secretly transported to the original capital of the Confederacy in Montgomery, Alabama.

moonshine Something that means nothing; e.g., "His speech was all moonshine about the Yankees trying to avoid a war."

moored torpedo An underwater mine ("torpedo") that remained in one place, moored to the bottom by a chain attached to a weight. An example is the STAKE TORPEDO.

mop and mow To make grimaces, especially in the manner of a monkey. In Harriet Beecher Stowe's UNCLE TOM'S CABIN, a plantation mistress complains about her slave children because "they are mopping and mowing and grinning between all the railings, and tumbling over the kitchen floor!"

more than you can shake a stick at A folksy expression to describe a large or uncountable number of people or things; e.g., "The cavalryman rode back from the hilltop and reported that he had seen more Yankees across the river than you can shake a stick at."

"Morgan's Mule" The nickname of a device, used for punishing Confederate prisoners in Union jails, which consisted of a tall sawhorse on which they were forced to sit. The derogatory nickname referred to the hated Confederate Brigadier General John Hunt Morgan who led his cavalrymen on rampages through Indiana, Ohio, and Kentucky. *See also* "terrible men."

morning roll call The day's uncomfortable first gathering of troops in camp. Having heard the "ASSEMBLY" bugle call, half-awake men would stagger into line dressed in various uniform pieces and stand at PARADE REST while duty sergeants would call the names of the 25 or so men under their charge. They would then report the number present to the orderly sergeant who passed this on to the officer of the day. Anyone who missed morning roll call without an excuse was usually put on the BLACK LIST.

morphia A common name for morphine, which was used to relieve pain during the war. It was taken orally and sometimes administered by injections. J.J. Chislom, who wrote the Confederacy's *A MANUAL OF MILITARY SURGERY*, dissolved one-third of a morphia grain in two MINIMS of water and injected it under the skin of the sternum. This, he found, relieved all the patient's pain within five minutes. The drug, derived from opium, became unavailable to Confederate surgeons during the Union blockade. Many patients, such as amputees, became addicted to it. *See also* chloroform; ether; laudanum.

mort or mott A slang name for a woman or girl.

mortally scared to death A common (and unusually honest) expression among soldiers during the war to express great fear.

mortar or siege mortar A short, stubby weapon used to lob shells over the walls of forts and other defenses to damage buildings, equipment, and soldiers within. Mortar fire was thrown high in the air, and soldiers became adept at dodging the shells, often yelling insults back at the mortar BATTERY. The mortar rested on a wooden base with its barrel elevated from 45 to 50 degrees; it fired a hollow shell filled with gunpowder or an incendiary material to cause explosions and fires. Mortars were part of the SIEGE ARTILLERY. *See also* "the Dictator"

mortar boat A boat built specifically to house a MORTAR. The boats were usually

Coehorn Model 1841 bronze mortar. *Copyright Inge Wright 1999.*

large schooners that carried one 13-inch mortar and two or more long 32-pounders. The ships were especially used to pound the enemy's seaside or river forts. Ten smaller mortar boats participated in 1862 in the Union bombardment of the Confederates' well-fortified Island No. 10 on the Mississippi River at the Missouri-Tennessee border. The boats were tied to steamers and pulled into positions along the bank. The iron-plated mortar boats were 60 feet long and 25 feet wide; each carried one mortar that weighed 17,210 pounds and fired 13-inch shells. The bombardment lasted from March 15 to April 7, after which the Rebels (seeing two enemy regiments arrive) withdrew. *See also* bummer.

mortify To decay or to develop gangrene. Confederate soldier Sam Watkins was horrified when he came across a dead Yankee, stripped naked and his body black and swollen. "He had mortified," recalled Watkins. The noun, mortification, was used by military field surgeons. Doctors diagnosed mortification in the death of Confederate Major General JEB STUART on May 12, 1864, after a bullet pierced his abdomen and caused peritonitis, inflammation of the peritoneum that lines the abdominal cavity.

Mosby's Confederacy An informal name for the western part of Virginia controlled by the PARTISAN RANGERS (43rd Battalion of Virginia Cavalry) of Colonel John Mosby, known as the GRAY GHOST.

"Moses" The nickname of Harriet Tubman, a title often expanded to "the Moses of her people." She was a slave originally named Araminta who escaped from her Maryland plantation in 1849 and the next year began 19 trips back to the South, helping some 300 slaves escape through the UNDERGROUND RAILROAD. A reward of $40,000 was offered for her capture. During the war, she was a Union scout and spy. On June 2, 1863, she led Negro Union soldiers up the Combahee River in South Carolina to burn plantations and set some 800 slaves free. In a more domestic role, Tubman served as a nurse, cook, and laundress under Union Major General David Hunter, who helped establish the army's first Negro regiment in South Carolina. After the war, she settled in Auburn, New York, and established a home for destitute former slaves. *See also* "General Tubman."

"Moses!" A mildly profane curse as a exclamation of surprise or anger. During the battle of Chickamauga on September 20, 1863, a Union soldier observed crows attacking a flying owl and declared: "Moses, what a country! The very birds are fighting."

"most largely circulated journal in the world" The persistent boast of the *New York Herald*, which daily printed 84,000 copies. *See also* "prince of darkness."

"most shot-at man in the war" The nickname for Professor Thaddeus Lowe, a civilian paid a colonel's salary, who organized and led the Balloon Corps of the Union army. Lowe piloted his observation balloons 1,000 feet over Confederate positions, well out of the range of gunfire, but Rebels could not resist continuous shooting at such a large, slow-moving target. *See also* Aeronautic Department; Silk Dress Balloon.

mother A dialect form of "grandmother" (not "mother") used by slaves. *See also* nanna.

"Mother" President Lincoln's special name for his wife, Mary Todd Lincoln. She was a native of Kentucky, and her brother and three half-brothers fought for the Confederacy. She had a quick wit, high spirits, and a quick temper. The Lincolns were a close couple, but after the death of their son, WILLIE, Mrs. Lincoln became depressed and held seances in the White House. Following her husband's assassination, Mrs. Lincoln's mental health declined until she was officially declared insane in 1875, although she was later ruled sane. *See also* "the Hell-cat."

"Mother Bickerdyke" Nickname for Mary Ann Bickerdyke, a famed Union nurse who survived 19 battles. She was also a SANITARY COMMISSION agent. Although she assisted doctors with amputations and other medical procedures, Mother Bickerdyke also foraged for chickens for "my boys," washed their clothes, and brewed their coffee. She was the only woman Major General W.T. Sherman allowed in camp because, he explained, "She ranks [outranks] me."

"Mother of Chickamauga" Nickname for Mrs. Thedford of Thedford's Ford on the Chickamauga River in Tennessee. The night before the battle of Chickamauga in September 1863, Confederate soldiers from Major General Alexander P. Stewart's division raided her potato patch. As an officer reprimanded them and ordered them away, she yelled, "Hold on, Mister Officer! Those are my potatoes and my boys. Let 'em take 'em." Mrs. Thedford, who had two sons wounded in the war, converted her home and yard into a temporary Confederate hospital after the battle.

"Mother of Presidents" The proud nickname of Virginia because 7 of the first 12 presidents were born there. When the Confederacy was urging that state to secede, Virginia Congressman Roger A. Pryor said "Give the old lady time. She cannot move with the agility of some of her younger daughters. She is a little rheumatic." Virginia was also called the "Mother of States."

"Mother of States" See "Mother of Presidents."

Mouchoir A pocket handkerchief. Confederate General William J. Hardee kept his collection in "an elegant blue satin Mouchoir case" that has his initials embroidered in white.

mountain dew Illegally distilled whiskey. The term had originated in the Highlands of Scotland.

"mountain fox" A nickname given to Confederate Lieutenant General "STONEWALL" Jackson by Charles H. Webb, war correspondent for the New York *Times*, because of the knowledge and craftiness displayed by Jackson while campaigning in the mountains around Virginia's Shenandoah Valley.

mouse A slang name for a black eye; e.g., "Mullins said he would give me hell, but all he gave me was a mouse, and I broke his front tooth."

"Movements of Mrs. Lincoln" The title of a daily column run in 1861 by the New York *Herald* detailing the activities of the president's wife, Mary Todd Lincoln. During this year, northern newspapers devoted more space to her personal life than that of her husband.

Mr. Banks A nickname given to Union Major General Nathaniel P. Banks by his own soldiers who were aware that he had little military training and was a poor tactician. *See also* "Commissary"; "Napoleon."

Mr. Grant The name publicly used during the war by Julia Dent Grant for her husband, Union General Ulysses S. Grant.

Mr. Lincoln's gun A nickname for the SPENCER CARBINE, because President Lincoln test fired it and personally ordered it issued to regiments.

Mr. Lincoln's war A southern name for the Civil War, first heard in 1861.

Mrs. President The name sometimes used for President Abraham Lincoln's wife, Mary Todd Lincoln. The honorary title was often used sarcastically because Mrs. Lincoln was known to meddle in the president's official business. *See also* "the Hell-cat"; "the She Wolf."

mud head An insulting nickname for someone from Tennessee.

mud hook or mud hooks 1. A slang name for an anchor. 2. A humorous slang name for boots when marching in mud, or for an especially large pair of boots.

Mud Lane A common name given by soldiers in winter camps to one of the main thoroughfares of the camp.

"Mud March" Union General Ambrose Burnside's disastrous march beginning on January 20, 1863, that resulted in his replacement as commander of the Army of the Potomac by General Joseph Hooker. Trying to recover from his defeat at Fredericksburg in December 1862, Burnside attempted to circle around, cross the Rappahannock River, and surprise General Robert E. Lee's left flank. His troops, however, were surprised by torrential rains and became bogged down in thick mud and their horses and mules began to die. As his soldiers slogged miserably around enemy lines in a howling wind, they encountered a makeshift Confederate sign: "Burnside Stuck in the Mud." During the trek, one Union soldier penned the following prayer:

> Now I lay me down to sleep
> In mud that's many fathoms deep;
> If I'm not here when you awake,
> Just hunt me up with an oyster rake.

mudsill A slang name used as an insult. Rebels particularly employed it for Yankees, and Union Major General W.T. Sherman's troops were derided in the southern press as a "grand army of mudsills." A mudsill was actually the foundation of a building, the lowest horizontal sill (level of timber or masonry) that usually rested on the ground.

mud truce A break in fighting when downpours turned roads into impassable quagmires.

"Mudwall" The humorous nickname given to Confederate Brigadier General William L. Jackson, because he was the cousin of Lieutenant General "Stonewall" Jackson, whom he had first served as an aide-de-camp. He was part of Major General Jubal Early's raid on Washington in 1864 and refused to surrender when the war ended, disbanding his men six days after General Robert E. Lee's surrender.

muggins 1. A slang name for a fool. One Confederate private described a Yankee deserter as "a considerable muggins and a great coward." The term is still used in British English. 2. A popular game of dominoes, often played by soldiers in camp and prisons. The players counted by fives or multiples of fives. *See also* Old Capitol.

mulatto A person with one white parent and one black; in the Old South, such a person was usually the child of a white slave owner and one of his female slaves. A common name for a mulatto was a YELLOW. The term mulatto was first applied in the late sixteenth century to the offspring of white Europeans and blacks, while a female was called a "mulatta." *See also* quadroon.

mule A derisive nickname given by Confederate soldiers to the tough meat included in their rations. *See also* Confederate beef.

The Mule Shoe The nickname for the Confederate's inverted V-shaped defensive line at the battle of Spotsylvania. Union General Ulysses Grant attacked General Robert E. Lee there with 18,000 men through a thick fog on May 12, 1864. The Mule Shoe, a SALIENT position, was breached and many lives lost at its BLOODY ANGLE, but the Rebels counterattacked to close it again.

multiform A nickname given by General Robert E. Lee's soldiers to their patched up uniforms. The word was created during their invasion of Maryland in September 1862.

mush Exaggerated, empty talk or nonsense. The term is still used, but less so than today's equivalent term of "baloney."

music A slang name for fun or liveliness; e.g., "General Forrest was a serious soldier but had a great deal of music in him."

musicianer A name for a musician that was sometimes used by poorly educated people.

musketry Muskets, rifles, and other small arms. Confederate Private Sam R. Watkins, writing about a sentry found guilty of sleeping at his post, noted that "by the rules of war he had to be shot to death by musketry." 2. The firing of muskets, rifles, and other small arms; e.g., "The cannonading and musketry of the enemy had ceased."

muss A slang name for a fight, commotion, or disorder. A soldier might "kick up a muss." The word dates back to Shakespeare. A verb also existed, meaning to confuse or put into disorder; e.g., "The new tactics mussed up the enemy's plans."

mustard plaster A common item employed by camp surgeons, especially used in misguided attempts to cure pneumonia.

muster out To die, especially in battle. This was a melancholy use of the original term created in the U.S. years before the war, meaning to be discharged from military service.

mutton-chop whiskers or mutton-chops Side whiskers that were wider and rounded at the bottom. The name appeared in 1865 and drew attention to the resemblance of the shape to a mutton chop of meat. The chin was always shaved. When mutton-chop whiskers were connected by a mustache, the fashion was called burnsides by 1875 and sideburns by 1887 because this style had been worn during the war by Union General Ambrose E. Burnside.

muttonhead This familiar insult for a stupid person was common during the war.

MVM The initials for the Massachusetts Volunteer Militia, which had 5,592 members when the war started. "MVM" was officially adopted for all the state's volunteer units on July 31, 1863.

"my bad old man" The nickname given by Confederate General Robert E. Lee to Major General Jubal Early, because Early was known to be an unemotional and bitter man. *See also* "Old Jube."

"my friends" An introductory greeting often used by President Abraham Lincoln when he addressed a group.

"my little bird" The coded name given by the Confederate spy, Mrs. Rose O'Neal Greenhow, to her intermediary in Washington, D.C. See also "Fort Greenhow"; trust bearer.

"my little family" A term sometimes used by senior officers for their staff.

"My Maryland" Often considered to have the best lyrics of all Civil War songs, "My Maryland" was a popular song in the South and one especially sung by soldiers on the march. They sometimes called it "Maryland, My Maryland." The Army of Northern Virginia sang the tune when it marched into Maryland in September 1862. The song was written by James Ryder Randall, a native of Baltimore teaching English literature at Poydras College in Louisiana. He used the tune of "Lauriger Horatius" by Jennie Cary of Baltimore and composed it within 24 hours of reading, in April 1861, about Massachusetts troops being attacked while marching through Baltimore. The song was first introduced to Confederate soldiers in 1861 by Jennie and her sister, Hetty Cary, who sang it to the troops of General P.G.T. Beauregard encamped at Centreville, Virginia. The last of the nine stanzas runs as follows:

> I hear the distant thunder-hum, Maryland!
> The Old Line's bugle, fife, and drum, Maryland!
> She is not dead, nor deaf, nor dumb;
> Huzza! she spurns the Northern scum—
> She breathes! She burns! She'll come! She'll come!
> Maryland! My Maryland!

"My name is Haines" or "My name is Hanes" A humorous announcement made by someone who is leaving suddenly, as from a party. It supposedly derived from President Thomas Jefferson's encounter with another horseman as he was out riding near his Virginia home, Monticello. The man, not recognizing Jefferson, berated the president until they neared the house. When the magnanimous Jefferson invited him in, the man asked his name. Told it was Thomas Jefferson, the stranger blurted out, "Well, my name is Haines" and dashed away.

"my old war horse" General Robert E. Lee's nickname for Major General James Longstreet, the longest serving corps commander in the Army of Northern Virginia. He gave him the name after the battle of Antietam in 1862. Longstreet had worn his old U.S. army uniform to fight the Yankees at the first battle of Bull Run in 1861. He also fought at such major battles as Fredericksburg, the Wilderness, and Gettysburg where, as second in command, his hesitation to attack probably contributed to Lee's defeat in that most crucial battle. Longstreet later helped defend Richmond and surrendered with General Lee at Appomattox Court House in April 1865. He was known for his poker playing and for wearing carpet slippers when he inspected his gun crews. He was distantly related to Union General Ulysses S. Grant by marriage. *See also* "Old Allegheny"; "Old Pete."

"my organ" Union General Ulysses S. Grant's tongue-in-cheek name for the New York *Herald*, a newspaper that urged a Grant-for-President campaign in the fall of 1863. Grant, with a twinkle in his eyes, would tell fellow officers that he read the *Herald* so "I can tell better what I'm going to do."

"My pen is bad, my ink is pale; my love for you shall never fail" A traditional phrase used to end a letter. It existed before the war, and became most appropriate for soldiers who often had to scratch out their correspondence using defective pens and endangered ink. One defender of Atlanta, Z.J. Armistead, concluded a letter to his brother with "The Yankees keep Shooting so I am afraid they will knock over my ink so I will close."

"my people" A plantation owner's euphemism for his slaves.

"my whip-lash" The nickname given by Union Major General W.T Sherman to the Army of the Tennessee, because of its rapid striking force and great wheeling movements in battle—the ability to swing quickly from one flank to the other. During his march through Georgia, Sherman preferred to have his fleet soldiers outflank the retreating Rebel forces. After the war, he recalled that his army "was never checked, always victorious, so rapid in motion, so eager to strike, it deserved the name of 'the whip-lash.'" General Ulysses S. Grant commanded the army up to Vicksburg; Sherman then took command and held it until March 26, 1864, when he turned the "whip-lash" over to Major General James B. McPherson.

N

nag This slang name for a horse did not have such a negative connotation during the war. It often meant a small horse but seldom an old or broken-down one.

"the nailhead" A nickname for Vicksburg, Mississippi, used by President Jefferson Davis, because he said the city "held the South's two halves together." *See also* "Gibraltar of the West."

nail keg A small barrel of nails. Nail kegs were common around camps and, when empty, were used by soldiers as tables and stools. When semi-permanent winter quarters were being built, soldiers finishing a chimney would sometimes crown it ceremoniously with a nail keg.

nanna A dialect form of "mother" (not "grandmother") used by slaves. *See also* mother.

Napoleon The best and most common cannon used by both sides. The 12-pounder Napoleon, officially designated the Napoleon gun-howitzer Model 1857, was a powerful smoothbore gun cast of iron or bronze. It had been designed by Napoleon III of France and adopted by the U.S. army in 1857. It weighed 1,227 pounds, was 5' 7" long and fired a 12.3-

A 12-pound Napoleon cannon. *Library of Congress, Prints & Photographs Division, LC-B8171-2582.*

pound solid shot to a maximum range of 1,680 yards when the muzzle was elevated to 5 degrees. The Napoleon was also cast in a 6-pounder version.

"Napoleon" A nickname given by his own soldiers, especially those from the West, to Union Major General Nathaniel P. Banks, a former congressman who, they believed, had Napoleonic military pretensions but few battlefield skills. *See also* "Commissary"; Mr. Banks.

Nashville Plow Works A farm equipment company in Nashville that switched to producing sabers during the war. The swords' brass guards were proudly marked "C.S.A." and "Nashville Plow Works."

"Nassau bacon" The nickname given by Confederates to the disgusting meat they had to eat toward the end of the war. Blockade runners brought in the dubious flesh, which was spotted, rancid, and dry, and stank when boiled. The name was sometimes corrupted, with grim humor, to "nausea bacon." One Rebel recalled that "the longer you chewed it, the bigger it got. Then, by a desperate effort, you would gulp it down. Out of sight, out of mind."

natheless or nathless An old form of "nevertheless." A southerner speaking of the hopeless war might add that "Natheless, I must defend my state."

National Army The name sometimes given in the North to the Union army. The adjective was used in many combinations, such as the "National flag," National forces," "National casualties," and the "National lines."

national game A descriptive wartime name for the fairly new game of base ball. By the twentieth century, this had changed to "the national pastime."

National Union Party The name adopted by the Republican Party for the 1864 presidential election that saw President Abraham Lincoln returned to the White House. The title was chosen partly to attract Democrats. Lincoln defeated the Democratic candidate, former Major General George McClellan, whom Lincoln had relieved of his command of the Army of the Potomac after the battle of Antietam in 1862.

National Volunteers An organization within the Democratic Party that supported southern rights during the election of 1860, in which the party's candidate, Stephen A. Douglas, lost to Republican Abraham Lincoln. The National Volunteers were an active and well-known group, conducting parades in several cities. *See also* Wide Awakes.

native American The name did not refer to Indians during the war, but to whites born in America. Many "native Americans" thought this was superior to being an immigrant, even though their parents might have been born elsewhere. A Native American Association had even been formed before the war as an anti-foreign, anti-Catholic organization.

nausea bacon *See* Nassau bacon.

Nauvoo Legion Militia A MILITIA of Mormons in the Utah Territory. It briefly had a mounted Battalion of Life Guards during three months in 1862.

Naval Rendezvous The name used by both sides for a recruitment center for sailors and marines.

navigate To walk, especially used with humor to describe such efforts by a drunk person.

navy bean A small white kidney bean. The name came from its frequent use by the U.S. navy, the Civil War being the first war in which it was used as a staple food. Military cooks soaked the dried beans before cooking.

necessaries A general term for a soldier's essential military equipment and personal items, from his rifle to his toothbrush. Civilians also spoke of necessaries, such as a war correspondent's pencils, paper, and binoculars.

necromancer A person, often a public performer, who foretold the future by communicating with the dead. A Mr. Wyman, "the unrivalled necromancer and ventriloquist," was performing in Washington, D.C., during the first battle of Bull Run in 1861.

Negress A common name for a Negro woman. It was used in eighteenth-century Britain and was considered a proper feminine form.

negro abolition traitors *See* dirty niggers.

"Negro cloth" or "nigger cloth" Any poor-grade coarse cloth used to make clothes for slaves. It was manufactured by northern textile mills specifically for this southern use.

Negro Hill A rundown district in Washington, D.C., located on a section of North Tenth Street that was outside of the main city.

"Neighbor" The nickname given by his men to Confederate Major General David R. Jones. He was the chief of staff for General P.G.T. Beauregard during the bombardment of Fort Sumter in 1861. His battles included both Bull Runs and Antietam before heart problems led to his death on January 15, 1863, in Richmond.

"Never kill a cat" A sailor's superstition in both navies. When the *Monitor* was sinking in high waves, Francis B. Butts, a crewman and new sailor, saw a cat sitting and howling on the breech of one gun. Butts recalled that no one "who is not filled with the superstitions which I had been taught by the sailors, who are always afraid to kill a cat," could appreciate the terror these howls raised in the sailors. With great fear—"I would almost as soon have touched a ghost"—he placed the doomed animal inside another gun.

The New Gymnastics for Men, Women and Children A book published in Boston in 1862 by Dr. Dio Lewis to promote his revolutionary idea that gymnastic training should be given to ordinary Americans, not just athletes. Lewis's program involved movements in which a person held devices to build up flexibility and general health. He advertised it for all ages of women and children and for fat and "feeble men."

"New Orleans, and home again by summer!" The slogan repeated by the troops of Union Major General John C. Fremont, who at the end of 1861 intended to invade the South from Missouri and join up with Union gunboats on the Mississippi River. "I think it can be done gloriously," wrote Fremont to his wife on October 7, "especially if secrecy can be kept." On November 7, after several lost battles, Fremont was relieved of his command by President Abraham Lincoln. Although Fremont posted guards to stop the relief order from arriving, a captain delivered it by disguising himself as a farmer. *See also* Fremont's proclamation.

newsie An informal name for a boy who sold newspapers on the street.

newsmonger A derogatory name for a journalist. "It is an infirmity of the President that he permits the little newsmongers to come around him and be intimate," complained U.S. Secretary of the Navy Gideon Welles of Abraham Lincoln.

news walker A soldier who liked to walk up and down the lines after a battle to collect and swap information. These eager communicators were also known for stealing HAVERSACKS and other items from the weary troops.

the New York game A descriptive name for base ball.

NHV The roman letters usually worn on the FORAGE CAPS of New Hampshire Volunteers. Each unit was independent, and there were no regulation uniforms.

Nicholson pavement A special street pavement in which wooden bricks were laid on a base of sanded planks and cemented into place with asphalt. The technique was used in such cities as New York, Chicago, and St. Louis.

nick A informal, shortened name for a NICKLE coin.

Nickajack The name selected for a new state proposed by anti-slavery people in north Alabama when the Confederacy was organized. After the war began, the idea was overcome by patriotism for Alabama and the South.

nickel A U.S. penny, because nickel formed 12 percent of the metal. This one-cent coin was authorized by Congress in 1857. The five-cent coin was then called a "half-dime," and the name of "nickel" was not transferred to it until years after the war.

nifty A slang word meaning stylish or smart looking. This term was first used just before the war ended.

nigger or nig Insulting names for a Negro, although whites in the nineteenth century did not consider them to be insulting. "Damn the niggers" complained Union Major General W.T. Sherman when the freed slaves slowed his advance through Georgia. Slaves and free blacks also used the name angrily or affectionately. The two names existed long before the war, with "nigger" heard in England in the eighteenth century. *See also* colored folk.

nigger-breaker *See* slave-breaker.

"nigger cars" An insulting name for cars on passenger trains, both North and South, set aside for black people, who were not allowed on regular cars. White people could use "nigger cars" and often did to smoke.

"nigger-driver" A derogatory name for a slave owner. An editorial in the *New York Herald* in late 1861 attacked "the insane faction of nigger-drivers at the South."

"niggerhead" A derogatory name for an abolitionist, being a word-play on COPPERHEAD. James Gordon Bennett, who published the New York *Herald*, made the crude contrast, saying Republicans suffered with niggerheads and Democrats with Copperheads.

"nigger heaven" An insulting name for a theater's highest gallery or the upper rows of its balcony. These were the cheapest seats. The expression was later applied to movie theaters in the first half of the twentieth century.

"nigger war" A derogatory name for the war that was, given the prejudices of the time, heard on both sides. Southern soldiers goaded their enemy for fighting a "nigger war," and most Union soldiers, especially in the conflict's early days, insisted that was not why they were fighting. One northerner wrote home saying "I came out to fight for the restoration of the Union and to keep slavery as it is without going into the territories & not to free the niggers."

nigger-worshipper A derogatory southern name for an abolitionist or northerner, but also used in the North for abolitionists. A *New York Herald* editorial at the end of 1861 noted that President Abraham Lincoln had been "mindful that the original cause of evil began with the machinations of fanatical nigger worshippers at the North, and that to them are mainly owing our present troubles."

night blindness The malady of being able to see virtually nothing at night, although daytime sight is not affected. Camp doctors sometimes thought soldiers were faking the rare problem, but medical research during the war pointed to a connection with scurvy.

night owl As today, a person who stays up late. Night owls in camp would often volunteer for overnight sentry duty. The word had been used for 15 years when the war began.

night rig A slang name (apt in the military) for night clothes.

nine-monthling A Union nickname for a nine-month army volunteer. Veteran soldiers cast scorn at "nine-monthlings hatched from $200 bounty eggs."

nobby A slang adjective meaning stylish, fashionable, smart, etc. A soldier could have a "nobby uniform" made by his family.

"No bottom." The welcomed call given by a ship's LEADSMAN to report no contact with the bottom of a river or bay. Warships required constant soundings in unknown water channels.

"No Colored People Allowed on This Car" Signs common on New York STREET-CARS during the war.

"no great scratch" or "no great scratches" Not important or outstanding, the same as "no great shakes." A private might say, "McClellan thinks he's something, but he's no great scratch."

nohow In no way or not at all, being a common dialect word during the war; e.g. "Our men can't defend this small hill, nohow."

nokum stiff A humorous name for strong liquor that was capable of knocking any soldier stiff.

non-com This informal shortening of "noncommissioned officer" is still used. It was common during the war, being a word from the eighteenth century.

noncombatant A person who ministered to a military unit without joining in battles. Captured noncombatants during the Civil War were always quickly released unharmed by both sides. This status was given to such people as chaplains, surgeons, nurses, SUTLERS, journalists, photographers, and civilians. This special understanding for the release of noncombatants was initiated by a Confederate surgeon, Dr. Hunter H. McGuire.

non-conscript An informal term for men who were not conscripted, because of age, physical problems, or otherwise. During a tour of the South in 1863, President Jefferson Davis urged non-conscripts to volunteer for garrison duty to free regular soldiers for battle duty.

no odds An informal term meaning "no difference"; e.g., "It's no odds whether they attack or we do. Our boys will whip them."

Norther A variant form of northerner used during the war. See also Southron.

Northman A northern man, meaning a Union man during the war. As the conflict began, Jane Stuart Woolsey of a socially prominent New York family, wrote of a friend: "He told me a month ago, *before Sumter*, that no Northman could be found to fight against the South."

no sabe Soldiers used the Spanish expression for not understanding or knowing something. It had been brought from the Southwest and had become common by the war.

nosegay A bouquet or bunch of fragrant flowers. Nosegays were popular in military hospitals, and the Union nurse Louisa May Alcott made a habit of laying them on soldiers' pillows.

nostalgia A medical term for home-sickness, deemed by military surgeons to be an illness of intense morbid longing and depression caused by "discomfort, hardships and exposures." Many soldiers who were shell-shocked, mentally disturbed, or suffering from combat fatigue, were diagnosed as having nostalgia.

not all the gold in California An expression used to indicate that immense wealth could not tempt one from a course of action; e.g., "Not all the gold in California could have kept me out of the war." The California Gold Rush had occurred only 12 years before the war. Today's equivalent would be "not all the gold in Fort Knox."

not born in the woods to be scared by an owl A useful rejoinder to anyone making threats or questioning your bravery. The expression meant you were too accustomed to threats and danger to be frightened.

not by a jugfull Not at all; not on any account; e.g., "I wouldn't share a tent with that Jonah, not by a jugfull."

"not care a sou" or **"care not a sou"** To care very little. A sou was a French coin of low value, usually 5 centimes. Union Major General W.T. Sherman said the aristocratic sons of southern planters "care not a sou for niggers, land, or any thing."

nothing to nobody A nonstandard southern expression meaning "nobody's business"; e.g., "Don't tell me what I need to eat, because it's nothing to nobody."

no touch to it No comparison, meaning the other item is that much better; e.g., "I'll take a breech-loading gun any day. A muzzle-loader is no touch to it."

not worth a continental cent A phrase used to describe something worthless; e.g., "In this war our lives are not worth a continental cent." The term derived from the nearly worthless paper money issued by the Continental Congress during the American Revolution. "Continental" became synonymous with "worthless" and is also heard in "not worth a continental" and "not give a continental."

not worth a pinch of shit A popular camp insult. An Ohio artilleryman shouted at his lieutenant: "You order me! You ain't worth a pinch of shit!"

noxious effluvia A medical term meaning harmful vapors or odors. Union physicians attributed bad health in overcrowded camps to noxious effluvia.

nullification The southern doctrine that said a state had the right to disobey a federal law that conflicted with its own state law or its rights. This idea, based on STATES' RIGHTS, was developed by Senator John C. Calhoun of South Carolina, and his state officially adopted it in 1832, nullifying a U.S. protective tariff and threatening to secede (but later backing down on both questions). The doctrine was ultimately used to justify the state's secession in 1860. *See also* nullifier.

nullifier A person who believed in NULLIFICATION—that a state had the right to refuse to obey a federal law. The term was in common use years before the war.

nuts for us A slang expression meaning "easy for us," as in "Taking that fort will be nuts for us boys."

O

Oath of Muster The oath taken by voluteers enlisting in the Union army. Its wording in full was as follows:

"I, _____ _____, do solemnly swear that I will bear true allegiance to the United States of America, and that I will serve them honestly and faithfully against all their enemies and opposers whatsoever, and observe and obey the orders of the President of the United States, and the orders of the officers appointed over me according to the rules and articles for the government of the armies of the United States."

obliged Obligated to someone because that person provided help or a kindness.

The word was used to mean "I'm in your debt" or even "Thank you." A soldier might say, "That skillet you loaned me helped a lot. I'm much obliged." The term is still used.

oblique order of attack *See* echelon attack.

obstruction sweeper A wooden and iron device on the bow of a warship to destroy torpedoes (mines). On the sweeper's underside were numerous iron stanchions (bars) to which were attached chains with hooks that grabbed the torpedoes, dragged them to the surface, and exploded them.

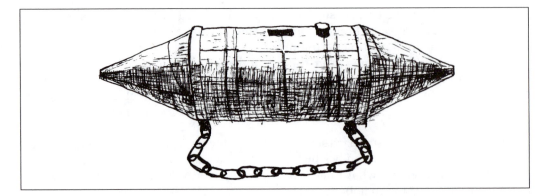

The obstruction sweeper discovered and exploded mines like this floating torpedo. *Copyright Inge Wright 1999.*

occasional A freelance journalist who was paid by the length of his report.

odd fish or queer fish An eccentric person or one who acts in a strange way. A variant name was "odd stick."

oddments Odds and ends, especially things left over; e.g., "The Yankees had deserted the camp minutes before, and we had our pick of their food and oddments."

office A witty name for a place of (somewhat sinful) enjoyment where one spends much time, especially a saloon or gambling house.

official intelligence The term used by the press for news obtained directly from someone in the government. The Washington *National Republican* published a column of "official intelligence" based on exclusive items fed to the paper by President Abraham Lincoln.

offish A shortening of "standoffish," describing someone who is aloof.

off the country An expression meaning "FORAGING." Food off the country was either taken, such as wild berries or mushrooms, or stolen, as was everything from corn to pigs.

off-wheel horse Of two horses pulling a carriage or wagon, the one on the right. An off-wheel is the wheel on the right.

"Oh, Be Joyful" A exuberant nickname for a strong, unpleasant type of whiskey. Louisiana soldier Charles Moore recalled "Emptying 3 canteens of 'Oh! be Joyful'" in camp with friends on his birthday.

"Oh, cow!" An exclamation of surprise, irritation, or disgust; e.g., "Look at that young lady spitting tobacco. Oh, cow!"

"Oh, Perdition!" A curse familiar to soldiers. Perdition is the theological name for damnation or hell.

oil-cloth A piece of cloth rubbed with oil to make it waterproof. During the war, oil-cloths served many purposes and were used to make everything from HAVELOCKS to bedding (one piece on the ground and one over the blankets), and even to mix and roll out dough for the MESS.

oil of gladness A descriptive name used in Union camps for alcohol.

O.K. Correct or all right. The expression was well established by the Civil War, having supposedly been first used on March 23, 1839, by C.G. Greene, editor of the Boston *Morning Post*, to mean "oll korrect," a humorous misspelling of "all correct."

okra coffee A coffee substitute made of okra by southern women during the restrictive war years when the price of coffee soared to $70 a pound. *See also* burnt sugar coffee; cane seed coffee; chinquapin coffee; grape coffee; pea coffee; potato and persimmon coffee; rye coffee; war coffee.

old Shrewd or cunning, because older people were thought to be crafty; e.g.,"I tried to bluff him in yesterday's card game, but he was too old for me."

"Old Abe" 1. A nickname for President Abraham Lincoln. Union Major General W.T. Sherman used the name in his letters and messages to others. 2. The live eagle mascot of the 8th Wisconsin Regiment, named for President Lincoln. An Indian had traded him to a soldier who pampered him throughout the war. During battles, Old Abe would soar high to safety and always return to the regiment. He suffered a single minor wound at Corinth, Mississippi, causing him to hide his head between his legs and demoralize the troops. Abe lived 15 years after the war, was then stuffed, and can still be seen in the Wisconsin State Museum.

"Old Allegheny" A nickname of Confederate Brigadier General James Longstreet. *See also* "my old war horse"; "Old Pete."

the Old Army The fond name given during the Civil War to the U.S. Army that had existed before the war began. It numbered about 13,000 men when Fort Sumter was attacked, most stationed in frontier outposts. More than a third of its 1,098 officers resigned to lead Confederate troops.

"Old Baldy" or "Old Bald Head" The nickname for Confederate Major General Richard ("Dick") S. Ewell, who had the tough job of taking over Lieutenant General "STONEWALL" Jackson's Second Corps after Jackson's death in May 1863. He lost a leg in action at Groveton, Virginia, during the second battle of Bull Run and was later strapped in his saddle to fight at Gettysburg. When a MINIÉ BALL thudded into his wooden leg at that battle, Ewell eyed Brigadier General John B. Gordon next to him and gibed, "Suppose that ball had struck you. We would have had the trouble of carrying you off the field, Sir. It don't hurt a bit to be shot in a wooden leg." *See also* "Popeye."

"Old Bed" The somewhat humorous nickname for Confederate Lieutenant General Nathan Bedford Forrest.

"Old Beeswax" The nickname given by his men to Confederate Admiral Raphael Semmes, because of his striking mustache which he kept stiffly pointed with beeswax.

"Old Billy" *See* "Uncle Billy."

"Old Blizzards" The nickname for Confederate Major General William W. Loring, because he would pace behind his firing lines yelling "Give them blizzards, boys! Give them blizzards!" He acquired the name after March 17, 1863, when his men, stationed on an island in the Tallahatchie River near Greenwood, Mississippi, in Fort Pemberton (built of cotton bales and sandbags), defeated a Union fleet of 10 ships, including two IRONCLADS and two TINCLADS. A lawyer, Loring had previously fought in the Seminole War and the Mexican War, where he lost an arm. His troops took part in the defenses of Vicksburg, Atlanta, and Nashville.

"Old Blue-Light" A nickname for Confederate Lieutenant General "STONEWALL" Jackson. A "blue-light" was a strict Presbyterian, and Jackson was an elder in the church who often prayed in camp. Lines in the poem "STONEWALL JACKSON'S WAY" read as follows:

Silence! ground arms! kneel all! caps off!
Old Blue-Light's going to pray.
Strangle the fool that dares to scoff!
Attention! it's his way.

"Old Bory" A nickname for Confederate Brigadier General P.G.T. Beauregard. He was a WEST POINTER who finished second in his class and was its superintendent for less than a week, being dismissed for his southern leanings. He directed the artillery attack on Fort Sumter against Major Robert Anderson, who had taught him artillery at West Point. Old Bory was a hero at the first battle of Bull Run and at Shiloh, where he shared the command. He later defended Charleston, South Carolina. *See also* "Little Creole"; "Little Napoleon"; "Man of Sumter"; Peter.

"Old Brains" *See* "Old Wooden Head."

"Old Buck" 1. The nickname given to Confederate Admiral Franklin Buchanan by Union Admiral David Farragut. Buchanan had helped establish the U.S.

Naval Academy at Annapolis and was its first superintendent. Buchanan commanded the *Virginia* (*Merrimac*) against the *Monitor* in their famous ironclad battle on March 9, 1862, at Hampton Roads, Virginia. During the battle of Mobile Bay on August 5, 1864, he impetuously steamed his *CSS Tennessee* at Admiral Farragut's overwhelming Union fleet. "I did not think Old Buck was such a fool!" exclaimed Farragut. After his leg was broken during the engagement, Buchanan surrendered. Farragut later wrote to his wife: "It was a hard fight, but Buck met his fate manfully." 2. A nickname for James Buchanan, the U.S. President when the southern states seceded. Buchanan always prayed before making a decision, and he hesitated before sending supplies to Fort Sumter in the "Star of the West." When the ship was fired upon on January 9, 1861, he did nothing, passing the problem to the new president, Abraham Lincoln, who took office on March 4. Buchanan's final appraisal of the presidency was that "The office of President of the United States is not fit for a gentleman to hold!"

old bull The nickname given by soldiers to especially tough SALT HORSE.

Old Capitol The name given to the domino game of MUGGINS by prisoners in the Old Capitol Prison in Washington, D.C.

Old Capitol Prison A prison in Washington, D.C., for Confederate soldiers as well as for political prisoners and important people suspected of being disloyal. The latter two groups were often denied the writ of habeas corpus. The granite prison building had once been the nation's temporary Capitol after the British had burned the Capitol during the War of 1812. It was then a hotel before becoming a prison in July 1861. It had an annex known as Carroll Prison. Famous Civil War pris-

Old Capitol Prison in Washington, D.C. *Library of Congress, Prints & Photographs Division, LC-B8171-1019.*

oners in the Old Capitol included the flamboyant raider Major John Singleton Mosby, known as the GRAY GHOST, and the Confederate spy, Mrs. Rose O'Neal Greenhow. The Old Capital also held prisoners from the battle of Gettysburg. One recorded happy ending involved the Confederate spy Miss Antonia Ford of Fairfax, Virginia, who wed her guard (Captain Willard of a distinguished hotel family) when she was released. After the war, the only person ever executed as a war criminal, Major Henry Wirz, the commander of the infamous Confederate prison at ANDERSONVILLE, was hanged at the prison on November 10, 1865, as soldiers chanted nonstop "Andersonville, Andersonville, Andersonville." The site of the Old Capital Prison is today occupied by the U.S. Supreme Court Building.

"Old Clubby" *See* "Old Club Foot."

"Old Club Foot" A nickname used by some of his men for Confederate General Edward Johnson, who limped because he had been shot in the leg. He was also more kindly called "Old Clubby" in reference to the strong hickory stick he used as a cane, waving it as he gave orders.

"Old Figgers" The nickname for Union Brigadier General Charles H. Grosvenor. The name meant "Old Figures," because he was also a Republican politician renowned for his accurate predictions of elections. Grosvenor also served as a U.S. congressman

the old flag A common Union term for the U.S. flag. The name created a fine comparison to the new Confederate flag and also reminded southerners in a nostalgic way that it was also their former flag.

"Old Folks at Home" One of the most popular songs with southern soldiers because of its lovely melody and nostalgic words. Many of Stephen Foster's songs, written years before the war, were heard in camps. Like the others, "Old Folks at Home" was traditionally sung in the dialect of the slave. Its first stanza and verse were as follows:

> Way down upon de Swanee ribber,
> Far, far away,
> Dere's wha my heart is turning ebber,
> Dere's wha de old folks stay.
> All de world am sad and dreary,
> Ebrywhere I roam;
> Oh, darkies, how my heart grows weary,
> Far from de old folks at home!

"Old Fuss and Feathers" A nickname of Union General Winfield Scott, because of his strict adherence to military procedures and regulations and because he wore fancy uniforms. When the war began, he was 75 and briefly commanded the Union army, devising the ANACONDA PLAN to blockade Confederate ports. Scott was also an unsuccessful Whig candidate for president in 1852.

"Old Gentleman Tipsy" A nickname for liquor, especially whiskey.

Old Glory This nickname for the U.S. flag was popularized during the war. The Massachusetts novelist Nathaniel Haw-

thorn, writing in the July 1862 issue of the *Atlantic Monthly*, described ships "wearing the Union flag,—'Old Glory,' as I hear it called these days." The name supposedly had first been used in 1831 by William Driver, a Massachusetts ship captain, who had been presented with a large flag and hoisted it up on his ship *Charles Doggett* on August 10, 1831, proclaiming "I name thee Old Glory."

"Old Graybacks" A nickname for the 7th New York State Militia because, somewhat confusing in this war, they wore light gray SHELL JACKETS and KEPIS trimmed in black. The members of the REGIMENT were from the socially elite class who paid for their own uniforms and equipment (including red blankets). New York's exclusive restaurant Delmonico supplied them with sandwiches. After Fort Sumter fell, the Old Graybacks spent a month in Washington, D.C., in case it was invaded. *See also* the Blue; standard gray.

old haymaker A sailor's humorous wartime nickname for a landsman.

"Old Heart of Oak" A poem written by William T. Meredith, an officer on the *Hartford*, a Union ship at the battle of Mobile Bay. The heart mentioned belongs to Admiral David Farragut who commanded that fleet. It begins as follows:

> Farragut, Farragut, Old Heart of Oak,
> Daring Dave Farragut, Thunderbolt stroke,
> Watches the hoary mist
> Lift from the bay,
> Till his flag, glory-kissed,
> Greets the young day.

"Old Hero of Gettyburg" The nickname for John L. Burns, a local man more than 70 years old who suddenly walked into the battle of Gettysburg with his musket. He was furious that Confederate troops had driven off his cattle. "Which way are the Rebels?" he asked, and then rejected the offer of a CARTRIDGE BOX because "I'm

not used to them newfangled things."
Burns had fought in the War of 1812, the
Seminole wars, and the Mexican War
(and was turned down for the Civil War
because of his age). He was captured at
Gettysburg but released after the battle.
He became such a hero, President
Abraham Lincoln asked to meet him
while visiting Gettysburg, and Burns was
an honored guest at the Manhattan Fair
of the SANITARY COMMISSION on April 14,
1864, in New York. In 1903, a memorial
statue was erected to him by the state of
Pennsylvania.

"Old Jack" A nickname for Confederate
Lieutenant General "STONEWALL" Jackson. Lieutenant General Richard S. Ewell
always called him "Old Jackson," although Ewell, himself known as "OLD
BALDY," was older.

"Old Joe" A nickname given to Confederate General Joseph E. Johnston by his
troops. Although he squabbled with
President Jefferson Davis and was briefly
relieved of duty after failing to halt Major General W.T. Sherman at Atlanta, Old
Joe was beloved by many. He was known
for his kindness, respect, and informal
friendliness with his men. When
Johnston took command of the Army of
Tennessee, Major General Benjamin F.
Cheatham introduced him to his men by
patting Johnston on his bald head and
saying, "Boys, this is Old Joe." During
the Atlanta siege, a southern editor wrote
that his reputation had "grown with every backward step." After the war,
Johnston served as an honorary pall-
bearer at the funeral of his old enemy,
Sherman. Out of respect, he refused to
wear his hat during the rain and died five
weeks later of pneumonia.

"Old Jube" or **"Jubilee"** The nicknames
given by his soldiers to Confederate Major General Jubal Early. He became famous in 1864 for clearing the Shenandoah
Valley of Union troops and conducting a

raid that threatened Washington on July
12. Early was a WEST POINTER who had
first strongly opposed secession. He
fought well from the first battle of Bull
Run in 1861 until his command was captured by Major General Philip H.
Sheridan's troops at the battle of
Waynesboro, Virginia, on March 2, 1865.
See also "my bad old man."

"Old Lemon-Squeezer" An early nickname given by his men to Confederate
Lieutenant General "STONEWALL" Jackson, from his health habit of sucking on
half a lemon. *See also* "Crazy Tom."

the Old Man 1. The affectionate name for
a commanding officer. The first U.S. military use was about 1850 in the U.S. navy.
2. A nickname for the Mississippi River
given by people living next to it.

"Old Man Green" *See* "Pop."

"old man" or **"old woman"** The two nicknames often assumed by tent-mates in
camp. The "old man" was generally older
or handled the tougher work.

Old North State A nickname for North
Carolina. During PICKETT'S CHARGE at
Gettysburg in July 1863, when Confederate Brigadier General James J. Pettigrew
from North Carolina gave a regiment the
order "for the honor of the good Old North
State, forward!" its members from Virginia, Alabama, Tennessee, and Mississippi failed to move and then rushed to
catch up with the North Carolinians when
they realized the order applied to all.

"Old Opium Pills" A nickname given by
soldiers to a military surgeon.

"Old Pap" *See* "Old Slow Trot."

"old peach" A nickname for peach
brandy. When the Confederate cabinet
escaped south by train from Richmond
at the war's end, the secretary of the trea-

sury, George A. Trenholm, somewhat revived their sadness with his inexhaustible "well-filled hampers of 'old peach.'"

"Old Pete" or "Old Peter" The nickname given to Confederate Lieutenant General James Longstreet at West Point and later used by his men. *See also* "my old war horse"; "Old Allegheny."

"Old Pills" The first nickname given to Union Major General W.T. Sherman during the war, because his men said serving under him was "a bitter pill to take." When he increased their supplies of items like tents and blankets, however, some began to call him "Old Sugar-Coated."

old plug or plug A slang name for a horse that is old, worn out, or inferior.

"Old Probabilities" The nickname for Union Colonel Albert J. Myer, the first signal officer for the U.S. Signal Corps. The name referred to his pioneering work in making weather predictions. Myer invented the WIG-WAG system of signaling by flags and adapted the BEARDSLEE TELEGRAPH system for military use.

"old puke" A insulting nickname sometimes given to an officer by his troops.

"old quinine" A popular nickname for a camp doctor.

"old red eye" A nickname for poor quality whiskey.

"Old Reliable" 1. The nickname Confederate Lieutenant General William J. Hardee acquired at the battle of Shiloh in April 1862. Later, General John B. Hood claimed that Hardee's unreliability led to an inconclusive result at the battle of Peach Tree Creek, Georgia, on July 20, 1864. Hood said Hardee's men "lay down," but Hardee said Hood had issued indefinite and incorrect orders. 2. The nickname

for Confederate Brigadier General John Bratton, who led the 6th South Carolina Regiment and then took over and successfully led the brigade of Brigadier General Micah Jenkins after he was killed on May 6, 1864. Bratton was a physician before the war and a farmer after it.

"Old Rock" *See* "Rock."

"Old Rosey" or "Old Rosy" The nickname given Union General William S. Rosecrans by his men of the Army of the Cumberland. They were delighted that the nickname was able to reflect Rosecrans's name and his large red nose. Old Rosey stuttered when excited but proved a successful commander until he was replaced after being defeated at Chickamauga in September 1863. *See also* "the wily Dutchman."

Union Major General William S. Rosecrans was known to his troops as "Old Rosey." *Library of Congress, Prints & Photographs Division, LC-B8172-2001.*

"Old Rye" A nickname for rye whiskey. Joseph Howard, Jr., a war correspondent with the New York *Times*, wrote on October 26, 1863, that distant cannon noises had interrupted his planned night's sleep and, remembering his readers, he "took a long swig of 'Old Rye', and shortly after cantered down the road."

"Old Scratch" A euphemism for the devil. It was used as a mild profanity, such as "What in the name of Old Scratch are the Rebs up to?" One Union soldier at the battle of Antietam recalled charging at Rebels through nearly impenetrable bushes "but we were so excited that the 'old scratch' himself couldn't have stopped us."

old sledge A popular camp card game played by two people. One enthusiastic player was Union General Ulysses S. Grant, who boasted that he had played old sledge with a future president, General Franklin Pierce, in Mexico City, when they served together in the Mexican War. The game dated back to the early eighteenth century, being known then as "all four" from the four requirements to win: high, low, Jack, and the game.

"Old Slow Trot" The nickname given to Union Major General George H. Thomas, commander of the Army of the Cumberland, for the leisurely pace of his troops when on the march. He was a West Point instructor when the name was pinned on him for his deliberate walk, and an injury from a train accident during the war reinforced his careful riding. He was also known as "OLD TOM" from his cadet days and then "Old Pap," having been 44 when he became a general. His most famous nickname, however, was the "ROCK OF CHICKAMAUGA." Thomas was a Virginian who stayed with the U.S. Army, and had once been commanded by Robert E. Lee. His family never spoke to him again, and his portrait in the family

home in Virginia was turned around to face the wall.

old soaker *See* soaker.

old soldier 1. A nickname for a cigarette or cigar butt. 2. A derogatory nickname for a soldier who feigned illness or injury to avoid duty, drill, or battle. *See also* play old soldier.

Old Sorrel or Little Sorrel The name of Confederate Lieutenant General "STONEWALL" Jackson's chestnut-colored horse that he captured in May 1861 at Harpers Ferry, Virginia. Soldiers thought the animal looked a bit awkward, but Old Sorrel had a superior long pacing stride in times of danger. When Jackson was accidentally and fatally shot in the saddle by his own men, Old Sorrel quickly carried him through thick bushes that knocked off the general's hat and scratched his forehead before Jackson fell and was caught by a captain. The horse then ran away into the Union ranks. Old Sorrel lived more than 20 years after this and was displayed at state fairs and other events where souvenir hunters would pluck hairs from his mane and tail.

"Old Straight" The nickname for Confederate Major General Alexander P. Stewart for his honesty and direct personality. The name was acquired when he taught mathematics at West Point and was perpetuated by his men, who greatly admired him. He was known for both his self-discipline and the strict discipline of his troops.

"Old Sugar-Coated" See "Old Pills."

"Old Tom" The nickname for Union General George H. Thomas since his days as a West Point cadet. Officers, such as his friend Major General W.T. Sherman, continued to use the name after the press and public began to honor Thomas as the ROCK OF CHICKAMAUGA.

"Old Unconditional" *See* "Unconditional Surrender."

"Old Virginny" The familiar nickname used by both sides for the state of Virginia.

"old woman" *See* "old man."

"Old Wooden Head" 1. A nickname for Union Major General Henry W. Halleck. He was general-in-chief of the U.S. Army from 1862 to 1864, but earned his disturbing nickname for his incompetent leadership on the battlefield. President Abraham Lincoln said Halleck was little more than "a first-rate clerk," and he was said to be one of the most unpopular men during the war. Halleck, however, graduated third in his West Point class, was a brilliant organizer of military staffs, being known in the OLD ARMY as "Old Brains," and had written the influencial *Elements of Military Art and Sciences* (1846) used during the war. 2. A nickname for Confederate General John B. Hood because of the poor judgment and disasterous overconfidence that led him to bold attacks on larger Union armies. *See also* Gallant Hood; "Yellow Rose of Texas."

old woodpecker A nickname for a soldier who was too seasoned or clever to be ambushed or surprised.

Old Wristbreaker A nickname given by calvalrymen to their heavy Model 1840 saber, a pre-war monster that was soon discarded.

"Ole Master" or "Ole Massa" The traditional name (and pronunciation) given by slaves to their owner.

"Ole Miss" The traditional name (and pronunciation) given by slaves to the mistress of their plantation. The name has been enshrined as a nickname for the University of Mississippi.

omnibus A common name during the war for a bus. "Omnibus men decorate their vehicles and horses" reported a Detroit *Free Press* article on patriotism printed on April 18, 1861, five days after Fort Sumter surrendered. The English writer Anthony Trollope, visiting New York during the war, noted, "The omnibuses, though clean and excellent, were to me unintelligible. They have no conductor to them. To know their different lines and usages a man should have made a scientific study of the city." The fare on New York omnibuses during the war was 6 cents.

"One-eyed Jeff" A rude nickname for Jefferson Davis, who had a chronic eye infection causing virtual blindness. One Confederate soldier in General John B. Hood's army, when retreating after the disastrous battle of Nashville, moaned, "Ain't we in a hell of a fix: a one-eyed President, a one-legged general, and a one-horse Confederacy!"

one-horse A description of anything small, such as a one-horse business, a one-horse college, or a one-horse wedding. The adjective survived in the phrase "one-horse town."

"One Irishman and three yards of flannel make a Zouave" A saying among Union troops in the West, making rude fun of both colorful ZOUAVE uniforms and Irish soldiers.

one-term principle The theory that a U.S. president should not serve longer than one term. This was used against Abraham Lincoln when he sought reelection in 1864, with Senator Samuel C. Pomeroy of Kansas saying the one-term principle was "absolutely essential to the certain safety of our republican institutions." The previous eight presidents had not served longer than one term.

(one's) cake is all dough. *See* cake is all dough.

on one's high horse An expression, still used, to describe someone who has become pretentiously proud and arrogant; e.g., "As soon as McClellan took charge, he got on his high horse." One could also climb down, as in "Pa said it was time Abe Lincoln got off his high horse."

on one's own hook On one's own volition. During the war, this phrase often meant doing something without permission. Confederate soldier Sam Watkins recalled that "no private soldier was ever allowed to shoot a gun on his own hook" to save ammunition. During hand-to-hand fighting at the battle of Gettysburg, a Union soldier noted that "Everyman fought on his own hook." A similar expression was "on one's own swing."

on the fly A variation of "on the run" or meaning in great haste. "A breakfast eaten 'on the fly' as it were, a rushing here and there," recalled Eliza Ripley, a southerner fleeing her sugar plantation on December 17, 1862, before Yankees arrived.

on the turf Working as a prostitute; a slang expression coined during the war.

"On to Richmond!" or "Forward to Richmond!" The northern cries, from virtually the beginning of the war, to capture the Confederate capital. "On to Richmond" was first urged on May 27, 1861, by Fitz-Henry Warren in the Washington office of the New York *Tribune* and constantly repeated by that newspaper. (Warren was later a Union major general.) After the Union defeat at the first battle of Bull Run in July 1861, many readers blamed the "On to Richmond" campaign for the disastrous confrontation and cancelled their subscriptions. By November 1862, however, the frustrated *Harper's Weekly* was calling for "On to Richmond once more!" *See also* "On to Washington."

"On to Washington!" A Confederate cry that became popular after the first victory at Bull Run in July 1861, but weeks slipped by before a real invasion was planned, allowing a sturdy defense to be organized around the capital. The South's efforts to defend its own capital quieted the call to take Washington. *See also* "On to Richmond."

O.P. An abbreviation for "Order on Paymaster," an I.O.U. used during camp card games. The credit supposedly lasted until the next payday.

open house A northern tradition on New Year's Day, in which homes were open to visitors who were greeted with wine, alcohol, and other refreshments. The tradition began to disappear in the South because "the observance being considered a Yankee fashion, the soldiers agreed to dispense with it."

open the ball To begin a battle by firing the first shots. Soldiers often referred to a battle as a ball, a humorous use of the name for a formal dance.

opera-glass A name sometimes used by soldiers for a military telescope. Confederate Private Sam Watkins of the First Tennessee Regiment recalled meeting General Robert E. Lee and noting that he had no sword, pistol, or anything to show his rank. "The only thing that I remember he had," Watkins wrote, "was an opera-glass hung over his shoulder by a strap."

operational organization The designation applied by both sides to a field army, infantry division, cavalry division, or army corps. *See also* territorial organization.

operator A surgeon, being a doctor who operated on patients.

opiumized Drugged on opium. The rector of New York's Trinity Church, Morgan Dix, once wrote during the war that U.S. Secretary of State William H. Seward "is drunk every day or opiumized."

Optic, Oliver The pen name of William Taylor Adams, whose books for boys were popular with northerners during the war. When smuggled South, his books also had an avid young readership, but mostly the adventure stories, not the patriotic ones. Living in Boston, Adams turned out more than 100 books in his lifetime and was well established seven years before the war with his "Boat Club Series." As the war ended, he began his popular "Army and Navy Series," which ran from 1865 to 1894. Most of the stories were published in *Oliver Optic's Magazine*, which he established and edited.

Order of American Knights *See* Knights of the Golden Circle.

Ordinance of Secession Legislation passed by each seceding state before the Confederacy was founded. Mississippi, for example, passed on January 9, 1861, "AN ORDINANCE to dissolve the Union between the State of Mississippi and other States united with her under the compact entitled 'the Constitution of the United States of America.'" The first section noted that Mississippi was "absolved from all the obligations, restraints and duties incurred to the said Federal Union, and shall from hence forth be a free, sovereign and independent State."

"Ordinanz numero eins!" The mock order ("Ordinance No. 1") that was given by Union Brigadier General Louis Blenker, a German, to have champagne served. This special signal was always given during visits by his commander, Major General George McClellan, who overlooked the violation of his ban on drinking.

Ordnance Department The U.S. department responsible for the army's arsenals and armories and for supplying all artillery and other military weapons with the ammunition, as well as the equipment needed for upkeep. It was headed by a chief of ordnance who was a brigadier general.

organized battle or pitched battle A battle in which troops on both sides were in fixed positions before it began.

"the Original Gorilla" A contemptuous nickname given to President Abraham Lincoln by his secretary of war, Edwin Stanton, and later repeated with relish by U.S. General George McClellan, the commander of the Army of the Potomac. Lincoln was often on bad terms with his military people, especially "LITTLE MAC" McClellan.

orison A formal name for a prayer. Captain Robert E. Lee once wrote to his cousin Martha Custis Williams about soldiers leaving for the Mexican War, saying "you must remember them in your orisons Markie."

orlop deck The lowest deck of a warship (or other ship). The name had been used since the fifteenth century and came from a Dutch word meaning "covering" because the deck originally covered the ship's hold.

"Orphan Brigade" The nickname for the Confederacy's 1st Kentucky Brigade because it became an outcast when the state did not secede. The brigade's banner was a cross with 13 stars (the 11 Confederate states with Kentucky and Missouri added because they had Rebel governments in exile). Most members of the brigade never saw their native state again. The "Orphans" were clever in both battle and camp. When orders came down prohibiting the use of a farmer's whole fence rails for firewood, the brigade's soldiers continued to steal rails but then broke each one before burning them.

orphan flag A battle-flag dropped and deserted on the ground during the conflict. Soldiers, many of them stragglers, who picked up friendly and enemy flags were often rewarded for gallantry and promoted. As one Confederate recalled, "had I only known that picking up flags entitled me to promotion and that every flag picked up would raise me one notch higher, I would have quit fighting and gone to picking up flags."

Osnaburg A heavy coarse linen or cotton woven plainly and used for linings, shirts, and sacks. Its name derived from Osnaburg (Osnabruck), Germany, where such linen was originally produced.

ostler *See* hostler.

Our American Cousin The British comedy that President Abraham Lincoln was watching at Ford's Theater in Washington, D.C., when he was assassinated. The American actress, Laura Keene, was the first to recognize the escaping assassin as John Wilkes Booth, the brother of Edwin Booth, with whom she had toured Australia. The play, by Tom Taylor, was popular in the U.S., where it was first seen in 1858 in Keene's own theater in New York.

"our best recruiting sergeant" The informal title given by President Abraham Lincoln to Thomas Nash, the famous illustrator for *HARPER'S WEEKLY* who captured Union heroics during the war, sketching battlefield scenes and life in camp. Nash was born in Germany and had come to the U.S. at the age of six. *See also* "Confederate War Etchings."

"Our Bob" The nickname given by the northern press to Union Major Robert

Anderson, the commander of Fort Sumter, who became an instant hero for refusing Brigadier General P.G.T. Beauregard's request to surrender until the Charleston batteries began a full bombardment that initiated the war.

"Our Country's Call" A poem by William Cullen Bryant published in 1861 as the war began. He intended the poem to arouse the North to the sacrifices ahead, as seen in the second of the seven stanzas:

> Our country calls' away! away!
> To where the blood-stream blots the green.
> Strike to defend the gentlest sway
> That Time in all his curse has seen.
> See, from a thousand covers—see
> Spring the armed foes that haunt her track;
> They rush to smite her down, and we
> Must beat the banded traitors back.

"Our George" An early nickname given by his troops to Union Major General George McClellan. *See also* "Little Mac"; "McClellan's Bodyguard."

ourn A substitution for "our," especially in the dialect of poorly educated white southerners and slaves, although the word was correct English usage in the fourteenth century. Similar terms are YOURN, THEIRN, HISN, and HERN.

"our own correspondent" A common anonymous byline used by newspapers during the war. Union Brigadier General Joseph Hooker created the modern newspaper byline in April 1863 when he insisted that all stories about the Army of the Potomac be signed to make reporters more responsible. He made this an official order on June 18, 1863: "Require all reporters' signatures to their published letters."

"our soil" A popular term used by Southerners and Northerners for their own territories. However, when Union Major General George Meade informed President Abraham Lincoln after the battle of

Gettysburg that the Confederate invaders had been driven from "our soil," the President reacted furiously, saying that all of the North and South was "our soil."

out-walker A person who walked alongside a carriage, for service, protection, or show. When Varina Davis, the wife of Confederate President Jefferson Davis, was driven to his inauguration in Richmond, Virginia, on February 22, 1862, she was surprised to see four black out-walkers accompany her carriage, two on either side, wearing black suits and white cotton gloves. When her black coachman told her this was usual for important ceremonies like funerals, she ordered the impressive out-walkers away.

over A shell purposely fired over a town or nonmilitary site to hit a distant target. Charleston was accidentally hit by several overs from Union guns aimed at its defending forts in late August and early September 1863.

over head and ears A descriptive expression for being completely overwhelmed; e.g., "I'm over head and ears in debt."

overseer The supervisor of work and production on a southern plantation. An-swering directly to the plantation owner, the overseer was usually the only white boss in the fields; he was assisted by the HEAD DRIVER and the other DRIVERS.

over the bay A slang expression describing someone who was drunk. See DRUNK for numerous other terms referring to intoxication.

OVM The abbreviation for the Ohio Volunteer Militia, which was etched on their metal belt plates. The organization was established on April 14, 1863, and renamed the Ohio National Guard in March 1864.

owning a body An expression used by Union prisoners at ANDERSONVILLE. Any prisoner who accompanied a burial party outside the walls had the opportunity to trade with southerners and then resell the items for exorbitant prices to other inmates. For this reason, prisoners used to "sell" the right to accompany a body (and 100 or more inmates died each day). Prices for "ownership" were pinned to the corpse, and those buried first in the day were often worth $3 while the last bodies, when the best goods had already been acquired outside, went for about 50 cents.

P

P.A.C.S. Provisional Army of the Confederate States. The Confederate Congress created it on February 28, 1861, in Montgomery, Alabama. It was designated as a volunteer force but all the South's soldiers were officially provisional ones because a regular standing Confederate Army was only drawn up on paper.

"Paddy" The nickname for Union Captain James Graydon, an officer of the OLD ARMY who was allowed to form an independent spy company of men from New Mexico. When Confederate troops under General H.H. Sibley moved into his territory, Graydon made a night attack on their camp with "torpedo mules." He tied boxes on the backs of two elderly mules and filled each box with a dozen 24-pound howitzer shells with their fuses cut. With a few men, Graydon led the mules through the night to within 150 yards of the Confederate picket line and lit the fuses. Unfortunately, the mules did not wander toward the enemy but immediately turned to follow their retreating owners. The torpedo mules exploded before they reached the horrified men, but the Confederate camp was alerted and stood ready to repel any attack.

Paddy-like Poor or poorly made, with a reference to supposedly low Irish standards. One officer writing about the quarters he had constructed in Virginia in the winter of 1862-63 explained, "It is Paddy-like, but much more comfortable than no house at all."

Paddy or paddy An insulting nickname, still heard, for someone born in Ireland or of Irish descent. It was first used about a decade before the war. As "Paddy," it was a provocative form of address.

Paff's Cave A New York bar used during the war as a rendevous and gossip spot for that city's war correspondents. It was located at 653 Broadway.

pair of stairs Another name for a flight of stairs.

pale-face 1. A nickname for a new recruit, especially one not used to toiling under the sun. 2. A witty nickname for whiskey.

paling A fence, especially one enclosing a yard or garden, made of "pales" (sharp stakes driven into the ground). When a Scotsman, David Macrae, visited a school for blacks in Philadelphia in 1868, he heard one student spell the word "pailing" and then watched the teacher provoke laughter by asking, "Then do you think the paling of the garden was made of buckets?" *See also* yard-paling.

palisade A fence of sharpened stakes pointed upward that was used as a defensive wall. The stakes were also called palisades. A row of these stakes were sometimes leaned over to point towards any enemy trying to attack an entrenchment, as was done at the Union's Fort Sedgwick ("FORT HELL") near Petersburg, Virginia.

Palmetto boys A nickname for South Carolina troops, the palmetto being the state's beloved palm tree. South Carolinians usually spelled it with a capital. During the bombardment of Fort Sumter in 1861, a local girl, Emma Homes, recorded that "our 'Palmetto boys' have won the highest praise from Beauregard."

Palmetto flag The state flag of South Carolina, bearing the palmetto tree. When Fort Sumter surrendered at the start of the war, South Carolina's Governor Francis Pickens declared on the same evening that "the proud flag of the Stars and Stripes, that never was lowered before to any nation on this earth, we have lowered it in humility before the Palmetto and the Confederate flags."

pan A slang name, still used, for the face.

panada *See* bully soup.

pantalets or pantalettes A woman's or girl's long drawers that extended beneath the skirt and had frills at the ankles. "Her point-lace pantalets attracted considerable attention," wrote the essayist Donald Mitchell (as IK. MARVEL) in 1855.

pantaloons Tight trousers that were fastened at the ankle or strapped beneath the boots. "Pants" is now the abbreviated form of this term. During one intense summer battle involving the Confederate ship *Arkansas*, after a record 120 degrees was recorded on the gun deck, Master's Mate John A. Wilson noted that the men and officers alike fought "clad only in pantaloons and undershirts."

pap-cup A baby's cup. A Union nurse treating the Confederate wounded after the battle of Gettysburg, recalled: "I even filled the silver pap-cup that a pretty boy from North Carolina had around his neck. . . . Yes, it was his baby cup, and his mother gave it to him; and he lay on the floor of the baggage car, wounded, with this domestic and peaceful of all little relics tied round his neck."

paper-collar soldier or paper-collar A soldier who still looked like a clerk or other civilian, usually because he had just come to camp from the recruiting station. The term was more familiar in the Union army, and western soldiers also generally used it as an insult for easterners on both sides. They also used the term "paper-collar dude." The paper collar referred to the DICKEY worn by clerks.

paper dickey *See* dickey.

parade rest A formal but relaxed position taken by soldiers, while in formation or in line, on the command of "Parade rest." If without weapons, a man clasps his hands behind his back and stands with his feet about 12 inches apart. If armed, he holds his rifle in his right hand with the gun upright and its butt on the ground and holds his left hand behind his back.

parapet A wall around a fort or earth bank to protect troops from enemy fire. It was often a chest-high barrier.

pard A short name for a partner, especially a best buddy, because many people pronounced "partner" as "pardner." This was first used about a decade before the war.

parlor Another name for a SITTING ROOM, although parlors were sometimes more formal. If so, a house might have both a sitting room for family gatherings and a parlor where guests were received and entertained. *See also* drawing room.

parlor house A euphemism for a house of prostitution.

parlor soldier An insulting name for a soldier who tried to avoid action and was not "one of the boys." Such a delicate man, it was assumed, would prefer to fight the war from a comfortable chair in a parlor. The name was sometimes also applied to officers who lacked great military skills and should have been in a parlor instead.

parole 1. A password given out each day by a commanding officer to be used by sentries and others to identify friend or foe. 2. A document releasing a military prisoner on his promise that he would not fight again. This was often done when prisoners were swapped but they were also sometimes freely given by one side. The most extravagant example was after Vicksburg fell on July 4, 1863. To avoid shipping the more than 31,000 defending Confederate soldiers back to Union prisons, General Ulysses Grant allowed them to march away free on their word to never again take up arms. He was later irate, but probably not surprised, to find some of them captured again, less than five months later, at Chattanooga, Tennessee. After General Robert E. Lee's surrender at Appomattox Court House in Virginia in April 1865, Confederate soldiers received paroles signed by their own commanders (and strictly honored by Union patrols) to return home, distinguishing them from deserters and men who refused to surrender. A typical parole, dated April 10, 1865, a day after the surrender, and signed by "L. F. Jones, Captain Commanding Second Company Howitzers" read as follows:

> "The bearer, Private _____, of Second Company Howitzers, Cutshaw's Battalion, a paroled prisoner of the Army of Northern Virginia, has permission to go to his home and there remain undisturbed."

paronychia *See* whitlow.

Parrott A common Union rifled cannon used by both sides. It was more accurate than the smoothbore NAPOLEON gun and had more than twice the range, up to 2,000 yards. The rear end was thick and the breech strengthened by a wrought-iron hoop. The guns ranged from 10-pounders to 300-pounders, with the heavier ones fired from fixed positions. The Union army acquired 1,684 Parrott guns of various sizes, the most (587) being 10-pounders. A 150-pounder navy version often burst during battle, killing and wounding sailors. The Parrotts were designed by Robert P. Parrott, the manager of the West Point Iron Foundry near Cold Spring, New York. *See also* "Long Tom"; "Swamp Angel."

A battery of Parrott guns near Fort Brady, Virginia, manned by Company C of the 1st Connecticut Heavy Artillery. *Library of Congress, Prints & Photographs Division, LC-B8171-2700.*

"Parson" The nickname for William G. Brownlow, a Unionist editor in Tennessee, because he was a former Methodist minister. During the war, he was imprisoned and his paper, the *Knoxville Whig*, was suppressed. Brownlow was elected as a Republican governor of the state during Reconstruction, but his portrait in the state capitol was a favorite target of tobacco-spitting legislators who had served the Confederacy. *See also* "Fighting Parson."

partisan rangers Cavalry units authorized by the Partisan Ranger Act of the Confederate Congress in April 1862 to fight behind Union lines in a guerrilla fashion, harassing the enemy. They operated in groups ranging from five to several hundred men. Although they wore Confederate uniforms and were part of the regular forces, many partisan ranger units behaved like murderous outlaw bands, such as Quantrill's raiders. General Robert E. Lee reported that the system gave license to "many deserters & marauders, who assume to belong to these authorized companies & commit depredations on friend & foe alike." With the single good exception of Colonel John S. Mosby's men, Lee recommended the units be disbanded, and in 1864 Congress abolished all units not approved by the secretrary of war. Almost all ranger groups, however, continued to operate. *See also* "Bloody Bill"; Gray Ghost; Hart, Charlie.

passengers *See* Underground Railroad.

"pass over the river" or "pass over" Euphemisms for dying. When the brother of Virginia Stinson of Camden, Arkansas, was wounded, she recorded that her family left for the battlefield but met a courier who said "that 'Hugh had passed over the river' and his body would be sent home next day."

passports The first passports in American history were required in 1861 during the war. Security fears led to a ban on anyone leaving or entering the Union states without a passport.

patchwork Patches, often decorative, sewn by soldiers over holes in their clothes. The Army of Northern Virginia developed a fad for hearts in the fall of 1863 after its Gettysburg defeat. One soldier patched a large red flannel heart on his torn trousers, and other heart designs, including those entwined or pierced by Cupid's arrow, brightened up the uniforms of the Army of Northern Virginia as it settled into winter quarters along the Rapidan River in Virginia.

"Pathfinder of the Seas" The nickname of Matthew Fontaine Maury, a Confederate naval officer, who was sometimes called the "Scientist of the Seas." He was first a U.S. navy officer who became head of the Depot of Charts and Instruments in 1841 and remained in charge as it added the U.S. Naval Obseratory and the hydrographic office. In 1855, he published *Physical Geography of the Sea*, the first textbook on oceanography, which helped establish that science. He also created charts for ocean currents and winds. Maury, a native of Spotsylvania County, Virginia, gave up his position in 1861 when the war began and returned South to head the Confederate coast, harbor, and river defenses. During this time, he invented an electric TORPEDO. After the war, he unsuccessfully tried to establish a Virginia colony in Mexico, then lived briefly in England before returning in 1868 to be professor of meteorology at the Virginia Military Institute (VMI).

Pattern 1853 A British cavalry saber frequently used by the Confederacy. German sabers were also bought, but Confederate cavalrymen generally used copies of the Union cavalry's MODEL 1840 and MODEL 1860.

patting The method used especially by slaves to keep time to music by patting with their hands and feet.

pavement An older name for a sidewalk; a term still used in Great Britain.

pavilion hospital A type of hospital consisting of long wooden buildings (pavilions), each able to handle 80 to 100 patients. The buildings often spanned out from a hub area that contained operating rooms and such medical support areas as pharmacies and kitchens. Pavilion hospitals were well ventilated and included flushing toilets with a continuous flow of water. The pavilion design was favored by both sides, and building programs were begun in 1862 by both armies. The larger Union buildings were often 120 feet long and up to 15 feet wide.

Paw-paw militia A nickname given to pro-Confederate militia operating in northwestern Missouri because it was believed they subsisted on this fruit when roaming the land. Numbering about 2,800, the Paw-paws were armed by the state government to protect peaceful Confederate sympathizers from Unionists.

Pay Department The U.S. department responsible for paying personnel, a vital flow of money that amounted to hundreds of millions of dollars. It was headed by a paymaster general, and units had paymasters at the rank of major and paymaster's clerks. A Union private from Massachusetts stated: "A paymaster's arrival will produce more joy in camp than is said to have been produced in heaven over the one sinner that repenteth." *See also* P.D.

P.D. The abbreviation of the PAY DEPARTMENT for Union forces. The letters were worn on department members' epaulettes and swords, while navymen in the department also had the initials within an oak leaf wreath on their caps.

Peace and Constitutional Society An organization established in 1861 in Arkansas by people loyal to the Union. It eventually had about 1,700 members and enough influence to provoke Confederate officials to try to disband it.

Peace Convention The common name for an unofficial convention called by Virginia's state legislature to resolve sectional differences and reverse the growing militarism in the months before the war. The timing was late and ironic; a day after Virginia's call on December 19, 1860, South Carolina seceded; and the day the convention began on February 4, 1861, in Washington, D.C., southern representatives met to form a provisional government in Montgomery, Alabama.

Peace Democrats A group within the divided Democratic Party who wished to end the war by holding peace talks with the Confederacy. They were powerful enough before the 1864 presidential election to add a "peace plank" to the party platform decreeing that "immediate efforts be made for a cessation of hostilities." President Abraham Lincoln wisely noted that the opposing party would only stay together if they "nominate a Peace Democrat on a war platform, or a War Democrat on a peace platform." When General George B. McClellan, the Democratic candidate, refused to run on the peace plank unless it demanded national reunion, the Peace Democrats split, and some WAR DEMOCRATS deserted to vote for President Lincoln, believing McClellan was still bound by the original platform. This chaos helped defeat the general's bid for the White House.

peace meeting One of several meetings held in the South in the latter months of the war to discuss ways to end the conflict through negotiations. In February 1864, Confederate Chaplain John Paris preached a sermon in which he fumed against such public gatherings, saying: "Some of these meetings have been dignified with the name of 'peace meetings' . . . but they have invariably been composed of men who talk more about their 'rights' than about their duty and loyalty to their country."

"Peace to his ashes" A blessing for a dead person. During the war, it was often used sarcastically. Confederate Private Sam R. Watkins recalled the demise of General Braxton Bragg: "Not a single soldier in the whole army ever loved or respected him. But he is dead now. Peace to his ashes!"

peach 1. To inform against or betray; to SQUEAL. The word is related to "impeach" and is still used in Great Britain. 2. A nickname for a pretty girl or young woman. It came into use near the end of the war.

pea coffee A coffee substitute in the South during the Union naval blockade. It was brewed from English peas roasted until they were a dark brown. *See also* burnt sugar coffee; cane seed coffee; chinquapin coffee; grape coffee; okra coffee; potato and persimmon coffee; rye coffee; war coffee.

peanut An adjective meaning small or insignificant. A soldier would use it in combinations like "peanut pay" or "peanut fortifications." This term was first heard about a decade before the war and is still used.

"Peas on a Trencher" The nickname in camp for the bugle call for breakfast. It came about 30 minutes after "REVEILLE." A trencher is a wooden bowl or plate.

peculiar institution A common southern euphemism for slavery. It was popularized by South Carolina's Senator John C. Calhoun, who in 1830 spoke of the "peculiar domestic institution."

peeler An extraordinary person or an amazing thing. A good example was a brave soldier.

peeling Stripping dead (or almost dead) bodies on the battlefield of valuables, a practice condoned by both sides and vitally needed by some Confederate units. Especially prized were guns, boots, coats, and other clothing.

pegs *See* pins.

pelerine A woman's mantle or cape that was popular during the war. Fashionable ermine pelerines were frequently seen at White House LEVEES. The name came from the French word for "pilgrim."

Pelican Rifles The nickname for the 3rd Louisiana Infantry regiment.

the Pen The nickname for a room kept in a barracks on New York's Park Row for soldiers who deserted and committed other crimes. Up to 77 men were confined at any one time for three to four months in the Pen, which measured 15 by 20 feet. While 45 men slept in the cramped spaces at night, the remaining prisoners were chained to trees outside until their turn to sleep.

penny ante The poker game with betting limited to a penny or other low amount. It was popular with the poorly paid soldiers on both sides.

penny packet A small amount. Commanders would sometimes split up their army in "penny packets." The Union army used its cavalry in penny packets early in the war until realizing the shock value of larger units.

pennyroyal A mint used as home medicine. It was steeped and the liquid used to cause perspiration and also to initiate or restore menstruation. One Massachusetts recruit, leaving his hometown with his unit, was mortified when his mother rushed after him with a bundle, calling, "Jack! Jack! You've forgotten to take your pennyroyal."

pen printing Using a fountain pen to print letters by hand. Many small news sheets in camps were pen printed, including the masthead.

"people's war" A phrase used by President Abraham Lincoln to emphasize democracy at work and the fact that the voices and actions of the public were the controlling factors in the conflict. The same term, however, was used against the government's censorship of war news. "This is a people's war," fumed the New York *World*, repeating Lincoln's exact words. "There must be freedom of information and freedom of speech."

pepper treatment A common method of spicing up bland soup by adding a pod of red pepper. Soldiers would sometimes do this secretly as they passed the cooking pot, and if more than one pulled off the trick, the mess-mates would wait in vain for the brew to cool.

percussion cap or cap The small container of explosive charge placed on the firing nipple of a musket and activated by the hammer to fire the gun's CARTRIDGE. Positioning the charge was called "capping a gun." During the heat of battle, soldiers sometimes forgot to add the cap, resulting in a misfire.

Perry's Saints The nickname of the 48th New York Regiment, because all the officers were ministers. Perry was their colonel.

personate To imitate someone or act out something. Robert E. Lee, in a letter to his cousin, Martha Custis Williams, wrote: "Roony has personated your extacies at the sight of the moonlight dancing on the water." *See also* extacy.

persuader A slang name for a weapon, such as a rifle, cannon, or sword.

petard A shell or half-cone of iron filled with powder and ball and used to blast open walls, doors, and other enemy obstructions. This bomb was normally attached to a plank that had hooks to fasten it to the barrier. The French term actually means to break wind.

Peter A familiar nickname sometimes given by his troops to Confederate General P.G.T. Beauregard, whose full name was Pierre Gustave Toutant Beauregard. See also "Little Creole"; "Little Napoleon"; "Man of Sumter"; "Old Bory."

Petersburg crater A Union tragedy that occurred during the first month of the siege of Petersburg, Virginia, in July 1864. Major General Ambrose Burnside approved a plan by Lieutenant Colonel Henry Pleasants (a coal-mine engineer) for the 48th Pennsylvania to dig a mine under a Confederate BATTERY. This dig was completed on July 23 after a month's digging; the mine was filled with 8,000 pounds of black powder connected to a 98-foot fuse. Union troops were to attack through the gap opened by the explosion. On the Confederate side, General P.G.T. Beauregard was aware of the digging and aimed large mortars at the likely point of detonation. The powder was exploded on July 30, blasting enemy soldiers and equipment into the air, creating a large crater (30 feet deep and up to 80 feet wide) and killing or wounding nearly 300 Confederates. The Union assault force of more than 15,000 men rushed in and were easy targets for the waiting artillery. Before their desperate retreat had ended, Burnside had lost 3,798 men to Beauregard's 1,500 casualties.

"the Petersburg Express" *See* "The Dictator"

"Pet Lambs" The ironic nickname given by the Washington *Star* to the rowdy Fire Zouaves regiment recruited from New York City fire departments. When on guard in Washington, D.C., at the start of the war, the "Pet Lambs" virtually terrorized the city with their drunkenness and disposition to fight any secessionist, as well as one another.

pet name A nickname, especially a personal one for a family member or someone special, such as a LOVER. The name is still used.

pet regiment The favorite regiment of a general. The 10th South Carolina, for example, was called General Braxton Bragg's pet regiment. Its officers were democratically elected, with ordinary soldiers choosing the lieutenants and captains, and the captains deciding among themselves who would be the field officers.

Philadelphia Confederate note One of several counterfeit Confederate notes printed in Philadelphia. Soldiers in Union Major General John Pope's army used them as currency when invading Virginia, paying for all kinds of purchases, even horses. The *New York World* correspondent reported on July 31, 1862, on "the passing of Philadelphia Confederate notes," by the army, saying: "Whenever we advance into a new section, the floodgates are immediately opened, and the *fac-simile* Confederate notes are poured out upon the land."

"Philippi Races" The local name given to the quick retreat of Confederate forces at Philippi, Virginia (now West Virginia), on June 4, 1861. Troops of Confederate General Robert S. Garnett had not posted sentries on the wet night and were surprised as they slept in the early morning darkness by soldiers of Major General George B. McClellan. The Rebels fled east and eventually escaped. Garnett, however, demonstrated his bravery to his nervous rear-guard by walking behind them and was killed by a sharpshooter, becoming the first officer to die in the Civil War. *See also* Buckland Races; Woodstock Races; Wildcat Stampede.

phiz A humorous name for the face or a facial expression, such as a grimace. First used in the seventeenth century, the term was a shortening of "physiognomy."

phonography Any type of shorthand based on using brief marks for spoken sounds, such as the Pitman system devised in England before the war. Phonography was one of several classes organized by 150 Union officers in 1863 in Richmond's LIBBY PRISON.

photo This shortening of "photograph" first occurred during the war when the demand for portrait photography greatly increased. Photos were prized possessions swapped between soldiers and their families and sweethearts.

photographist An alternate name for a photographer.

phrenology The pseudoscience of determining a person's character by reading the shape and bumps on his or her head. It became the rage, and a popular book during the war was *New Illustrated Self-Instructor in Phrenology and Physiology* published in 1859 by the brothers Orson and Lorenzo Fowler. In 1861, a New York City phrenology company, Fowler and Wells, offered half-price examinations to men enlisting for the war.

physic A medicine or remedy. In his 1858 book *The Impending Crisis of the South*, Hinton Rowan Helper, a southerner, noted that the South depended on the North for most things in life, until "in old age we are drugged with Northern physic."

pianoforte The formal name for a piano. As the war began, the upright pianoforte was the most popular one in homes, almost replacing the older "square" version that resembled a coffin on four legs. "Pianoforte" means "soft-loud" in Italian, and the instument was first called "fortepiano" in eighteenth-century England.

piazza *See* veranda.

pick A name used in weaving for thread. A merchant determined the quality of cotton cloth by the number of picks to an inch.

pickaninny or piccaninny A black child. The term was heard in the North as well as the South. President Abraham Lincoln's wife asked him in April 1863 how many of "those piccaninnies" would he guess were named after him. (He said two-thirds under the age of two.) As with other names for African-Americans (NIGGER, NEGRESS, UNCLE, etc.), white speakers did not consider it derogatory. This name came from the Spanish or Portugese language, and sailors heard it used by black natives of the Spanish West Indies. It was also common in Australia and South Africa, introduced there by the English (who also used the word humorously for white babies).

picket A soldier assigned as a watch some distance from a camp, often a quarter mile away. The name came from pickets (sharp stakes) driven in the ground to mark the location of this duty. Some soldiers liked the freedom and isolation from camp duties, but the picket line was a dangerous area, especially vulnerable to snipers. The captain of the picket was in

Union pickets outside Atlanta, Georgia, in 1864. *Library of Congress, Prints & Photographs Division, LC-B8171-3628.*

charge of the detail for picket duty, usually four or five men in each area, marching them to the picket line and later calling them in. A man was said to be "picketing" an area, and a cavalry would "ride picket." *See also* drive in the pickets.

picketed To be assigned as a PICKET to a certain location; e.g., "He was picketed at the foot of Lookout Mountain."

Pickett's Charge The heroic but disasterous assault of 42 Confederate regiments on Cemetery Hill on July 3, 1863, the third day of the battle of Gettysburg. Its failure has been blamed for the loss of the battle and even by some for the loss of the Civil War. About half the 12,500 men who made the attack were killed. The Confederates charged against heavy artillery fire and 27 Union regiments comprising up to 10,000 men. Although the name of Major General George E. Pickett was blackened that day, this is only because Lieutenant General James Longstreet ordered him to organize the brigades on the field before the attack. Pickett did not lead the charge, and the men of his division were a minority of those involved. Before the charge, the nervous Confederates had a "battle" with green apples to relieve the tension. Confederate artillery had been pounding the enemy's position and the Union cannons suddenly went silent, convincing the southerners that the guns had been destroyed. In fact, they were saving ammunition. Just after 3 p.m., the order was given, and the Rebels marched (rather than charged) resolutely forward over the nearly mile-wide field covering 100 yards a minute, forming a straight front that stretched more than half a mile, with banners flying and their field officers mounted. They had been instructed not to fire or give their frightening Confederate yell. The sight awed the waiting Yankees who described it as "splendid," "like a dress parade," and "the most beautiful thing I ever saw." Then the Union's 1,700 rifles and 11 cannons opened up, shattering the enemy. The highest point of the advance was when the Union line was breached by about 150 men under Brigadier General Lewis Armistead, but they were soon either killed (including Armistead) or captured by troops of the 72nd Pennsylvania. After the survivors retreated and General Robert E. Lee ordered Pickett to prepare his division for a counterattack, Pickett replied, "General, I have no division." In the distance, Union soldiers dragged the fallen Confederate flags behind their horses to add insult to injury. Years after the war, Pickett still blamed General Robert E. Lee for the disaster, saying "That old man had my division massacred."

pick-lock journalism The name given by the New York *Tribune* to war or government news obtained in dubious, illegal, or secret ways, such as having inside informers. Rumor said the New York *Herald* was able to print excerpts from President Abraham Lincoln's first State of the Union message (before Congress knew what was in it) because the paper's Washington correspondent, Henry Wikoff, was a close personal friend of Mrs. Lincoln. Wikoff claimed the White House gardener had memorized and repeated it to him.

pick-up or pick-up dinner A northern name for a dinner of leftover meats.

"Pie-cake" *See* "Daughter of the Confederacy."

piece A general name for a cannon, rifle, or revolver. Carlton McCarthy, a private in the Confederate Army of Northern Virginia, wrote that it was impossible to wear gloves and "handle a rammer at the piece." The term is still used for small arms. *See also* field piece.

pie eater A nickname for a rural man, especially a country bumpkin.

"the pie order" An informal name for a humorous Special Order issued by Union Brigadier General Ulysses S. Grant in 1861 during his campaign in eastern Missouri. Grant stopped by a wayside house in search of a meal, only to find that a Lieutenant Wickfield of the Indiana Cavalry had earlier in the day presented himself and his advance guard as "General Grant and his staff" and eaten everything in the house but one pumpkin pie. Grant paid the woman a half dollar to keep the pie until it was collected. Later that evening at a dress parade, he published his special order, saying that Lieutenant Wickfield "having on this day eaten everything in Mrs. Selvidge's house, at the crossing of the Ironton and Pocahontas and Black River and Cape Giradeau roads, except one pumpkin pie, Lieutenant Wickfield is hereby ordered to return with an escort of one hundred cavalry and eat that pie also."

Pigeon A popular pet name for a female sweetheart.

piggin A small wooden pail whose handle was formed by making one of its staves longer than the rest.

pike To leave quickly or depart with haste. A regiment might have to "pike" from a losing battle.

pile All of a person's money. The slang name was first used by California miners to mean all their accumulated gold dust and nuggets. This usage has evolved to today's meaning of any large amount of money.

pilot-engine A locomotive engine sent ahead of a regular train to make certain the track is clear. When Abraham Lincoln traveled from Illinois to Washington, D.C., in February 1861 for his first inauguration, pilot-engines preceeded his different special trains.

pimp This name for a procurer of prostitutes was commonly used during the war. The Memphis *Bulletin* complained on May 1, 1863, that "Memphis is the great rendezvous for prostitutes and 'pimps.'" The word has been used in England since the beginning of the seventeenth century.

pinchbeck Cheap jewelry, worn during the troubled days of war by both respectable women and prostitutes. It was made of pinchbeck, a yellow alloy of five parts copper and one part zinc that resembled gold. It was invented in the eighteenth century by an English jeweler named Christopher Pinchbeck.

pins An informal name for legs, which were also called "pegs."

pintle An iron pin. They were found on the back of a LIMBER. The LUNETTE (ring) on the end of a cannon's STOCK TRAIL was connected to it when the lunette towed the cannon. Pintles were also used under stationary cannon mounts to allow the guns to be rotated 180 degrees.

"The Pioneer" The name of the first Pullman railroad car, which was used to carry President Abraham Lincoln's body from Chicago to Springfield, Illinois, the final stage of his funeral procession by train. George M. Pullman, a cabinetmaker born in Brocton, New York, had built the luxurious car during the war in 1863 in Chicago, but it proved too large for existing stations and was kept on a siding until Lincoln's death, when Illinois cut back station platforms and raised bridges for Lincoln's final journey. The car was so impressive, Andrew Carnegie joined Pullman two years after the war to establish the Pullman Palace Car Company that built the famous Pullman sleeping cars.

Pioneer Corps The unit of engineers in each of the Confederate armies for the first half of the war. It was run by the army's professional engineers but had to fill the ranks with ordinary infantry soldiers transferred from different brigades, or even by forcibly rounding up civilians. The Pioneer Corps was replaced in 1863 by two engineer regiments that each had 10 companies of 100 men.

pipe down This familiar command, to stop talking or to hold down noise, was already common during the war. The expression was possibly related to a boatswain's pipe or whistle, since he would sound it to dismiss, or "pipe down," sailors.

pipe-laying In politics, bringing in outside or illegal voters during an election. The name derived from a New York Democrat's accusations, later proved false, that the city's Whig Party had sent an agent to Philadelphia to bring Whig voters into New York. The accusation said the agent tried to conceal his true mission by saying he was traveling to Philadelphia to buy water pipes to be laid in New York.

piss-pot An insult heard in the camps of both armies. "God damned little piss-pot!" yelled one Massachusetts private to the sergeant escorting him to the guard-house.

Pittsburg Landing The alternative name for the battle of Shiloh. It took place on April 6 and 7, 1862, at Pittsburg Landing, Tennessee, where some Union troops had camped around Shiloh Church.

pitched battle See organized battle.

plank down To table or put down money on something or to pay on the spot. It comes from the idea of slapping cash on the planks of a table. The expression began about a decade before the war and is still heard.

plank road A road laid with sturdy planks, providing a smoother surface

than a CORDUROY road. Before their victory at the battle of Chancellorsville in 1863, Confederate generals Robert E. Lee and "STONEWALL" Jackson held their main strategy meeting on a plank road about a mile southeast of the town. Plank roads were especially needed in swampy areas.

plant To bury a body. This informal verb was first used as the war began.

planter The term used in the South for the owner of a plantation and slaves. The principal crops were cotton, sugar, or rice. Owners of less than about 20 slaves were called "small planters," while those with only a few (or none) were referred to as farmers. See also yeoman farmer.

platoon A small military unit on both sides, composed of two SECTIONS. A platoon might have from 40 to 50 men. Two platoons together composed a COMPANY.

play off To shirk military duties; e.g., "I ended up cooking while my mess-mates played off."

play old soldier An expression meaning to fake an illness; e.g., "He plays old soldier every time he hears the long roll." See also old soldier.

play-out A solder who was played out, or worn out, often to the point of a breakdown. The name was also used for men suspected of malingering. See also about played out; "All played out!"

play smash To wreck something. One Union soldier reported in 1863: "We are going on a big scout to Columbus, Mississippi, and play smash with the railroads." The expression was often used by southern soldiers when they destroyed their own equipment and supplies to keep it from enemy hands.

plebe The nickname for a first-year cadet at the U.S. Military Academy at West

Point, New York. The word, still used there, is derived from the Roman "plebeian," describing the common person or class.

pledging ceremony A ceremony held in Confederate units asking men to pledge to re-enlist. This often followed hell-fire speeches by officers or visiting politicians. Some officers then held a dress parade, moved the flags forward, and asked men to advance to the colors if they intended to re-enlist. Pledging ceremonies often inspired soldiers to extend their service for more than three years. The 20th Mississippi Regiment wanted re-enlistments for 99 years or the duration of the war.

plough A common spelling of "plow." Many British spellings and words were still used during the war era, such as "axe," "grey," "favourite," "haemorrhage," "whilst," and "pavement" (sidewalk). Confederate General Robert E. Lee used the British double "l" for his horse, Traveller.

plucking board An informal name for a board of officials or professionals who examined applicants for positions and then rejected, or plucked out, the failures. For instance, during the war, northern governors had the authority to commission surgeons in the Union army, but the U.S. surgeon general could remove unwise choices by having them reexamined by plucking boards.

plug 1. A slang name for a top hat or tall silk hat. Some new soldiers would arrive in camp with the item. 2. The insulting nickname given to any plain-looking or ugly man. 3. The name was also used for the PLUG UGLIES. *See also* old plug; tile.

plug a tooth To fill a tooth. When Alabamian Samuel Kelly with the Army of Northern Virginia wrote his wife, Amie, that he intended to have two teeth pulled, she replied on July 17, 1862: "I would dislike to have them pulled unless they ached. Could you have them plugged and save them?"

"plug uglies" Ruffians from Baltimore who supported the Confederacy. The name came from either the PLUG hats they wore or the spikes on the toes of their boots, used to kick their enemies ("plug them ugly"). As the war began, these gangs roamed the state, attacking northerners and burning bridges to delay the progress of Union troops. On April 19, 1861, six days after Fort Sumter surrendered, their rock and brick attack on the troops of Major General Benjamin F. Butler marching through Baltimore provoked the soldiers to open fire. Twelve civilians and four soldiers were killed. During the war, "plug-ugly" was generalized to mean any tough hoodlum.

Plug Ugly The name of the horse of Union Brigadier General Alpheus Williams.

plunging fire A common expression for intense gunfire.

pocket money An allowance given to children. The term is still the only one used in Great Britain.

"poet laureate of the South" The unofficial title given to Henry Timrod, who wrote poems extolling the South, including "Ethnogenesis" and "The Cotton Boll."

the Point The shortened nickname, still used, for West Point, the United States Military Academy.

points and blunts A surgeon's common name for chisels and hammers used for amputations and other operations on bones, such as trimming them.

poisonous vapors The mist, fog, and gases from swamps and ponds that doctors believed caused several diseases, such as malaria, meningitis, and peritonitis. Treatment consisted of opening windows in the hospital.

poke-bonnet A woman's bonnet with a large brim in front.

poker This card game was played in both armies, but had long been a southern favorite. Soldiers intent on marking their cards profited from the recent innovation of decorations on the back. Until a decade before the war, cards normally had white backs to eliminate this form of cheating. Draw poker was a favorite game. Confederate General John B. Hood was an avid player who, while recuperating in Richmond from the amputation of his leg, reportedly bet $2,000 on a hand without a pair, and won. Union Brigadier General Joseph Hooker, according to a friend, "could play the best game of poker I ever saw, until it came to the point when he should go a thousand better, and then he would flunk." Confederate Lieutenant General James Longstreet stopped playing poker as a penance after three of his children died of scarlet fever in one week in 1862.

pokerish An informal word to describe something frightening, such as a "pokerish looking old convent." The word was often used in conversations with children, but also in serious newspaper articles. A "poker" was a frightening thing, like a boogeyman in the dark.

polack This insulting name for a person from Poland or a descendant of Poles, was well known during the war and dates back to the seventeenth century. Although used as an insult, the name is the German version of *Polak*, which is simply the Polish word for Pole.

polar star Someone who was a guiding light or strong leader. Confederate diarist Mary Chesnut wrote on January 1, 1864, that southerners who disliked President Jefferson Davis had one champion (who felt the same): "Joe Johnston is their polar star, the redeemer!"

"Polecat" The nickname given by his Louisiana and Texas men to the Confederate Brigadier General Camille Armand Jules Marie, the Prince de Polignac from France. They could hardly pronounce his name and also resented his foreignness and the idea that his title, not his leadership, might have earned his rank. Polecat earned their loyalty, however, by his bravery under fire.

police descent A police raid. The term was familiar during the war in New York City where disreputable concert saloons suffered regular police descents.

policing The military word, still used, for cleaning up a camp or other area of litter. Soldiers were assigned "police duty" as regular duty or as mild punishment, their names often coming from the BLACK LIST. Most considered this cleaning duty to be degrading work. The term was also sometimes used for heavier work, such as felling trees before setting up camp.

political general A general appointed because of his political connections. These appointees were generally inept and despised by the regular officers and men. One exceptionally successful example was Confederate General John C. Breckinridge, who later became the Confederacy's sixth and final secretary of war. W.T. Sherman enlisted as a colonel in the Union army, turning down a higher rank to avoid being a political general. (His brother was a U.S. senator.)

Poliute The pen name used by Franc Bangs Wilkie, the New York *Times'* war correspondent (only "correspondent," not the later term "war correspondent," was used). He once noted, "Whiskey flowed for correspondents with the coming of Grant." He was known for his sharp, unflattering descriptions of the nation's military leaders, describing Union Major General W.T. Sherman as "built narrow and almost effeminate" and having the attitude of "cynical indifference." Wilkie covered the action west of the Allegheny Mountains until 1863, when he became an editorial writer for the Chicago *Times*.

polka A popular dance with young men and women but condemned by most of their parents because they believed passions were aroused by the rapid tempo, galloping movements, and closeness of the couples (the man embracing the woman's waist with one hand). The dances also usually had very un-American names, such as "The Celebrated Varsovienne." As early as 1845, U.S. Captain Robert E. Lee wrote from Fort Hamilton, New York, that "The Polka has been a favourite dance."

polka jacket A tight fitting military jacket worn by some units, such as the New York MILITIA. The name, originally given to a woman's knitted jacket, came from the dance.

Polly The nickname of Maggie Davis, the daughter of Confederate President Jefferson Davis.

polt A northern name for a blow, especially heard in New England and New York; e.g., "He gave the Rebel a polt over the head with his rifle."

poltrune A fancy name for a coward. It is related to "poultry" and, thus, being a chicken.

pontonier A soldier who builds pontoon bridges. Military engineers were in charge of such projects and served as pontoniers themselves. The work was of-

Photographed in May 1864, this pontoon bridge across Virginia's North Anna River was constructed by pontoniers of the 50th New York Engineers. *Library of Congress, Prints & Photographs Division, LC-B8171-0746.*

ten done under enemy fire, as on December 10, 1862, when Mississipi sharpshooters easily picked off pontoniers for hours as they constructed a bridge over the Rappahannock River at Fredericksburg. The Union men would work rapidly until the devastating fire drove them away, only to have their officers order them back to the deadly task.

the pony or pony post Familiar names for the Pony Express, the famous mail relay system from St. Joseph, Missouri, to Sacramento, California. It began on April 3, 1860, but went out of business on October 24, 1861, six months after the first shots of the war were fired at Fort Sumter. The completion of the transcontinental telegraph was the death knell for "the pony."

"Pook Turtle" A later version of Union IRONCLAD warships built by Samuel M. Pook. Unlike the original flat-decked *Monitor* with its gun turret, the Pook ships resembled the Confederate's *Virginia (Merrimac)*, with a slanted upper housing containing four gun holes on each side. The first Pook Turtle was the U.S.S. *Carondelet*, one of several such ships that secured control of the Mississippi. Altogether seven were built to control western rivers.

poor as Job's turkey A common simile for poverty or lack of funds; e.g., "Every time the sutler comes around, I'm as poor as Job's turkey."

poor white trash (or white trash or mean trash) A contemptuous southern name for a poor, uneducated white person, said even by slaves who looked down on white servants. "Poor white," less of an insult, was also used for a better type of white person lacking money and education.

"Pop" The nickname given by his men to Union Major General George S. Greene,

who was 62 years old when he took part in the battle of Gettysburg in 1863. They also called him "Old Man Greene." The name fit his relaxed dress of a civil engineer, but he was known for his harsh discipline and rough manners. Greene, who had taught engineering and math at West Point, saw action at such battles as Chancellorsville and Antietam. A bullet passed through his face at Wauhatchie, Tennessee, in October 1863, but he returned to the field on April 9, 1865. After the war, Greene developed the infrastructures for several cities, including the elevated railroad and water supply for New York City and the sewer system for Washington, D.C. He lived to the age of 98.

"Pope's headquarters is where his hindquarters belong" A humorous popular saying among Union soldiers, because a journalist had asked Union Major General John Pope where his headquarters was, and he supposedly had said "In the saddle." The pompous Pope denied the quote and called the saying "cheap wit," but it continued to flourish. The notion was not confined to Pope. Confederate Lieutenant General Nathan Bedford Forrest headed some of his poorly-spelled letters "Hed Quaters in Sadle."

"Popeye" A nickname given by his men for Confederate Major General Richard ("Dick") S. Ewell. He was described as being "bald, pop-eyed and long beaked, with a piping voice that seems to fit his appearance as a strange, unlovely bird." *See also* "Old Baldy."

poppycock This familiar slang name for foolishness or nonsense was coined toward the end of the war. The word comes from *pappekak*, the Dutch name for soft dung.

pop-skull A descriptive term used by Confederate soldiers for strong, illegal liquor.

pork and eggs A popular combination during the war, as was ham and eggs. The pork was the uncured meat.

"Porte Crayon" The pen name of Union Colonel David H. Strother, who supplied articles and pen sketches of military life and the South to *HARPER'S WEEKLY*, becoming one of its best-paid contributors. When John Brown was hanged in 1859, Strother had violated protocol (and good taste) by lifting the dead man's blindfold as he still swung on the rope, to sketch his face. *Harper's Weekly* turned down the gruesome portrait and Strother's accompanying article, which it considered too inflammatory.

portmanteau A bag or trunk used to carry apparel on journeys. The literal meaning of the French name was "carry mantle (or cloak)."

port-monnaie A woman's purse or pocketbook. The French word literally meant "carry money."

port stopper A device used on warships to block the gunports while the guns were being loaded. This protected the dangerous powder and shot from enemy fire. The Union's first IRONCLAD ship, the *Monitor*, had usual port stoppers of heavy iron sheets that were pulled like shutters over the gunports.

possum A humorous but affectionate name for a good buddy or a special friend.

posted Informed or in the know. An army officer could "post up" his troops about an imminent battle, and anyone "well posted up" was well informed. The expressions came from the bookkeeping term of "posting," or transferring, figures from a journal to a ledger.

postillion A man who rode and guided the left-hand horse of two pulling a carriage without a driver, or a man who rode the leading left-hand horse when four or more were used with a driver. In the army, drivers and postillions were used for six-mule teams that pulled the wagons.

Post Office Department The Confederacy's postal service. At the beginning of the war, the cost of sending a letter weighing half an ounce was 5 cents and newspapers and other printed matter cost 1 cent. In two years, the prices rose to 10 cents and 2 cents, respectively. The Constitution of the Confederate States required that the department have a balanced budget, and it actually made a profit in 1863. The Confederate postmaster general was John H. Reagan.

potato and persimmon coffee A southern coffee substitute used during the blockade, made of persimmon seeds that were boiled and parched, with mashed potatoes mixed in for body. Coffee was also made of dried and parched sweet potatoes (yams). *See also* burnt sugar coffee; cane seed coffee; chinquapin coffee; grape coffee; okra coffee; pea coffee; rye coffee; war coffee.

potato chips Potatoes served in slices, which, by modern standards, were very thick.

potato grabbers A slang name for hands that was an appropriate term for the hands of soldiers foraging off the land.

powder boat Any kind of boat filled with powder and exploded near enemy ships or forts. Powder boats were not always successful. Union General Benjamin F. Butler tried to demolish Fort Fisher (protecting the mouth of the Cape Fear River in North Carolina) by filling an old steamer, the *Georgiana*, with 215 tons of powder and exploding it at 1:30 a.m. on December 23, 1864. After the explosion, Butler's flagship approached Fort Fisher at full speed, only to have all the fort's guns fire away. Butler's ship quickly reversed course. "The last we saw of her, she was running east as fast as her engines could carry her," recalled Robley D. Evans, a Union sailor on another ship. "The powder boat had proved a failure, and the General was grievously disappointed." So was General Ulysses S. Grant, who soon had Butler relieved of his command. *See also* fire raft; fire ship.

powder manufactory A company or facility that manufactured gunpowder.

powder monkey A young boy on a warship who carried powder or shells from the magazine to the cannons. Powder was originally carried in powder buckets or canvas bags.

a power A dialect term for a large number of people or things. "They are killing off a power of the boys," noted one Union prisoner in ANDERSONVILLE.

pox Another name for syphilis.

practicable breach *See* breach.

"Prairie Dog Village" The nickname given by Union soldiers sieging Vicksburg, Mississippi, to the approximately 500 caves local residents had dug to live in during the bombardments. Some of the more elaborate caves had several furnished rooms and were served by slaves. *See also* gopher hole.

"Prayer of Twenty Millions" An open letter in the New York *Tribune* to President Abraham Lincoln, written by the owner, Horace Greeley. Published on August 20, 1862, it asked the president to enforce the CONFISCATION ACTS that freed slaves. Lincoln responded negatively, saying "what I forbear, I forbear because I do *not* believe it would help to save the Union." Twenty million was the population of the northern states.

the Presidential grub The overwhelming desire to be president of the United States. The grub (larva of an insect) has today become the "presidential bug." Abraham Lincoln was uncertain whether being bitten by the grub helped his leaders or not. He thought it might distract General Ulysses S. Grant but might produce more work from Secretary of the Treasury Salmon P. Chase.

"president of the Underground Railroad" *See* Underground Railroad.

pretty man A handsome man.

"Prince John" The nickname given by his soldiers to Confederate Major General John B. Magruder because of his expensive tastes, lavish parties, fashionable clothes, and pompous but elegant manners. A popular song described him as "the hero for the times." He loved plays and during the Mexican War had staged *Othello*, for which young Ulysses Grant donned crinolines to try for the part of Desdemona. Magruder was famous for moving his troops about in a great DEMONSTRATION of false strength; his small force routed the army of Major General Benjamin F. Butler at the battle of Big Bethel, Virginia, on June 10, 1861. After the war, he lived in Mexico.

"prince of darkness" One of many nicknames for James Gorden Bennett, the Scottish-born founder and editor of the politically independent *New York Herald*. He fashioned the paper into an internationally known scandal sheet because he believed a newspaper's function was "not to instruct but to startle." Bennett was often hostile to President Abraham Lincoln's policies and was publicly beaten on four occasions. Among his other derogatory nicknames were "murderer of reputations" and "venomous reptile." *See also* "most largely circulated journal in the world"; "nigger-drivers"; "nigger worshippers."

"prince of humbugs" The title given to the showman P.T. Barnum, who entertained northerners during the war with BARNUM'S AMERICAN MUSEUM in New York, and circus performances in Washington, D.C., and elsewhere. Barnum proudly used the title himself and was known for his blatant motto, "There's a sucker born every minute."

"prince of rails" A humorous nickname for Robert ("Bob") Todd Lincoln, the oldest son of President Abraham Lincoln, because his father was known as "the RAIL-SPLITTER." Robert was an 18-year-old Harvard student when the war began and, at his mother's insistence, finished his education and spent four months at Harvard Law School. The public criticized this avoidance of duty, and in 1865 he was appointed a captain and joined General Ulysses S. Grant's staff. Earlier that year, Robert's life was possibly saved at the Jersey City, New Jersey, train station when a man grabbed his coat collar as a crushing crowd pushed him toward the track. His rescuer was the actor Edwin Booth (brother of John Wilkes Booth, who would assassinate President Lincoln). Robert was supposed to join the family at Ford's Theatre the evening his father was killed but said he was too tired. He regretted this decision the rest of his life. He was the only one of Lincoln's four children (all sons) to live to adulthood and was U.S. secretary of war under President James Garfield.

private-hand letter A letter delivered by hand and not through the official postal services. This system was especially used in the early days of the Confederacy when normal mail deliveries ceased between the North and the South. The later disruption of war often forced southerners to rely on letters brought by the private hands of family members, travelers, merchants, and others.

A Proclamation of Amnesty and Reconstruction President Abraham Lincoln's proclamation on the treatment of citizens of the Confederate states, delivered during his message to Congress on December 1, 1863. It promised a full executive pardon for most citizens (with such exceptions as major military officers and former U.S. congressmen) who would take a LOYALTY OATH and pledge of support for the EMANCIPATION PROCLAMATION. A former Confederate state would be readmitted to the Union and send representatives to Congress if 10 percent of its 1860 voters took the oath.

progressive order of attack *See* echelon attack.

prolonge An arrangement of strong ropes attached to a cannon with a hook on one end and a toggle on the other. Men sometimes used the prolonge to haul the cannon under dangerous conditions when horses would be more conspicuous and vulnerable.

Promises-to-Pay The nickname for paper money, especially Confederate bills, because of the wording "Will pay one dollar to the bearer on demand."

Provost Marshal Department The U.S. department responsible for policing the army and for organizing conscription. It was established on March 17, 1863, in Washington, D.C., and was headed by the provost marshal general, who was a brigadier general. Each field army had policemen, usually cavalry members, serving under a provost marshal. Because their duties included curtailing alcohol and prostitutes, provosts were not popular with soldiers or businessmen. At camps, they were jeered and insulted and accused of avoiding true military duty. One soldier summed it up with "they loll and roll in their glory." Also, each state in the Union had an acting assistant pro-

Four provost marshals from the 3rd Army Corps of the Union Army of the Potomac pose for a photo at Brandy Station, Virginia, in December 1863. *Library of Congress, Prints & Photographs Division, LC-B8171-7402.*

vost marshal to chase down draft-dodgers, deserters, and traitors.

Pshaw! A common expression of disbelief, impatience, dislike, disgust, or contempt. Confederate diarist Mary Chesnut noted that "Everyone said at first, 'Pshaw! There will be no war.'" The word dates back to the seventeenth century.

puddler An iron worker who turned cast iron into wrought iron by "puddling," a process in which the cast iron was heated and stirred along with oxidizing agents.

puerperal fever Blood poisoning during childbirth. During the period of the war, it was often fatal.

puff To promote or build up someone or something, a practice usually ascribed to the press. Newspapers during the war generally either puffed or ran down the reputations of various commanders. The New York *Herald* regularly puffed Major Union General George B. McClellan who, in return, invited their reporter to visit him on a daily basis.

puffing For women's clothes, a type of flounce designed in several puffs. They were especially popular on the hems of skirts. One Confederate lady wrote with delight that she had found an old satin cloak "to make a puffing round the bottom of my three year old brown silk [dress] to make it long enough."

pull foot A slang term meaning to run or walk quickly; e.g., "When I saw the Union cavalry down the plank road, I pulled foot and disappeared into the woods."

"Pull her off!" An informal order to fire a cannon that was sometimes heard in the desperate heat of battle, when common language replaced learned military terms. It meant to jerk the LANYARD to ignite the PRIMER that fired the CARTRIDGE and discharged the shell.

pumpkin A slang name for an important person. This was often heard in the expression "some pumpkins," as in "General Hood is some pumpkins."

pumpkin slinger A humorous nickname for the type of antique rifle that some recruits brought with them to camp. Some were Belgian rifles with crooked barrels. Pumpkin slingers were heavy and inaccurate, causing Union General Ulysses Grant to comment that such a gun could "fire at you all day without you ever finding it out."

punching Naval high-velocity gunfire used to punch holes through the armor of IRONCLAD warships. Such fire required a RIFLED gun using an elongated shell to penetrate the iron plating. The Union navy preferred an 8-inch PARROTT cannon firing a 152-pound solid shot. *See also* racking.

puny list A disparaging name for a SURGEON'S CALL or sick call.

puppy love An adult's descriptive name, still common, for love between an immature teenage or preadolescent couple.

The term was well established before the war.

pup tent *See* dog tent.

pushing up daisies A flowery euphemism for lying buried in a grave. It was first heard about when the war began and is still used today.

pus in the blood A descriptive name for blood poisoning. About 90 percent of soldiers with blood poisoning died.

put one to the blush To make someone blush with embarrassment. "Nanny puts me to the blush continually," despaired one Virginia lady. "She is so patriotic and unselfish."

put on style Another version of the more common "put on airs," to be snobbish or act refined. A western soldier might grumble, "Have you ever seen a bandbox soldier who didn't put on style?"

putrid fever A medical name for typhus or sometimes diptheria.

put the licks in To run fast; e.g., "It was some scene at Bull Run with the whole Federal troops fleeing and even the officers putting the licks in."

put through To process the enlistment of a new recruit. It included recording his personal details, giving a simple physical examination, and having him sign the enlistment papers. Men were put through an enlistment office before being assigned to a training facility, such as Brigadier General Silas Casey's camp in Washington, D.C.

Q

Q.M. or q.m. The abbreviation for quarter-master. An 1862 poem, "The Johnny Reb's Epistle to the Ladies," by a Confederate soldier (known only as "W.E.M."), asked the ladies to knit more socks because:

> To speak of shoes, it boots not here;
> Our Q. M.'s, wise and good,
> Give cotton calf-skins twice a year
> With soles of cottonwood.

See also Quartermaster Department.

quadrille A popular square dance of French origin in which four or more couples (at right angles or lined up opposite one another) perform different movements. It was popular during the war and a feature of President Abraham Lincoln's first inaugural ball. *See also* the German.

quadroon A person who is one-fourth Negro, three grandparents being white and one black. A quadroon is thus a child of a MULATTO and a white person. A common name used was YELLOW.

Quaker gun A false gun. When Confederate General Joseph E. Johnston was forced to pull his troops back from Centreville, Virginia, and closer to Richmond in October 1861, he left dummy guns (logs painted black) and dummy sol-

diers at their posts. This deception slowed the progress of General George McClellan's forces and embarrassed the North. Newspapers quickly applied the Quaker name, chosen for the pacifist doctrine of that religion.

Quartermaster Department The U.S. department composed of quartermasters who were responsible for troop quarters and transportation, as well as the storage and movement of supplies and equipment and for each horse and WAGONER. It also constructed coffins and buried the dead. The department was headed by the quartermaster general with the rank of brigadier general. J.F. Rusling, a Union quartermaster, said the department followed the army "with its outstretched and sheltering arms, dropping only mercies, wherever it goes." The Confederate government had a similar "Quartermaster's Department" also headed by a quartermaster general.

quartermaster hunter A humorous nickname given by front-line soldiers to an enemy shell that flew overhead to land in the rear where quartermasters were staying in presumed safety.

quarter section or quarter An informal name for the 160 acres (a quarter of a

Photographed in March 1862, these Quaker guns defended the Confederate winter quarters at Centreville, Virginia. *Library of Congress, Prints & Photographs Division, LC-B8171-0334.*

square mile) provided to each HOME-STEADER during the war by the U.S. Homestead Act of May 20, 1862.

"the Queen of Sheba" The black cook of Union Major General George Armstrong Custer, because she rode with his brigade in an old family carriage that he provided especially for her. When Custer and his men were ambushed on June 11, 1864, in Virginia, he escaped but the Queen was captured along with his personal possessions. Before daybreak, however, she strode smiling into his camp carrying his valise, having slipped away from the Confederates.

Queen of the Valley A popular brand of chewing tobacco in Union camps.

"Queen Varina" A southern nickname for Varina Howell Davis, the wife of Confederate President Jefferson Davis. The title was not derogative, but was warmly given in recognition of her position as first lady of the South. Born in Natchez, Mississippi, Varina was known to be a clever, perfectly mannered lady "brimming with zest for life."

queer fish *See* odd fish.

the quiet man A nickname for Colonel Ulysses S. Grant, given by volunteer soldiers of his first command during the Civil War, the Illinois Seventh District Regiment at Camp Yates.

quinine A medicine commonly prescribed by camp doctors, when available, to treat malaria and other diseases. It was often mixed with whiskey to produce an evil-tasting drink that soldiers still requested for its alcohol. A valuable product in the Confederacy, quinine was brought in by blockade runners and sold for a high price. Money was made on both sides by smuggling it from the North, sometimes sewed in the hems of women's dresses and hidden in the soles of shoes or the false bottoms of trunks.

"Quinine" A nickname given by enlisted men to an army doctor.

"Quinine Brigade" The nickname assumed by 175 incapacitated Union cavalrymen, suffering from everything from saddle sores to dysentery, when they were ordered to leave a force raiding Mississippi. The column of 1,700 men under Colonel Benjamin H. Grierson had left La Grange in western Tennessee on April 17, 1863, and penetrated 80 miles south by April 20 when the sick horsemen were sent back (with about a dozen Confeder-ates captured the first three days). Major Hiram Love led their return, with the men riding four abreast to obliterate their cavalry's outward tracks and give the impression that the entire force was retreating. This deception helped the success of Grierson's 16-day raid, which covered 600 miles and destroyed railroad tracks, telegraph wires, and military equipment before he reached Union-held Baton Rouge, Louisiana. General Ulysses S. Grant called it "one of the most brilliant cavalry exploits of the war." *See also* Butternut Guerrillas.

quoin A wedge used on navy warships to elevate a cannon. It was pushed between the breech of the cannon and the wheeled TRUCK CARRIAGE on which the gun rested.

quoits A game resembling horseshoes that was played in camps on both sides. Soldiers tried to throw rings, often made of ropes, to encircle pegs.

R

Raccoon Roughs A company of Georgia mountaineers put together by John B. Gordon, a lawyer and businessman with no military experience, who became their captain. Told they were not yet needed by Georgia, the company joined the 6th Alabama Infantry. During the war, Captain Gordon became a major general and commanded one of General Robert E. Lee's corps. His wife, Fanny, went along on all his military campaigns, causing Major General Jubal Early to proclaim to others his wish that Union forces would capture the lady.

rackansacker or rackensacker A nickname for a rough soldier, such as a militiaman, especially a Confederate one. The term was first common in the Mexican War for members of state militias. It probably simply means a soldier who will wrack the enemy and sack his towns.

racking Naval gunfire that racked (strained) an IRONCLAD warship, causing its iron plates to bend and crack and hopefully fall off, or causing splinters to explode from the wooden walls behind the plates thereby endangering the crews. Racking required smooth-bore guns that fired the heaviest iron balls, such as the 15-inch Rodman cannon that fired 15-inch balls weighing 453 pounds. *See also* punching.

Radical Republicans Members of an extremist group in the Republican Party who wanted President Abraham Lincoln to issue an Emancipation Proclamation early in the war and to severely punish the South after the war. Their efforts caused Lincoln to complain, "If there is a hell, I am in it." Secretary of War Edwin M. Stanton and Secretary of the Treasury Salmon P. Chase, members of Lincoln's cabinet, were Radicals. The Radical leaders in the Senate included Thaddeus Stevens of Pennsylvania and Charles Sumner of Massachusetts. After Lincoln's assassination, the group resisted President Andrew Johnson's moderate Reconstruction program and failed by one vote to impeach him. They then imposed a strict military and political Reconstruction on the southern states, which they considered "conquered provinces."

raffling The usual term for a raffle. Soldiers raffled almost anything, from watches to blankets. Some addicted men would lose their entire pay on, as one described it, "a painful spell of Raffling."

raft torpedo A Confederate mine ("torpedo") that was a tank of powder simply placed in a box on a raft and moored in a harbor. The Union gunboat *Gertrude* discovered and disabled one in Mobile Bay on January 30, 1864. Its gunpowder tank was three feet high and two and one-quarter feet square.

ragbag A woman's bag or sack containing rags and cloth scraps. During the war, they were often searched for odd pieces that could be turned into gifts for soldiers, such as handkerchiefs, bandages, and clothes patches.

raglan A loose waterproof overcoat. It was named for Lord Raglan, the British commander in the Crimean War. When Confederate President Jefferson Davis was captured by Union troops on May 10, 1865, near Irwinville, Georgia, he was wearing his wife's raglan and a shawl over his head. This provoked stories that he had dressed as a woman to escape. Davis, however, said he had taken his wife's raglan, similar to his, by mistake in his dark tent, and she had thoughtfully thrown the shawl over his head as protection from the damp, chilly morning.

raid around the army A Confederate expression for the daring raids by General "JEB" Stuart and his cavalrymen to taunt and attack invading Union armies. The first raid began on June 11, 1862, when Stuart, 1,200 cavalry, and a section of artillery circled General George McClellan's troops in Virginia to gather military intelligence, having only one man killed during encounters. When he returned with 165 prisoners and 260 captured horses and mules, Stuart was met by a furious General Robert E. Lee (who seldom was angry), fuming that he had not known Stuart's whereabouts.

rail it An informal expression meaning to travel by railroad; e.g., "The Confederate troops railed it to the junction at Manassas."

"Railroad *Merrimac*" *See* "Dry Land *Merrimac*."

railroad time Fast time or quickly. The expression arose in 1864, when a soldier might have said, "The cavalry arrived in railroad time." The verb, "to railroad," meant to move fast.

"Rail-Splitter" A nickname for Abraham Lincoln, because of the power and skill he had displayed with an ax as a young man, clearing and fencing his father's farm in Illinois. Once during the war, he saw soldiers hewing logs for a hospital and told them he "used to be pretty good on the chop."

raise blazes To create excitement or turmoil; e.g., "We knew the enemy was near because the officers were raising blazes all over the camp."

The Rakish Rhymer A book of erotic songs that was published in the North during the war. The vulgar volume found its way into many Union knapsacks. *See also Cupid's Own Library.*

"Rally" The bugle call or drum signal that ordered scattered troops to regroup.

"Rally on the sutler!" A call feared by SUTLERS, for it meant his soldier customers were about to raid and distribute his goods freely.

rambunctious A slang adjective, still used, meaning boisterous, noisy, wild, or disorderly. It evolved from the earlier forms of "rumbustious" and "rambustious," which were related to "robustious," meaning robust.

rammer The artillery position of gunner number 1, who shoved the cartridge of ball and powder down his cannon's barrel with a long pole. The pole was also called a rammer. It was a dangerous job because the artilleryman was exposed to enemy fire and to the possibility that the charge would go off prematurely due to embers still in the tube. At the battle of

New Hope Church in Georgia from May 25 to 27, 1864, three Louisiana brothers were killed one after the other as they served as rammers for the same gun.

rampart A protective mound of earth or wall surrounding a fortification. "The Star-Spangled Banner" had made them well known with the words, "O'er the ramparts we watched." Civil War ramparts were often made of sandbags or log walls filled with earth.

ramrod A long rod used to ram a charge into a muzzle-loading musket. It was attached below the gun, protruding a bit in front to make it easy to grasp. The burned powder from a soldier's ramrod was soon smeared over his fingers and hands. Ramrods also had other uses. When Union Major General W.T. Sherman made his infamous march through Georgia, his men used the gun rods to poke into gardens and lawns for hidden food and valuables.

ranch The slang term, created in Washington, D.C., during the war, for a house of prostitution. Charles Mackay, correspondent for *The Times* of London, noted that "a whole army of brazen courtesans and 'painted Jezebels' had invaded the city" to follow the soldiers, and "the Provost Marshal and his officials make little or no effort to interfere with them." Mackay also explained to his British readers that a ranch is "a word that in Texas signifies an enclosure for cattle."

rank To have a higher military rank than another soldier. When his officers insisted to Union Major General W.T. Sherman that it was the responsibility of the newly arrived General John A. McClernand to pay a courtesy visit, Sherman announced that he would have to pay the call "for he ranks me." President Abraham Lincoln thought it was ridiculous how much importance officers put on outranking

someone, and he wrote Major General William S. Rosecrans in 1862 that the world "will never care a fig whether you rank Gen. Grant on paper, or he so ranks you."

ransom The word had a specialized meaning for the Confederate cavalry which sometimes demanded a large ransom from northern towns to buy off their destruction. In July 1864, Major General Jubal Early threatened to burn Frederick, Maryland, if it did not pay a ransom of $200,000. This sum was finally raised and handed over, but the city did not pay off this public debt until October 1, 1951. Earlier in the month, Early had sent Brigadier General John McCausland, nicknamed TIGER JOHN, to demand a ransom of $200,000 from the merchants of Hagerstown, Maryland, to prevent his troops from burning down its business district. McCausland mistakenly asked for $20,000, which was quickly paid. On July 30, Early sent him with the same threat to Chambersburg, Pennsylvania, to demand $500,000 in paper money or $10,000 in gold; when that sum was not paid, McCausland's men burned down the business district.

The Rapid Ann A camp newspaper produced by the soldiers of the Army of Northern Virginia. Copies were turned out in pen and pencil. Much of the content was humorous, such as the parody of HARDEE'S TACTICS, which was called "Tactics of Kissing." This concerned firing a rifle, with the advice to "pucker the mouth, and apply the lips smartly to the muzzle mouldings" but warned, "Break off promptly on both legs, to escape the jarring or injury should the piece recoil."

raspberry tea A tea substitute made of raspberry leaves by southern women during the war's lean years. Other substitutes were blackberry, huckleberry, and holly-tree leaves.

ratherish To a slight degree or somewhat; e.g., "Last night was ratherish cool."

the Rattlesnakes A military company formed in Savannah, Georgia, when the state seceded. Many town rowdies were in its ranks. Members were called to meetings by announcements in local newspapers that began, "Attention, Rattlesnakes! Come out of your holes," and were signed "By order of President Grand Rattle; POISON FANG, Secretary." The next day's paper would instruct, "Crawl into your holes."

razor A clever saying, such as a pun or a sharp joke.

RC The abbreviation for the Rifle Corps MILITIA of New Jersey. It was used on FORAGE CAP badges along with the letters "NJ" and crossed rifles. The organization was formed in 1863 and had about 40 companies by the end of the war. The members wore blue and gray CHASSEUR uniforms.

reading linen A common camp activity in which a soldier held his shirt up to a light to examine it for vermin. This was also called a "skirmish drill."

ready-finder A Union solder's nickname for a civilian who hung around troops to pick up any items that they discarded. Men joining the army usually brought too many possessions, and these proved a burden on the march, especially in summer. Ready-finders collected overcoats, long-tail coats, flannel shirts, and gloves. Regularly issued items were also shed for the taking, including KNAPSACKS used to carry clean clothes and heavy CARTRIDGE BOXES and cap boxes (whose contents soldiers could carry in their pockets).

the real Simon Pure The real thing; e.g., "This beef is the real Simon Pure."

the real South Another name for the Deep South, used mostly by people living there. A Confederate misconception was that Union armies could not conquer "the real South" because their supply lines would be too long.

Rebel chiefs A Union name for the Confederate leaders.

Rebel rag A scornful Union nickname for the Confederate flag.

Rebel yell The wild yelping shout given by Confederate soldiers as they attacked. It was supposedly first heard at the first battle of Bull Run in 1861, when Brigadier General Thomas Jackson ("STONEWALL" after this battle) told his troops to "yell like furies!" It soon spread throughout the southern armies. One Union veteran called it "shrill, exultant, savage." Another recalled, "There is nothing like it this side of the infernal region." When Confederate Major General Jubal A. Early ordered an attack on Yankee positions and was informed that the ammunition had run out, he recalled the enemy's fear of the Rebel yell and told his officers, "Damn it, holler them across" After the war, a Confederate veteran from Tennessee, asked to give the yell after a banquet, said it would be "worst than folly" to make the attempt "with a stomach full of food and a mouth full of false teeth."

receiving ship In the Union and Confederate navies, the ship or station that received and trained new sailors who would serve there. New recruits were given medical examinations by the surgeon, were issued uniforms and other items, and received their basic training.

reconnaissance in force A large number of troops that advance to find the enemy or attack to test the enemy's strength. Union Brigadier General Joseph Hooker sent a reconnaissance in force of about 11,000 men to discover General Robert E. Lee's movements at Brandy Station, Virginia, on June 9, 1863.

reconnoissance A wartime spelling of "reconnaissance." It is the older version, but both spellings were in use by the early nineteenth century.

red *See* red cent.

Red The nickname given by his soldiers to Confederate cavalry leader Brigadier General William H. Jackson, who had red hair. Among his many battles, he commanded cavalry units at Vicksburg and Atlanta, then ended in command of all the Tennessee cavalry.

redan The simplest type of FIELDWORK, being two raised levels that form a SALIENT angle toward the enemy.

red cent An informal name, still used, for a penny or an insignificant amount. It is almost always used in a negative statement; e.g., "We had fought two battles, and the army still hadn't paid us one red cent." The red color refers to the copper in the coin, and a penny was also called a "red" during the war.

red-eye A slang name, still used, for cheap, raw, and fiery whiskey or other liquor.

red-letter pass A special pass signed in red ink by President Abraham Lincoln, allowing the holder to travel anywhere in the war area. Lincoln presented many of these cardboard passes to journalists.

redneck A descriptive name, still used, for a southern farmer or other rural worker, because of his weather-beaten neck. This demeaning name dates from the early nineteenth century and has usually implied that the person is poor, uneducated, and prejudiced. The term "hillbilly" was unknown during the war, being first heard just before the twentieth century.

redoubt A defensive breastwork in the field, closed on all sides and usually square. It was most often of earth and proved to be an easy burial place after a battle. Sometimes a type of redoubt was

On June 14, 1864, Union forces captured this redoubt in the outer line of Confederate fortifications around Petersburg, Virginia. *Library of Congress, Prints & Photographs Division, LC-B8171-0784.*

constructed within a fort to serve as the defenders' last stand.

Red Strings The nickname for the Heroes of America Society in the South, because of the red threads worn on their lapels. The secret society, which sometimes also called itself Sons of America, was composed of a mixture of mostly poor southerners who supported the Union or opposed the war (as pacifists or as realists who saw the war as hopeless). Mainly located in North Carolina, Virginia, Alabama, and eastern Tennessee, the group encouraged and hid deserters, helped spies, and did spying themselves. The society became larger and more open and vocal as Union troops won victories and occupied the South.

red tape This familiar term, meaning official delay because of paperwork or routine, was popularized during the war, coming from the red ribbon used to tie up official U.S. military and government documents, even before the nation divided. When Lieutenant Isaac N. Brown was made commander of the Confederate warship *Arkansas*, one admirer wrote "there is nothing of the Red Tape about him."

refractory A common word for "stubborn." After Union troops burned her home in Jefferson, Tennessee, in February 1864, and she had moved into her old kitchen building, Rebeccah Ridley recorded in her diary: "my negroes refractory and insolent and not supporting themselves."

refreshment saloon A canteen, especially in the North, run for soldiers. Philadelphia had a large VOLUNTEER REFRESHMENT SALOON "supported gratuitously" by its citizens. Volunteer soldiers could receive free meals in its "dining saloon" or just hot coffee, water, and refreshments in another area, and they could clean up in the "washing department." About 100,000 soldiers had taken advantage of this one facility by January 1862.

refugeeing This term for the flight of wartime civilians was especially used by southerners fleeing SHERMAN'S BUMMERS. The refugees took or hid as many possessions as possible as they moved between houses or towns ahead of the invaders.

refused A military term to describe an army wing that has been swung back from its normal position for strategic reasons; e.g., "McClellan waited, his army now in a semicircle with the right wing refused and extended to the river."

regiment A military unit on both sides, consisting in the infantry of 10 COMPANIES or sometimes 2 or more BATTALIONS, in the artillery of 8 to 12 BATTERIES (or "companies" using REGULAR ARMY terminology), and in the cavalry of 8 to 12 companies or 2 to 3 battalions. The average Union regiment had from 845 to 1,025 officers and men. A regiment was designated by its state's name, such as the First Tennessee Regiment and the 97th Pennsylvania Regiment. The official title would be longer, like the 10th Michigan Volunteer Regiment, but all these units were normally just called, for example, the "First Tennessee," "97th Pennsylvania," and "10th Michigan. Usually 2 or 3 regiments made up a BRIGADE.

regiment hospital tent *See* field hospital.

"Rest in Peace" *See* "Rip."

"Retreat" 1. The bugle call or drum signal ordering troops to retire to the rear. 2. A roll call for soldiers as they retired from their day's duties.

"Retreating Joe" The nickname given to Confederate General Joseph E. Johnston for his tactics in 1864 in Georgia of trying to avoid engagement with the forces of Major General W.T. Sherman. Johnston was soon replaced by General John B. Hood.

retrograde movement A euphemism for a retreat, used in military reports and by supportive newspapers.

"Reveille" The bugle call in camp to assemble the troops for the MORNING ROLL CALL. It was blown in the infantry just before the men stepped into line. Soldiers improvised different words to the notes, the most popular being the following:

I can't get 'em up, I can't get 'em up,
I can't get 'em up, I tell you.
I can't get 'em up, I can't get 'em up,
I can't get 'em up at all.
The corporal's worse than the private,
The sergeant's worse than the corporal,
The lieutenant's worse than the sergeant,
But the captain's worst of all.

Reveille is now the bugle call to rouse soldiers in the morning, but during the Civil War this wake-up call was known as "Assembly of Buglers." *See also* "The devil is loose, the devil is loose."

reverent whiskey A southern term for strong whiskey that was not diluted; e.g., "We had men who survived the whole war without tasting a drop of reverent whiskey."

revetment In military fortifications, a stong retaining wall. Usually made of wood or stones, but sometimes of sandbags or GABIONS, it was used to keep a trench from collapsing and also placed on the outside of a RAMPART.

the Revolution A southern name for the Civil War during its early days.

rhino A slang name for money, first used in seventeenth-century England.

"rich man's war, poor man's fight" An often repeated phrase by soldiers on both sides. When the Confederacy passed a Conscription Act that exempted a person who owned 20 slaves, Sam Watkins of Company H of the First Tennessee Regiment recalled, "It gave us the blues; we wanted twenty negroes. Negro property suddenly became very valuable, and there was raised the howl of 'rich man's war, poor man's fight.'" A Union soldier, Levi Ross, wrote his father: "I believe that a poor man's life is as dear as a rich man's" and added that the latter should sacrifice more in the war to "save their property, homes and liberty." *See also* "twenty-nigger law."

Richmond The first horse ridden by Confederate General Robert E. Lee in the war in the spring of 1861. The steed proved too nervous for combat and died in July 1862 after Malvern Hill, the last of the Seven Days' battles. *See also* Ajax; Brown-Roan; Lucy Long; Traveller.

Richmond Howitzers A Confederate battalion formed in Richmond, Virginia, and noted for its intellectual members. Its ranks formed the Howitzer Glee Club, led by Frederick Nicholas Crouch who had written a popular song, "Kathleen Mavourneen," and formed the Howitzer Law Club. Robert Stiles, a battalion member, recalled the burial service for a pet crow (witnessed by the entire unit and hundreds of local townspeople) that included a Latin oration and a Greek ode.

Rienzi The strong black horse of Union Major General Philip H. Sheridan. A colonel of the 2nd Michigan Cavalry had given him the horse in 1862 near Rienzi, Mississippi, where they were stationed in 1862. The animal had taken several wounds, and Sheridan changed its name to Winchester in 1864 after winnng a victory at Winchester, Virginia. When the horse died, it was stuffed and placed in the Smithsonian Institution.

Rifle and Light Infantry Tactics *See* Hardee's Tactics.

rifled gun A gun, such as a rifle or cannon, with spiral grooves cut inside the barrel to make the bullets or shells rotate when fired. This rotation created a better accuracy and distance. Many of the older SMOOTHBORE guns were rifled throughout the war.

rifle knock-knee A humorous camp name for strong alcohol made of strange concoctions.

rifle pit A hole dug out by soldiers as a temporary protection while engaging the enemy.

right wheel *See* left wheel or right wheel.

ring-tailed snorter A nickname, still heard, for an energetic, powerful man.

ring tournament A contest staged in camps by cavalrymen or other horsemen who tried at full gallop to snatch a suspended hoop with a lance.

Rio A nickname for genuine coffee, a rare item in camp, especially southern ones. When President Jefferson Davis visited General Joseph E. Johnston in Chattanooga, Tennessee, in December 1862, the general's wife eagerly let friends know she had served her honored guest the "real Rio." The name came from Rio de

Taken in September 1862, this Alexander Gardner photo shows Confederate dead lying in a rifle pit on the battlefield at Antietam, Maryland. *Library of Congress, Prints & Photographs Division, LC-B8171-0565.*

Janeiro because of the fame of Brazilian coffee.

rip A wild, dissolute person. One Confederate captain moaned, "I think my company is composed of the wildest set of rips in the world!"

"Rip" The nickname of Confederate Colonel John S. Ford, who commanded the raggedy Cavalry of the West. His nickname stood for "Rest in Peace," because Ford sent many of his enemies to the cemetery. A former physician, newspaper editor, and Texas Ranger, Ford won the last real battle of the Civil War, a month after General Lee had surrendered. His troops were attacked by Colonel Theodore H. Barrett's on May 12, 1865, at Palmito Ranch on the east bank of the Rio Grande, 12 miles from Brownsville, Texas. The two-day battle resulted in 30 Union soldiers killed and 113 captured, with Ford's men suffering only five minor wounds. To avoid the official humiliating surrender of his cavalry to the Yankees, Rip disbanded his unit 13 days after winning the war's final battle.

Rip-Raps The military punishment of breaking up rip-raps, the ragged rocks used to build walls or thrown into a harbor or other water to create a foundation for a breakwater. Once when Union Major General Benjamin Butler was scolding a colonel whose men had been accused of vandalism, he roared, "I'll send your whole regiment to the Rip-Raps!"

ripsnorter A nickname for a remarkable or wonderful person or thing. It was first used about a decade before the war and is still heard. "Ripsnorting" did not appear until the early twentieth century.

"Rip Van Winkle" The nickname given to Union Brigadier General James Ripley, chief of the U.S. Ordnance Bureau, because in 1861 he opposed the new breech-loading Henry and Spencer rifles.

"Rising of the People" A patriotic Union song composed by M. Colburn with words by N.P. Beers. It included the line, "The drum-tap rattles through the land."

"Roast Beef" The camp nickname for the bugle call for DINNER. The infantry and artillery had different calls for this.

"Rob" or "Bob" The nicknames of Confederate Major Chatham Roberdeau Wheat, who led the tough Louisiana company of "TIGER RIFLES." Wheat, born in Virginia, was a soldier of fortune who had been an officer in the Mexican Army and fought in Italy with Garibaldi. Wounded in both lungs at the first battle of Bull Run in 1861, and told he would die, Wheat huffed, "I don't feel like dying yet" and recovered to lead his terrible Tigers until killed in 1862 at the battle of Gaines' Mill in Virginia.

Robber's Row A nickname for the area of a camp occupied by SUTLERS. Their goods were more appreciated than their inflated prices.

robbing the cradle and the grave An expression used in the South for the conscription age limit of 18 to 45 years.

Robert Lee or Bob Lee The name of the (mongrel) canine mascot of the Troupe Artillery of the Army of Northern Virginia. The missing middle initial was no doubt a wry way of distinguishing him from their commanding officer. The mascot, however, was spied hiding behind a tree during the battle of Chancellorsville in 1863.

rock To stone something or someone, especially heard in the South and West; e.g., "We rocked the windows of the house."

"Rock" The nickname given by Confederate General Robert E. Lee to Brigadier General Henry Lewis Benning of Georgia. His soldiers expanded this to "Old

Rock." Part Cherokee Indian, Benning was an associate justice of the Georgia Supreme Court prior to the war. He led troops at numerous battles, including the second Bull Run, Antietam, the Wilderness (where he was badly wounded), Fredericksburg, Gettysburg, and, despite having two horses killed as he rode them, Chickamauga.

rockaway A type of civilian light carriage with a top and open sides. When Major General W.T. Sherman occupied Atlanta and expelled its citizens, one lady called upon him and convinced him to let her keep her horse and rockaway. The carriage name came from Rockaway, New Jersey, where they had first been built.

rocking someone Throwing rocks at someone, used in the same manner as "stoning someone."

rock me to sleep mother A camp name for strong and usually unpleasant alcohol.

"Rock of Chickamauga" The nickname of Union Brigadier General George H. Thomas of Virginia, because he was seen "standing like a rock" against overwhelming odds at the battle of Chickamauga in northwest Georgia. On September 20, 1863, the troops of Confederate Lieutenant General James Longstreet broke through to put the center and right of the Union lines into a panic retreat, which was joined by Major General William Rosecrans, the commanding general. Thomas placed his back against a large rock and refused to budge; his courage and that of his men holding the left wing saved the retreating Union army. *See also* "Sledge of Nashville."

rocket-propelled submarine torpedo The name given to the world's first self-propelled torpedo, invented by Pascal Plant and loaned in December 1862 to the Union navy for trials. Two were launched

Union Major General George H. Thomas earned the name "Rock of Chickamauga" for his defiant stand at the battle of Chickamauga in September 1863. *Library of Congress, Prints & Photographs Division, LC-B8172-6480.*

from a barge on the Potomac River; one attacked the mud on the river bottom and exploded and the other veered out of control and sunk a schooner. A second trial also failed the next year, so the device was deemed useless.

rocky A slang word for being drunk, groggy, or unsteady. See DRUNK for numerous other terms referring to intoxication.

rod This measurement of distance was commonly used during the war. It is equivalent to 16.5 feet or 5.5 yards. One Union nurse noted that the regiment's large hospital "lies a few rods outside the lines."

"The Rogue's March" A depressing march played in camp when soldiers were punished, especially when they were paraded before the ranks. Often only a fife and drum provided the tune, but regimental bands were employed for the grandest examples of humiliation.

rolla pot The name given by Union prisoners at ANDERSONVILLE for a "luxury" soup-like dish." They created it by rolling the soft part of bread into balls about an inch in diameter and boiling them in a stewpan with meat (normally too rancid to eat alone) and rice.

roll-book The book listing the members of a company. The list was kept up to date by an officer. When Union Lieutenant John L. Bailey of Company D, 27th New York Regiment, was shot and killed by a Rebel picket, his roll-book was found punctured by the bullet that entered his heart. The picket was shot dead by Corporal H.M. Crocker, whose name in the roll-book had been blotted out by blood stains.

rolling mill A company or facility that produced (rolled) iron plate. The Confederacy's first IRONCLAD ship, the *Virginia (Merrimac)*, was armored by the TREDEGAR IRON WORKS in Richmond, Virginia, the only rolling mill in the South that was capable of rolling iron plates two inches thick.

Roll of Honor An honor roll published by the Confederate Congress after each battle, listing those soldiers who had fought with bravery. Since the Congress did not award medals, it was the South's highest recognition of an individual soldier. Rolls of Honor were published in newspapers, kept on file in the adjutant general's office, and read at the dress parades of units. *See also* "Thanks of Congress."

The Roan *See* Brown-Roan.

"Rooney" The nickname of Confederate Major General William Henry Fitzhugh Lee, the son of General Robert E. Lee (who, in his early letters, spelled it "Roony"). The name came from his resemblance to the Lee's Irish gardener, Mr. Rooney. Lee's son became a cavalry brigadier general under Major General "JEB" Stuart, fighting bravely at the second battle of Bull Run, Antietam, Fredericksburg, and Chancellorsville. He was wounded and taken prisoner on the march to Gettysburg. U.S. Secretary of War Edwin Stanton declared that he would be hanged if the Confederacy hanged any Union officers. Lee was in prison when his wife died; the U.S. turned down an appeal by his brother, Brigadier General Custis Lee, to replace him so Rooney could see her one last time. After several months, however, he was exchanged and then, as the South's youngest major general, led troops into action until the end of the war. At Appomattox Court House, he was seen weeping outside the McLean House as his father surrendered.

"Root, hog, or die" An expression meaning you had to create your own shelter or die. It was popularly used in prisons, such as ANDERSONVILLE, where prisoners had to fashion shelters out of virtually nothing or live exposed to the blistering sun and pounding rain. In the war, a failure to actively work to provide for yourself might well lead to death. First recorded by Davy Crockett, this southern expression took note of a hog's ability to fend for itself successfully by rooting through the ground.

rope in To swindle, cheat, or deceive, a slang expression still familiar.

rose hip sauce A thin cream sauce produced by boiling the seeds of rose hips with white wine and sugar.

rot or rot of pop skull Humorous names given to almost unbearable alcohol. "Who wouldn't get drunk a thousand miles from home," wrote one Union soldier, "and 'rot' only two dollars a quart?"

The Rough and Ready Guards The nickname for the mountaineers of Company F of the 4th North Carolina Infantry Regiment. They fought at many important battles, including Antietam, Chancellorsville, and Gettysburg. The Rough and Readies were organized by Captain Zebulon B. Vance, who after the war said he had been "awfully rough, but scarcely ever ready." Vance had been a U.S. senator who opposed secession until his state left the Union. After the war, he became governor of North Carolina and then returned to the Senate.

round 1. A single shot from a rifle, cannon, or other piece. 2. Shots from many guns fired at the same time, usually on the order of "Fire." 3. The ammunition for a single shot. *See also* cartridge.

roundabout A short coat or jacket that fit closely, worn by men and boys.

route step An order of marching in which soldiers are not required to keep in step. It was often given when marching in mud or crossing over a bridge that might shake and sway under a CADENCE STEP.

rowed up Salt river To be politically defeated; e.g., "The Democrats' candidate was again rowed up Salt river." The expression supposedly came from the Salt River in Kentucky, a small stream with shallows and sand bars that were difficult to navigate.

rowel On a spur, the small revolving wheel with points projecting from it. A cavalryman would say he roweled his horse, meaning he spurred it.

Rowlands, John The birth name of Henry Stanley, who fought in the war on both sides. Born in Wales, he had sailed to New Orleans and been taken care of by Henry Morton Stanley, who gave him his name. Stanley joined the Confederate army, deserted to the Union navy, and then deserted again. He later became a journalist with the *New York Herald* and was sent to Africa to find Dr. David Livingstone, whom he greeted with the famous words, "Dr. Livingstone, I presume?"

rubber A common name for a rubber blanket. It was a normal blanket on one side that was attached with eyelets to the "rubber cloth." An average soldier could carry only one. On a march, it was rolled with the rubber outside and bent into a loop with the ends tied together, then usully carried over the left shoulder with the connected ends under the right arm. Soldiers often used them to fashion a good waterproof tent, tying two rubbers together at their eyelets and propping them up with fence posts or other wood. James Kendall Hosmer described this process in camp in 1862 with the 52nd Regiment of Massachusetts Volunteers. He shared a rubber tent with his brother, Ed, and a Corporal Buffum. The roof was created with his and Corporal Buffum's blankets. "Then," he noted, "we spread Ed's rubber on the ground underneath, put our luggage at one end, and crowd in to try the effect."

rub out This well-known American slang expression, meaning to kill, was common during the war. It supposedly came from Indian sign language in which the hands make a rubbing motion for killing someone. *See also* wipe out.

rub the wrong way This expression for irritating someone was first recorded during the war.

ruche A ruffle worn on a lady's dress, usually at the neck or wrists. It was often a pleated or fluted ribbon or piece of muslin.

rum-bud A slang name for a red splotch on the face, especially the nose and cheeks, caused by drinking too much alcohol.

rum-hole A disreputable saloon or other drinking place, usually run-down and fairly dangerous. *See also* groggery.

rummy or rummie A slang name for someone who was intoxicated; a drunkard. It was first heard about the start of the war. See DRUNK for numerous other terms referring to intoxication.

rum-sucker A slang name for someone who was intoxicated; a drunkard. It was used before RUMMY, appearing about three years before the war. See DRUNK for numerous other terms referring to intoxication.

run The name, especially used in the South and West, for a small stream or brook. Bull Run in Virginia is an example.

running a battery The attempt of a ship to pass the enemy's defensive BATTERY onshore without being sunk or damaged. Battery running, done almost always by Union ships, occurred on rivers and channels and in harbors.

running-bag A nickname employed by southern women for a large bag used to carrying valuables and personal articles quickly from the house. The women would usually be running from artillery fire or advancing Union troops.

running the guard The feat of avoiding your own camp guards, especially to visit a nearby community or to plunder the countryside and its farms for food.

run (one's) gait To act as one wishes or do anything. After Union Major General W.T. Sherman decided on marching through Georgia without knowing what his adversary, General John B. Hood, planned to do, President Lincoln told one of his secretaries that "Sherman was inclined to let Hood run his gait for a while, while he overran the Gulf States in Hood's rear."

run out a gun On a warship, the action of rolling a cannon into firing position, thrusting its barrel through the gun portal. The order to load and run out the guns was given by a division officer. *See also* run up a gun.

the runs An apt name for diarrhea.

run up a gun The artillery term for returning a gun to its firing position after the rebound, which could be several feet. Seasoned gunners enjoyed watching new men try in vain to avoid the hard work of "running up" by holding onto the HANDSPIKE at the end and putting weight on the STOCK TRAIL. *See also* run out a gun.

rush To court a woman or girl ardently. The noun was also common; e.g., "He gave her the rush."

Rush's lancers The nickname for the 6th Pennsylvania Cavalry, who were the only lancers in the Union army. The regiment was named for its colonel, Richard Rush. In 1863, they replaced the clumsy lances with carbines. The lances, which were nine feet long, had a red pennant attached near the point.

Russian stove A type of all-brick stove used to heat SITTING-ROOMS or other similar rooms. It was economical, with only a little wood required to give out an abundance of even heat.

"Russian thunderbolt" The nickname of Union Brigadier General John Basil

Turchin, who was born in Russia as Ivan Vasilovitch Turchinoff. A veteran of the Crimean War, he earned the thunderbolt name for his daring and powerful attacks in battle. He was so abusive to everyone, Turchin was court-martialed but later reinstated by President Abraham Lincoln.

rusticate To expel a student from college. The word is still used in Great Britain. It is derived from a Latin word meaning to live in the country, which also provides "rustic."

rye coffee A substitute coffee in the South during the blockade. Rye was boiled until the grain burst, and it was then left in the sun to parch. Some southerners vowed it was the closest to real coffee of all the imitations. *See also* burnt sugar coffee; cane seed coffee; chinquapin coffee; grape coffee; okra coffee; pea coffee; potato and persimmon coffee; war coffee.

S

sabot A soft lead base attached to a cannon shell in a RIFLED GUN. When fired, it flatted toward the grooves cut inside the barrel, giving spin to the shell. This action also created small cuts in the sabot that produced the frightening scream of the flying projectile.

sabots Heavy coarse-leather shoes that had thick wooden soles. The name, a joke on the shoes' heaviness, came from wooden shoes once worn in Belgium and France. One southern lady, Sarah Morgan of Baton Rouge, Louisiana, pitied the war's restrictions that forced her to change shoes "from my pretty English glove-kid, to sabots made of some animal closely connected with the hippopotamus!"

sack To dismiss a person from employment. This term was first heard about five years before the war, and it is still the main word used in Great Britain for firing someone.

sack coat A short, loose coat whose back hung straight from the shoulders. A military version existed for infantrymen.

sacking A coarse-woven cloth made of such materials as hemp and flax. Although mostly used for sacks, southerners sometimes patched their clothes with the rough cloth during the hard times of the war.

sack posset A hot alcoholic drink composed of milk curdled with sack (dry white wine), with sugar and grated nutmeg added and biscuits or a French roll crumbled into it. Possets are such drinks combining hot milk with ale or wine and spices.

sacredamn "Holy damn," a French-English expression invented and frequently used by the famous "LITTLE CREOLE," Confederate General P.G.T. Beauregard.

saddle-skirt The lower part of a saddle or the part of a horse's flanks that it covers. Confederate Colonel Bedford Forrest, escaping Fort Donelson in Tennessee before its surrender on February 16, 1862, described the backwaters of an icy creek he had to cross as being "saddle-skirt deep."

sail in To attack or act boldly. A soldier might say "They outnumber us, but we just have to sail in and surprise them." This slang term originated about five years before the war.

sailmaker's gang On a navy ship, the company of men who repaired the sails and awnings. They answered to the sailmaker's mate, a petty officer.

St. Paul's Episcopal Church The church in Richmond, Virginia, attended by Confederate President Jefferson Davis and his family. It's high gray spire was a familiar landmark in the city. Davis was attending church there on April 2, 1865, when a messenger strode up the aisle as a lesson was being read and handed him the despatch from General Robert E. Lee announcing that Richmond should be evacuated because his lines had been penetrated at Petersburg. Davis quietly left the church, his last services there as president of the Confederacy.

salad A northern name for lettuce, because it was often the main part of a salad. This usage still exists in the both the U.S. and Great Britain.

salamander stove A portable stove that burned coke. The name came from the belief that the salamander could live in extreme heat.

saleratus Baking soda used in camp cooking. It became scarce in the South, and in the summer of 1862 Union prisoners in Macon, Georgia, reported paying $2.50 for a pound.

salient The defensive line or section of a fort closest to the enemy. It is often the angle of fortification projecting toward the attackers. A famous example was THE MULE SHOE at the battle of Spotsylvania in 1864.

salt horse The irreverent name given on both sides to beef that was salted or pickled. This described both its leathery texture and the men's distrust about the source of the meat. Union army salt horse was supposed to last for two years and had to be soaked in water for hours to remove enough salt to be consumed. Several occasions were recorded of soldiers holding a mock funeral for a particularly odious piece of salt horse, bearing it in a box (festooned with pieces of an old harness) to the SINKS where they tossed it in, uttered a few religious sentiments, and fired a volley over the grave. *See also* old bull.

salt junk Old pork or a poor grade of it that Confederate blockade runners supplied to Confederate troops late in the war. It was discarded from other ships and usually was the meat in "NASSAU BACON."

salts Various mineral salts commonly dosed out by military doctors, especially as a restorative or purgative medicine. They were sometimes given for dysentery, making the problem worse. Complained a Pennsylvania soldier of his camp surgeon, "He prescribes 'salts' to everybody."

"Sam" The nickname given by friends to Ulysses Grant when he attended West Point. He was still known as Captain Sam Grant when the Civil War began. *See also* "Company"; "Country Sam"; "Uncle Sam."

Sambo An derogatory name for a Negro. When Union Rear Admiral David D. Porter (not considering it an insult) addressed a freed Louisiana slave in this manner in 1863, the man replied, "My name aint Sambo, sah. My name's Tub." After the war, the name became well known through the 1899 book *The Story of Little Black Sambo* by the British writer Helen Bannerman. The word was derived from *zambo*, a Spanish-American name for "Negro." *See also* "Uncle Sambo."

"Sambo's Right to Be Kilt" A strangely named poem by Union Brigadier General Charles G. Halpine, who issued the order for Major General David Hunter creating the first troop of black soldiers, the First South Carolina Regiment. Halpine's poem appeared in the *New York Herald* in 1862. Born in Ireland, he had first worked for P.T. Barnum, writing advertising copy, and then became the Washington correspondent for the *New York Times*. *See also* chloroform; United States Colored Troops.

sand Grit or courage. After Texans unsuccessfully attacked the 1st Regiment of Colorado Volunteers at the battle of Pigeon's Ranch on March 28, 1862, one of the defenders, Ovando J. Hollister, wrote of the enemy's attempt, "It was right, of course, if they had the 'sand' to do it."

sand-bag battery A BATTERY built out of barrels filled with sand. When the war began, southerners quickly constructed these along their coasts, with some directing the cannons at Union forts.

sand-itch An annoying itch acquired by soldiers in camps built on sandy soil. It was a serious problem in the Confederate prison of ANDERSONVILLE where the inmates' thighs became so encrusted, they had to lie face-down for relief. The agony was often increased by the presence of sandfleas.

sand lappers The good-natured nickname given to soldiers from South Carolina by Confederate troops from other states.

sand shot Small lead balls, about one inch in diameter, used as ammunition. They were packed together to create GRAPE SHOT. *See also* canister; spherical case shot.

Sanitary Commission A private relief organization for the Union Army, performing in a similar way to today's Red Cross. Its general secretary was Frederick Law Olmsted, who designed New York's

An April 1865 photograph of workers and relief wagons of the U.S. Sanitary Commission near Washington, D.C. *Library of Congress, Prints & Photographs Division, LC-B8171-7711.*

Central Park. Officially named the United States Sanitary Commission, it was established in 1861 and grew to about 7,000 chapters of mostly women volunteers who sent boxes of food, blankets, and other personal items to soldiers. The commission's most important work was carried out by their agents who established field headquarters at camps to ensure sanitary conditions and provide medical supplies and assistance. Members visited and nursed patients in hospitals, their most famous hospital agent being MOTHER BICKERDYKE. The organization also ran the HOSPITAL TRANSPORT SYSTEM of boats to move patients to base hospitals, and it was also in charge of convalescent homes. During the war, it received nearly $5 million and another $15 million in supplies, with much more money raised through SANITARY FAIRS. The Confederacy had no equivalent organization.

Sanitary Fair or Sanitary Commission Fair One of several regular events held in the North to raise money for the SANITARY COMMISSION. The total money and produce raised in three years was estimated at $60 to $70 million, with some events, such as the Manhattan Fair on April 14, 1864, in New York, raising up to $1 million. All of them sold donated articles and included special events, such as balls and quilting bees. One woman sold her kisses for $10 a time. President Abraham Lincoln (reluctantly) gave his own copy of the EMANCIPATION PROCLAMATION to the first such event, the Great Northwestern Sanitary Commission Fair in Chicago, held on October 28, 1863. The document was auctioned for $3,000 (winning Lincoln a gold watch for making the largest contribution); he later spoke at another fair in Washington, D.C., on March 18, 1864.

Sanitary shirt A common name for one of the many clean shirts dispensed to Union soldiers by the SANITARY COMMIS-

SION. Wounded Confederate soldiers in Union hospitals also received them.

sap A narrow trench used by besieging forces to approach or undermine a fortification. They were usually part of a complex system known as a SAP AND PARALLEL. The trenches were dug by "sappers," soldiers from the "sapper corps," who advanced behind a "sap roller" made of cylindrical baskets thick enough to stop a bullet and resembling a gigantic whicker basket rolled on its side. One sapper corp from Maine was composed of woodcutters.

sap and parallel A trench system used by besieging troops to advance on a fortification. It consisted of parallel trenches (dug closer and closer to the fortification) connected by advancing trenches called SAPS that were dug in a zigzag pattern to avoid gunfire. Before digging began, siege artillery and mortars were set up in protective pits to harass the defenders.

saphead A slang name for a stupid person, simpleton, or fool. The name became popular in the early nineteenth century, evolving from the adjective "sap-headed," which had been used since the seventeenth century.

Saratoga trunk A large trunk, mostly used by women when they traveled. It was often called just a Saratoga. After Yankee soldiers searched her Mississippi home for arms in 1863, Cordelia Scales wrote, "I wore my pistol (a very fine six shooter) all the time & stood by my saratoga, and would not permit them to search it."

sardine box A nickname for a soldier's tin CAP BOX.

sass This word, used then and now to mean impudent talk or backtalk, began less than a decade before the war. The verb, to sass someone, appeared as the war began.

sassafras tea An aromic drink made from sassafras bark. It was used as a tea substitute by Confederate soldiers and officers.

saucy Impertinent, imprudent, or rude. The New York *Herald* described the Confederate ironclad *Merrimac* as looking "terribly saucy." When Union Major General W.T. Sherman saw Confederates standing on Pine Mountain peering at U.S. guns that had shelled the position, he remarked, "How saucy they are." The adjective is still often heard in Great Britain.

savage as a meat axe An expression meaning the same as "hungry as a horse." The simile was mostly heard in the North and West. A soldier might say, "All this marching makes me savage as a meat axe." The British spelling of "axe" was still used.

Saviour of the Valley The nickname given to Confederate Brigadier General Thomas L. Rosser by residents of the Shenandoah Valley in Virginia, because of his successes there, including the BUCKLAND RACES. Rosser also saw action at both battles at Bull Run, and at Chancellorsville, Gettysburg, and Peterburg and was at Appomattox Court House during the surrender.

"Sawbones" A common name given by soldiers to an army doctor.

sawyer A tree that has collapsed into a river and is being swept down by the current, bobbing (sawing) up and down. Boats were sunk by sawyers, and the danger was always anticipated on large rivers, such as the Mississippi, where the Union fleet battled the defenders of Vicksburg. *See also* snag.

scallawag or scalawag or scallywag The popular name for a rascal. One prisoner gave the critical opinion that his military guards were "the worst looking scallawags." The name existed in New York State before the war for a mean person and was also used in the North, perhaps first, for a sickly cow. During Reconstruction, southern Democrats used "scallawag" for a white southerner who supported Reconstruction.

scape-grace A derogatory name for a graceless man or boy, especially a rogue or rascal; e.g., "Washington became infested with scape-graces as the war wore on."

scarce as hen's teeth This still current expression, meaning rare or scarce, was common during the war; e.g., "Good field officers in this company are as scarce as hen's teeth."

the scare An informal name for a military action done to frighten and demoralize the enemy. This was often done by loud noises or troop movements back and forth. Confederate Lieutenant General Nathan Bedford Forrest was more direct, once ordering, "Shoot at everything in blue and keep up the scare." *See also* the Chinese game; demonstration.

schottische A dance similar to the POLKA but at a slower tempo. They were popular at balls in both the North and South. The name was the German word for "Scottish."

"Scientist of the Seas" *See* "Pathfinder of the Seas."

scorbutus The medical name for scurvy, also called a scorbutic disease.

Scott's Anaconda *See* Anaconda Plan.

Scott's (Great) Snake *See* Anaconda Plan.

Scott's Nine Hundred A New York regiment that, despite its rowdy reputation, was assigned to provide the first cavalry escort for President Abraham Lincoln as he moved around Washington, D.C. Lincoln disliked the restriction of such bodyguards, but was convinced by his friend, the district marshal Ward Hill Lamon, to accept the protection in the summer of 1862. The regiment was replaced by the UNION LIGHT GUARD more than a year later.

scour This word, meaning to clean by polishing or rubbing, was used by a disappointed President Abraham Lincoln in November 1863, immediately after his Gettysburg address, which seemed to draw a half-hearted reaction from the crowd. Returning to his seat next to his friend, Ward Hill Lamon, Lincoln said under his breath: "Lamon, that speech won't scour." In this case, Lincoln was thinking of plows that did not scour themselves while turning up wet soil.

scout To reject an idea or statement as absurd. U.S. Congressman G.W. Julian said of Vice President Andrew Johnson: "He always scouted the idea that slavery was the cause of our trouble."

scow A flat-bottomed boat, such as a ferryboat. They were sometimes used during the war for river transportation, but their slow speed created dangers. On October 21, 1861, a Union regiment of 1,700 men under Colonel Edward D. Baker, Lincoln's personal friend, leisurely crossed the Potomac on scows and were ambushed on Ball's Bluff near Leesburg, Virginia. Many had to retreat in the scows, which held 40 to 60 men. The boats were swamped and some sunk with the loss of lives. The total Union losses were 48 killed (including Baker), 158 wounded, and more than 700 taken prisoner or missing.

scratch gravel To run quickly, especially to run away. This slang expression, first heard about a decade before the war, came from the fact that many good roads were still surfaced with gravel. *See also* cut dirt.

scuppers running blood A naval expression for a bloody battle. Scuppers are the openings in the side of a ship to let water run off the deck, and the gory expression was often accurate, as Union Lieutenant John C. Kinney noted at the battle of Mobile Bay on August 5, 1864.

scuttlebutt A slang naval word for gossip or rumor, still used in today's navy. It evolved from sailors' conversations around the scuttlebutt, the water barrel. Something "scuttled" had a hole cut in it, and a "butt" is a large barrel or cast. Richard Dana, in his book, *Two Years Before the Mast* (1840), wrote about "filling the 'scuttled butt' with fresh water."

sea lawyer A sailor who pretended to be an expert on matters and who dispensed unwanted advice. He usually was quick to argue and complain. This name was also popular in the U.S. navy in World War II.

sea pie A dish served on warships on both sides. It was a bland layered mixture of crust and various types of meat.

seat of war The general term for the fighting zone or a battle ground.

Secesh A short and scornful northern form of "Secessionist." One Union spy informed a Confederate private, "I would not trust a Secesh on his word, oath or bond." A less common name was "Secesher."

Secessia A comic early name in the North for the Confederate States.

The Second War for Independence A southern name for the Civil War, also called the Second American Revolution and the Second War of Secession.

Secret Service The spying organization established in 1861 for the Union by Allan Pinkerton, a Scottish-born detective who had protected Abraham Lincoln during his first inaugural, foiling an assassination attempt during his train's stopover in Baltimore. The Secret Service, which Pinkerton also headed for a year (using the name of E.J. Allen), had erratic success. One reason that Union General George McClellan failed to advance on Richmond was because the spying organization overestimated the number of Confederate defenders. Before the war in 1850, Pinkerton had founded his famous

Detective Allan Pinkerton (left), shown here with President Abraham Lincoln and General John A. McClernand, headed the Union Secret Service. *Library of Congress, Prints & Photographs Division, LC-B8171-7929.*

Chicago detective agency, which was continued by his sons after he died. The Secret Service Bureau that today protects the U.S. president is not the same. The Confederacy used the same name for its spying organization. *See also* "The Eye."

section The smallest military unit on both sides, consisting of from 20 to 25 men who were usually sent on details together. Two sections formed a PLATOON.

seed A young man, a slang name first used about a decade before the war.

see how the cat jumps To find out what people think or what trend is developing; e.g., "We'll add the 'peace plank' to the platform and see how the cat jumps." The expression means the same as "see how the wind blows."

see the elephant To see the wonders of the world, especially if they prove disappointing. Soldiers used the phrase to mean seeing the war and its horrors. After taking his first trips on a steamboat and train, an Ohio recruit wrote home, "Since I seen you last I have seen the elephant." The expression originated with farmers who had seen their first circus elephant. Soldiers in the Mexican War used it to describe the letdown they experienced after their expectations of glory. A similar expression was "to see the monkey show."

Seidlitz powder A laxative commonly prescribed by camp doctors, even in combination with other medicines, to cure malaria.

seining Catching fish with a net, a popular and rewarding sport when camps were located near rivers and streams.

sell A slang term for a deception or lying joke. A patient at a Confederate hospital was so angry at the matron in charge, he yelled, "I always did think this government was a confounded sell, and now I am sure of it, when they put such a little fool to manage such a big hospital as this."

"Seminole" The nickname for Confederate Lieutenant General Edmund Kirby Smith. It was first pinned on him by his West Point classmates. *See also* Kirby Smith-dom.

"Semmes the pirate" The name often used by the U.S. State Department and northern newspapers for Confederate Admiral Raphael Semmes, captain of the commerce raider *ALABAMA*.

sending a boy to the mill Sending a boy to do a man's work.

servant or house-servant The usual names for a plantation slave who worked in the house. "Maid" was also a common name.

set-down A proper full meal, so called because one sat down at a table. The term began about two or three years before the war.

set store by To have great esteem or love for. One slave was promised she could remain with her husband because "mistress knew we set stores by one another."

setting pickets The expression used for deploying PICKETS around the edges of a camp.

seven devil A nickname given by Confederate soldiers to the Union army's SPENCER carbine, because it was a repeating rifle that could shoot seven shots without reloading.

sewing society A sewing circle. During the war, these ladies turned their hands to such tasks as making tents for soldiers and sheets and pillow cases for hospitals.

shackly Shaky or rickety; e.g., "Mother eventually had to go around town in a shackly old carriage."

shade An insulting nickname for a black person in both the South and North.

shadow A nickname for a DAGUERREOTYPE photograph, which produced a slightly ghostly image. *See also* ghost.

shafts A wagon's or carriage's two front poles to which a horse was harnessed; e.g., "The sergeant put the horse in the shafts."

the shakes A common name for malaria.

shako A solder's tall stiff dress hat that was cylindrical, the crown tilted a bit forward, with a flat top and visor. Inspired by the French style, it was generally worn with a chinstrap, a plume or pompom on top, and a badge or metal insignia in front. The Auburn Guards of the Alabama Volunteer Militia wore an impressive version—Pattern 1851 Albert shakos made of black leather and sporting a red-and-white striped feather pompom. The FORAGE CAP was a floppy variation of it.

"Shanks" The nickname friends gave Confederate Brigadier General Nathan G. Evans, because of his skinny legs. He was a famed braggart and drinker whose orderly always carried along the general's keg of whiskey. He made his brigade very independent, and his ruffian character helped him (then a colonel) lead half a brigade to glory at the first battle of Bull Run, when his 400 men held down a division of nearly 10,000 Union troops. Evans, from South Carolina, survived a court-martial for drinking, but eventually lost his command in 1863.

shank's mare A humorous name for an infantryman's "horse," which was his legs. He would say "I'm riding shank's mare today."

sharper A swindler or cheat; e.g., "The government was a victim of sharpers selling their shoddy blankets to the army."

"sharp sabers and sharp spurs" The motto of Union Brigadier General Philip St. George Cooke, because he believed the cavalry's stength lay in saber charges. By the 1850s, his bravery fighting Indians and in the Mexican War made him one of the most admired cavalry officers in the OLD ARMY. Cooke was a Virginian who split with his Confederate family. His son, John Rogers Cooke, was a Confederate brigadier general and "JEB" Stuart (whom he once tried unsuccessfully to capture) was his son-in-law.

Sharpsburg The Confederate name for the battle known in the North as Antietam. The fighting took place on September 17, 1862, around Sharpsburg, the town in Maryland located near Antietam Creek.

Sharps carbine An accurate .52-caliber breech-loading carbine, the most desired Union gun in the war after the SPENCER

Linen cartridge for a Sharps carbine. *Copyright Inge Wright 1999.*

carbine. Sharps models of 1859 and 1863 were manufactured, with the Union ordering more than 80,000. The gun's lever was the trigger-guard, pulled down to expose the rear of the chamber. A paper cartridge with powder and ball was inserted into the chamber. If the gun was not cleaned regularly, powder built up and clogged the breech, so ramrods were supplied for muzzle loading between cleanings. The carbine was patented by Christian Sharps in 1848. *See also* sharpshooter.

sharp-set An informal word meaning "hungry"; e.g., "The marching had made the men exhausted and sharp-set."

sharpshooter A person having great accuracy with a rifle or carbine. They were excellent soldiers in a SKIRMISH or as individual snipers. Famous Union sharpshooters included Henry C. Foster, known as COONSKIN, of the 23rd Indiana Volunteers, and Truman Head, called CALIFORNIA JOE, of BERDAN'S SHARPSHOOTERS. The word was first used in England at the beginning of the nineteenth century and did not therefore come from SHARPS CARBINE, as often reported.

shavetail An unbroken or newly broken Army mule, because their tails were shaved to mark them as not properly trained. After the war, the name was applied to inexperienced young men, and then, beginning with the Spanish-American War in 1898, to a second lieutenant.

shaving glass A soldier's small mirror that was primarily used in camp for shaving.

shebang A simple camp structure built to provide shade in the summer. Shebangs, from about 8 to 12 feet high, had frames constructed of poles or fence rails (often nailed to trees) and were covered on top with brush, such as pine branches in the South, and sometimes oil clothes.

sheep dip A humorous name for harsh alcohol because of its foul taste. The term was first heard in 1865 in Union camps.

sheep rack The nickname given by western soldiers to the CHEVAL-DE-FRISE.

sheep's head soup A soup made of the head, lungs, and liver of a sheep, cooked with barley, such vegetables as turnips, carrots, and onions, and such spices as cloves, parsley, thyme, and marjoram. A tureen was usually filled with a glassful of sherry before the soup was poured in. Sometimes a sheep's heart was added to create a pudding.

sheep-skin This slang name for a diploma was first heard about two years before the war.

sheet-iron crackers A descriptive camp name for tough HARDTACK crackers. The camp stoves were made of sheet-iron.

shellback A humorous slang name for an experienced, usually older, sailor.

shell jacket A close-fitting military jacket that was cut evenly to waist length, such as those worn by cavalrymen, light artillerymen, and buglers. A modern example is a waiter's formal jacket.

shell out As still used today, it means to pay, spend, or contribute money. It was a common expression in camps.

shell road A road, especially near the Gulf coast, laid with shells. Bay oysters and other fish provided a critical source of food for the South during the U.S. navy's blockade. Major shell roads were maintained in New Orleans and Mobile, Alabama, where the name Old Shell Road lingers on in a major city street.

shelter tent *See* dog tent.

shenanigan or shenanigans Trickery or mild mischief, terms first heard about five years before the war. The singular form has now disappeared.

Sherman's bummers The southern name for troops of Union Major General W.T. Sherman who plundered farms and homes for food and other items during their 300-mile march through Georgia. This plunder included staples such as chickens, pigs, potatoes, corn, peanuts, bacon, lard, candles, fence rails, wagons, and carriages. The practice was encouraged by Sherman in his Special Field Order 120 on November 9, 1864: "As for horses, mules, wagons, etc., belonging to the inhabitants, the cavalry and artillery may appropriate freely and without limit; discriminating, however, between the rich, who are usually hostile, and the poor and industrious, usually neutral or friendly." He later admitted that "many acts of pillage, robbery and violence were committed by these parties of foragers usually called 'bummers,' for I have since heard of jewelry taken from women, and the plunder of articles that never reached the commissary." The name BUMMER originally meant a lazy person.

Sherman's gorillas The nickname given to themselves by western and midwestern soldiers under the command of Union Major General W.T. Sherman.

Sherman's monuments or Sherman's sentinels or Sherman's tombstones Facetious nicknames for the trail of lonely chimneys left standing after Union Major General W.T. Sherman's troops had burned homes in Louisiana, Mississippi, and Georgia. *See also* Chimneyville.

Sherman's neckties A facetious name for the southern railroad tracks that Union General W.T. Sherman's army destroyed during their march through Georgia. They were less often called "Billy Sherman's neckties," "iron neckties," "Sherman hairpins," "Jeff Davis neckties," and "Lincoln gimlets" (a right-angled boring tool). The destruction was done to make the tracks unusable to the Rebels. Track was taken up in sections as long as a regiment and broken up rail by rail. Soldiers then piled up railroad ties for a bonfire, heated the rails, and twisted them with special hooks or around trees or telegraph poles to cool in the necktie shape. Sometimes, the men would bend the rails into the letters "U" and "S" and display them on a hillside.

the Sherman torch The name given by Confederate General Robert E. Lee to Major General W.T. Sherman's policy of burning his way through Mississippi in 1863. Sherman called it "a swath of desolation fifty miles broad across the State of Mississippi which the present generation will not forget." Lee said three-fourths of the destruction was to private property, and he put the total damage at $5 million.

"the She Wolf" The derisive nickname given to Mary Todd Lincoln, wife of President Abraham Lincoln, because of her tempermental nature. *See also* "the Hellcat"; Mrs. President.

"shield of the South" A nickname for Tennessee, given by Confederate General Joseph E. Johnston, because the long state was supposedly a protective buffer for the Deep South.

shift To change clothes. A soldier might have to "shift into a new uniform" when on furlough.

shilly shally Uncertainty or irresolution. It was also used as a verb. In March 1864, U.S. Brigadier General T. Kilby Smith wrote his mother from Louisiana to say,

"Our western troops are tired of shilly shally, and this year will deal their blows very heavily." The word came from "Shall I? Shall I?" and changed under the influence of "dilly dally."

"Shiloh" A mournful poem written by Herman Melville after the bloody battle of Shiloh on April 6 and 7, 1862, at Pittsburgh Landing, Tennessee. Melville concentrated on the tragedy of young men who could only find peace in death, as seen in the following lines:

> Foemen at morn, but friends at eve—
> Fame or country least their care:
> (What like a bullet can undeceive!)
> But now they lie low,
> While over them the swallows skim,
> And all is hushed at Shiloh.

shindy A big commotion or noisy disturbance or an uproar.

shine a frog To use a torch or other light to stun and catch a frog at night. This was a common practice among soldiers subsisting on the land.

shinplaster A contemptuous term for a U.S. or Confederate Treasury bill, because a few soldiers supposedly used them to cover wounds. The name, taken from the paper used to heal cuts, was first applied to the Union's paper GREENBACKS originally issued in 1862 to make up for a lack of silver coinage. An oversupply of Confederate paper money followed and caused an irritated southern editor to complain, "two hundred and fifty different sorts of shinplasters, and not one dime in silver to be seen." One Yankee's opinion of Confederate shinplasters was that "the notes depreciated the paper on which they were printed." Another joke, recalled George W. Cable of Company 1 of the 4th Mississippi Cavalry, was that a person could pass the label of an olive-oil bottle off as a shinplaster, because "it was greasy, smelt bad, and bore an autograph."

ship over To re-enlist, used both in the navy and army.

ship's fever *See* jail fever.

shirk A shirker; someone who avoided his military duties. Shirks tried especially hard to avoid battles.

shit ass A vulgar insult that was common on both sides. The name was most often pinned on the enemy, officers, fellow soldiers, and politicians.

shit house A vulgar slang nickname for a GUARD HOUSE. A North Carolina soldier writing to his brother on June 13, 1864, decided it was more respectable to spell it "sh_t house."

shit-house adjutant A soldier's common insult for a staff officer.

the shits A soldier's profane but common slang term for diarrhea.

shiv *See* chiv.

shoddy Inferior, artificial, poorly made, or cheap. The name during the war referred to Union uniforms that were made by deceitful suppliers from a material called "shoddy," a short-fiber mixture of many poor and reused bits of wool and cloths (even from carpets). When wet, the short fibers fell to pieces. *Harper's Monthly* called it a "villainous compound." The name was soon used for many items and even for the times. "This is the age of shoddy," complained the New York *Herald* on October 6, 1863. The nineteenth-century name had originated in Yorkshire, England, for a poor quality of stone and coal.

shoot A new channel carved out by a river, often connecting the ends of an oxbow bend. Perceptive river boat captains would wait for a shoot to deepen and then use it as a shortcut.

shote or shoat A derogatory slang name for a lazy or worthless man; e.g., "The camp was full of sarcastic shotes who had joined for the bounty." A real shote is a young pig that has been weaned.

shot in the neck A southern term, often reduced to "shot," meaning: 1. A drink of straight whiskey, usually downed in one gulp. 2. Intoxicated or drunk. See DRUNK for numerous other terms referring to intoxication.

shoulder strap A slang name for an officer. "If there is one thing that I hate more than another it is the sight of a shoulder strap," wrote Union soldier George Gray Hunter of Pennsylvania, "for I am well convinced in my own mind that had it not been for the officers this war would have been ended long ago."

Shove it up your ass! A well-know profanity during the war. One Kansas cavalryman was sentenced to confinement and hard labor for telling his lieutenant "You may shove it up your ass" when the officer asked why he had given whiskey to prisoners he was guarding.

shovel fleas To try to do something that is virtually impossible. This was a favorite idiom of President Abraham Lincoln. At the end of 1862, he complained that Major General George McClellan was calling for more troops, but the deserters and furloughed men outnumbered the recuits. And he added: "To fill up the army is like undertaking to shovel fleas. You take up a shovelful, but before you can dump them anywhere they are gone." *See also* like shoveling flies across the barnyard.

shower bath The punishment famously given by the police in Washington, D.C., to drunk soldiers. They were doused with a stream of icy water, which was particularly dreaded in the winter.

shrapnel *See* spherical case shot.

shucks The humorous southern name given to BLUEBACKS, the Confederate bills, because they soon became as worthless as corn shucks.

Sibley tent A tepee-style military tent in a bell shape 12 feet high and 18 feet in diameter. It was made of canvas with a door flap and supported by a center pole. One southern soldier compared it to "a large hoop skirt standing by itself on the ground." Because it resembled a bell, the Sibley was sometimes informally called a bell tent. It was heated by a Sibley stove designed in the same cone shape. The tent was intended for 12 men but, if raised on a stockade four-feet high, could sleep up to 20 or more (like spokes, with their feet at the hub). Designed in 1857 by Henry H. Sibley, a WEST POINTER who later became a Confederate brigadier general, the tent was popular in the early days of the war but proved too expensive and cumbersome for a rapidly moving army. The DOG TENT replaced the Sibley, which was out of service by the Union army in 1862.

Stove for use in a Sibley tent. *Copyright Inge Wright 1999.*

Sibley tent. *Copyright Inge Wright 1999.*

sick call *See* surgeon's call.

sick nurse *See* doctor woman.

sick-permit An official paper signed by a camp surgeon verifying that a soldier was ill and unfit for fighting. The permits quickly came out of pockets as a unit moved into battle, and a sick soldier unfortunate enough to have lost his paper was seldom able to talk his way out of the upcoming engagement.

Sic semper tyrannis The state motto of Virginia, which means "Thus always to tyrants." After John Wilkes Booth assassinated President Abraham Lincoln, the actor leaped from the presidential box onto the stage below, breaking his leg and shouting "Sic semper tyrannis. The South is avenged."

sidling movement Soldiers' common term for the sideways movement of a military unit during combat. It was normally a shift to test different parts of the enemy's line.

siege artillery Heavy artillery guns used against forts and other strong defenses. The heaviest gun was a smooth-bore 24-pounder, known as a "battering gun" because it could fire balls from a long range through thick stone or earth walls. Because its overall weight on the move was 10,155 pounds, it required a 10-horse team. SIEGE MORTARS were also used against defenses.

siege mortar *See* mortar.

sight A great many things or people; e.g., "We came upon a sight of wagons." The word was mostly used in the North and East. "Heap" was the equivalent in the South and West.

signalize A variant of "to signal," used in speaking about the new telegraph, as well as about WIGWAG communications; e.g., "Has the lieutenant signalized General Grant for reinforcements?"

Silk Dress Balloon The popular name given to a Confederate observation balloon that was put together using hundreds of silk dresses, including wedding-gowns, that southern women sent to Richmond, Virginia. Captain E. Porter Alexander was in charge of the operation that saw the balloon filled with town gas, transported on a locomotive, and tranferred to a steamboat that eventually ran aground, allowing Union forces to capture both boat and balloon. The South hardly used balloons because, lacking portable gas generators, they had to be filled in Richmond. *See also* Aeronautic Department; "most shot-at man in the war."

Simon A slang name for a dollar. It was first heard about two years before the war and was obviously transferred from the British sixpence, which had been called

a Simon since the beginning of the eighteenth century.

simple intermittant fever *See* intermittant fever.

singling The first crude spirit produced by distillation. Soldiers would sometimes come across a small distillery in the woods, fire it up, and consumed the singling while it was still hot. This was not an ideal drink.

singular Unique, remarkable, or odd. The word was popular during the war. "It was a singular sight," wrote one Union soldier, after observing his troops fraternizing with the enemy during a break in the fighting. The wife of a Georgia plantation owner, describing the deprivations of war to her friend in England, said "when our intercourse with the rest of mankind is revived we shall present a singular aspect."

sinker A military biscuit, because it was hard and heavy.

the sinks A euphemism for the regimental latrines. They were often no more than a shallow straight ditch about 30 feet long. Fresh earth was sometimes thrown into the ditch and sometimes not.

Sis, Sissy, or Cissy Short forms of "sister," commonly used in families during the war.

Sisters of Charity Catholic nuns who helped in military GENERAL HOSPITALS on both sides. They performed nursing and mothering duties for the patients who tended to call all hospital nuns Sisters of Charity, although many came from other orders, such as the Sisters of Mercy, Sisters of the Holy Cross, and Sisters of St. Joseph.

sitting room The main family room in a house, sometimes called a PARLOR or DRAW-

ING ROOM. The term "living room" was introduced about two years after the war.

"The Situation" A standing heading run in many northern newspapers for a summary of the day's war news. Other papers were more blunt, using "The War."

"sixty days" A popular early estimate in the North for the length of the South's secession or for the war. U.S. Secretary of State William H. Seward, speaking in New York only two days after South Carolina left the Union, told the crowd that "Sixty days' more suns will give you a much brighter and more cheerful atmosphere."

skedaddle To run off or scurry away quickly. The noun—a hasty retreat or flight—had been known in the U.S. since the 1820s and was used for the GREAT SKEDADDLE of Union troops at Bull Run in 1861. The verb was created during the war, and used especially by Union troops to describe how Rebels fled.

skeesicks A slang name for a rascal. In camp, it was often applied to a tentmate.

skeeter A dialect name for a mosquito. First used about a decade before the war, it is still heard.

skid One of several thin logs placed across a defensive trench. This arrangement was to protect the men in it from being crushed or injured if the enemy's artillery fire blew the large HEAD-LOG back to the trench. Confederate Private Sam R. Watkins of the First Tennessee Regiment recalled Colonel H.R. Field "when he fell off the skid from which he was shooting right over my shoulder, shot through the head." (He was only wounded.)

skillygalee A fairly indigestible Union camp meal said to "make the hair curl." It was prepared by soaking HARDTACK pieces in cold water before frying them in pork fat and salting to taste. They were often toasted to be crumbled in coffee or buttered. During the toasting on the end of a split stick, if a skillygalee fell off into the fire, as often happened, soldiers still ate the charred remains, which were thought to cure "weak bowels."

skin *See* whiskey skin.

skipper A small maggot. An Ohio soldier complained the meat was "so damned full of skippers that it could move alone." Cheese infested with maggots was said to be "skippery."

skirmish An irregular battle between a few soldiers or two small military groups. The participants were called skirmishers, and a military unit often moved with "skirmishers out" in a "skirmish line" ahead of a force's main line, to prevent surprise attacks. The verb "to skirmish" was also used.

skirmish drill *See* reading linen.

skirmishing A popular slang camp word for killing lice.

skittles A nine-pin bowling game in which a wooden ball or disk shaped like a small flat cheese was rolled at the pins ("skittles"). It was originally played in a skittle-alley about 60 feet in length, but soldiers were limited to an outdoor version, often using a cannon ball. Skittles originated in Great Britain where it is still played. *See also* ten-pins.

skrimmage or scrimmage A western variant for "SKIRMISH," as in "We had a few skrimmages with Indians." The word goes back to fifteenth-century England. It survives as a specialized term in football, while rugby uses "scrummage."

skunk A special term of abuse that soldiers usually reserved for a hated officer.

skylarking Frolicking, having fun, or playing around; e.g., "Between battles, we would quickly be skylarking, sometimes racing or wrestling." The word was originally a naval one and is still heard in the navy.

slangwhang To use violent or abusive language (to someone). An abusive speaker or writer was called a "slang-whanger."

slapjack 1. A flapjack, especially one made to fit the whole frying pan. 2. A meal created in Confederate camps by altering the greasy concoction called SLOSH OR COOSH. Less water and grease were used so the flour turned into a paste that could be browned on both sides and sweetened with sugar or sorghum syrup.

the slashes The area of trees cut ("slashed") down in front of a fort or BATTERY. The trees were felled at about a three-foot level, and their tops faced the advancing enemy, who found the slashes a difficult obstacle to overcome.

slat To throw something down in a violent way; e.g., "Kelly slat his rifle down and walked away."

slave-breaker or nigger-breaker An informal name for a man who was an expert at training young slaves and turning disobedient or lazy ones into good servants. He could be of any social class, including a poor farmer who rented his land and received the slaves free in exchange for his training, often for a year. The former slave, Frederick Douglass, in his autobiography, recalled his year under a cruel slave-breaker, Edward Covey, who became less aggressive after Douglass (facing a lashing) overpowered him.

"slave hound of Illinois" A nickname for Abraham Lincoln given by abolitionists because he been elected on a Republican platform promising no interference with slavery, and he reiterated this pledge in his inaugural address in 1861.

slave songs The old name for traditional songs, especially those later called "spirituals," that were sung by plantation slaves.

Slavocracy A northern name for the southern ruling class or for the South itself.

"Sledge of Nashville" The nickname given Union Major General George H. Thomas after his overwhelming victory at the battle of Nashville on December 16, 1864, over the forces of General John B. Hood. The name, short for "sledgehammer," was popularized for a while by the press but could not compete with Thomas' famous sobriquet of the ROCK OF CHICKAMAUGA.

sleeper An alcoholic drink made of rum, egg yolks, sugar, and, for flavoring, cloves, cinnamon, and coriander seeds. The mixture was whisked and strained.

Sleepy Hollow chair An large, comfortable armchair with a concave upholstered seat and high upholstered back. It was sometimes an armchair-rocking chair.

slewed A slang name for being moderately drunk. See DRUNK for numerous other terms referring to intoxication.

sling a nasty ankle or sling a nasty foot A slang expression meaning to dance like an expert or professional.

sling cart A two-wheeled unit used to transport and position cannons. "Sling" in this case means a device for supporting and carrying something. At the end of the war, the Confederates built one gigantic sling cart with wheels 11 feet high to transport two 12-inch cannons that weighted almost 50,000 pounds each.

slip A narrow church pew. A member of a congregation might say he preferred to sit in "the back slips."

slip up To fail or make an error. The noun, which is still heard, was also used for an accident, failure, or mistake. The terms became common during the war, having been created about seven years before it began.

slope A slang verb meaning to run away; e.g., "The captain rode up, but we sloped before he could identify us."

slops A sailor's slang name for new clothes issued on ship by the paymaster.

slop water A common insult, often accurate, for a miserable brew of coffee.

slosh or coosh A poor meal in Confederate camps. A small amount of bacon was fried until the pan was half filled with boiling grease. Flour was watered down until it "flowed like milk," then poured on the grease and quickly stirred into a dirty brown mixture. One version was called SLAPJACK.

slouch hat The soft-brimmed felt hat beloved by Confederate troops. The wide brim provided shelter from the sun, and the hats could be turned into comfortable pillows. The design was based on British hats first imported in the 1830s.

slow bear A deceptive nickname given by foraging troops for any farmer's pig they had stolen and eaten.

the slows The characteristic of being generally hesitant and slow to action. When Union General George McClellan held back his Army of the Potomac from engaging the enemy, Abraham Lincoln fumed that "Little Mac has got the slows."

slumgullion or slum A campfire stew made from any ingredients that were at hand. The name was created by the Forty-niners during the California Gold Rush to describe the sludge remaining after gravel was sluiced for gold.

slush fund Money that is put aside to influence or bribe politicians. The term was introduced about a year before the war began.

slush lamp A homemade lamp in camp. A typical lamp was a sardine box filled with cooking grease containing a wick made of a piece of rag inserted in one corner. The whole device was then hung from the ridge pole in a soldier's tent by a wire, often taken from bales of hay for the horses.

small-arms men A navy landing party. Such a unit was useless when facing regular soldiers. During the Union capture of Fort Fisher in North Carolina on January 15, 1865, the U.S. navy's small-arms men attacked with revolvers and swords but beat a quick retreat when they encountered Rebel infantry and artillery.

"Smart Aleck" A nickname for the Confederacy's vice-president, Alexander Stephens of Georgia. Stephens was so named because he was a lawyer and had a quick mind, although the name served equally well as a put-down by his opponents. He and President Jefferson Davis were often at odds, with moderate Stephens opposing conscription and taxes for the war. He described his leader as "weak and vacillating, timid, petulant, peevish, obstinate." *See also* "Little Aleck."

"Smash 'em up! Smash 'em up!" Concise advice on how to defeat the enemy, given to his men by Union Major General Philip Sheridan.

smear-case An informal name for cottage cheese, because it was smeared (spread) on bread.

smell powder To take part in a military engagement or battle. It was usually said to distinguish between soldiers who had smelled powder and those who had not yet met the enemy. Confederate soldier Allen C. Redwood of the 55th Virginia Regiment recalled that "Our brigade [Field's] was rather a new one in organization and experience, most of us having 'smelt powder' for the first time in the Seven Days before Richmond."

smile A slang name for whiskey. A soldier might ask "Do you have any smile?" It was also used as a verb; e.g., "I saw the general smile a glass."

"Smiler" The nickname for Schuyler Colfax, the speaker of the U.S. House of Representatives from 1863 to 1869, because his face wore a perpetual smile. He was a Radical Republican who did not agree with President Abraham Lincoln on many matters, including how the defeated South would be handled. At his last cabinet meeting the day he was assassinated, Lincoln told Colfax he was happy Congress was not in session because he could deal directly with the South. Colfax continued to lead opposition to President Andrew Johnson's moderate Reconstruction views. In 1868, Colfax was elected vice president on the Republican ticket with President Ulysses S. Grant.

smite 1. To hit hard. 2. To defeat or kill, especially in battle.

smoke ball A CARCASS shell filled with materials that gave off a thick smoke when exploded. This shell was used both to send the enemy gasping and to conceal attacking forces.

smoke box A wrought iron box inside the later *Monitor*-class ironclads that collected the smoke and blast of the gun. This device was needed because larger 15-inch guns had replaced the 11-inch ones for which the *Monitor*'s gun ports had been designed. Since the 15-inch barrel could not be pushed through the port (although the fired shell went through), the smoke box was devised. It also absorbed much of the noise.

smoked Yankee A Union soldier, such as a mess cook, who had labored hard over the cooking fire. The name was a familiar joke in Union camps.

smoke pole A nickname for the large .69 and .75 caliber guns that some soldiers brought with them into camp when the war began.

smoke wagon A slang name for a train, because of the engine smoke that blew back into the passenger cars.

smooch To smudge or smear something, such as ink.

smoothbore gun A gun, like a rifle or cannon, with no spiral grooves cut inside the barrel to make the bullets or shells rotate when fired. The advantage of the spinning MINIÉ BALL and artillery shell (instead of a cannon ball) led to older weapons being converted to RIFLED GUNS that had better accuracy and distance. Union soldiers often hurled taunts at any Rebels discovered to be still fighting with smoothbores.

smoothing iron A delightfully descriptive name for the common device used to iron clothes.

smudge A smoldering fire with dense smoke, used to fumigate an area. When Sara Rice Pryor, a volunteer Confederate nurse, returned to her home in Petersburg, Virginia, in the fall of 1863, she had to wait outside in the cold "while a colored boy made a 'smudge' in the house to dislodge the wasps that had tenanted it for many months."

snack This contemporary word for a quick meal was used during the war and, in fact, dates back to the mid-eighteenth century. In the seventeenth century, it referred to a small taste of liquor.

snag An obstruction on a river, especially a floating tree trunk with its roots anchored in the water. Sometimes visible and sometimes not, snags were always a peril to navigation. They were particularly dangerous to Union boats on the Mississippi River, where local river-boat pilots seemed to have a sixth sense, even at night, to help them avoid the "hidden monsters." *See also* sawyer.

snake medicine A light-hearted name given strong whiskey by Union soldiers in 1865 because of the facetious idea that it was an antidote for snakebite.

snakeroot The common name for a plant with a medicinal root used for the general treatment of ill soldiers, especially by Confederate surgeons during the blockade. Several varieties of snakeroot were available. The name comes from it being a supposed remedy for snakebite.

snap A slang word for vitality or energy. One war correspondent for the New York *Tribune* complained that his fellow worker "lacks energy and snap to an almost fatal degree."

snapped A southern slang word for being drunk; e.g., "Tom had a furlough to Richmond and got snapped on rum before the sun set." See DRUNK for numerous other terms referring to intoxication.

snatch A slang word meaning to arrest someone. It was introduced as the war began.

snatch bald-headed To steal something, especially after carefully planning. Soldiers also used the term when food or equipment was confiscated.

snollygoster A politician, often without principles, who gains office by overwhelming the voters with his verbosity. Unethical lawyers were also called snollygosters. The name was apparently related to "snallygaster," a type of dangerous spirit, being a term derived from *snel geist*, Middle High German for "fast spirit."

snowball An insulting name for a Negro, especially an old person with white hair.

snow balling *See* Great Snowball Battle.

snub A slang word meaning to tie up something. An officer might order a private to "Snub that mule to the tree with a strong rope."

snug as a bug in a rug This well-known simile, meaning to be very contented or comfortable, was popular during the war. It was probably coined in the eighteenth century by Benjamin Franklin.

SNY The abbreviation for the State of New York, worn on the metal belt plates of the state MILITIA. The New York State Militia was organized in 1861 and renamed the National Guard in April 1862. Its members wore blue SHAKO uniforms.

soaker A slang name for a person who was a hard drinker. An "old soaker" usually meant a drunk. One Confederate complained about a barrel of whiskey that was "such villainous stuff that only the old soakers could stomach it."

soap A slang name for money, especially when it was used to grease someone's palm.

sobby Soggy or saturated with moisture. "The land was low and sobby," a Confederate private reported about his camp in a Virginia woods.

social An informal gathering of up to 30 or 40 friends and acquaintances, usually in the evening and often without food or drink served. Beside general conversation, ladies brought their knitting and there were such entertainments as music performances, readings, and charades.

soda biscuit A biscuit that uses soda and buttermilk or sour milk as the leavening agents. One Confederate private described it as "yellow and odoriferous."

soda-pop gun or soda-water bottle The nicknames given the Dahlgren gun because its shape resembled such a bottle.

softhorn Another name for a green horn. This description of an inexperienced person was applied to new soldiers.

soft money Another name for paper money. The term was introduced as the war began.

soft-tack A soldier's humorous name for soft wheat bread. *See also* hardtack.

"so help me, Hannah!" A mild oath expressing determination; e.g., "I'll be home by Christmas, so help me, Hannah!"

sold down the river *See* sold South.

soldier of the Republic A name sometimes used in the North for a Union soldier.

Soldier's Aid Society One of the numerous private organizations throughout the North that sent necessities to wounded and dying Union soldiers. Tens of thousands of women contributed their time sewing and knitting, rolling bandages, preparing home medicines, cooking jams and jellies, and making or collecting other gifts. There was even a Hebrew Ladies' Soldiers' Aid Society.

Soldier's Friend League A private league of southern women who provided for the well-being of Confederate soldiers, sending them bandages they had rolled, shirts they had sewn, and gloves, soap, candles, and other personal and useful items.

Soldiers' Home One of a system of homes run by the military for Union soldiers who were honorably discharged. Many of the staff came from the SANITARY COMMISSION. They provided care, treatment, and refreshments for those in the transition phase between military and civilian life, as they waited for their proper discharge papers and final pay. During hot summers, President Abraham Lincoln slept in a Soldiers' Home three miles north of Washington, D.C. *See also* Wayside Home.

The Soldier's Hymn Book A collection of 271 hymns published as a pocket-sized booklet for Confederate soldiers by the South Carolina Tract Society. Another popular hymn book was *The Army Hymn Book* of 191 selections that was distributed by the Richmond Presbyterian Committee of Publications.

"Soldier's Joy" A brand of tobacco popular with pipe smokers in Confederate camps. (Cigarettes were a new commodity that only became available to the general public after the war.) One of the few material advantages Rebel soldiers enjoyed over their enemy was tobacco grown in Virginia and North Carolina. Union soldiers often had to make do with a mixture of ground chickory, cabbage, and sumac leaves. "How the Yankees did enjoy smoking the Rebel tobacco!" noted one Confederate after watching wounded Union soldiers accept the gift after the second battle of Bull Run in 1862. In another fellowship at the Rappahannock River in Virginia, Union PICKETS on one bank sailed newspapers on toy boats 200 yards across to their Rebel counterparts in return for 20 pounds of cut plug tobacco pushed over on a plank. Several incidences were recorded of Confederate tobacco being swapped for Union coffee.

sold South A term describing a slave from the Upper South who was sold to someone in the Deep South. A similar expression was "sold down the river," meaning the Mississippi. It was estimated that about 30 percent of the slave children living in the Upper South in 1820 had been sold South by 1860. Slaves usually feared this, since some owners tried to keep them loyal by a threat to sell them South where, they had heard, brutality was more common. This movement away from the border states decreased the chance of a slave fleeing on the UNDERGROUND RAILROAD. *See also* kidnapping; viginital crop.

solid shot A solid round cannon ball used in smooth-bore guns. The plural name was the same.

"Somebody's Darling" A sentimental song sung by both sides. It was so well known, when a dead soldier's body was encountered by troops on the march, some hardened veteran would often point it out and add, "That's somebody's darling." The end of the song went as follows:

> Somebody's watching and waiting for him,
> Yearning to hold him again to her heart;
> There he lies—with the blue eyes dim,
> And the smiling, child-like lips apart.
> Tenderly bury the fair young dead,
> Pausing to drop on his grave a tear;
> Carve on the wooden slab at his head,
> "Somebody's darling slumbers here!"

some pumpkins *See* pumpkin.

"Song for Our Soldiers" A patriotic Union song about freeing the slaves. It went in part as follows:

> Where you find the white men,
> Union-hating white men,
> Ribald rabble white men,

> Let your cannon play.
> Where you find the black men,
> Union-loving black men,
> True and loyal black men,
> Let 'em run away!
> Break off their chains, boys!
> Strike off their chains, boys!
> Knock off their chains, boys,
> And let 'em run away.

son of a bitch The most commonly used name to curse both an officer and a fellow soldier, but also a familiar name of companionship among buddies. When someone blatantly used the expression to insult a superior, he was usually given time in the guard house.

Sons of Liberty *See* Knights of the Golden Circle.

sora A popular game bird known as the short-bill rail. So many were served at the banquet following the wedding of Confederate General George E. Pickett on September 18, 1863, it was called the "wedding-sora-supper." This was during the hard times in the South, just over two months after the same general had ordered the fatal charge at Gettysburg. Ammunition was so restricted, the soras were killed at night with paddles.

sorgum molasses A sweetner used by Confederate troops later in the war as sugar became rare. Sorgum was easy to obtain in the South, but the molasses was inferior to that produced from sugar. It was used in camp coffee made with roasted rye. "The mixture of rye and sorghum," noted one Confederate, "was enough to produce deadly illness in any one who swallowed it, not excepting a Rebel soldier. But we learned to love it."

sound on the goose A slang southern description for someone who was rich or well off; e.g., "Carrie says she only wants to marry some fellow who's sound on the goose." The expression was coined during the pre-war troubles in Kansas and originally described a solid supporter of the slavery question.

sour milk Buttermilk, a name especially used in the southern mountains, where many people thought it was not fit for drinking.

Southern Bureau The research department of the New York *Herald* that collected and filed background information on the Confederate states for use by its journalists.

Southern Confederacy A common name used for the Confederacy.

Southern Cross A popular southern name for the Confederate battle flag, which was designed by General P.G.T. Beauregard, based on a suggestion by Colonel William P. Miles and a Colonel Walton. It had a red background and diagonal blue St. Andrew's cross trimmed in white and filled with 13 white stars, the number of states expected to secede, although Missouri and Kentucky only had Confederate governments-in-exile. (The U.S. flag flown in the North continued to show a star for each Confederate state.) The Southern Cross was square and not, as often portrayed today, shaped like the Stars and Stripes.

Southern Field and Fireside A popular magazine in the South, often read and passed around in camps.

Southern Illustrated News A weekly newspaper established in 1862 in Richmond, Virginia. Based on *The Illustrated News* of London, it became the leading weekly throughout Dixie. The in-depth articles included biased analyses of battles (calling Gettysburg "a great victory" for General Lee) and such matters as the EMANCIPATION PROCLAMATION and Great Britain's failure to recognize the Confederacy.

Southern Mothers' Association A relief organization for Confederate soldiers. It was well known for establishing temporary hospitals.

Southern Punch A satirical magazine based on the famous British publication. Its humor ribbed both Yankees and Rebels. In 1863, it even reprinted the burlesque Vicksburg mule meat menu from the *Chicago Tribune. See* Confederate beef.

Southern Republic An informal name for the seceded states before the Confederate name was adopted. U.S. Colonel Robert E. Lee wrote a letter on January 22, 1861, to his cousin Martha Custis Williams about his son and her younger brother "looking forward to captancies in the Army of the Southern Republic!"

Southron A southerner, a form of the name used during the war. It was originally a Scottish term. *See also* Norther.

sowbelly An informal name on both sides for salt pork. It was boiled or fried, and even eaten raw between two HARDTACK biscuits, although it was often rancid and stringy. Union sowbelly was supplied by a Chicago pork-packing factory.

Spades Lee *See* Ace of Spades.

span A pair of horses that were harnessed side by side. They were chosen to look as identical as possible, especially in color. A person might talk about buying "a span of Virginia horses." The verb was also used, as seen in the compliment, "Those gray horses span well."

"The Spanish Fandango" A popular guitar piece that was a favorite of "accomplished" young ladies who had been taught the instrument.

spanish fly *See* cantharide.

spanking good A common expression for something that was especially good; e.g., "The meadow along the river made a spanking good site for the camp."

spark it A slang expression meaning to engage in kissing, cuddling, or other sexual play. "Sparking," a term that lasted into the twentieth century, was also used. A Missouri cavalryman wrote his brother: "Let me know what Girl you are sparking."

spar torpedo An underwater mine ("torpedo") pushed ahead of a small boat to explode on contact with an enemy ship. The canister of explosive gunpowder was attached to the boat by a 20-foot to 30-foot spar (pole). The attacking boat would approach the enemy at night, and the torpedo would be detonated under the water on contact or by a line pulled by the crew to set off a firing pin. The attackers were also always in danger of sinking. The Confederate ship *Albemarle* was sunk by a spar torpedo.

special hospital A hospital specializing in one or related types of medical problems. To treat their soldiers, the North established a neurological hospital in Philadelphia, and the South had ophthalmic hospitals. Both sides operated special hospitals to treat venereal diseases.

specie Coined money. Betty Maury of Fredericksburg, Virginia, suffering during the Union occupation, complained on June 12, 1862, that "A pair of shoes are worth so much in Specie, so much more in Yankee paper, and double their real value in Virginia money."

speculator In the South, a businessman who bought slaves from a plantation with the hopes of selling them for a higher price. Some speculators even bought, for a bargain price, the ownership of slaves who had run away, hoping to catch and sell them for a large profit. In Harriett

Beecher Stowe's *UNCLE TOM'S CABIN*, the small slave Topsy says she was never born or had parents because "I was raised by a speculator, with lots of others."

Spencer carbine A short rifle used by the Union army, considered the best rifle in the war and the first repeating rifle to be used. It was invented and patented a year before the war began by Christopher M. Spencer, 20, a Quaker. The trigger-guard lever was pulled down to inject one of seven self-contained metallic cartridges into the barrel and pulled back to ready the gun to fire; operating the lever again ejected the spent shell and loaded another cartridge. Toward the end of the war, the gun was upgraded to fire 15 shots a minute. More than 94,000 Spencer carbines were issued to the Union forces, and about 11,400 regular-sized Spencer rifles were also used. Confederate General Robert E. Lee disapproved of repeating rifles because he felt soldiers would waste ammunition, and the South lagged behind in copying the Spencer carbine.

sperm candle The common name for a spermaceti candle. Spermaceti is a fatty substance taken either from sperm whales, other whales, or dolphins. Confederate Kate Cumming, serving in a military hospital in Corinth, Mississippi, met a woman searching for her wounded husband, and noted, "Her mother, on leaving, presented me with some very nice sperm-candles."

spherical case shot The official American military name for a shrapnel shell in which a cannon shell was filled with some 350 small lead balls. Fired from a smoothbore cannon, the shell was exploded by a fuse within and was able (far beyond the range of a rifle) to rain the equivalent of rifle fire in all directions for a distance of 44 yards. Shrapnel shells were invented by a British soldier, Henry Shrapnel, who became that country's inspector of artillery in 1804. *See also* canister; grape shot; sand shot.

"Splice the main brace" The command given by captains in both navies to issue the GROG RATION to the crew.

spider *See* creeper.

spike the gun An order to make a cannon unusable by driving a spike into the vent hole. The call to "spike the guns" was given to artillerymen before a quick retreat so the weapons left behind could not be used by the enemy. Just before the war began, U.S. Major Robert Anderson had the guns spiked at Fort Moultrie in Charleston harbor before moving his troops into the more protected Fort Sumter.

spill skull A nickname for homemade whiskey that was strong and vile.

spinning bee A gathering of women to make yarn for soldiers' clothes. In the South, spinning wheels, cards, and cotton would be loaded in a wagon and proceed to a designated home, often under a banner of loose cotton waving from a long twig. Up to eight spinning wheels might be whirring together during one meeting, which was often called together by members of a SEWING SOCIETY.

spirit photograph A double-exposure photograph taken by disreputable "spiritualist photographers" to picture a customer next to a ghost. The client is photographed alone but a second shadowy person often appeared at their side when the film was developed. If a "spirit" made such an appearance, the photographer charged an extra $5. Spirit photographs became popular during the wartime vogue for SPIRITUALISM.

spiritualism The desire to contact the dead was intense during the war, and bereaved family members became gull-ible customers of charlatans. Even Mary Todd Lincoln, the president's wife, held a few seances in 1862 in the White House after their son WILLIE died and later ones to ask the spirits if her husband would be renominated. For his part, Lincoln said the contradictory voices of the spirits at the sessions reminded him of his cabinet meetings.

splendiferous A humorous corruption of "splendid." A soldier might say, "General Grant had bought himself another splendiferous horse."

spondulicks or spons A made-up slang word for money. It may have come from *Spondylus*, a species of mussel, drawing a connection with primitive shell money. It was also variously spelled spondulics, spondulix, spondoolicks, spondoolics, and spondoolixs.

sponge A sponge used to put out embers in a cannon barrel between rounds. This kept the next CARTRIDGE from firing prematurely. Gunner Number 1, informally called the "sponger," soaked the sponge in the sponge bucket hanging from the gun's STOCK TRAIL. After his cannon fired, he quckly rammed the sponge into the barrel before Gunner Number 2 inserted the next cartridge.

spooney A slang name for an ignorant or silly person; e.g., "The war would end tomorrow if the government wasn't full of spooneys."

spoon-fashion A sleeping position of men sharing a tent with limited space. They faced the same way in the manner of spoons close together. In permanent log cabins in winter quarters, bunks were made of several plank decks, and each accommodated two men also sleeping spoon-fashion. In the larger SIBLEY TENTS, up to 22 men slept spoon-fashion. If one wanted to turn over, he would call "Spoon!" and the whole line would roll over into a reverse position.

"Spoons" The nickname given to Union Major General Benjamin F. Butler, commander of troops occupying New Orleans during the war, after stories circulated that he and his soldiers were stealing silver and other items from the homes of wealthy residents. *See also* "Beast"; Butlerize.

sportsman A euphemism for a gambler.

spot To mark your own officer for death. Some soldiers openly "spotted" their commanding officer to be killed at the first opportunity during a battle. Confederate Brigadier General Charles Winder, a tough discliplinarian, was spotted by a group of his men in August 1862 but a Union shell killed him first. Union General Thomas Williams was the target of his own soldiers of the 6th New Hampshire, but their repeated shots during battles all missed him.

"Spot Lincoln" A mocking nickname for Abraham Lincoln early in his political career. While serving as a U.S. congressman (1847-49) from the Whig Party, he had questioned Democratic President James K. Polk's assurance that Mexico had shed the first blood on American soil, thereby initiating the Mexican War. Lincoln introduced "spot resolutions" demanding to know exactly the spot that this occurred. He also voted to condemn the war and President Polk.

Spotswood Hotel A hotel in Richmond, Virginia. Its bar was a special gathering place for Confederate soldiers.

spotted fever A common name for typhus.

spread A slang name for a newspaper; e.g., "Have you finished reading that lying spread."

spread down To settle down for the evening, usually while on the march. A tent was pitched or a makeshift bed prepared in the open, and any required items, such as cooking utensils, were spread out. One Confederate wrote that he "spread down" for the night under the pole of a wagon.

Springfield rifle One of the most valued guns of the war. Soldiers liked the comfort of its smooth stock, which was shaped to the curve of the shoulder. The first important Springfield used in the conflict was the .58 caliber muzzle-loading Model 1855 rifle musket. It fired the MINIÉ BALL, used MAYNARD TAPE PRIMING, and came equipped with a bayonet. This gave way to the improved Springfield Model 1861 U.S. Percussion Rifle Musket, with about 700,000 produced. The Springfield Armory in Massachusetts then introduced simplifications to speed production of its Model 1863 Rifle Musket, making 270,000 before switching to an even more simple "Type 2" of which 255,000 were turned out. The Confederacy's Richmond Armory also made the 1855 version of the gun with machinery captured in 1861 at the Union's armory at Harpers Ferry, Virginia, and Rebel soldiers often picked the enemy's weapons off the battlefield.

sprung wagon A wagon riding on springs. Sprung light wagons were used by the Union army as ambulances to provide a more comfortable ride, but the Confederate wounded usually made a rough journey in regular wagons.

squadron A cavalry unit on both sides, consisting of two COMPANIES. Two squadrons together made up a BATTALION.

squeal To inform on someone or to PEACH. The word, still used, was introduced two years before the war and popularized during it.

squiffed or squiffy A slang word for being slightly drunk. "Squiffy" is still used in Great Britain. See DRUNK for numerous other terms referring to intoxication.

stack The common name during the war for a ship's smokestack, now called a funnel. The cylindrical stack drew the smoke from the furnace, creating a draw.

stag dance A special dance in camp when soldiers danced together as partners, often to polkas, reels, or square dances. It was also called a "gander dance" and "bull dance." The event was not considered unmanly, but rather an opportunity to have fun and practice an important social skill.

Stainless Banner The nickname for the Confederate National Flag, Second Pattern, officially adopted to replace the STARS AND BARS. This adoption happened on May 1, 1863, under Senate Bill No. 132. The flag was white with a smaller version of the famous SOUTHERN CROSS battle flag in the upper inside corner (where the stars are located on the U.S. flag). Its first official use was to drape the coffin of Lieutenant General "STONEWALL" Jackson. Southerners criticized the Stainless Banner for resembling a white truce flag, so on March 4, 1865 (about a month before the war ended), the Confederate National Flag, Third Pattern, was officially adopted. It had a wide red stripe added from top to bottom on the outside edge.

stake torpedo An defensive underwater mine ("torpedo") positioned in a river or bay. It was usually a canister of gunpower attached to a stake that was anchored to the bottom by a chain and weight. The stake was pointed in the direction of the enemy by using a longer chain and weight at its top. A ship would set off the explosion by touching firing devices on the top of the canister. The stake torpedo was a type of MOORED TORPEDO.

standard The name for a flag when carried by the cavalry. *See also* color.

standard gray A uniform color worn by many Union troops early in the war. Gray was worn by some regiments in such northern states as Maine, Vermont, New York, Indiana, Nebraska, and Kansas. This use of gray caused immense confusion on the battlefield before blue uniforms became standard for the U.S. Army. *See also* the Blue; "Old Graybacks."

standee A person forced to stand in a crowded church, theater, or other public place.

stand in one's own light To be the cause of one's own problems or lack of success; e.g., "General McClellan was always standing in his own light by hesitating to attack the enemy."

stand the gaff To stand up to the fear or pressure of battle. Many soldiers worried more about disgracing themselves as cowards than about the bullets that could kill them. "I may run," wrote one Confederate soldier to his family, "but if I do, I wish that some of our own men would shoot me down."

Starry flag A northern nickname for the Stars and Stripes.

Stars and Bars Nickname for the first Confederate flag, officially called the First National. It had the same format as the U.S. flag, but with only three wide stripes (top and bottom red ones, a central white one) and 11 stars, one in the center circled by 10. Prussian-born Nicola Marshall designed it, originally with a circle of seven stars for those first states that had seceded. The flag was approved on March 4, 1861, and first flew over the Alabama capitol in Montgomery. Because of its similarity to the Stars and Stripes, which caused Confederate troops to fire on it by mistake, the Stars and Bars was replaced unofficially by the SOUTHERN CROSS and then officially on May 1, 1863, by the STAINLESS BANNER.

Starvation Alley A popular name in winter camps for one of the main thoroughfares.

starvation party Social gatherings held by southerners in the hard times near the end of the war. Despite the name, elegant suppers were sometimes served. The atmosphere was one of frivolous doom (beans sold for $60 a bushel), but the social seasons continued in cities like Richmond, New Orleans, Charleston, and Mobile. One lady descibed the parties as events "where young persons meet for innocent enjoyment, and retire at a reasonable hour." On Christmas Day, 1864, with advancing Union troops within an hour of Richmond, President Jefferson Davis' neighbor held a starvation party attended by Confederate officers from nearby camps who "defiantly made merry." During Reconstruction, however, "starvation parties" were often held as social events without refreshments.

State Rangers An organization of Virginia MILITIA formed on March 27, 1861. Its several companies of 75 men each were sent to the western part of the state to operate behind Union lines, but the State Rangers became part of the Confederate army on February 28, 1863.

states' rights The doctrine that convinced southern states they could continue with the institution of slavery. It was sometimes called "states' sovereignty" by Confederate Vice President Alexander H. Stephens and others. The Articles of Confederation ratified in 1781 had given each state "sovereignty, freedom and independence." This grant was reduced by the 10th Amendment to the U.S. Constitution, which says: "The powers not delegated to the United States by the Constitution, nor prohibited by it to the States, are reserved to the States respectively, or to the people." Southern states interpreted this in a liberal fashion, with South Carolina even claiming the right of NULLIFICATION of federal laws that conflicted with its own state laws. The South's interpretation of states' rights was then used to support the theory that a state had the right to voluntarily leave the union that it had voluntarily joined. An early southern name for the Civil War was the War for States' Rights. During the war, however, states' rights conflicted with a strong Confederate government and military organization, especially in the matter of conscription.

states' sovereignty See states' rights.

stations See Underground Railroad.

steam ironclad floating battery The name used by the Union navy when it was seeking designs and bids for its first IRONCLAD warship. John Ericsson met the specifications with his design for the *Monitor*. See Ericsson's folly.

steel-pen coat See clawhammer coat.

stereoscope A device for viewing stereographs, a pair of photographs, so that a three-dimensional image is created. The photographs, "stereoscopicdaguerreotypes" or "card stereographs," were of the same scene or person shot at slightly different angles, and the stereoscope's two eyepieces fused them together. The instrument, which was more common in the North, had been introduced in London at the Great Exhibition of 1851.

stewart A white man assigned to run two or more southern plantations for an absentee owner. The stewart would generally depend on a black DRIVER for the day-to-day running of each plantation. This system was especially used on large plantations in Georgia and South Carolina.

stiff This common slang name for a corpse was coined in the U.S. and first used about two years before the war.

"That's a stiff 'un" was a usual observation of soldiers.

still-house A common name for a distillery. This term and "still" can be traced back to the sixteenth century in England, but Americans settled on the latter term before the twentieth century.

Still Waters Run Deep A play performed in Washington, D.C., on March 17, 1865. John Wilkes Booth orginally planned to kidnap President Abraham Lincoln as he traveled to the matinee performance in his BAROUCHE. The president and his cabinet had been invited to see Tom Taylor's popular comedy at Campbell Hospital on North Seventh Street. Booth and his conspirators laid in wait, but Lincoln was unable to attend.

stock trail The long wooden piece that was the base of a cannon, often just called the trail. It rested on the ground when the gun was in battle position and was attached to the LIMBER to transport the cannon (by connecting the stock trail's LUNETTE to the limber's PINTLE). At the upper part of the stock trail were the CHEEKS that sat on the axle and held up the cannon.

stomach-jumped Frightened to the point of having an upset stomach. It was an apt description of a soldier awaiting an enemy attack.

stone-bruise A bruise or often serious injury caused by rocks and pebbles during a march. Confederate soldiers especially suffered toward the end of the war when they were reduced to wearing thin-soled boots and shoes or no footwear at all.

stone fence An iced southern drink made of bourbon and sweet cider.

Stonewall The name of the canine mascot of the Richmond Howitzer Battalion. He was taught to join roll call and sit up at attention in the line with a tiny pipe between his teeth. Stonewall proved brave under fire and was transported around the battlefield in an artillery LIMBER chest.

"Stonewall" The nickname of Confederate Lieutenant General Thomas J. Jackson. It came from the description given of him by Brigadier General Bernard E. Bee to his men at the first battle of Bull Run in July 1861: "There is Jackson standing like a stone wall. Rally behind the Virginians!" Some Confederates claimed at the time that Bee was angry because Jackson's troops were not advancing, and "stone wall" was intended as a criticism. Jackson was known for his brilliant maneuvers, defeating three Union armies in three months during his Shenandoah Valley campaign in 1862. His men were fiercely loyal and greatly enjoyed Jackson's many eccentricites, which led others to question his mental stability, such as his habit of sucking lemons, refusing to eat pepper because it made his left leg ache, always sitting bolt upright to keep his internal organs in correct alignment, wearing his Mexican War cap into battle, and laughing soundlessly with his mouth open. In the midst of incoming artillery fire, he could be seen astride his horse, pouring molasses from a canteen onto his meal of a cracker. Jackson was fanatically religious, praying constantly. After the first victory at Bull Run, he sent his pastor an envelope containing a donation to the church's "colored Sunday School." He was killed, along with two of his aides, when two of his own PICKETS mistook them for the enemy in the dark at the Battle of Chancellorsville in May 1863. When General Lee heard that Jackson's arm had been amputated, he said sadly, "He has lost his left arm, but I have lost my right." Jackson died eight days after being shot.

Stonewall Brigade The 1st Virginia Brigade of five regiments from the Shenandoah Valley, organized, trained, and led by Confederate Colonel, later Lieutenant General, Thomas J. Jackson. It was the only brigade with a nickname officially approved by the Confederate Congress (on May 30, 1863). They assumed his nickname of "STONEWALL," but there was initial confusion about whether Jackson or his soldiers had resembled a stone wall at the first battle of Bull Run in 1861. Three days after it, the Confederate diarist Mary Chesnut wrote about "Jackson, whose regiment stood so stock still under fire that they were called 'a stone wall.'" Later in the war, Jackson was heard to call during a furious battle, "Where's my Stonewall Brigade? Forward, men, forward!" Jackson led the regiment until his death in 1863, after his men accidentally shot him on May 2, during battle of Chancellorsville. The brigade, still called "Jackson's Own Brigade," then fought at Gettysburg, the Wilderness, and Spotsylvania, having six more commanders, three of whom were killed. Other units during the war, such as the 20th Mississippi Regiment, were described during various battles as "standing like a stone wall," but none assumed the nickname.

"Stonewall Jackson of the West" The somewhat overstated nickname for Confederate Major General Patrick R. Cleburne, who was born in Ireland. He earned such respect for his strong leadership, demonstrated at the battles of Shiloh, Stones River, Chickamauga, and Atlanta. Cleburne was one of the five generals of General John B. Hood to be killed at Franklin, Tennessee, on November 30, 1864.

"Stonewall Jackson's Way" A Confederate poem by John Williamson Palmer that was published in 1862. In part it went as follows:

He's in the saddle now. Fall in!
Steady! the whole brigade!
Hill's at the ford, cut off—we'll win
His way out, ball and blade!
What matter if our shoes are worn?
What matter if our feet are torn?
"Quick-step! we're with him before dawn!"
That's "Stonewall Jackson's way."

Stonewall's foot cavalry *See* Jackson's foot cavalry.

stool pigeon A person used as a decoy. This term derived from the practice of hunters sometimes tying a pigeon or other bird to a "stool" (a piece of wood) and moving it up and down to lure in wild birds. The underworld meaning of an informer was not generally used until the twentieth century.

store-bought bread Soft white bread made of bleached flour. It became a new popular item during the war and was sometimes called bakery bread.

storm A slang term for a dance, especially a large, festive one.

"Stovepipe" The nickname of Confederate Brigadier General Adam R. Johnson, because on July 18, 1862, he forced a Union garrison to surrender at Newburgh, Indiana, by attacking with 12 Kentucky partisans and "artillery" made of pieces of stovepipe and old wagon parts.

straggler A soldier who dropped behind his unit. "Stragglers," said General Robert E. Lee, "are usually those who desert their comrades in peril." If this happened heading into a battle, it usually indicated cowardice but could be caused by such problems as illness, exhaustion, hunger, or lack of shoes. Being late for a battle was considered close to desertion, since a large number of stragglers could cause a defeat. After the battle of Antietam in 1862, Confederate Major General Daniel H. Hill complained about the "enormous straggling," and added, "Had all our stragglers been up, McClellan's army would have been completely crushed or annihilated." For his part, Major General George McClellan had handbills distributed to his troops on September 10, 1862, a week before the battle of Antietam, that threatened, "Should an able-bodied man leave ranks without orders and become a straggler, he will be tried by a drumhead court martial and shot." *See also* straggler's camp.

straggler's camp A guarded camp that housed STRAGGLERS and deserters under arrest. Mary Livermore, from the Chicago branch of the SANITARY COMMISSION, recorded at the end of 1862 that the Union's straggler's camp in Alexandria, Virginia, had within a period of three months returned 75,000 stragglers and deserters to their units.

streaky or streaked An informal adjective describing someone who was confused or alarmed; e.g., "I wasn't frightened in my first battle, but afterwards I felt a little streaky."

street-car or horse-car A long OMNIBUS that ran on rails and was pulled by one or more horses. The system was called a street railway. This mode of transportation was found in large cities, such as New York, Boston, Philadelphia, Baltimore, Cincinnati, and St. Louis, with a street railway built during the war in Washington, D.C. (although blacks were banned from it until a special car was built for them). The fare on New York street-cars during the war was 5 cents and the capacity was 40 passengers, with a driver and conductor.

stretcher An informal name for a blantant lie; e.g., "Jack could gamble as well as he could tell a stretcher."

strop A thick leather strip used to sharpen a razor. They were common items in soldiers' KNAPSACKS.

studying The name the Union's black troops gave to their quiet contemplation of serious news, such as an upcoming battle. The studying phenomenon was noted by Major General Henry G. Thomas, who contrasted the excitement and criticisms of white soldiers after receiving such orders, with the long silence that pervaded groups of blacks who sat together and waited "like the Quakers, for the spirit to move."

stuff and nonsense A popular expression (still heard) for ideas, opinions, or information considered to be wrong or foolish, as in "just a lot of stuff and nonsense." It was also used as an exclamation: "Oh, stuff and nonsense!"

stuffening A western version of "stuffing" used with turkey and other meats.

stump To challenge someone to do something difficult; e.g., "He stumped us to enlist in the regular army."

sub As used today, this was a common word for someone who replaces a person in a job or activity. During the war, it referred to substitutes paid to take the place of a person who was conscripted.

subaltern A commissioned army officer below a captain, which would be a first lieutenant or a second lieutenant.

submissionist A name, usually derogatory in the South, of a southerner who was willing to submit to defeat to achieve peace.

Subsistence Department The U.S. department that supplied food to military units. It was headed by the commissary general of subsistence, who was a brigadier general. A commissary officer, with the rank of lieutenant, and a regimental commissary sergeant were assigned to each regiment.

sucker 1. This well-known slang name for a person who is easily tricked or cheated, was commonly used during the war. 2. A slang name for a drunk. 3. A country bumpkin or greenhorn, used in the West. 4. A native of Illinois, supposedly because pioneers crossing the plains used to suck water with reeds from holes made by crawfish.

sugar cracker A simple, improvised sweet consisting of sugar sprinkled over a cracker. It was an easily made treat to please children. When Betty Maury was escaping south through Union lines as the war began, she was horrified when her young daughter began to sing "Dixie." She solved this by giving her a sugar cracker when they encountered a sentinel. Her daughter soon figured out the game and would call, "Mama here is another soldier. Give me a sugar tacker."

sulky A light two-wheeled carriage pulled by one horse. It had only room for the driver, and the name derived from the idea of the lone individual sulking. Sulkies are still seen today in harness racing.

summerset Another form of "somersault" that was common during the war.

sun fuel A popular name for kerosene, then a fuel newly created from petroleum. In 1861, the U.S. put a tax on alcohol-based camphene lamp fuel, and this greatly increased the demand for kerosene.

Sunday battle Superstition said a battle on the Sabbath should be avoided. A folk saying on both sides warned that anybody who started a battle on that day would not win it. A Union attack began the first battle of Bull Run on a Sunday (July 21, 1861) in which the North was routed, and a Confederate attack began the battle of Shiloh on a Sunday (April 6, 1862), and the South suffered a major defeat.

Sunday soldier An insulting name for a soldier considered to be a poor or reluctant fighter, because Sunday was the civilian day of rest.

supporting distance A distance that would allow one military unit to come in time to support another one, as is done in a CONCENTRATED FORCE.

supports A common word for "supporting troops." Soldiers often complained, "Why don't they send us supports?"

sure as a gun An informal expression to emphasize that something was absolutely certain; e.g., "He talked himself into a court-martial, sure as a gun."

sure thing As used today, this term described something that was a certainty.

surgeon A general name for any military doctor or medical officer, with one who performed operations officially called an "operating surgeon." Union surgeons wore green sashes around their waists. The broader sense of the word is still used in Great Britain, where a "surgery" is the office of a general practitioner. *See also* contract surgeon.

surgeon's call or sick call The daily gathering of ill or slightly wounded men to see a doctor and receive medication. Such soldiers were not serious enough to stay in a hospital. Union nurse James Kendall Hosmer described the routine at his military hospital in 1863: "Every morning, just at light, 'surgeon's call' is beaten; and from each company a sergeant marches off at the head of a long line of sick men to be prescribed for."

surgical fever A general name for gangrene or deadly pyemia (blood poisoning).

sutler A civilian merchant allowed to sell his wares at permanent military camps.

Sutlers had to be officially licensed as vendors by the army. They sold such items as tobacco, sugar, candy, razors, knives, books, and newspapers. They tended to bring out their best cakes and other DAINTIES around payday. Molasses cookies, selling at six for 25 cents, were the most popular item sold by Union sutlers. Lacking competition, many sutlers became rich by selling shoddy products at inflated prices (which was officially illegal), and this practice often provoked soldiers to raid sutlers' supplies to even the score. Sutlers in the field also served to take messages to miliary bases. *See also* "Rally on the sutler!"

sutler's pie A small pie that was an uninviting but still popular snack item for Union soldiers. The pies sold for 25 cents, and the ingredients within the thin crust were usually a mystery. One soldier described them as "moist and indigestible below, tough and indestructible above, with untold horrors within."

"Swallowed a bass drum?" A common insult for a fat person.

"Swamp Angel" The nickname of the rifled eight-inch, 200-pound PARROTT gun used by Union forces of General Quincy A. Gillmore to bombard the city of Charleston, South Carolina, with incendiary projectiles on August 21, 1863. It was mounted behind a sandbag parapet in marshes southeast of the city. Gillmore had threatened the action if the defending forts of Sumter and Wagner did not surrender. On the first night, 16 shells filled with GREEK FIRE were hurled at the city. Southerners were outraged at fire aimed at civilians, but the Swamp Angel was fairly inaccurate and went out of action on August 23 when it cracked while firing its 36th round.

A sutler's tent at Union Army of Potomac headquarters near Bealeton, Virginia, in August 1863. *Library of Congress, Prints & Photographs Division, LC-B8171-7216.*

swamp fever A name sometimes used in camp for typhoid fever.

Swampoodle An Irish colony in Washington, D.C., in a sordid district located on marshy land near North Capitol Street.

swanga buckra A name used by slaves to describe an elegant or dandy white man. "Swanga" was originally a name meaning any "elegant" thing in an African language, but was almost always used with BUCKRA by blacks in the South.

"The Sweet Little Man" A 15-verse poem by Oliver Wendell Holmes that railed against northern men who avoided the war. It was dedicated to "the Stay-at-Home Rangers." One verse went as follows:

> "Bring him the buttonless garment of a
>   woman!
> Cover his face lest it freckle and tan;
> Muster the Apron-string Guards on the
>   Common,
> That is the corps for the sweet little man."

sweet oil A descriptive name commonly used for olive oil.

Sweet Water Branch The ironically named polluted stream that ran through the South's infamous ANDERSONVILLE prison. Usually stagnant, it was a sewer, bathing place, and source of drinking water, assuring the spread of disease.

swell A slang name for a fashionable and often rich and sophisticated person from the city; e.g., "About a dozen of us from Company C walked into town, had a few drinks and got into a fight with a bunch of swells."

swellhead As used today, the name referred to a conceited person.

"Swine Hotel" A popular name given by soldiers to their camp accommodation, usually a more permanent cabin in winter quarters.

switchel A drink of molasses and water and sometimes with rum, vinegar, or ginger added. It was especially popular in New England.

the Sword Test A contest to select the Union's most popular general, held at the Manhattan Fair of the SANITARY COMMISSION on April 14, 1864. Each vote cost $1, and a sword would be presented to the winner. The polls were to close at midnight, and Major General George B. McClellan was far ahead until five minutes before closing, when the Union League of Philadelphia telegraphed 500 votes for General Ulysses S. Grant, who won. The result was disputed by Democrats in the crowd—McClellan was the party's presidental candidate that year—and, as one observer noted, "only the general refinement and restraint of the surging, self-respecting crowd prevented an outbreak."

Sykes' yellow dog A fictional dog used by President Abraham Lincoln in one of his humorous, instructional stories. It involved a gang of boys feeding Sykes' dog an explosive wrapped in meat that blew the animal to pieces. The owner ran out in great distress, held up the largest piece he could find, with part of the tail attached, and said sadly, "Well, I guess he'll never be much account again—as a dog." When a Washington delegation visited Lincoln to complain about General Ulysses S. Grant allowing Vicksburg's Confederate defenders under Lieutenant General John C. Pemberton to leave the city freely on PAROLE, the president asked, "Have you ever heard about Sykes' yellow dog?" After telling the story, he added: "I guess Pemberton's forces will never be much account again—as an army."

syllabub or sillabub A drink of wine or cider mixed with milk, then sweetened, flavored, and whipped into a froth. A solid dessert version was made by adding gelatine and water and boiling. As the nation began to split apart in 1860, U.S. Senator Wigfall from Texas called on his fellow congressmen to act, complaining, "You cannot save this Union by making 4th of July speeches. Whipped syllabub is not the remedy for the patient."

System of Infantry Tactics The standard military instruction manual for the Union army after its official adoption in 1862. The three-volume manual, written by 55-year-old Union General Silas Casey the previous year, was also used by some Confederate units. It was notable for replacing traditional French and German military terms with simple and clear ones in everyday English. Casey then published *Infantry Tactics for Colored Troops* in 1863.

T

T The letter branded on soldiers guilty of theft, usually on their foreheads, cheeks, or hands. Indelible ink was commonly used, but major thefts could call for hot irons. *See also* C; D; W.

tableau vivant A popular entertainment in which a scene, often a historical event or a famous painting, is represented by real people wearing costumes and frozen in silent poses. It was a popular diversion for society women.

tactical articulation Immediately before a battle, the quick and accurate movement of troops into their correct positions in a battleline. Officers had to learn and use a series of commands to make this operation go as smoothly as possible.

Tad President Lincoln's nickname for his favorite son, Thomas, because Lincoln thought he looked like a tadpole when he was born. He was the youngest of the Lincolns' four sons, born on April 4, 1853. He was named Thomas for Lincoln's father. The boy, who had a cleft palate and lisp, did not learn to read until the age of nine. In 1864, the president took him on a visit to General Ulysses S. Grant and his army at City Point, Virginia. Lincoln often worried about Tad and once tele-

graphed his wife, when she and his son were visiting Philadelphia in 1863, to ask her to put Tad's pistol away because "I had an ugly dream about him." Several days after Lincoln's assassination, Tad told a servant: "I am not a president's son now. I won't have many presents anymore." Tad died in 1871, probably of tuberculosis.

tailor fashion *See* Turk-fashion.

take an image To have your photograph taken; e.g., "Do take an image before leaving for the regiment."

take a shine to The slang expression, still used today, means to take a liking to or to begin to like someone or something.

take off A euphemism for dying. One Confederate wrote that the battle-worn soldier "becomes utterly fearless and holds his 'taking off' in indifference, if not in disdain."

take the cake An informal expression meaning to win the top prize in something, such as a poetry competition or oratory contest. The modern usage, meaning to be audacious, amazing, or unusual, did not exist during the war.

take the shine off someone To surpass someone in ability, fame, or beauty. A Rebel might say, "McClellan had more men and artillery, but Lee soon took the shine off him."

take the shortening out of a gingercake without breaking the crust An expression for stealing without anyone knowing it. Southerner farmers used it to describe Yankee foragers.

taking a twist at the tiger Taking part in a card game, especially faro or one involving gambling. *See also* bucking the tiger; tiger den.

A Tale of Two Cities This 1859 novel by Charles Dickens was one of the most popular novels during the war, as was *Great Expectations*, published as the conflict began, and *Our Mutual Friend*, which first appeared in 1864. Dickens's work was beloved by both sides, and he made a successful tour of the United States two years after the war ended.

talking-iron A humorous name for a gun, being a variant of "shooting-iron".

talking torch A method of military signaling at night, replacing flags with torches. A torch, often turpentine in a copper container, was lit and attached to the end of a pole, normally a flagstaff. The signalman sent the message by waving his "flying torch." Since a point of reference was needed to read the sweeping movements, he stood just behind a "foot torch" stuck into the ground.

talk large To talk in a boasting way or to brag.

tall An informal word, especially in the South, for "great" or "excellent." A soldier might brag about "a pretty tall victory."

talma A loose overcoat with a hood, the soldiers' version often made of rubber.

The name was also used for a woman's loose hooded cloak.

tampion A plug inserted in the muzzle of a cannon not being used. This was done primarily to protect the gun from dampness that caused rust.

tangle-foot or tangle-leg Union names for alcohol, especially cheap whiskey, because it produced an unsteady walk. A tangle-foot or tangle-leg person was drunk. The expressions were mostly used by western troops.

taper A small candle. A small light from such a candle or other device was called a taper light.

"Taps" The mournful bugle or trumpet call used by the Union armies for funerals and in their camps to "EXTINGUISH LIGHTS." It was a revision of the "TATTOO" and was created in 1862 by Brigadier General Daniel Butterfield in camp at Harrison's Landing, Virginia, on the James River. One night, he brought a bugler into his tent to help make the old call more "smooth, melodious and musical." Butterfield changed the first note, slowed the tempo and altered the rhythm, creating the sad, haunting "Taps" now associated with a military funeral.

tarantula juice A facetious nickname devised by Union troops in 1861 for illegal whiskey because its bite was dangerous.

"Tardy George" A satirical poem written in the North by George H. Boker concerning the delays and slow troop movements of Union General George McClellan. One of the seven verses went as follows:

Now that you've marshaled your whole command,
Planned what you would, and changed what you planned;
Practiced with shot and practiced with shell,

Know to a hair where every one fell,
Made signs by day and signals by night;
Was it all done to keep out of a fight?
Is the whole matter too heavy a charge?
What are you waiting for, tardy George?

tarletan or tarlatan A gauze-like muslin cloth popular during the war for ladies' ball gowns. It was thin but stiff. White tarletan was in fashion during President Abraham Lincoln's second inaugural ball in 1865.

tartar emetic Antimony potassium tartrate, used as a medical drug to cause patients to vomit, expectorate, or perspire. It was called a "double salt." U.S. Surgeon General William A. Hammond banned it and CALOMEL because army doctors overused them, but the doctors resisted and he was in effect replaced.

tar water A witty name for strong liquor.

tatterdemalion A ruffian or ragged fellow, often said of boys. "I forgot that I had called the little tatterdemalion a 'nuisance' every day for months," wrote Mary Ashton Livermore, a SANITARY COMMISSION worker, after a poor lad who sold matches on the street donated 50 cents of his meager earnings to help Union soldiers in 1863.

"Tattoo" The bugle or trumpet call to "EXTINGUISH LIGHTS." A drum was sometimes used. The Tattoo had long been played in the OLD ARMY before the Civil War and had been used at military funerals during the Mexican War. The name "tattoo" came from the Dutch word meaning "the taproom (bar) is now closing." *See also* "Taps."

T.E. The initials for the Corps of Topographical Engineers of the Union army. The initials in Old English letters were worn on the members' epaulettes under a gold-embroidered oak leaf wreath. *See also* topographical engineer.

Teacher's Regiment The nickname of the 33rd Illinois Regiment, because it had many college teachers in its ranks. Other regiments joked that its officers would not obey an order unless it was framed in perfect English and correctly spelled.

"teakettle" A sailor's nickname for an IRONCLAD warship. This term alluded to both the metal and the heat it generated. "Hot, hotter, hottest," wrote a *Monitor* crew member from James River in Virginia. In the South, the summer temperature inside an ironclad could rise above 120 degrees, and outside decks were watered down for sailors to sleep on overnight.

teamster A person who drove a team of horses or mules. The name came to mean a truck driver in the twentieth century and remains in the union name, the International Brotherhood of Teamsters.

tea party The British formal tea party was still an important social event during the war. The best families on both sides had an impressive "tete-a-tete" tea service displayed on a special tea table.

"Tecumseh the Great" The title given by northern newspapers to Union Major General William Tecumseh Sherman after his march through Georgia from Atlanta to Savannah in November and December 1864.

Ted The nickname given by his family to Confederate General Edmund Kirby Smith. *See also* Kirby Smith-dom. *[See photo on the following page.]*

teeth dullers or tooth dullers Humorous names for HARDTACK crackers.

telegraphic account A news story quickly sent by a reporter to his newpaper by telegraph. The danger of wires breaking and interrupting transmissions from the battlefield led reporters to invent the "inverted pyramid" style giving the most

Confederate General Edmund Kirby Smith was nicknamed "Ted" by his family. *Library of Congress, Prints & Photographs Division, LC-B8172-2013.*

important facts first (who, what, when, and where), the form still used. *See also* telegraphic message or telegraphic dispatch.

telegraphic message or telegraphic dispatch Terms coined about 1852 and commonly used during the war for a telegram. *See also* telegraphic accounts.

telephone A megaphone or speaking tube used to increase the volume of the voice. Alexander Graham Bell later adopted the name for his "Electric Speaking Telephone" introduced in 1876. *See also* trumpet.

"Tell that to the Marines" An expression meaning a fact is unbelievable and ridiculous. Sometimes "Tell it to the Marines"

was used. When southerners found handcuffs left by Union soldiers after their retreat from the first battle of Bull Run in 1861, the Confederate diarist Mary Chesnut asked: "For whom were they? Jeff Davis, no doubt, and the ring-leaders. 'Tell that to the marines.'" The phrase apparently originated from English sailors' contempt for the marines' ignorance of seamanship. The older, fuller English saying is "Tell that to the marines—the sailors won't believe it."

tell tuther from which Tell one from another. This phrase was an especially southern expression. Confederate veteran Sam Watkins recalled his First Tennessee Regiment unpacking to make camp in Staunton, Virginia, when they "found everything so tangled up and mixed that we could not tell tuther from which."

ten-forty bonds U.S. government bonds issued in 1864 to raise $75 million that would help cover war expenses. The bonds had a 6-percent interest rate and a maturation date of from 10 to 40 years.

Tennessee quick step or Tennessee two-step A dancing nickname for diarrhea. It was sometimes called the "Tennessee trots" and the "Virginia quick step."

Tennessee Tories The nickname given in the South to people from Tennessee who joined the Union army or were loyal to the United States.

Ten Percent Plan President Abraham Lincoln's proposal in 1864 that a Confederate state would be allowed to reenter the Union after the war if 10 percent of its 1860 voters affirmed their loyalty to the United States. *See also* Proclamation of Amnesty and Reconstruction.

ten-pins This bowling game took many forms in camps, including the novel substitute of rolling cannon balls at holes in the ground. *See also* skittles.

"Tenting on the Old Camp Ground" One of the saddest but most popular war songs, sung by soldiers and families on both sides. Walter Kittredge, a Union soldier and native of New Hampshire, wrote it in a few minutes in 1862 while waiting to go to the front. It was at first turned down by publishers but then became immensely popular. The chorus went as follows:

Many are the hearts that are weary tonight,
Wishing for the war to cease;
Many are the hearts looking for the right,
To see the dawn of peace.
Tenting to-night, tenting to-night,
Tenting on the old camp ground.

The last chorus changed "tenting" to "dying." Kittridge was a singer and composer who also published the "Union Song-Book" of his original songs in the first year of the war.

terre-plein The platform or surface behind a rampart or parapet of a fort on which cannons were mounted. Its destruction during a bombardment would be a disaster. The French word means "filled with earth."

"terrible door of death" The nickname given by Union Major General W.T. Sherman for Rocky Face Ridge in northwest Georgia. A railroad line ran through its Buzzard Pass, and the high rocky gorge was defended by the massed guns of General Joseph Johnson's Confederate army. After more than a week, Sherman eventually made a flanking movement south through Snake Creek Gap and Johnson deserted the "terrible door."

"terrible men" The nickname for the famous raiders of Confederate Brigadier General John Hunt Morgan. They spread terror with their raids into Indiana, Ohio, and Kentucky. In July 1863, President Lincoln remarked, "They are having a stampede in Kentucky." Most of the "terrible men" were eventually killed or imprisoned. Morgan also spent four months in an Ohio jail before escaping with six of his men, digging their way out with knives and spoons. Their exploits were the subject for a song that said, in part:

I'm sent to warn the neighbors, he's only a mile behind,
He's sweeping up the horses, every horse that he can find.
Morgan, Morgan the raider, and Morgan's terrible men,
With bowie knives and pistols are galloping up the glen.

See also "Morgan's Mule."

"terrible wound" Confederate Lieutenant General "STONEWALL" Jackson's favorite name for a great defeat inflicted upon the enemy.

territorial organization The designation applied by both sides to a territorial department, territorial division, territorial district, or military post. *See also* operational organization.

tete de pont A fortification defending the approach to a bridge. Union troops protecting Washington, D.C., built Fort Runyon as a *tete de pont* on the Virginia side of the LONG BRIDGE. The French term literally means "head of bridge" or "bridgehead."

Thanksgiving Although Thanksgiving had been officially proclaimed by President George Washington on November 26, 1789, celebrations were sporadic and becoming less until the middle of the war in 1863, when President Abraham Lincoln first proclaimed Thanksgiving Day as August 6 and then decided that the celebration should be the last Thursday of November "as a day of thanksgiving and praise to our beneficent Father who dwelleth in the heavens." This celebration first took place on November 26, 1863.

"Thanksgiving Day" A well-known poem among soldiers on both sides. It was written in 1857 by Lydia Maria Child and begins as follows:

> Over the river and through the woods,
> To grandfather's house we go;
> The horse knows the way
> To carry the sleigh,
> Through the white and drifted snow.

"Thanks of Congress" Official resolutions passed by both the U.S. Congress and the Confederate Congress to recognize military bravery and, also in the Confederacy, special wartime service. Only 15 Union officers received such resolutions. The Confederate ones were of special value because congressional medals were not awarded. *See also* Roll of Honor.

the go A slang term for something that was trendy or fashionable; e.g., "She particularly liked the colonel because uniforms were now the go."

theirn A substitution for "their," especially in the dialect of poorly educated white southerners and slaves, although the word was proper English in the fourteenth century. Similar terms are OURN, YOURN, HISN, and HERN, all originating in the English Midlands and South.

"there's no ho in him" An expression meaning there is no stopping a person. "Ho" is the same as "whoa," with both words having been used by drivers to halt their horses. A soldier might observe, "The general may have a wooden head, but there's no ho in him."

thicker than fleas on a dog's back A descriptive phrase for a lot of anything. In 1862, a Union captain at Shiloh officially reported, "The Rebels are out there thicker than fleas on a dog's back!" Other versions include "thicker than lice on a hen" and "as thick as flies in August."

thin Insufficient, inadequate, or limited. When one Tennessee soldier was stopped by a captain because he lacked a pass through the lines, he explained that he was wounded and going to the hospital. "Well, sir," came the reply, "that's too thin. Why did you not get a pass?" (He had not known one was required.)

thirsty A common word used by soldiers in regard to their desire for tobacco; e.g., "I'm really thirsty for some tobacco."

"this damned old house" The term President Abraham Lincoln used for the White House after finding that his wife had overspent an appropriation of $20,000 to remodel it "when," Lincoln noted, "the soldiers cannot have blankets."

Thompson, Franklin The assumed name of Sara Emma Edmonds, a woman born in Canada who fought with the Union army for more than two years without revealing her sex. She also served as a spy, blackening her skin to pose as a Negro. Edmonds had first used the disguise to represent a Connecticut book publisher and on May 25, 1861, at the age of 20, she was mustered in as an army nurse to serve in Washington and then the field. She was said to have had many lady friends. After the war, she published her memoirs, *Nurse and Spy or Unsexed, the The Female Soldier*, which sold 175,000 copies.

"those people" Confederate General Robert E. Lee's usual term for the Union forces. He seldom called them "the enemy."

"three days' cooked rations and 40 rounds" The Union army order that, as every soldier knew, indicated an upcoming battle was expected.

three-hundred-dollar clause The popular name for the stipulation in the Union's

Enrollment Act (draft law) that conscripted men would be exempt from service if they paid $300 to the government.
One who did was the future president
Grover Cleveland. This exemption fueled
the charge of "RICH MAN'S WAR, POOR MAN'S
FIGHT."

three-months man The popular name for
a member of the Union's first volunteers
in 1861. President Abraham Lincoln
asked the governors of the U.S. states and
territories to furnish 75,000 volunteers to
serve 90 days. They would be used especially to defend Washington, D.C. More
men volunteered than were needed. After their enlistments were up, many
three-months "veterans" returned home
to organize regular units for the war, for
Lincoln was now asking for three-year
volunteers.

throw down the gage A figurative expression meaning someone has thrown down
a challenge (that should be answered), the
same idea as "throw down the gauntlet."
A gage is a pledge. After President
Abraham Lincoln ordered Fort Sumter
resupplied on March 29, 1861, the
Charleston Mercury editorialized, "The
gage is thrown down and we accept the
challenge."

thug The name for a rough type of character in New Orleans during the war (before the word came into general use).
*Harper's Pictorial History of the Great
Rebellion in the United States* (1866) explained that during Union Major General
Benjamin F. Butler's capture of New Orleans in May 1862, "The scoundrels of the
city, known by the Hindoo name of
'Thugs,' were those who thronged the
streets, and with whom the Union commander had first to do."

thumbstall A leather device used by Gunner Number 1 in the artillery to protect
his thumb, which he held over the

cannon's vent when he loaded the gun
and when he sponged down embers in the
barrel after firing.

"The Thunderer" The nickname, originating in Great Britain, for *The Times* of
London. The paper covered the war with
such famous correspondents as William
Howard Russell and Charles Mackay. Its
thundering voice was considered to be
powerful enough to sway British opinions
about the war and Parliament's decision
on whether it would recognize the Confederacy (which it did not despite *The
Times'* bias toward the Confederacy).
When Russell met Abraham Lincoln in
1861, the president told him, "*The London Times* is one of the greatest powers
in the world. In fact, I don't know anything which has much more power, except perhaps the Mississippi."

thundering A word used to emphasize
almost anything. A soldier might observe,
"You're looking thundering sick" or
compliment "a thundering good breakfast." He also would "fight like thunder,"
"run like thunder," and even "try like
thunder."

Thunder! or Good thunder! A common
exclamation of surprise or anger.

tick A pillow case or mattress case. They
were generally stuffed with feathers, cotton, straw, or hair.

the ticket A slang name for the ideal or
the very thing needed; e.g.,"What do I
want for Christmas? Now a furlough ...
that's the ticket." The name may have
come from the idea of a winning lottery
ticket. *See also* the checker.

tidy or tidy-cover The common name for
a loose cover to protect the back of a settee or chair (and arms of an armchair).
Also used for ornamental reasons, they
were popular gifts during the war, with

women producing a new fancywork version, often muslin or embroidery edged with lace. The more proper name was an antimacassar, indicating their original role in protecting such furniture from hair grease, since Macassar was a trade name for a hair oil.

tierce A cask that held 42 gallons, being in size between a barrel and a hogshead. It was called a tierce because it was one-third of a pipe, a cask containing 126 gallons. Confederate Private Carlton McCarthy recalled a detail sent into Cumberland, Virginia, where they "found a tierce of bacon surrounded by a ravenous crowd, fighting and quarreling."

"Tige" The nickname for Confederate Brigadier General George T. Anderson of Georgia. It was short for "Tiger" and reflected his ferocious nature. Despite being wounded at the second Battle of Bull Run in 1862 and more seriously at DEVIL'S DEN during the battle of Gettysburg in 1863, Anderson fought through the war to Appomatox Court House. After the war he became the chief of police in Atlanta, Georgia.

tiger den A gambling house, or in a military camp, a tent, that specialized in the card game FARO because the faro table was nicknamed "the tiger." *See also* bucking the tiger; taking a twist at the tiger.

"Tiger John" The nickname for Confederate Brigadier General John McCausland, a graduate of and professor at the Virginia Military Academy, who led cavalry brigades from that state and specialized in RANSOMS.

"Tiger Rifles" or "Wheat's Tigers" Nickname for the 1st Special Battalion of the Louisiana Infantry, a rowdy Confederate company from New Orleans composed of many former convicts. One officer said the battalion was "so villainous that every commander desired to be rid of it."

Led by Major ROB Wheat, it was a ferocious fighting machine from the first battle of Bull Run in 1861 until Wheat's death in 1862. The company's main motto was "Lincoln's life or a Tiger's death" and other slogans included "Tiger by Nature" and "Tiger—Try Me."

tight place A common term for the thick of a battle or its critical point. Many regiments boasted that they had proved themselves under fire and were chosen to "occupy tight places."

tile A slang nickname for any hat, especialy a PLUG one. A Union soldier recalled a drunk Irish comrade who traded his greasy cap for a nicer plug worn by a Negro simply by "lifting the darkey's tile from his head and giving it an elegant poise on his own."

"till death or distance do us part" An expansion of the usual marriage vow for slaves, since spouses were sometimes separated when one was sold.

tin A slang name for money, especially silver.

"tin can on a shingle" One of the ungracious nicknames for the Union's IRONCLAD ship, the *Monitor*.

tinclad The name for a warship whose wood was protected with a tin covering. This covering could stop only rifle and musket fire, so a tinclad assiduously avoided battle with an IRONCLAD. (Sometimes the name "tinclad" was used derisively for an ironclad.)

tintype A photographic process that was introduced about a year before the war and gradually replaced the popular AMBROTYPE. The process was cheaper than glass, a negative was not required and the metallic plate would not break. It was the most popular type of photograph for soldiers. The tintype was misnamed, since the image was fixed on a sheet of iron. It was also called a melainotype.

title A slave's word for a surname. Plantation owners used first names only for their slaves, but many slaves gave themselves surnames to help identify their family in case members were sold to other owners. Owners often did not know such "titles" existed. Robert Smalls, a former slave, explained in 1863 that titles were used among slaves, but "before their masters they do not speak of their titles at all." Many freed slaves assumed the surnames of their masters.

titty A dialect form of "sister," used by slaves.

to An incorrect substitution heard in the North for "at," "in," and "for." Someone might say, "We played cards to camp" or "I live to Boston."

toad stabber A slang name for a sword or bayonet.

tobacco bag An essential possession of nearly every soldier, who normally tied it to his buttonhole. They were especially prized not only because they held the treasured tobacco, but also because the bags were usually handmade and beautifully embroidered by their mother or sweetheart.

toe the mark To do the job; e.g., "Half the men in this company are not toeing the mark."

toilette A style of dress or a particular item of dress; e.g., "I was surprised to see President Lincoln's wife wearing such a stylish toilette."

tombola A type of raffle. They were often used on the home front to raise donations for the war effort on both sides. One large tombola in Baton Rouge, Louisiana, in 1862 raised $6,000 Confederate dollars, with community donations including "every imaginable article from a toothpick to a cow!" Each ticket won something, although Eliza Ripley complained "I cannot remember anyone who secured a prize worth the price of the ticket. I invested in twenty tickets, for which I received nineteen lead-pencils and a frolicsome old goat." The name is still used in Great Britain for raffles at fetes and fairs.

"Tom Fool" *See* "Fool Tom Jackson."

ton A fashionable tone or the current vogue or mode. A fashionable lady was referred to as a leader of the ton. In one of his social satires, Donald Mitchell (writing as IK. MARVEL) wrote about "the utmost height of society and of ton."

"Too many pigs for the tits." A favorite expression of President Abraham Lincoln, especially when referring to persistent office seekers.

toot This slang name for a drinking spree was popular during the war, coming from the Scottish slang term "tout," which also meant a bout of drinking. Soldiers might say they planned to "go tooting all night."

topical engineer Any of the Union army's engineers who were in charge of reconnaissance, surveying, and the production of military maps. Their organization was the Corps of Topographical Engineers, and the members were all staff officers, with civilians added during times of increased demand. The army's regular Corps of Engineers was responsible for the same type of work, so the topical engineers were merged into that unit on March 31, 1863.

top rail number one An expression used to describe someone or something that was top class or first class; e.g., "We built our cabin for winter quarters, and it was top rail number one."

"torpedo mules" *See* "Paddy."

Tory A southerner who was loyal to the Union. The name, of course, became derogatory in the South. In 1862, President Jefferson Davis announced that "the Toryism of East Tennessee" was greatly exaggerated. The word came from the American Revolution, when colonials loyal to Great Britain were dubbed Tories.

touching a tiger's cubs An expression meaning to do something that is guaranteed to end in disaster. Writing in 1864 about a well-protected Confederate PLANK ROAD, Union Colonel Theodore Lyman wrote that "It is touching a tiger's cubs to get on that road."

tough nut A stubborn or tough person to deal with. This well-known expression was new and popular during the war.

town ball *See* base ball.

traces The two straps or chains that connected a horse's harness to the wagon or carriage it pulled. The rattle of trace-chains was a familiar sound when an army was on the march.

track-hound A southern name for a bloodhound. They were used to find escaped Union prisoners and some plantations kept such dogs to track down runaway slaves. Union Major General W.T. Sherman's troops killed one notorious track-hound at a plantation in Georgia, much to the joy of the freed slaves there.

train-boy A boy on a passenger train who sold such items as newspapers, magazines, books, nuts, apples, and candy. Different items were dispensed, at inflated prices, during the train-boy's series of trips through the cars.

"Tramp, Tramp, Tramp, the Boys Are Marching" A Union war song written by George F. Root, who also wrote "Just Before the Battle Mother" and "THE BATTLE-CRY OF FREEDOM." The sentimental words were easily sung by Rebels as well. It began as follows:

> In the prison cell I sit,
> Thinking, mother dear, of you,
> And our bright and happy home so far away,
> And the tears they fill my eyes,
> Spite of all that I can do,
> Tho' I try to cheer my comrades and be gay.
> *Chorus:* Tramp, tramp, tramp, the boys are marching,
> Oh, cheer up, comrades, they will come,
> And beneath the starry flag we shall breathe the air again,
> Of freedom in our own beloved home.

Trans-Mississippi The region west of the Mississippi River. The Confederacy extended as far as the western border of Texas, and President Jefferson Davis often emphasized the need to protect Vicksburg, Mississippi, and Port Hudson, Louisiana, as the links to the Trans-Mississippi. The Confederacy maintained a Trans-Mississippi Department (informally known as KIRBY SMITH-DOM) that was virtually one-third of its entire area. The Union's Division of West Mississipi was also called the Trans-Mississippi Division. *See also* the further West.

traps A soldier's gear or a civilian's clothes and belongings; e.g., "After four hours of marching, we had shed most of our traps."

trash gang A group of slaves on a plantation assigned to light work, like picking up debris, planting the garden, or weeding the yard. The gang was usually made up of children and old or decrepid adults.

Traveller Confederate General Robert E. Lee's horse, a gray charger that he bought for $200 in South Carolina from its Virginia owner. Lee described Traveller as having "fine proportions, muscular figure, deep chest, short back, strong haunches, flat legs, small head, broad forehead, delicate ears, quick eye, small feet, & black mane & tail." And he once told his wife that "Traveller is my only companion. I may say my only pleasure." On May 12, 1864, Traveller inadvertently saved Lee's life during the battle of Spotsylvania by rearing wildly at an exploding shell. As Lee struggled to control him, the horse stood on his hind legs and a shot passed under his belly that would have otherwise killed horse and rider. Traveller ended the war with Lee on April 9, 1865, at Appomattox Court House. The horse was unbridled to nibble grass as the surrender was signed. When Lee emerged from the house and rejoined him, a cavalry major later recalled that "as the orderly was buckling the throat latch, the general reached up and drew the forelock out from under the brow band, parted and smoothed it and then gently patted the gray charger's forehead in an absent-minded way, as one who

loves horses, but whose thoughts are far away." In 1868, Lee obtained Traveller's pedigree from the breeder. The horse outlived Lee and marched behind his hearse in 1870. *See also* Ajax; Brown-Roan; Lucy Long; Richmond.

traverse An earthwork within a fort that is built at right angles to a wall (running from the wall toward the center of the fort) to limit the damage of exploding shells. The large traverses at Fort Fisher in North Carolina were 35 feet tall, or 12 feet higher than the parapet, and ran back 30 feet.

treble shot *See* double shot.

Tredegar Iron Works The Confederacy's largest iron works, located on the James River at Richmond, Virginia. It had been Virginia's arsenal before the war. It produced 1,100 cannons during the conflict and everything from nails, tools, and

Alexander Gardner took this photograph of Richmond's Tredegar Iron Works in April 1865. *Library of Congress, Prints & Photographs Division, LC-B8171-7542.*

machines to armor for IRONCLAD warships. This was done despite a fire that caused about $250,000 damage and also a strike. Next to the iron works was a weapons factory.

Trent Affair A naval and diplomatic incident off Cuba that nearly brought Great Britain into the war on the Confederate side. On November 7, 1861, the Union ship *San Jacinto*, commanded by Captain Charles Wilkes, fired two shots across the bow of the *Trent*, a British mail steamer, to stop it and seize two newly appointed Confederate envoys, John Slidell of Louisiana (to France) and James M. Mason of Virginia (to Great Britain). Saying Wilkes's actions violated the freedom of the sea, Great Britain sent 8,000 troops to Canada, put its fleet on alert, and demanded the release of the envoys. The *Times* of London said Wilkes had showed the characteristics of "the Yankee breed," which were "swagger and ferocity, built on a foundation of vugarity and cowardice." The New York *Times* headlined "Great Preparations for War." The two countries held desperate negotiations (which included Prince Albert). U.S. Secretary of State W.H. Seward actually thought war with Great Britain might bring the South back into the Union, but President Abraham Lincoln told him, "One war at a time." He also needed 2,300 tons of saltpeter from India, used for gunpower, that the British had embargoed. The affair cooled after Seward sent a note regreting the action and in December released the agents, who had been imprisoned in Fort Warren at Boston. They resumed their travel on New Year's Day 1862.

"Triple Sheets" The boasting term used by the New York *Herald* when it expanded during the war to 12 pages.

trooper Another name for a cavalryman and also applied to his horse.

trophy An item taken as a souvenir, often from the battlefield or the enemy's camp. Soldiers were more interested in rifles, shoes, canteens, and other useable military equipment, but such booty as flags, badges, and buttons also became trophies. Civilians were also avid collectors; after the bombardment and capture of Fort Sumter, all the shell splinters quickly disappeared.

A canteen could be scavenged as a trophy from the battlefield if this useful item was not first found by soldiers. *Copyright Inge Wright 1999.*

trou de loup A defensive work consisting of a hole shaped like a funnel or cone and having a sharpened stake pointing up from the bottom. Rows of these were dug in front of a fortification. Originally used against cavalry, they became a standard defense against the infantry. The French word means "wolf hole."

truck carriage A four-wheel wooden rolling device beneath a cannon on a warship. The cannon sat between two side CHEEKS connected to them by the gun's TRUNNIONS. The cheeks were secured to each other by cross-transoms (beams). When the cannon was fired, the truck carriage recoiled strongly and had to be rolled back into position.

truckle bed A low bed on wheels that can be stored under another bed; a trundle bed.

true as the needle to the pole An expression denoting loyalty and sincerity in a person; e.g., "I cried when a Rebel ball brought down David. He was my mess mate and as true as the needle to the pole."

true Yankee grit Real Yankee courage or fortitude, a common northern term during the war expressing belief in this inherent quality; e.g., "General Thomas showed them true Yankee grit at Chickamauga."

trumpet A megaphone-type conical tube with a wide mouth used to communicate between ships. The original full name was a "speaking-trumpet." In good conditions, the voice could be heard more than a mile away. Union Admiral David G. Farragut used a trumpet to shout orders from his flagship to other ships of his fleet during the battle of Mobile Bay on August 5, 1864. *See also* telephone.

trunnion One of the two side knobs on a cannon. They supported the gun in the middle near its center of gravity by fitting into two side CHEEKS on its wooden carriage.

trust bearer A term signifying that the person so named is loyal and can be trusted. When Mrs. Rose O'Neal Greenhow, a Confederate spy in Washington, D.C., had information on Union troop movements, a messenger was sent to her by Brigadier General P.G.T. Beauregard's command. On July 15, 1861, the messenger, named Donellan, showed her a scrap of paper with the coded message, "Trust bearer." She then handed him her message, also in code: "Order issued for McDowell to march upon Manassas tonight." When that information reached Beauregard, he was able to prepare fully for what became the first battle of Bull Run. When she was later banished to the South, President Jefferson Davis visited her with the greeting, "But for you, there would have been no battle of Bull Run." *See also* "Fort Greenhow"; "my little bird."

Truth, Sojourner The name taken by the slave Isabella Baumfree, who was freed in 1827 by New York State's emancipation law. She changed her name in 1843 because she said God told her "to travel up and down the land, showing the people their sins and being a sign unto them." Although illiterate, she spoke throughout the North advocating the freeing of slaves and rights for women. She also called for a state to be set aside in the West for blacks. During the war, she carried supplies to the Union's Negro troops and was invited to the White House by President Abraham Lincoln, who appointed her to the National Freeman's Relief Association in Washington, D.C., to counsel and resettle freed slaves. After the war, she worked for the education and employment of former slaves. In 1997, the National Aeronautics and Space Administration honored her by choosing the name Sojourner for the robotic vehicle it landed on Mars.

trying to catch a seagull with a pinch of salt An expression to describe an ineffective or hopeless effort. It was sometimes used to criticize various military tactics.

tucking-comb A woman's small comb for tucking and holding the hair in place.

tuck-out *See* blow-out.

tumble bug A more delicate name for the dung beetle. H.A. Stephens, a Confederate private from Mississippi, was bemused by a riddle posed by a woman he met in 1863 during the war: "If a Tumble Bug can roll an ounce ball up a hill perpendicular how much can he shoulder on a level?"

tumbled over Killed, especially in battle.

"Tumble up!" A cry to get up and begin working. It was an overseer's traditional call to slaves resting in the field.

turkey bumps Another name, especially in the South, for goose bumps.

turkey hunt *See* turkey shoot.

turkey on one's back If you had a turkey on your back, you were drunk. See DRUNK for numerous other terms referring to intoxication.

turkey shoot A nickname used by soldiers for an easy kill, especially in picking off individual members of the enemy. Sharpshooters often used the term. A "turkey hunt" was a search for individual enemy soldiers, such as a detail sent out to locate and bring down the sharpshooters.

Turk-fashion or tailor-fashion Cross-legged, describing a way of sitting with the ankles crossed and the knees spread. The expressions were replaced by "Indian-fashion." Describing an overcrowded transport ship, a Union sergeant reported: "This morning I took breakfast in the berth—dining-room, study, and parlor, as well. There is room enough, sitting Turk-fashion, and bending over." Henry O'Conner of the 1st Iowa Volunteer Regiment explained his letter's lack of "elegance of style" by writing "I am sitting tailor fashion with the tail-board of a wagon across my knees for a writing desk."

Turtle torpedo An underwater mine ("torpedo") that would explode if the enemy tried to raise it. The Turtle was invented after warships began to send out small boats to look for torpedoes and haul them out of the water. The new invention was an iron MOORED TORPEDO shaped like a hemisphere with a firing pin that would be released if someone began to pull up the Turtle.

Twain, Mark The pen name of Samuel Clemens, the renown humor writer, who fought briefly for the Confederacy for a few weeks in the spring of 1861 with a unit of Missouri MILITIA. This experience was later used in his short story, "The Private History of a Campaign that Failed." After the war, he published the *Personal Memoirs of U.S. Grant*, the former general and president who, broke and ill, had become his friend. "Mark Twain" was a river term meaning "two fathoms deep."

Twelve Apostles The nickname given by Union sailors to the 12 enemy cannons guarding Vicksburg, Mississippi, from a WATER BATTERY near the levee. *See also* "Matthew," "Mark," "Luke," and "John."

"twenty-nigger law" The nickname for an amendment to the Conscription Act of the Confederacy that allowed people in charge of 20 or more slaves to be exempt from military service. Passed on October 11, 1862, the amendment was despised by ordinary soldiers who saw rich plantation owners use it to avoid the war. The Confederate government, however, knew the risks of leaving slaves without normal supervision. *See also* "rich man's war, poor man's fight."

twenty-one A card game that was popular on both sides. It is often called "blackjack" today. A player wins by receiving cards totaling 21 points or less, while the dealer has less points or more than the allowed 21 points.

Twenty Questions A popular game during the war, still played, in which 20 questions are allowed players to guess the identity of a person, item, or word selected by one player. The questions can only be answered "yes" or "no."

twist Tobacco leaves twisted into a roll. Confederate Admiral Raphael Semmes of the *ALABAMA* recalled capturing the Union merchant ship *Alert* and his men being delighted at finding several cases of "Virginia twist."

"two years and a but" A Union soldier's conventional reply during the first year of the war when asked how long he had left in the army: "It's only two years and a but." A volunteer's normal enlistment was for three years.

"the tycoon" The nickname given Confederate General Robert E. Lee by his staff officers, because Lee tried to coor-dinate all the planning and accept all the responsibility. The name first arose in March 1863, when Lee was irritable and angry during his first illness of the war, a chest infection. He performed his "tycoon" role magnificently, but some battles, such as Gettysburg, exposed the weakness of his staff in carrying out or modifying his orders. Grant, conversely, relied more on the abilities of his staff. The name "tycoon" was the title of the shogun of Japan and was first heard in the U.S. during the Civil War.

tying up The general name given to the humiliating camp punishment in the summer in which a soldier was tied up on the ground with his arms and legs extended and left without a hat in the bright sun.

U

U.H. Grant. *See* Grant, U.H.

Uncle A male slave, usually elderly. It was used with his first name, such as Uncle Joe.

Uncle Abe or Uncle Abraham Affectionate nicknames for President Abraham Lincoln. During his second presidential race in 1864, a popular book of quotations was *Lincolniana; or, The Humors of Uncle Abe.*

Uncle Billy A personal nickname given by his soldiers to Union Major General W.T. Sherman. He liked the name and continued to use it himself after the war, as in his speech on August 11, 1880, to Union veterans, in which he said "every soldier here today knows that Uncle Billy loves him as his own flesh and blood." The men also called him "Old Billy" or just "Billy." *See also* Billy.

Uncle Dick The nickname for Union Major General Richard J. Oglesby. He had been in the Mexican War and California Gold Rush before joining the Union army to lead divisions of the Army of the Tennessee. In 1862, he was wounded at Corinth, Mississippi. Oglesby, who was noted for his pleasant personality and keen wit, was later elected governor of Illinois and then a U.S. Senator.

Uncle George The nickname for Union Major General George Crook. He fought at Antietam in 1862 and in campaigns in Tennessee and the Shenandoah. Captured in 1865 in Maryland, he was later exchanged and commanded the cavalry of the Army of the Potomac. Four years before the war, Crook had survived a poisoned arrow taken while fighting Indians; he returned to Indian fighting after the war and achieved more success than any other former Union soldier, including George Armstrong Custer. The Indians called him "Gray Fox."

Uncle Gideon A nickname for Gideon Welles, President Abraham Lincoln's secretary of the navy, who took the office at the age of 60. A former Democrat, Gideon had previously published the *Hartford Times* of Connecticut, and Lincoln enjoyed teasing him for not knowing a ship's bow from its stern. *See also* "Father Neptune."

Uncle Joe An affectionate nickname for Confederate General Joseph E. Johnston. *See* "The Yellow Rose of Texas."

Uncle John The nickname his soldiers gave to Union Major General John Sedgwick. A confirmed bachelor, he was one of the kindest and most beloved generals in the war. He led the VI Corps of the Army of the Potomac at Chancellorsville, Gettysburg, the Wilderness, and finally Spotsylvania, where he was killed by a sniper. His last words were to reassure his troops about sharpshooters, saying with a smile, "Don't duck. Pooh! They couldn't hit an elephant at that distance." The next shot entered his brain and killed him. His statue now stands at West Point and cadets superstitiously twirl the spurs to help them pass their final exams.

Uncle Robert An early nickname given by his men to Confederate General Robert E. Lee.

Uncle Sam A nickname given by fellow cadets to Hiram Ulysses Grant in his first year at West Point, when he was incorrectly registered as Ulysses S. Grant and the name was posted on the bulletin board in his North Barracks as U.S. Grant. Some students also called him "United States Grant." *See also* "Company"; "Country Sam"; "Sam."

Uncle Sambo An abusive term for a black man, especially a slave. One northern newspaper headline in 1863 declared: "Willing to fight for Uncle Sam but not for Uncle Sambo." *See also* Sambo.

Uncle Tom's Cabin Copies of Harriet Beecher Stowe's antislavery novel, originally published in 1852, were distributed in the thousands to Union troops by religious organizations. In August 1864 alone, the Episcopal Book Society sent 67,000 copies to the United States Christian Commission for distribution. The book was also read by curious Confederate soldiers. Harry St. John Dixon of Mississippi recorded in his diary on May 19, 1862, that he had spent all day "coughing and read-

ing that d____d Yankee lie Uncle Tom's Cabin."

unco Very or exceptionally. After they captured Vicksburg on July 4, 1863, Union Major General W.T. Sherman wrote General Ulysses Grant as follows: "Surely I will not punish any soldier for being 'unco happy' this most glorious anniversary of the birth of a nation." The word came from the Scottish language.

"Unconditional Loyalty" A term that became popular in the North during the war. It was first used in a sermon by Henry Bellows, the minister of All Souls Church in New York, who said that criticism of President Abraham Lincoln during a crisis was criminal. Bellows later preached another sermon to moderate this view, and some New Yorkers began to question his unconditional loyalty.

"Unconditional Surrender" A nickname for Union General Ulysses S. Grant, who was the first person to use the expression. This was on November 16, 1862, when Major General Simon B. Buckner, besieged by Grant's troops in Fort Donelson, Tennessee, asked for the terms of surrender. Some 14,000 Rebels were captured. Since the new term fit the Grant's initials, he was soon nicknamed in northern newspapers as "Unconditional Surrender Grant." (Grant and Buckner had been classmates at West Point, and Buckner had loaned Grant desperately needed transportation money when he resigned from the army.) Grant was also sometimes called "Old Unconditional." *See also* "Company."

Underground Railroad The secret network that helped up to 100,000 slaves escape to northern states and Canada. It was not a real railway, for the fugitives traveled by any available means, including their feet. The system had a loose organization dependent on individual efforts, such as those made by the former slave

Harriet Tubman, known as "Moses"; Levi Coffin, a Quaker nicknamed "the president of the underground railroad" for organizing the flight of at least 3,000 slaves; and Thomas Garrett, who supposedly helped more than 2,000. Workers on the railroad were called "conductors," their fugitive slaves were "passengers," and the homes and other safe places along the escape route were known as "stations," such as the ones provided by Harriet Beecher Stowe (who wrote Uncle Tom's Cabin) and by Allan Pinkerton (who later established the Secret Service) in his cooper's shop.

underpinnings A humorous and euphemistic nickname for a person's legs.

Uniform and Dress The short title for *Uniform and Dress of the Army of the Confederate States*. The official guide was published as the war began, but the standards for uniforms were seldom followed by underequipped Rebel soldiers.

Union bonnet A hat worn by northern women, especially early in the war, that had alternate layers of red, white, and blue. For their part, men often stuck a U.S. postage stamp on their hat as a show of partriotism.

Union Light Guard A squadron of Ohio cavalry assigned in 1863 to protect President Abraham Lincoln during his movements around Washington, D.C. The unit replaced Scott's Nine Hundred. The president distained protection, however, and during his second inauguration in 1865 had the Union Light Guard escort his wife to the Capitol so he could drive there alone.

Union Meetings Meetings held throughout cities and towns in the North as the war began, in which speakers and audience members vowed to save the Union. On April 20, 1861, eight days after the bombardment of Fort Sumter, a rousing Union Meeting was held in New York City, appropriately in Union Square. Mayor Fernando Wood urged New Yorkers to "speak trumpet-tongued to the people of the South," and a resolution was passed saying all citizens should help maintain the Union to save the country from "universal anarchy and confusion." However, three months earlier, on January 7, Wood had supported the southern cause and proposed that New York secede from the Union as an independent city.

Union Refreshment Saloon The name given by Mary W. Lee, a Sanitary Commission volunteer born in England, to a facility she established in 1861 for Union soldiers in a boathouse in Philadelphia's waterfront district. More than 4 million men visited it. Lee provided food and coffee and, before the war ended, added a medical center, sleeping quarters, and baths. A similar facility nearby was Cooper's Shop Saloon opened by Anna Maria Ross.

Union Repeating Gun *See* "coffee-grinder."

Union-saver A derogatory name used by abolitionist Republicans, especially during the 1860 election, for politicians who wanted to compromise on slavery to save the union of free and slave states. A well-known one was Edward Everett, a former U.S. Senator and governor of Massachusetts who was the Constitutional Union Party's vice-presidential candidate in 1860. Abraham Lincoln, the Republic candidate, was neither an abolitionist nor an extreme Union-saver through compromise, as his resupplying of beleagured Fort Sumter demonstrated.

Union tie A blue tie that was sold in New York City soon after the bombardment of Fort Sumter in April 1861. The blue tie was worn as a symbol of patriotism and became a best-seller.

"United South" A Confederate joke at the beginning of the war to explain the "U.S." on uniforms still held by southerners who had been soldiers and sailors before the nation divided.

"United States are . . ." The plural verb was used for the United States before and during the Civil War, because the union was considered to be a confederation of independent states. The plural verb had been used since the American Revolution, but after the Civil War secured a strong union, "United States is . . ." became the permanent form.

United States Christian Commission *See* Christian Commission.

United States Colored Troops The official designation for Negro troops in the Union army, who eventually numbered some 180,000. They made up 100 regiments and 16 companies of infantry, 11 regiments and 4 companies of heavy artillery, 10 batteries of light artillery, and 6 regiments of cavalry. They were organized under a Bureau of Colored Troops, created after President Abraham Lincoln authorized the recruitment of black soldiers in the fall of 1862, with the first unit being the First South Carolina Regiment. Lincoln's decision arose from growing military casualties and large numbers of runaway slaves entering the North. About 7,000 white officers were eventually in charge of these units; most of these officers were supporters of abolition, but some

Company E of the 4th U.S. Colored Infantry, photographed during the war at Fort Lincoln, part of the defensive works around Washington, D.C. *Library of Congress, Prints & Photographs Division, LC-B8171-7890.*

took the assignment for higher pay, including the officer who said "I would drill a company of alligators for $120 a month." One advantage of black troops was pointed out by Iowa Senator James W. Grimes, who said he preferred to see "a negro shot down in battle rather than the son of a Dubuquer." Dozens of blacks rose to become officers, the highest being Major Martin Delaney of the 104th United States Colored Troops. Blacks fought well. They took part in the siege of Petersburg, Virginia, and other engagements, but were decimated at the FORT PILLOW MASSACRE. Despite the urgings of Confederate General Robert E. Lee, the South only authorized black units 10 days before Richmond fell in 1865. Even then, it had 35 recruits in uniform, including a dozen free blacks who wanted to fight for the South. During Reconstruction, United States Colored Troops were among those occupying the South. *See also* "Sambo's Right to Be Kilt."

United States Military Railroads The military rail system created by Congress on January 31, 1862. Tracks were built into the South by its Construction Corps, which was mostly composed of civilian workers supervised by engineers. During the war, they laid 641 miles of track and, at their peak, had 24,964 men controlling more than 2,000 miles of track and operating 419 locomotives and 6,330 cars. After the war, the Military Railroads were sold to private owners and any railroad companies that had been nationalized were returned.

United States Sanitary Commission *See* Sanitary Commission.

the unknown land A euphemism for heaven.

unman To take away one's masculinity. When one woman wept as young soldiers in Manassas, Virginia, left for battle, the mother of the boys scolded her: "How could you let them see you crying? It will unman them."

unmentionables A pair of trousers. The meaning did not shift to underclothes until the early twentieth century.

the Unpleasantness An informal early southern name for the Civil War, first heard in 1861.

"Up!" The word to be yelled by the first crew member whose endurance failed when submerged in the Confederate's crude submarine, the *H. L. Hunley*. At that point, officers on board would pump out the ballast to surface. The nine-man crew carried with them one candle that would usually be extinguished by lack of oxygen in less than a half-hour. After tests asphyxiated three crews, the fourth survived underwater for 2 hours and 35 minutes before the men gasped, virtually together, "Up!"

up a tree Being in a dilemma; this well-known expression was often used during the war.

upper ten or upper ten thousand The upper classes, a term especially used in large cities in the North; e.g., "It looked like all of the upper ten had driven out to watch the battle at Bull Run."

the Uprising The common name given to the burst of patriotism in the North following the bombardment and surrender of Fort Sumter in 1861. During the Uprising, proclamations of loyalty were published, flags were flown from public buildings and in front of homes, patriotic poems were penned, and volunteer military units were formed.

U.S.A. Hosp Dept or U.S.A. Hospl Dept The abbreviation used by the United States Army Hospital Department. It was inscribed on surgical sets and some medical instruments.

us-all A southern term meaning "all of us," although it has not survived like YOU-ALL. Near the end of the war, Confederate prisoners asked the passing Union Major General Philip Sheridan, "Where do you want us-all to go to?"

U.S.C.T. The abbreviation for the UNITED STATES COLORED TROOPS. Soldiers preferred to use the initials.

"Useless" A taunting nickname given by schoolmates to the boy Ulysses S. Grant, who was then named Hiram Ulysses Grant.

use up To destroy or kill, as in "Three Yankees tried to escape, but we used them up."

U.S.M.A. The abbreviation for the United States Military Academy at West Point, New York. The initials, surrounded by a U-shaped wreath, were worn on the cadet's blue FORAGE CAP.

U.S.M.R.R. The abbreviation for UNITED STATES MILITARY RAILROADS. The initials were placed on locomotives and cars.

V

---

valerian A medicinal drug used as a nerve sedative and as an antispasmodic. A teaspoon was often put into a pint of water. Valerian was produced from the garden heliotrope plant.

Valiant Val A nickname given by his supporters to Clement L. Vallandigham, the Ohio COPPERHEAD who led the PEACE DEMOCRATS. He labeled the war unconstitutional and called for soldiers to desert on both sides. Union Major General Ambrose E. Burnside, who commanded the Department of the Ohio, ordered that Vallandigham be thrown into a military prison for two years, but President Abraham Lincoln commuted this to banishment to the Confederacy. However, Valiant Val left the South immediately for Canada, and returned to Ohio in June 1864 to help create the Peace Platform that split the Democratic Party and assured Lincoln's reelection. Vallandigham, a lawyer, died during a court case on June 16, 1871, accidentally shooting himself while demonstrating how his client may have accidentally shot himself. *See also* Vallandighammer.

Vallandighammer A nickname for followers of Clement L. Vallandigham, a leading COPPERHEAD who sought peace rather than victory for the North. *See also* Valiant Val.

vamose or vamoose The Mexican word for "let us depart" had become American slang for leaving, especially in haste, a few years before the war and became popular during the conflict. In the summer of 1863, a Union signalman ended his WIGWAG flag communications during the siege of Port Hudson, Louisiana, with "We will vamose now. Come again tomorrow."

vandal chief A southern nickname for Union Major General W.T. Sherman because of his army's destruction of property in the South, especially Georgia. He acknowledged the title in a letter written during his army's occupation of Savannah, Georgia, where he had been stationed before the war: "There are some elegant people here whom I knew in better days, who do not seem ashamed to call on 'the vandal chief.'"

Vandyke collar A woman's wide lace or linen collar with a border having points and indentations. It was often just called a "Vandyke." During the war, women produced knitted and crocheted woolen versions. The name came from the collars shown in portraits by the seventeenth-century Flemish artist, Sir Anthony Vandyke.

the vapors Hypochondria, melancholy, or depressed spirits. The vapors often afflicted soldiers in camp who were contemplating the next battle. Some physicians thought it was brought on by smoking and chewing tobacco.

variola The medical name for smallpox. A mild form, varioloid, slowed down President Abraham Lincoln in 1863 soon after his Gettysburg Address, causing him to remark, "There is one good thing about this. I now have something I can give everybody."

vaunt A vain display. In 1861, the poet Walt Whitman wrote as follows about the scene of Union troops streaming into Washington, D.C., after losing the first battle of Bull Run: "Where are the vaunts and the proud boasts with which you went forth?"

veal A slang name for raw recruits. A soldier watching fresh troops arriving in camp might exclaim, "We asked for men and they send us veal!"

vedette or vidette A mounted sentry who was posted beyond the army's normal outposts to observe enemy movements. *See also Vidette.*

veranda A wide porch covered by a roof supported by light pillars. The name was especially associated with southern plantations, where slaves would often wait on the veranda to receive instructions or to make their personal appeals. It was sometimes called a piazza.

a very long grace for a thin plate of soup A great effort for a small result. President Abraham Lincoln used it to describe Union Rear Admiral Samuel F. Du Pont's detailed preparations before his IRONCLAD fleet was defeated at Charleston on April 7, 1863.

vet A common abbreviation for a VETERAN VOLUNTEER who had re-enlisted. It indicated an older, experienced soldier.

veteranize To complete one's military service; e.g., "Foster said he would never veteranize until the last battle was won."

Veteran Reserve Corps The Union corps created in 1863 of soldiers who were disabled, convalescing, or otherwise no longer fit for combat duty. It was first called the Invalid Corps, but the name was changed in March 1864 because the initials I.C. were the same as the army's "Inspected Condemned." A comic song, "The Invalid Corps," was even published. To free others for front-line duty, they were assigned as support personnel, such as recruiters, guards, cooks, and nurses. The Corps, which wore pale blue uniforms, began with two battalions: the 1st battalion was for soldiers who could handle a weapon, and the 2nd was for amputees, who often served in hospitals. Later, room was found for normally healthy veterans. In July 1863, its members helped quell the DRAFT RIOTS in New York City. After seven months in existence, the Corps had 20,000 members in more than 200 companies.

veteran volunteer or volunteer veteran Any of those 200,000 or so Union soldiers who re-enlisted for three years or the length of the war, after orders in June 1863 requested this. They each received a bonus of $400 and a 30-day furlough, as well as red and blue chevrons to wear on their left sleeves. Their re-enlistment greatly strengthened the Union army's ability to carry the war South to victory.

"Victory, General Grant" The prophetic message attached to the wing of a pigeon that the magician Senior Blitz pulled from President Abraham Lincoln's hat in early July 1863. The English conjurer was performing for the president and others outdoors in Washington, D.C., while the battle of Gettysburg was being fought.

"Victory or Damned Badly Wounded" A revision of "Victory or Death" suggested by Mexican War veterans when they viewed banners in Indiana towns staging celebrations to send their hometown boys off to war.

Vidette A camp newspaper issued irregularly in 1862 and 1863 by the cavalry troops of Confederate General John Hunt Morgan. The title came from VEDETTE OR VIDETTE, the name for a type of sentry. The publication contained news and humor, as well as disparaging opinions about Yankee soldiers. During Morgan's raids, copies were sometimes left to annoy the enemy.

viginal crop A name that was used to describe the raising of slaves for the market, because slaves were generally sold about the age of 20 when they would bring their highest price. *Viginti* was the Latin word for 20. Most slaves were produced in Virginia, which was described as "a Negro-raising state for other states." The trade brought in tens of millions of dollars to Virginia each year. *See also* sold South.

village A common name for the slave quarters on a plantation, consisting of a group of cabins. These buildings were located a good distance from the owner's BIG HOUSE and, if possible, out of sight from it, an option appealing to everyone—the owner could avoid a view of the slum housing, and the slaves could acquire some privacy from their master.

vinum A military doctor's name for wine or brandy, written on prescriptions.

Virginia The name of Confederate Major General "JEB" Stuart's favorite horse. Virginia once easily leaped a ditch that was up to 15 feet wide to allow Stuart to escape Union troops who had trapped him against it on June 30, 1863, at Hanover, Pennsylvania, during his Gettysburg raid. *See also* Highfly.

The Virginia Cavalier The name of a southern military melodrama that provoked soldiers to attack the stage of a Richmond theater in March 1863. The realistic scenery of a Confederate camp and the dramatic story of a Yankee hand-to-hand attack enraged drunk Texas and Arkansas soldiers (sitting with their unloaded muskets) who stormed the stage with wild yells to repulse the "Yankees." As the orchestra dived for cover, the lights were extinguished and the manager, D'Orsay Ogden, urged the soldiers to return to their seats. He then strode to the footlights to announce that he considered the audience's attack to be a compliment and a tribute to the staging of play, "unparalleled in the history of the stage."

"Virginia Creeper" The nickname given by Union General Philip Kearny to his commander, General George B. McClellan, because of his slow advances and avoidance of battles.

Virginia quick steps *See* Tennessee quick step.

Virginia State Line An organization of Virginia MILITIA formed on May 15, 1862. Its members were exempt from conscription into the regular Confederate forces, but many made the transfer when the State Line was abolished on February 28, 1863. *See also* Georgia State Line.

Virginia weed A slang term for tobacco. It was seldom heard after the war.

vitiate To morally corrupt or pervert someone; e.g., "Robert's mother made him pledge not to be vitiated by bad associations in the army."

vivandiere A woman who served as a nurse and general attendant with a military unit, especial French and European troops on both sides. The position had been a European tradition since the Thirty Years' War in the seventeenth century.

VMM The initials for the Volunteer Militia of Maine, worn on metal belt plates, although the organization had no regulation uniforms.

volunteer veteran *See* veteran volunteer.

vomit An informal name for any medicine prescribed to make the patient vomit, such as TARTAR EMETIC; e.g., "Our regimental surgeon's usual cure was to administer bleeding and vomits."

W

W The letter branded on soldiers considered to be worthless, usually on their foreheads, cheeks, or hands. Officers would hand down the sentence in camp. The branding, however, was usually in indelible ink. *See also* C; D; T.

wafer A thin disk of paste or adhesive paper used to seal letters or documents.

wag A common camp name for a habitual joker or witty person. The sixteenth-century English word is still sometimes used.

wage slave A southern name for northerners who had to work long hours under harsh conditions for their wages. This popular southern retort to abolitionists included the idea that plantation slaves were better taken care of (free food, free medicine, free housing, etc.) and had less problems than the North's wage slaves under their economic "bondage."

wagon dog A nickname give by Confederate soldiers to those among them who became ill and joined the wagons. This retreat was often suspiciously viewed as avoidance of battle.

wagoner The driver of an army wagon that carried supplies, food, and equipment. The U.S. Quartermaster Department was in charge of hiring master wagoners, who were paid at the rank of cavalry sergeants, as well as civilian wagoners, paid like cavalry corporals.

waiter A tray used for serving food and drinks. A Confederate returning with his brigade to Richmond after the battle of Seven Pines in 1862, noted that "Ladies stood in front of their homes with waiters of food and drink, luxuries and wine, which they dealt out unsparingly to wounded soldiers that passed them."

waiter girl A lovely but supposedly sinful woman who served drinks in concert saloons in New York City, such as the Gaieties and the Eagle Concert Saloon. "Pretty waiter girls" were often highlighted in the saloons' advertisements during the war, and the naughty women often drew as many customers to the establishment as did the singers and comics.

walking ticket or walking papers A dismissal from work or discharge from the military. The second term became predominant over the years.

walk-over An easy victory. On the first day of the battle of Gettysburg in July 1863, Confederate Brigadier General James J. Archer was captured and Union

Assistant Adjutant-General E.P. Halstead later recalled that "He evidently had expected an easy 'walk over,' judging from his disappointed manner after he was captured."

wallpapered A delightfully strange slang word for being inebriated.

War Against the States The name given the Civil War by Confederate General Joseph E. Johnston.

War Between the States The traditional southern name for the Civil War, still heard today. This term emphasized a war between states with equal rights, being opposed to the northern name of the War of the Rebellion.

war coffee A coffee extender used in the southern states during the Union blockade. One spoonful of real coffee was mixed with one spoonful of toasted cornmeal and then boiled well. The recipe was published in the *Tri-Weekley Watchman* newspaper of Sumter, South Carolina, on July 8, 1861. It was sent by a reader who urged, "Try it, and see if we can't get along comfortably even while our ports are blockaded by he who would be king." *See also* burnt sugar coffee; cane seed coffee; chinquapin coffee; grape coffee; okra coffee; pea coffee; potato and persimmon coffee; rye coffee.

War Democrats Members of the Democratic Party who supported Republican President Abraham Lincoln's efforts to unite the country by pursuing the war vigorously. When Lincoln was first elected in 1860, the War Democrats were opposed by the COPPERHEADS in their party. In the 1864 election, their opposition was the PEACE DEMOCRATS.

war department The section of a large newspaper that covered the war. Important metropolitan papers had large war departments, with the New York *Herald* spending about $500,000 to cover the conflict.

ward-master A person in charge of a hospital ward. He assisted the surgeon, supervising the treatment of the patients on his ward.

"war dog" A nickname for any cannon.

War for (or of) Independence A southern name for the Civil War, which in the South was also called the War for Southern Independence, the War for Southern Freedom, and the War for Southern Rights. A year after the war ended, Confederate Major General Jubal Early wrote *A Memoir of the Last Year of the War for Independence in the C.S.A.* (1866) and Confederate Major Heros Von Borcke penned *Memoirs of the Confederate War for Independence*.

War for Separation A descriptive early southern name for the Civil War.

War for Southern Nationality or War for Nationality Early southern names for the Civil War, first heard in 1861.

"War is hell." A shortening of the sentiments of Union Major General W.T. Sherman, as expressed in his speech in Columbus, Ohio, 15 years after the war on August 11, 1880. Sherman told Union veterans of the Grand Army of the Republic that "There is many a boy here who looks on war as all glory, but, boys, it is all hell. You can bear this warning voice to generations yet to come."

"War is war" A simple idea often repeated by Union General W.T. Sherman to justify his harsh treatment of southerners and their property. The words have been virtually forgotten because of his stronger post-war quotation that "WAR IS HELL."

war-look A soldier's expression as he enters battle. His men always spoke of Confederate Lieutenant General "STONE-WALL" Jackson as having "his war-look on him" when his face turned grave and stern as he rode into battle.

War of 1861 An optimistic name for the Civil War during its first year, for many people felt it could never last longer. The name was engraved on some IDENTITY DISCS worn by soldiers. A similar name was the War of the Sixties.

War of Secession An early southern name for the Civil War.

War of the Rebellion The official name used by the U.S. Congress for the Civil War while it was happening and until the end of the nineteenth century, when it was printed on the U.S. government publication, *Official Records of the Union and Confederate Armies*. The name was commonly used in the North, along with "the Great Rebellion."

"warrant officers' champagne" The nickname given by sailors to a drink of grog mixed with ginger ale. *See also* grog ration.

wash To withstand a test or to prove itself. Still used, this term was new when the war began, as was the expression "Republicanism will wash."

washing-machine A machine for washing clothes owned by the rich. It was a 10- to 20-gallon cylinder container with a boiler below that provided hot water and steam. The clothes were put in first followed by soap, and the cylinder was made to revolve from 5 to 10 minutes. Introduced in 1854 at the Crystal Palace Exhibition in New York City, the washing-machine cost $50 or, with an additional boiler for rinsing, $75. It supposedly cleaned clothes "without spot or blemish."

Washington City A common name for Washington, D.C. "The capture of Washington City is perfectly within the power of Virginia and Maryland," wrote the Richmond *Examiner* on April 23, 1861.

"Washington slave-pen" See "The Blue Jug."

wash kettle A nickname for a large, wide military shell.

wash-tub on a raft An early humorous nickname for the Union's first IRONCLAD ship, the *Monitor*, because of the round turret on its flat deck.

watch and ward A common expression for guarding, in the manner of a sentinel. In Petersburg, Virginia, the wife of a Confederate captain wrote as follows in her diary about her slave's loyalty: "When the city was given up to the enemy, Becky still kept 'watch and ward' over our things, though threatened with . . . even death by some of the Yankee soldiers if she did not give up her master's property."

water battery A BATTERY of cannons directed toward a stretch of water, such as a bay or river. A large water battery was the Confederate's TWELVE APOSTLES overlooking the Mississippi River from Vicksburg, Mississippi.

water-filterer A device bought by some soldiers early in the war to protect them from polluted water. It was a GUTTA-PERCHA (rubberlike gum) tube about 15 inches long and a half-inch in diameter, with an air chamber midway. One end was attached to a metal mouthpiece through which the water was sucked, and the other end contained a small suction chamber perforated at the bottom and containing a filter made of bocking, a coarse woolen cloth. A simpler version had rubber tubing attached to a pumice stone as a filter. These devices were quickly discarded because of the effort required (and the derision of fellow soldiers).

watermelon juice A "cure" often given by camp doctors for the common cold.

watermelon sherbet A cool alcoholic drink for summer, not the ice sherbet of today. It was made of a strained mixture of pulped watermelon, sherry, rosewater, and sugar. The name "sherbet," still used in Great Britain for a fruit-flavored effervescent drink, came from an Arabic drink of fruit juice and water sweetened and cooled.

"Waterspout Man" The nickname given by northern war correspondents to one of their number, Henry Bentley of the Philadelphia *Inquirer*, because of his continuous chatter and bragging. Confederates captured Bentley in his tent at Shiloh in 1862 and stripped him down to his pantaloons and boots before he escaped.

way-bill An official list of passengers booked on a train, stage coach, ship, or other form of public transportation.

Wayside Home or Wayside Hospital One of a southern system of private homes open to soldiers and sailors moving to and fro, and of buildings serving as hospitals. These homes provided rest, food, and medical care that local governments could not afford. As in the North, they were sometimes called a SOLDIERS' HOME, although they were not quite the same. Some of the facilities were described by soldiers who stayed there as practicing humbug medicine.

weak sister A slang nickname for a cowardly or undependable soldier or person.

"We Are Coming, Father Abraham" A rousing popular poem in the North, written by James Sloane Gibbons, a Delaware native living in New York City. He penned it after President Abraham Lincoln called for 300,000 volunteers in 1862, and it helped inspire enlistments. The poem was first published anonymously in the New York *Evening Post* on July 16, 1862. The first of the four stanzas reads as follows:

> We are coming, Father Abraham,
> three hundred thousand more,
> From Mississippi's winding stream
> and from New England's shore;
> We leave our ploughs and workshops,
> our wives and children dear,
> With hearts too full for utterance,
> with but a silent tear;
> We dare not look behind us,
> but steadfastly before:
> We are coming, Father Abraham,
> three hundred thousand more!

Gibbons was an abolitionist who was one of the editors of the *Anti-Slavery Standard*. He was nearly killed in the New York DRAFT RIOTS of 1863, but friends helped him escape over rooftops to a waiting carriage. *See also* commutation fee.

webfoot 1. A nickname for a sailor. When praising his army in 1863, President Abraham Lincoln added, "Nor must Uncle Sam's web-feet be forgotten." 2. A jocular nickname for a common infantryman, often hurled by a cavalryman.

weed 1. A cigar, especially a cheap one made of poor tobacco. 2. Tobacco in general; e.g., "Most people in camp chew the weed."

"We'll Hang Jeff Davis from a Sour Apple Tree" New words created and sung by Union soldiers to the tune of "JOHN BROWN'S BODY." This version appeared before Julia Ward Howe used the tune for "THE BATTLE HYMN OF THE REPUBLIC."

wench A name for a black girl or woman, although in England it originally meant a country girl, then a female servant or an immoral woman.

West Pointer A graduate or former student of the U.S. Military Academy at West Point, New York. Both armies had many leaders who had been West Pointers. Charles Mackay, a journalist for *The Times* of London, reported that "innuendo is daily made that the West Pointers on both sides love each other too well to fight very desperately, and that some fine morning before anyone suspects the manoeuvre they will unite their armies, and make an end of the Republic."

we-uns A substitution for "we," especially in the dialect of poorly educated white southerners and slaves, being the pronunciation of "we ones." A similar term is YOU-UNS.

whaler A big, strongly built man; e.g., "We tried to force him down, but he was a whaler."

"Whar's you? Whar's you?" The words that slaves in Petersburg, Virginia, put to the sound of incoming shells during the long Union siege of the city in 1864-65.

"the Whatisit" The nickname given by soldiers to the mobile darkroom used by war photographer Matthew Brady. The strange hard-topped wagon had been converted from Brady's own buggy. The Whatisit was usually occupied by his assistants who did most of the developing of the wet-plate glass negatives.

Wheat's tigers *See* "Tiger Rifles."

wheel A slang name for a silver dollar.

wheel pair The pair of horses closest to a cannon being pulled by three pairs.

"When Johnny Comes Marching Home" This popular war song was written in 1863 by Irishman Patrick Gilmore, who was then the Union army's bandmaster in occupied New Orleans. He set it to the old Irish tune "Johnny I Hardly Knew Ye." It later became the most popular song of the Spanish-American War. The first verse goes as follows:

> When Johnny comes marching home
> again,
> Hurrah, hurrah!
> We'll give him a hearty welcome then,
> Hurrah, hurrah!
> The men will cheer and the boys will shout,
> The ladies they will all turn out,
> And we'll all feel gay when Johnny comes
> marching home.

"When This Cruel War Is Over" A popular song among Union soldiers and civilians, written by Charles C. Sawyer of Brooklyn, New York, and published in the fall of 1861. The first of the four stanzas and the verse go as follows:

> Dearest love, do you remember
> When we last did meet,
> How you told me that you loved me,
> Kneeling at my feet?
> Oh, how proud you stood before me,
> In your suit of blue,
> When you vowed to me and country
> Ever to be true!
> Weeping, sad and lonely,
> Hopes and fears, how vain;
> Yet praying
> When this cruel war is over,
> Praying that we meet again.

whicker A descriptive word for the neighing of a horse.

whipped The most common term used for defeat in battle. After the first battle of Bull Run in 1861, W.H. Russell of *The Times* of London reported that fleeing Union soliders cried "We're whipped" and "We're pretty badly whipped." Following the battle of Fair Oaks in 1862, the *Richmond Examiner* noted that "the enemy was well whipped." Union Brigadier General Robert Mitchell's message after the battle of Murfreesboro was, "The Lord is on our side. The rebels are whipped." When the Union's Major General Don Carlos Buell asked General Ulysses Grant at the battle of Shiloh if he had made any plans to retreat in the face of the enemy, he replied, "I have not yet despaired of whipping them, General."

whipple hat A soldier's hat of light-blue felt, having a rounded top and a brim running two-thirds around it from a leather visor. Confederates called it an Excelsior hat, and another name was the havelock cap because it was designed to add a protective HAVELOCK at the rear. The whipple was named for its inventor, J.F. Whipple of New York, who patented it in 1861.

whirl-a-gust A whirlwind or other fast destructive force. The Confederate veteran Sam Watkins recalled a brigade that "swooped down on those Yankees like a whirl-a-gust of woodpeckers in a hail storm."

whiskey cobbler An alcoholic drink created in 1862 and popular in the South. It was whiskey mixed with fruit and sugar and served with cracked ice.

whist A popular card game on both sides. It was played by four people, two on each team, and eventually evolved into bridge.

"Whistling Dick" The nickname for a Confederate cannon on the heights of Vicksburg that played havoc with Union boats on the Mississippi, including sinking the *Cincinnati* on May 27, 1863. It has been called the most famous gun in the war. The name came from the strange sound its wobbling shells made, a result of the uneven spirals cut into the orginal SMOOTHBORE gun to transform it into a RIFLED gun. "Whistling Dick" was produced by the TREDEGAR IRON WORKS at Richmond, Virginia. The gun disappeared just before Vicksburg surrendered and has never been found. Some believe Confederate soldiers buried it in the river to keep it out of Yankee hands.

white black A light-skinned black person.

white gold A southern nickname for cotton. Confederate leaders overestimated European reliance on the South's crop, hoping to bargain it for military assistance or diplomatic recognition. This effort failed because of the Union blockade and the European switch to other cotton suppliers in Egypt and India.

White House The nickname for the first home of Confederate President Jefferson Davis in Montgomery, Alabama, when the Confederate capital was located there in 1861. The 1835 Italianate style home, still dubbed "the first White House of the Confederacy," can be visited today at 644 Washington Avenue.

white nigger A demeaning term for an abolitionist or other supporter of Negroes. It was heard early in the war on both sides, and in the South was eventually applied to Union soldiers. On April 19, 1861, when Massachusetts troops marched through Baltimore, Maryland, on the way to Washington, D.C., the epithet was hurled at them during a riot that killed 12 civilians and 4 soldiers.

white oak chip A nickname for a HARD-TACK biscuit because it seemed as hard as a piece of oak wood.

white trash *See* poor white trash.

whitewash To win a game without the other team scoring. This well-known word came into usage when the war began and usually referred to BASE BALL. The noun was sometimes expanded to "a whitewash bath."

whitlow A painful sore or swelling, accompanied by pus, around the fingernail. It was sometimes called paronychia.

whittling The relaxing art of applying knife to wood was a popular pastime in camp. Union General Ulysses Grant was an avid whittler. During thoughtful sessions, he would often fish his penknife from his pocket, select a suitable branch, and intently carve away. New Englanders were especially known for the art. When fuse plugs were desperately needed for the Union's bombardment of Fort Pulaski in Georgia, the ordnance officer remembered a regiment of Connecticut Yankees back in camp. The *New York Times* correspondent wrote, "all Yankees are whittlers; if this regiment could be turned out to-night, they might whittle enough fuse-plugs before morning to fire a thousand rounds." The men of the 6th Connecticut were ordered out to whittle and "did whittle to advantage," supplying all the plugs needed for the next two days.

"Whoopee!" An exclamation of joy, excitement, or approval. The word was first heard in the U.S. about the start of the war to describe a joyous celebration or revelry; e.g., "They are having a Fourth of July whoopee in town this Saturday." The term was derived from the British word "Whoop!," which had meant the same since the sixteenth century. The expression, "to make whoopee," meaning to make love, was not used until the twentieth century.

whorehouse pimp A soldier's term of abuse, frequently leveled at an officer.

whoreson A common term of contempt used by profane name-callers.

"Who steals my purse steals trash." A favorite Confederate quote from Shakespeare, often heard after the devaluation of the South's money.

Who wouldn't be a soldier? A strange expression of unconcern meaning "Who cares?" A private might say, "The colonel turned down my furlough, but who wouldn't be a soldier?"

Wide Awakes Members of the Wide Awake Clubs, which were formed within the Republican Party during the presidential election of 1860 to support their ultimately successful candidate, Abraham Lincoln. The first club was founded in Hartford, Connecticut. The name was a pun on their hats made out of a fabric with "no nap." The Wide Awakes, who numbered about 400,000, were vocal and visible, escorting speakers to campaign meetings and conducting parades in which they wore oilskin caps and capes and carried swinging lamps. Some southerners believed the marching Wide Awakes were preparing for the eventual invasion of the South. *See also* National Volunteers.

"Widow Blakely" The nickname for a well-known cannon in Vicksburg, Mississippi, that covered the river with ferocious fire. It is now on display at the U.S. Military Academy in West Point, New York.

wiggle-waggle To sway from side to side, a western term introduced about when the war began.

wig-wag A system of communicating by flags. Colonel Albert J. Myer, a surgeon, was the Union's first chief signal officer in the U.S. Signal Corps, which was created during the war. Myer had invented the coded flag system before the war during campaigns against the Navajos. Helping him develop the system was Second Lieutenant Edward P. Alexander, an engineer from Georgia who left to join the Confederates when the war began. The South was the first to use signalmen, employing them at the first battle of Bull Run in 1861. Confederate flags measured 4 by 2.5 feet. Dark blue flags were used against the sky, white ones in front of a darker background, and scarlet ones if it had snowed. The centers of the flags were of different colors. Union signalmen used a white flag with a red square in the center and a red one with a white center. The flags were positioned differently to spell out the messages. When Confederate General Leonidas Polk (who was also a bishop) was fatally hit by a shot from an enemy battery on June 14, 1864, at Pine Mountain, Georgia, the northern gunners first learned they had killed the famous general when they read the Confederate wig-wag communication.

wigwam A nickname for a SIBLEY TENT.

wild bear *See* bear.

"Wild Bill" The nickname of James Butler Hickok, who was a Union scout during the war. He claimed to have killed 50 Rebels with 50 shots. He later won fame as a frontier marshal.

Wild Cat Stampede The nickname for the panicked Union retreat from Wild Cat Mountain in eastern Kentucky by the First Brigade of the Army of Ohio, commanded by Brigadier General Albin Schoepf. On October 21, 1861, his troops had temporarily pushed a Tennessee brigade of some 4,000 men led by Brigadier General Felix Zollicoffer into the Cumberland Gap before the military reversal occurred. *See also* Buckland Races; Philippi Rces; Woodstock Races.

wild fire Unorganized gunfire, often in all directions. When Confederate Lieutenant General "STONEWALL" Jackson was mortally wounded by his own men in 1863, his first words to the officer who ran up to hold his horse, were "Wild fire, that, sir; wild fire."

Wild's African Brigade A Union brigade of black soldiers. General Edward A.A. Wild organized them in North Carolina in 1863 and also led them. *See also* United States Colored Troops.

wild West This term for the lawless West was first heard about a decade before the war.

Willard's Hotel The most famous wartime hotel in Washington, D.C., Willard's was located on Pennsylvania Avenue and 14th Street two blocks from the White House. It remains popular today as the Willard Inter-Continental Hotel. During the war, it was a main meeting place for politicians and military officers. President Abraham Lincoln stayed in its Parlor 6 before his inauguration on March 4, 1861, and Willard's served dinner to 1,500 people on the Sunday before. After the first Union defeat at Bull Run in July 1861, Walt Whitman accused the officers by saying, "Sneak, blow, put on airs there in Willard's sumptuous parlors and barrooms." General Ulysses Grant made it his headquarters when visiting the city, and Julia Ward Howe wrote the "Battle Hymn of the Republic" in her room. The bustling hotel was not admired by all, however. Its lobby was composed of "heat, noise, dust, smoke, and expectoration," noted one Englishman. And George Templeton Strong, a New York lawyer, said of Washington: "Beelzebub surely reigns here and Willard's Hotel is his temple."

Willie 1. President Lincoln's nickname for his son, William Wallace Lincoln, who was named for Dr. William Wallace, the husband of Mrs. Lincoln's sister, Frances. The family's tutor, Alexander Williamson, said the blue-eyed boy was the brightest of Lincoln's four children. Willie's death on February 20, 1862, from BILIOUS FEVER and typhoid at the age of 11, devastated the Lincoln family, and the president gave permission for his wife to hold a few seances in the White House to contact their son. Mrs. Lincoln remained in mourning dress for two years. 2. The nickname for Union Major General William T. Sherman's young son and namesake. Willie died of typhoid in 1863 at the age of 9, when Sherman took his family with him to the South. The general went into a deep depression as his wife returned North with his first-born son's body. He wrote her asking, "Why was I not killed at Vicksburg and left Willy to grow up and care for you?"

wilt someone To weaken someone. After a box fell on a Union prisoner in ANDERSONVILLE prison, he later wrote that "it 'wilted' me, to use an army expression, and I could not walk a step for several weeks."

"the wily Dutchman" A nickname for Union General William S. Rosecrans that only referred to his name and ancestry, for Rosecrans was born in Kingston, Ohio. *See also* "Old Rosey" or "Old Rosy."

Winan steam gun An odd-looking mobile gun invented for the Rebels by a Mr. Winan of Baltimore as the war began. It was built on a four-wheeled vehicle with a protective pointed nose that opened for firing. A furnice and tall smokestack were in the rear. The weapon was being sent to Harpers Ferry, Virginia, then controlled by the Rebels, but was intercepted by General Benjamin Butler on May 10, 1861. The unworkable machine, built to revolutionize artillery warfare, never saw action.

Winchester *See* Rienzi.

windage The space between a cannon ball and the inside of the cannon muzzle. This space was needed in smooth-bore guns because air would otherwise be trapped inside the muzzle as the ball was loaded, slowing the process. When the gun was fired, however, the windage let gas escape that could have propelled the ball farther. Windage also led to an uncertain accuracy because the fired ball bounced around the inside of the muzzle and no one knew where the last bounce would throw it. More windage, therefore, resulted in less accuracy.

wing A Confederate military unit formed early in the war and containing several DIVISIONS. Major General James Longstreet led the Right Wing at the battles of Fair Oaks and Seven Pines and commanded a wing of five DIVISIONS in the Army of Northern Virginia at Antietam.

Winnie Confederate President Jefferson Davis's pet name for both his wife, Varina, and their daughter, Varina Anne. *See also* "Daughter of the Confederacy."

winter fever An informal name for pneumonia.

wipe out As today, this slang expression meant to kill a group and was often applied to military units. It was first heard in the U.S. (and Britain) during the war, although to "wipe away" was used as early as the sixteenth century in England. *See also* rub out.

wire entanglements A "devilish contrivance" used by Union forces and consisting of telegraph wires stretched between tree stumps to hinder and bring down the enemy. Confederates considered this a violation of normal warfare. On May 16, 1864, wire entanglements trapped Rebel troops and led to many casualties at Drewry's Bluff, Virginia.

"Wizard of the Saddle" The nickname for Confederate Lieutenant General Nathan Bedford Forrest, the dashing cavalryman known for his brilliant raids. His delightfully simple rule of war, "Get there first with the most men," became a famous saying. He was the only Confederate cavalryman that Union General Ulysses S. Grant was said to fear. Forrest was a slave trader who joined the army as a private, was made a brigadier general in July 1862 and by 1864 commanded all the cavalry of General John B. Hood in the Tennessee campaign. He also fought at Shiloh and led the capture of Fort Pillow on April 12, 1864, which resulted in a massacre of black Union troops and Forrest being labeled the "Fort

Pillow Butcher" by northern newspapers. After the war, he became a member of the Ku Klux Klan.

"Wizard of the Valley" A nickname for Confederate Lieutenant General "STONE-WALL." Jackson, for his military successes in the Shenandoah Valley of Virginia in 1862.

The Wolf's Den A house of prostitution in Washington, D.C, run by a Mrs. Wolf.

A Woman in White A popular mystery novel during the war, written by Wilkie Collins of England, the son-in-law of Charles Dickens. Collins helped develop the early mystery story and reached more wartime readers in 1862 with *No Name*.

wood bee or wood spell A group of soldiers assigned to chop wood for camp fires. It was a name taken from community get-togethers to cut firewood for old or ill citizens or for the local church or school. The second term was first used during the war.

wooden coat or wooden overcoat A morbid nickname for a coffin.

Woodstock Races A Union nickname for Major General Philip H. Sheridan's victory in a cavalry clash with Confederates on October 9, 1864, near Tom's Brook, Virginia. "Either whip the enemy or get whipped yourself," Sheridan instructed Major General Alfred T. Torbert, who then sent Brigadier General Wesley Merritt and Major General George Armstrong Custer after the Rebels. Merritt's troops chased them 20 miles south past Woodstock to Mount Jackson. About 300 Rebels and 11 guns were captured during the "Woodstock Races," a name chosen as a revenge echo of the BUCKLAND RACES a year earlier in which Custer had fled before the cavalry of Major General "JEB" Stuart. *See also* Philippi Races; Wildcat Stampede.

wool To pull someone's hair in anger or as a joke; e.g., "He wooled him badly during the fight." The punishment of shaking a soldier by the ear was also called "wooling."

woolly head An insulting nickname for a Negro, used mostly in the South but also in the North.

Woolly Head The insulting nickname given by some members of the Democratic Party in the North to an abolitionist or person who sympathized with slaves.

work *See* fieldwork.

work off a dead horse To work on a job for which you were already paid in advance.

worm A device shaped like a screw and used by soldiers to remove unfired bullets from their rifles. A soldier would "worm a bullet" by attaching the device to his ramrod, push it into the rifle barrel and screw the worm into the bullet to bring it out.

worm castles A humorously gruesome camp nickname for HARDTACK.

the worse for wear 1. An item that has become delapidated from use. 2. A person who is worn out because of work, travel, conflict, etc. A Confederate woman finding her brother after a battle wrote, "He looks rather the 'worse for wear.' But, thank God, he is safe."

wrapper A general name for a loose-fitting gown or dress.

wrathy Another word for "wrathful." Ovando J. Hollister of the First Regiment of Colorado Volunteers wrote of a friend as follows: "Jem soon learned that he was charged with sundry plugs of tobacco on the Sergeant's books, and as he made no use of the weed he naturally became wrathy."

wrinkle An informal name for an idea or notion; e.g., "Our plan was to retreat, but the general's wrinkle was to attack."

write someone down To write a critical report or article about someone. When Union Major General W. T. Sherman arrested Thomas W. Knox, the war reporter for the *New York Herald*, on January 31, 1863, for an article criticizing his leadership and behavior, the reporter told him, "I have no feeling against you personally, but you are regarded as the enemy of our set and we must in self-defense write you down."

Y

---

the Yankee anniversary An ironic southern name for the Fourth of July, a date which the South had been so instrumental in creating.

"Yankee Doodle" The popular American song that became taboo in the South following secession. Mary Boykin Chestnut, the daughter of a South Carolina governor, recorded in her diary that Mrs. Scott, a northerner visiting in 1861 before the war, had played the tune on a piano and "the Judge came in and calmly requested her to 'leave out the Yankee while she played the Doodle.'"

the Yankee Invasion A southern name for the Civil War, coined in 1861.

Yankeeized In the South, the process of adopting northern ways. The term was heard during the war in areas occupied by Yankees and was common during Reconstruction.

"the Yankee nurse" The sarcastic nickname given by the southern press and public to President Abraham Lincoln's wife, Mary Todd Lincoln, because she visited Union soldiers in hospitals, bringing them fruit and wine.

yard-paling A PALING or other type of fence around a yard. Confederate Major General Daniel H. Hill, called to a meeting at General Robert E. Lee's headquarters in a Richmond house, rode up and recognized Major General "STONEWALL" Jackson "leaning over the yard-paling, dusty, travel-worn and apparently very tired."

"Yates' Hellions" The nickname for the wild new regiment that, in June 1861, became Ulysses Grant's first command. Officially the 21st Illinois Volunteers, it was named for the state's governor, Dick Yates. Grant, a 39-year-old colonel, was mortified to find a regiment of hell-raising, hard-drinking, hen-house-robbing farmboys. "I guess I've come to take command," he announced, and soon he had the Hellions shaped into tolerable soldiers. Eight months later, they had two victories in northeast Tennessee, capturing Fort Henry and Fort Donelson, where Grant earned his nickname of "UNCONDITIONAL SURRENDER." He was immediately elevated to brigadier general.

yawper A person who yelps and shouts. A Union soldier, noticing General Ulysses Grant paying no attention to troops cheering him, remarked, "Grant wants soldiers, not yawpers."

yearling The nickname for a second-year cadet at the U.S. Military Academy at West Point, New York. The term was derived from the word that describes an animal that is a year old or in its second year.

yellow 1. This slang term meaning cowardly was first heard about a decade before the war and was commonly used by both sides. 2. A descriptive term for the skin coloring of a MULATTO or dark-skinned QUADROON person. Invading Union troops often commented on the beauty of the "fair yellow girls" they encountered in the South.

yellow boy A slang nickname for a gold coin. The name was borrowed from Britain where it had been used since the seventeenth century for sovereigns and guineas.

yellow dog A derisive name among Confederate troops for a staff officer, courier, or other noncombatant. When one would pass by, soldiers would take the opportunity to give such calls as "Here, dog, here, come here" or whistle for the "yallow dog." After a horrific battle, however, some soldiers wished aloud that they could become yellow dogs. *See also* hanger-on.

yellow hammers The teasing nickname given to Alabama soldiers by Confederate troops from other states, because of the many yellowhammer woodpeckers in Alabama. *See also* flicker.

yellow jack or yellow jacket A common name for yellow fever.

"The Yellow Rose of Texas" The rousing and popular marching song of Confederate soldiers. Its origins, perhaps in 1853, are lost in the mists of history, but many

believe the woman was a "high yellow" former slave, Emily Morgan West, who was captured by Mexican General Santa Anna during the Texas Revolution and distracted him so badly that he lost the battle of San Jacinto in 1836. The song's author is known only by the initials "J.K.," and some claim he was a black soldier whose original lyrics used "darky" in place of "soldier." After the war, the tune became popular with the U.S. Cavalry in the West. The best known version begins as follows:

> There's a yellow rose in Texas
> That I am going to see
> Nobody else could miss her,
> Just half as much as me.
> She cried so when I left her,
> It like to broke my heart,
> And if I ever find her
> We never more will part.
> *Chorus:* She's the sweetest rose of color
> That Texas ever knew,
> Her eyes are bright as diamonds,
> They sparkle like the dew.
> You can talk about your Clementine
> And sing of Rosa Lee,
> But the Yellow Rose of Texas
> Is the only gal for me.

During the Confederate retreat after General John B. Hood's disasterous defeat at Nashville on December 16, 1864, soldiers of the Army of Tennessee sang their own version of the song:

> So now I'm marching southward,
> My heart is full of woe;
> I'm going back to Georgia
> To see my Uncle Joe.
> You may talk about your Beauregard
> And sing of General Lee,
> But the gallant Hood of Texas
> Played hell in Tennessee.

See also Gallant Hood; "Old Wooden Head."

yeoman farmer A southern farmer who usually had no slaves but made a decent living by growing crops for his own family and selling his extra produce at local markets. Admired throughout the South for his industry and independence, the yeoman farmer joined planters in looking down on the poor whites. In British history, a yeoman was a respected commoner who owned and cultivated a small land holding.

yep This regional version of "yes" was coined in the United States in the first half of the nineteenth century.

"Yorkshire" The name of the first family home of Wilmer McLean, a retired grocer whose two houses were involved in the war's beginning and ending. "Yorkshire," retaining the name of its previous English-born owner, sat on the banks of Bull Run and was in the midst of the war's first major battle there in 1861. One shell barreled down the kitchen chimney to destroy a stew being cooked for Confederate General P.G.T. Beauregard. Desperate to avoid the war, McLean moved his family to a two-story brick home in Appomattox Court House, Virginia. When Generals Grant and Lee needed a place for the official surrender on April 9, 1865, McLean's house was chosen, even though he tried to direct them to an abandoned building. After the famous event in his parlor, soldiers bought or looted souvenirs from the unlucky family.

you-all The well-known southern term of address for several people. "Y'all" was the usual pronunciation. "You-all at the North have been taught to look upon this war as a contest inaugurated in the interest of slavery," a Charleston gentleman told a captured Union prisoner, Ohio Hospital Steward Solon Hyde. *See* us-all.

You can't catch a weasel asleep An expression meaning you cannot surprise or trick an alert person. A typical usage would be: "The Yankees tried to lure us across the river, but you can't catch a weasel asleep."

"Young Bloods of the South" Nickname given by Union Major General W.T. Sherman to young southern military fanatics. "War suits them," he warned, "and the rascals are brave, fine riders, bold to rashness." He advised that the Young Bloods "must all be killed or employed by us before we can hope for peace."

"Young Napoleon" A nickname for Union General George McClellan, because he was a great admirer of Napoleon, but also because of his vain self-confidence and short height. Some wits turned the nickname into "Young McNapoleon."

Your Excellency A common form of address for both President Abraham Lincoln and President Jefferson Davis. They were referred to as "His Excellency the President." Even General Robert E. Lee referred to "Your Excellency" in his messages to Davis.

yourn A substitution for "your," especially in the dialect of poorly educated white southerners and slaves, although the term was correct English usage in the fourteenth century. Similar words are OURN, THEIRN, HISN, and HERN.

you-uns A substitution for "you," especially in the dialect of poorly educated white southerners and slaves, being the pronunciation of "you ones." A similar term is WE-UNS. During Union Major General W.T. Sherman's march through Georgia, a rural woman complained to one of his officers, "You'uns don't fight we-uns fair."

Z

Zouave A member of any of the volunteer regiments on both sides that dressed in the dashing, colorful uniforms of the French Zouaves, Algerians recuited in the 1830s for the French army. The usual uniform was baggy red pants, a short jacket,

Dressed in Zouave uniforms, Company H of the 114th Pennsylvania Infantry was photographed near Petersburg, Virginia, in August 1864. *Library of Congress, Prints & Photographs Division, LC-B8171-7077.*

a waist sash, and a red fez hat adorned with a black tassel. By war's end, many units had abandoned the bright uniforms, which were easily spotted by snipers. Well-known units included the first famous one, the United States Zouave Cadets from Chicago, known for winning competitions with their military drills; the infamously rough New York Fire Zouaves from the New York City Fire Department; and the even more rowdy WHEAT'S TIGERS who had supposedly been signed up at recruiting booths in local jails.

"Zou! Zou! Zou!" The yell given by some ZOUAVES as they charged into battle.

Zu-Zu A nickname for a Zouave soldier.

BIBLIOGRAPHY

The following volumes were indispensable in providing Civil War terms and examples, and they are recommended to those pursing further reading for research or enrichment.

Allen, Thomas B. *We Americans*. Washington, DC: National Geographic Society, 1975.

Arnold, James R. *The Armies of U. S. Grant*. London: Arms and Armour Press, 1995.

Beckett, Ian F.W. *The War Correspondents: The American Civil War*. London: Grange Books, 1997.

Billings, John. *Hardtack and Coffee*. Boston: George M. Smith, 1887.

Boatner, Mark M., III. *The Civil War Dictionary*. New York: Vintage Books, 1991.

Bode, Carl. *Midcentury America*. Carbondale, IL: Southern Illinois University Press, 1972.

Bradley, William J. *The Civil War*. New York: Military Press, 1990.

Butcher, Margaret J. *The Negro in American Culture*. New York: New American Library, 1957.

Chapman, Robert L. *The Dictionary of American Slang*. New York: Harper & Row, 1987.

Craven, Avery, ed. *"To Markie."* Cambridge, MA: Harvard University Press, 1933.

Dannett, Sylvia G.L. *Noble Women of the North*. New York: Thomas Yoseloff, 1959.

Davis, Burke. *The Civil War: Strange & Fascinating Facts*. New York: The Fairfax Press, 1982.

Davis, Kenneth C. *Don't Know Much About the Civil War*. New York: Avon Books, 1996.

Davis, William C. *Battlefields of the Civil War*. London: Salamander Books, 1991.

——. *Brothers in Arms*. New York: Smithmark, 1995.

——. *The Commanders of the Civil War*. London: Salamander Books, 1990.

——. *The Fighting Men of the Civil War*. London: Salamander Books, 1989.

Dickson, Paul. *War Slang*. New York: Pocket Books, 1994.

Foote, Shelby. *The Civil War: A Narrative*, Vol. 1, *Fort Sumter to Perryville*. New York: Random House, 1958; Vol. 2, *Fredericksburg to Meridian*. New York: Random House, 1963; Vol. 3, *Red River to Appomattox*. New York: Random House, 1974.

Garrison, Webb. *2,000 Questions and Answers About the Civil War*. New York: Gramercy Books, 1992.

Girard, Charles. *A Visit to the Confederate States of America in 1863*. Tuscaloosa, AL: Confederate Publishing Company, 1962.

Gragg, Rod. *The Civil War Quiz and Fact Book*. New York: Harper & Row, 1985.

Grant, U.S. *Personal Memoirs of U. S. Grant*. New York: Smithmark, 1994.

Green, Jonathon. *The Cassell Dictionary of Slang*. London: Cassell, 1998.

Hart, Albert B. *The Romance of the Civil War*. New York: Macmillan, 1903.

Harwell, Richard B., ed. *The Civil War Reader.* New York: Konecky & Konecky, 1957.

Hendrickson, Robert. *Word and Phrase Origins.* New York: Facts on File, 1997.

Henry, Robert S. *The Story of the Confederacy.* New York: Bobbs-Merrill, 1936.

Hogg, Ian V. *Weapons of the American Civil War.* London: PRC Publishing, 1987.

Horn, Stanley F., ed. *The Robert E. Lee Reader.* New York: Bobbs-Merrill, 1949.

Howe, M.A. DeWolfe, ed. *Marching with Sherman.* Lincoln: University of Nebraska Press, 1995.

Hunt, O.E., ed. *The Photographic History of the Civil War,* Vol. 3, *Forts and Artillery, The Navies.* Secaucus, NJ: The Blue and Grey Press, 1987.

Hunter, Alexander. *Johnny Reb and Billy Yank.* New York: Konecky & Konecky, 1904.

Hyde, Solon. *A Captive of War.* Shippensburg, PA: Burd Street Press, 1996.

Johnson, Rossiter. *Campfire and Battlefield.* New York: Bryan, Taylor & Company, 1999.

Jones, Katharine M., ed. *Heroines of Dixie.* New York: Smithmark, 1955.

Katcher, Philip. *The American Civil War Source Book.* London: Arms and Armour Press, 1992.

——. *The Army of Robert E. Lee.* London: Arms and Armour Press, 1994.

Kraus, Michael, and Vera Kraus. *Family Album.* New York: Gross & Dunlap, 1961.

Leech, Margaret. *Reveille in Washington 1860-1865.* New York: Harper & Brothers, 1941.

LeVert, Suzanne. *The Civil War Society's Encyclopedia of the Civil War.* New York: Random House, 1997.

Lewis, Lloyd. *Captain Sam Grant.* Boston: Little, Brown, 1950.

——. *Sherman: Fighting Prophet.* New York: Smithmark, 1992.

MacDonald, John. *Great Battles of the Civil War.* London: Michael Joseph, 1988.

MacRae, David. *The Americans at Home.* New York: E.P. Dutton, 1952.

McCarthy, Carlton. *Detailed Minutiae of Soldier Life in the Army of Northern Virginia 1861-1865.* Lincoln: University of Nebraska Press, 1993.

McKay, Ernest A. *The Civil War and New York City.* Syracuse, NY: Syracuse University Press, 1990.

Randall, J.G., and Richard N. Current. *Lincoln the President,* Vol. 4, *Last Full Measure.* New York: Dodd, Mead, 1955.

Robinson, Charles M., III. *Shark of the Confederacy.* London: Leo Cooper, 1995.

Sandburg, Carl. *Storm Over the Land.* London: Jonathan Cape, 1944.

Scharf, J. Thomas. *History of the Confederate States Navy.* New York: Gramercy Books, 1996.

Sorrel, G. Moxley. *Recollections of a Confederate Staff Officer.* New York: W.S. Konecky, 1994.

Starr, Louis M. *Reporting the Civil War.* New York: Collier Books, 1962.

Stern, Philip Van Doren, ed. *Soldier Life.* Greenwich, CT: Fawcett, 1961.

Strode, Hudson. *Jefferson Davis,* Vol. 1, *American Patriot.* New York: Harcourt, Brace, 1955; Vol. 2, *Tragic Hero.* New York: Harcourt, Brace, 1964.

Swinton, William. *Army of the Potomac.* New York: Smithmark, 1995.

Van Horne, Thomas B. *The Army of the Cumberland.* New York: Smithmark, 1996.

Ward, Geoffrey C., with Ric Burns and Ken Burns. *The Civil War.* New York: Alfred A. Knopf, 1990.

Watkins, Sam R. *"Co. Aytch."* New York: Collier Books, 1962.

Wentworth, Harold, and Stuart B. Flexner. *Dictionary of American Slang.* New York: Thomas Y. Crowell, 1975.

Wiley, Bell I. *The Life of Billy Yank.* Baton Rouge: Louisiana State University Press, 1998.

——. *The Life of Johnny Reb.* Baton Rouge: Louisiana State University Press, 1999.

Woodward, C. Vann, ed. *Mary Chesnut's Civil War.* New Haven, CT: Yale University Press, 1981.

INDEX

Page references in **bold type** refer to main entries in the encyclopedia.

About the Author

JOHN D. WRIGHT is a reporter with *Time* magazine in its London bureau. He has taught journalism at three universities. He has also written extensively for *People* magazine. Wright has contributed to numerous reference works, including *Collins Dictionary of the English Language*, *Bloomsbury Thesaurus*, and *Oxford Guide to British and American Culture*.

(J 4